airy Tail volume 46 is a work of fiction. Names, characters, places, and incidents 're the products of the author's imagination or are used fictitiously. Any :semblance to actual events, locales, or persons, living or dead, is entirely oincidental.

Kodansha Comics Trade Paperback Original.

ublished in the United States by Kodansha Comics, an imprint of Kodansha SA Publishing, LLC, New York.

ublication rights for this English edition arranged through Kodansha Ltd., okyo.

rst published in Japan in 2014 by Kodansha Ltd., Tokyo
BN 978-1-61262-797-7

rinted in the United States of America.

ww.kodanshacomics.com

8 7 6 5 4 3 2

ranslation: William Flanagan
ettering: AndWorld Design
diting: Ben Applegate
odansha Comics edition cover design by Phil Balsman

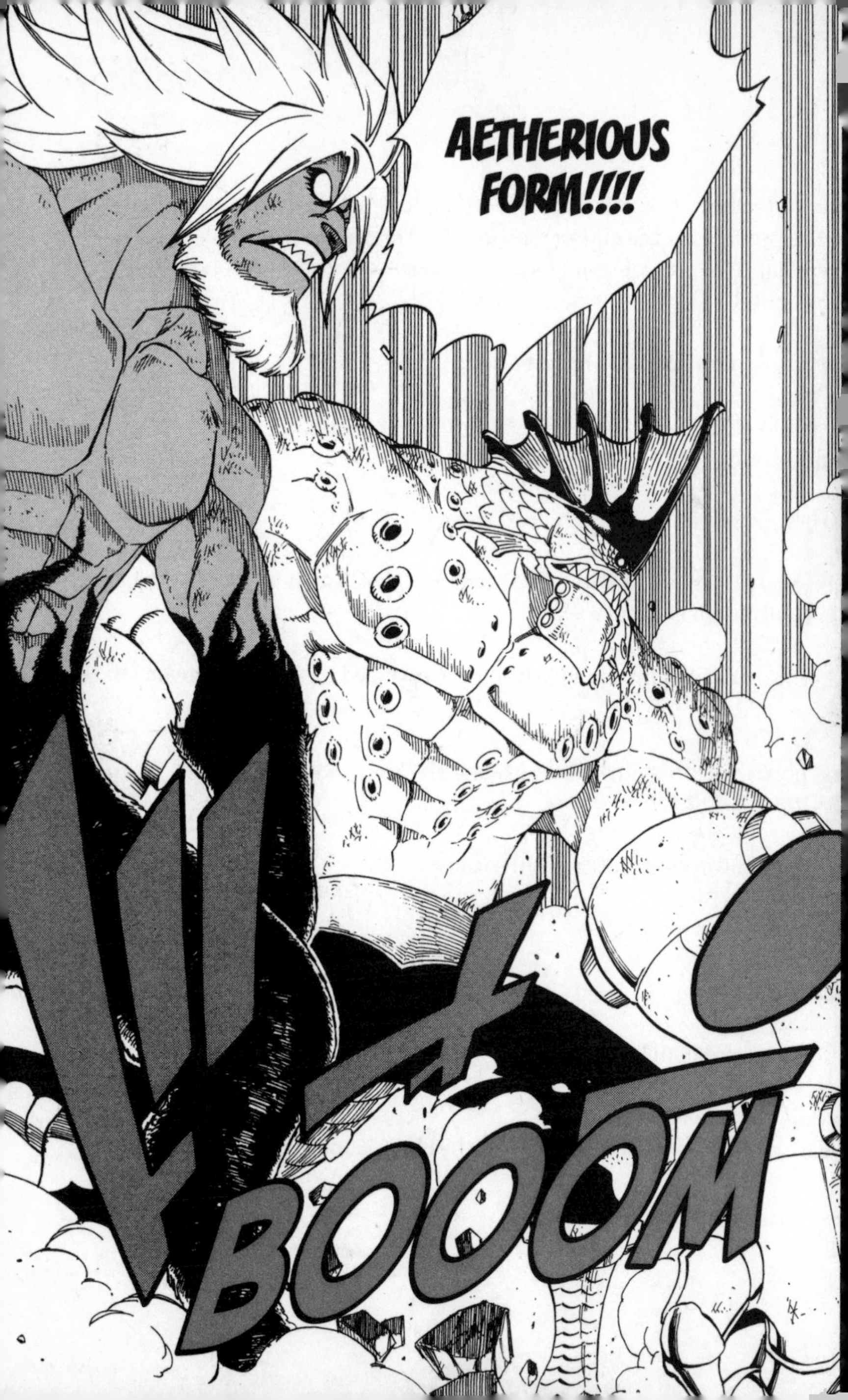
AETHERIOUS FORM!!!!
BOOOM

FAIRY TAIL

46

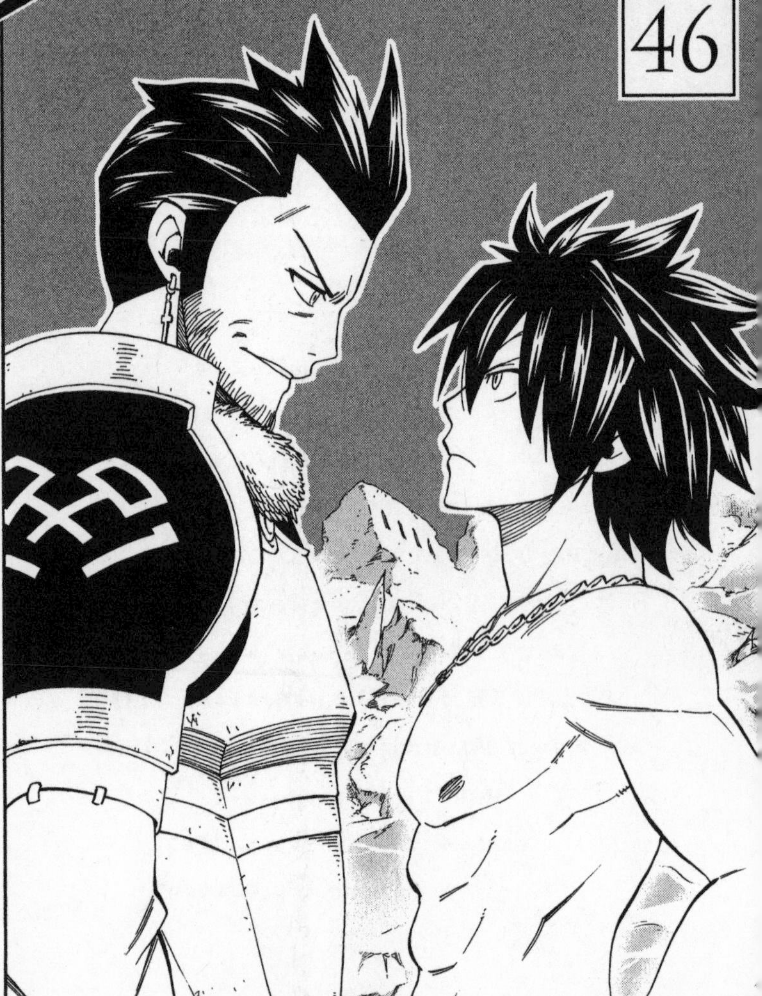

HIRO MASHIMA

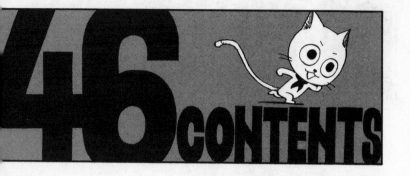

CONTENTS

FAIRY TAIL

フェアリーテイル

Chapter 387: Tartaros Arc, Part Four: Father and Son

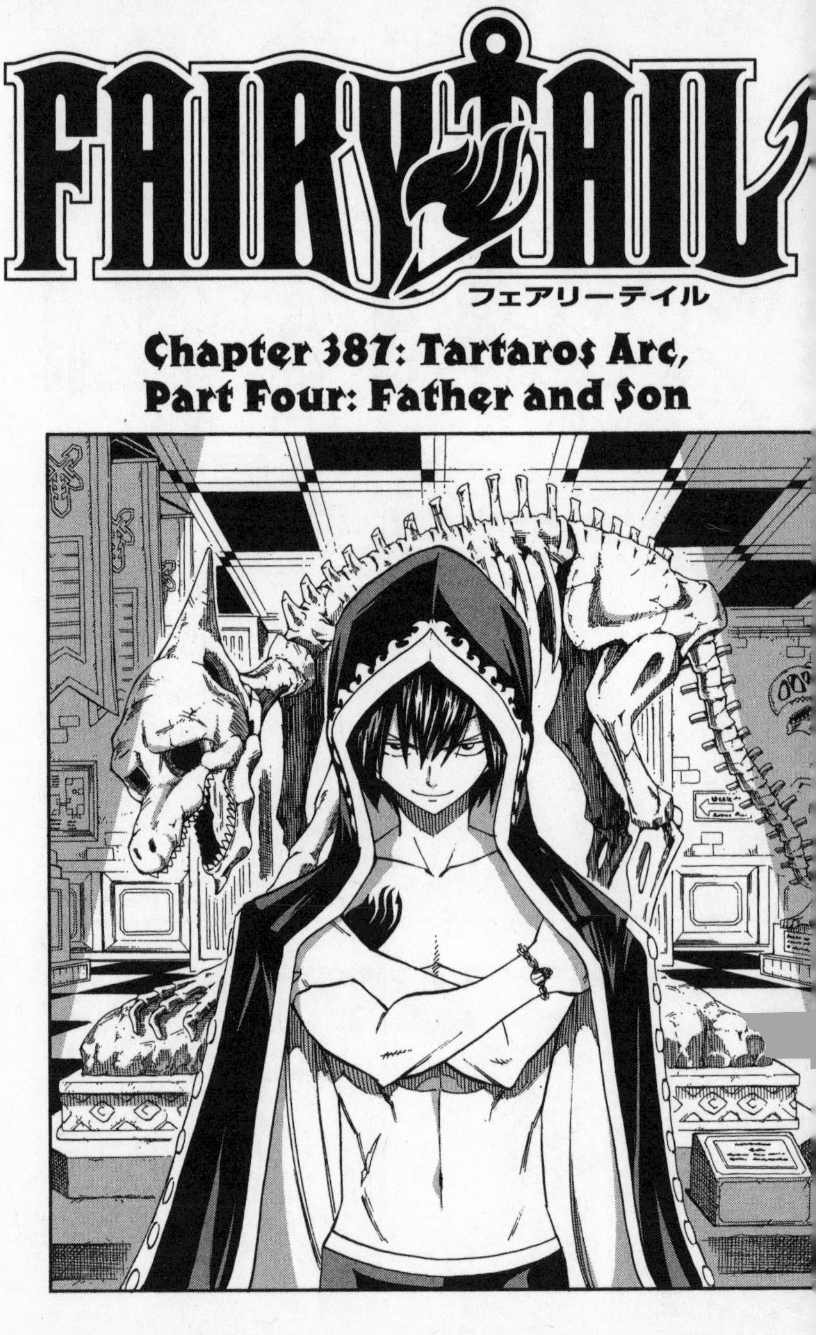

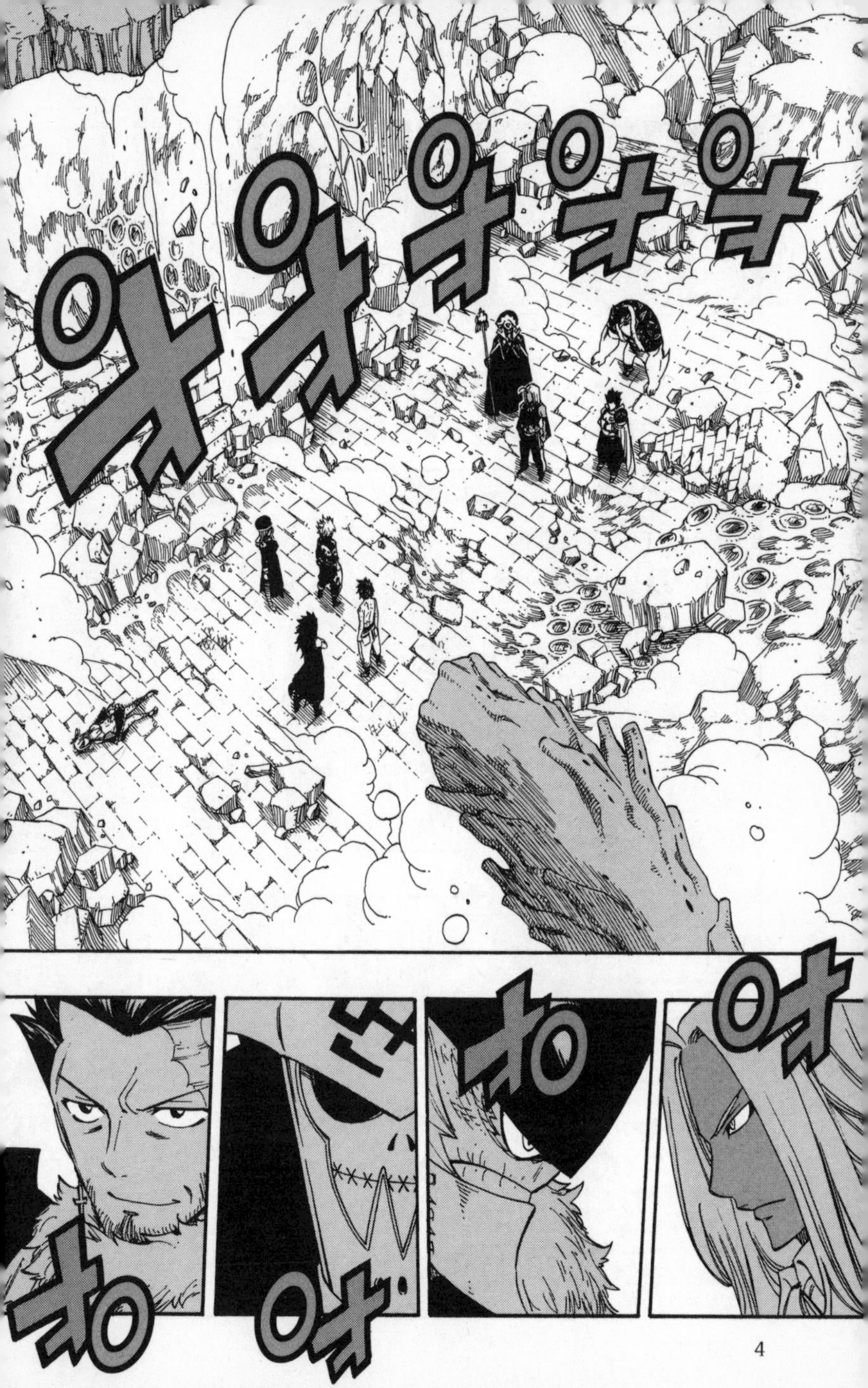
オオオオオ
オ
オ
オ
オ

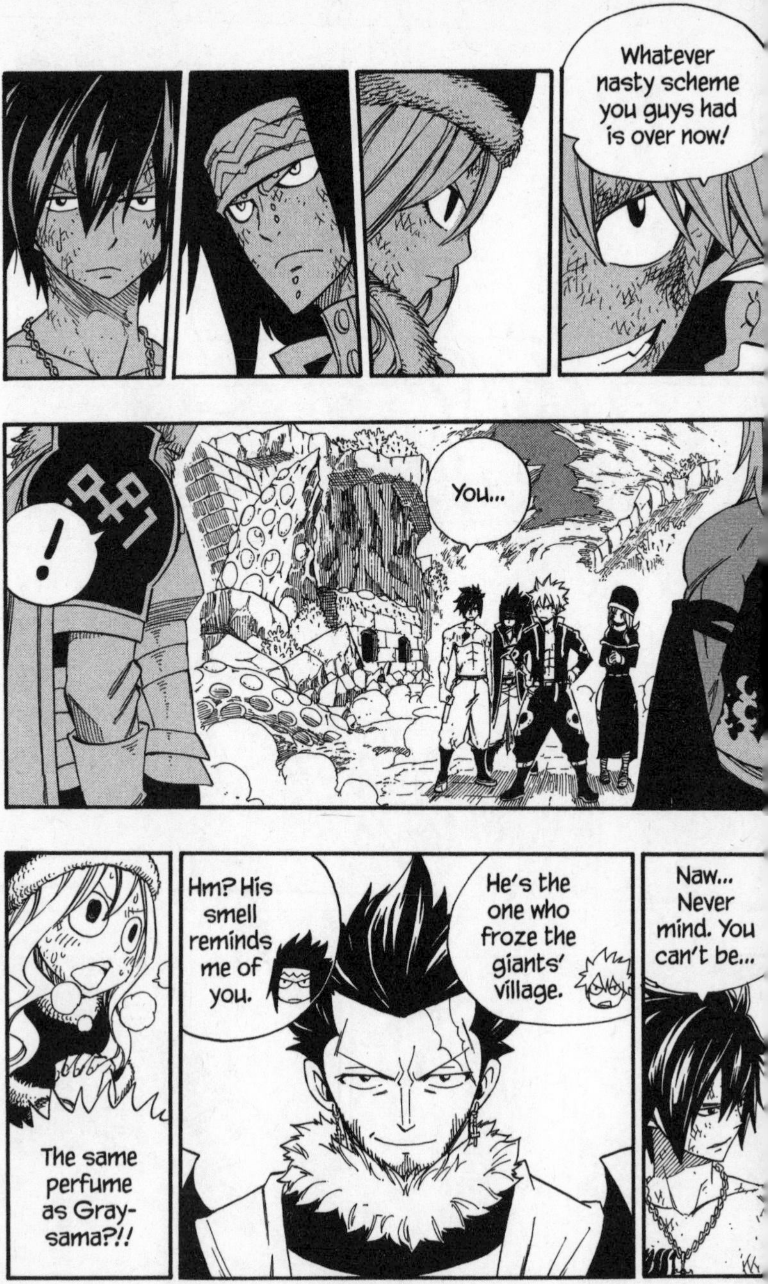
Whatever nasty scheme you guys had is over now!
You...
!
Naw... Never mind. You can't be...
He's the one who froze the giants' village.
Hm? His smell reminds me of you.
The same perfume as Gray-sama?!!

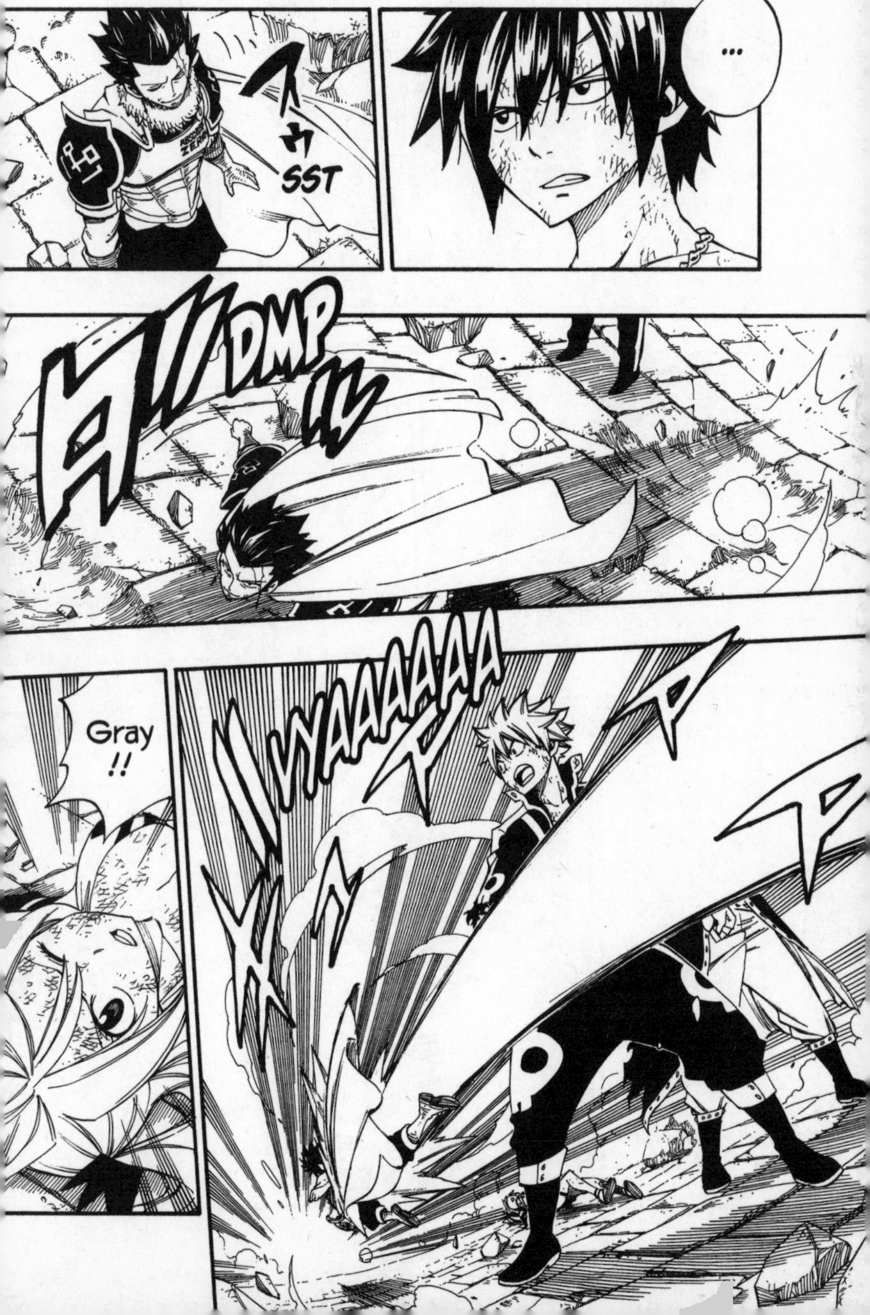
...
SST
DMP
WAAAAAA
Gray !!

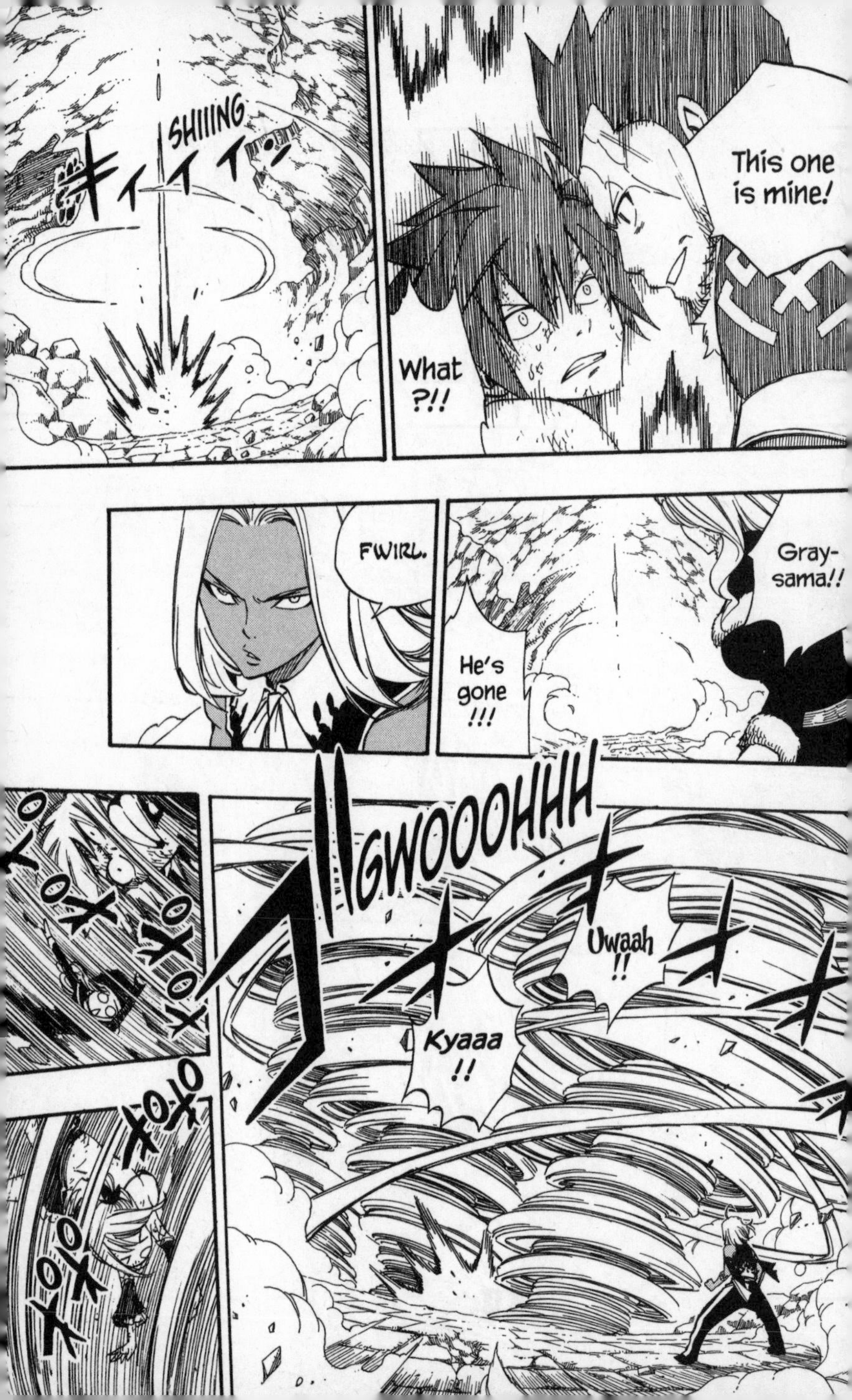
This one is mine!
What?!!
SHIIING
Gray-sama!!
He's gone!!!
FWIRL.
GWOOOHHH
Uwaah!!
Kyaaa!!

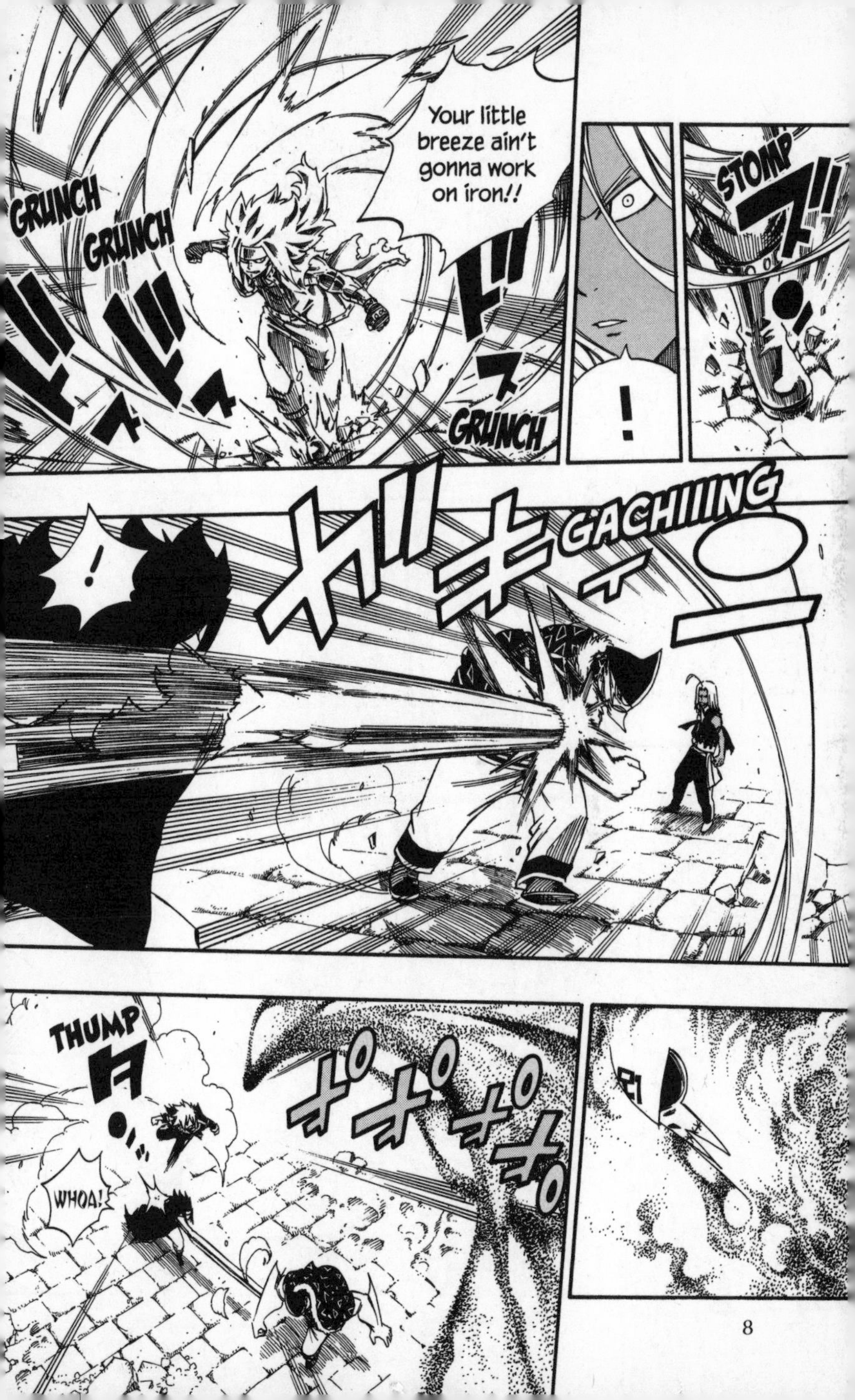
STOMP
!
Your little breeze ain't gonna work on iron!!
GRUNCH
GRUNCH
GRUNCH
!
GACHIIIING
THUMP
WHOA!

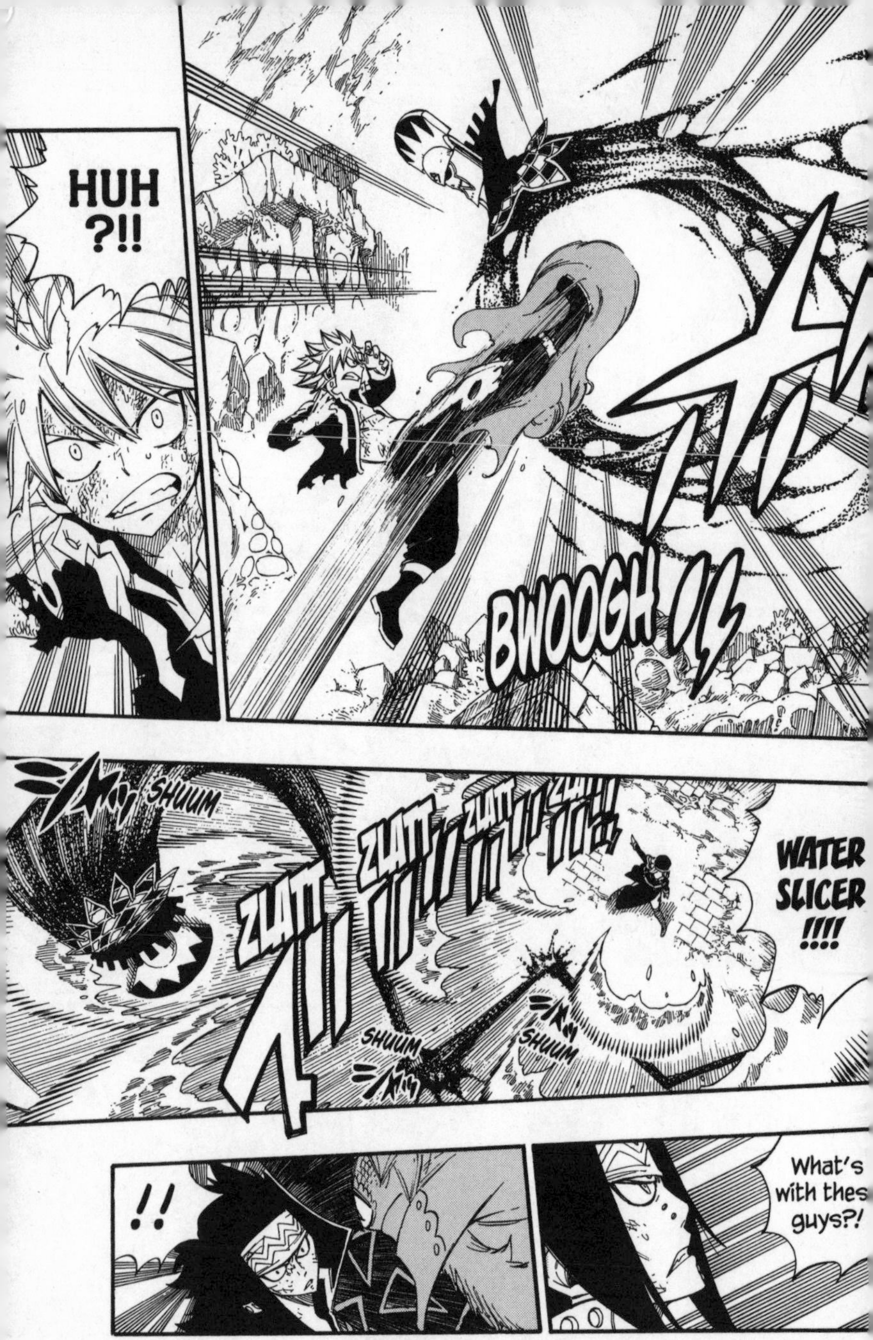
BWOOGH
HUH ?!!
WATER SLICER !!!!
ZLATT
ZLATT
ZLATT
ZLATT
SHUUM
SHUUM
SHUUM
What's with thes guys?!
!!

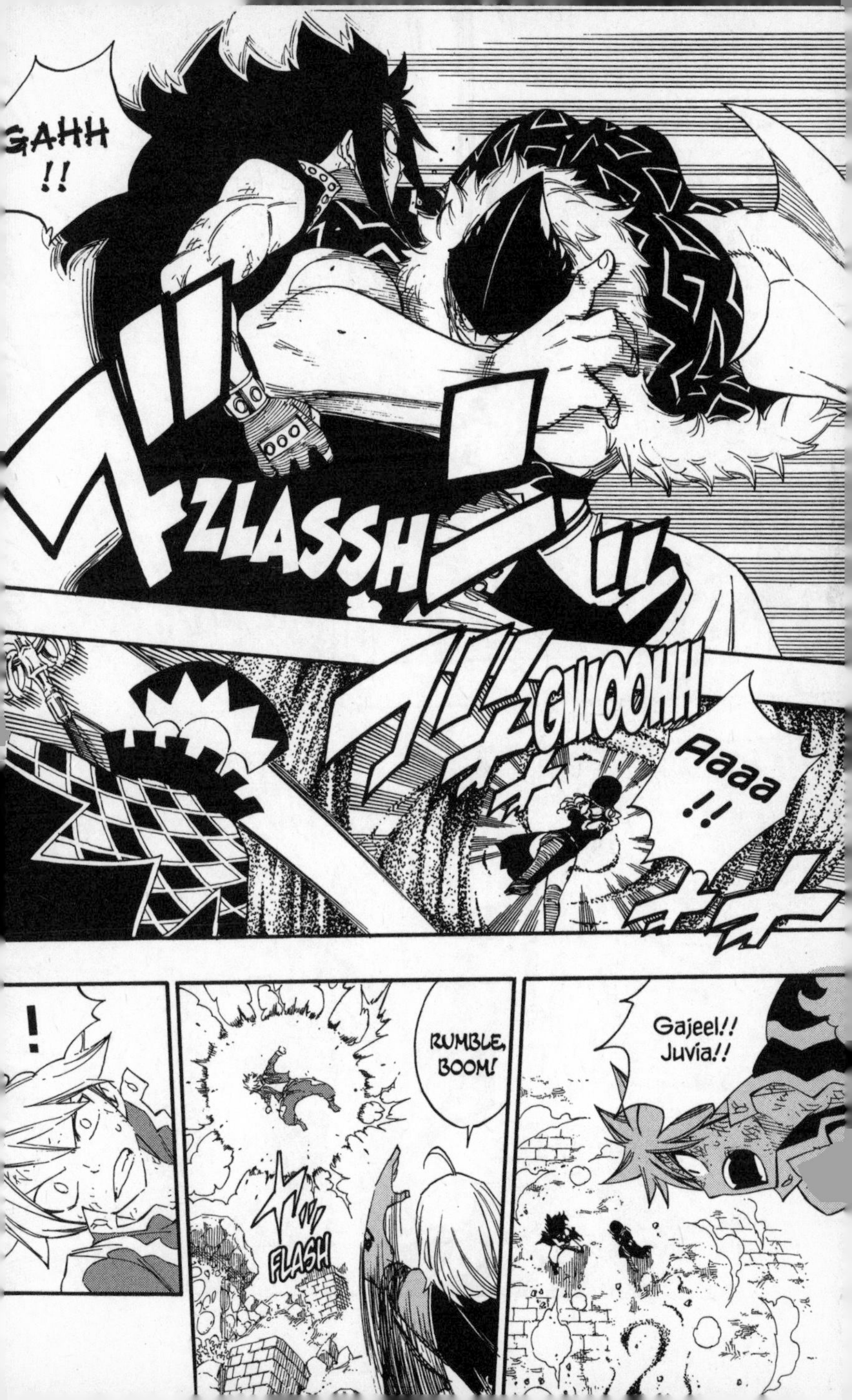
GAHH !!
ZLASSH!!
GWOOHH
Aaaa !!
Gajeel!! Juvia!!
RUMBLE, BOOM!
FLASH
!

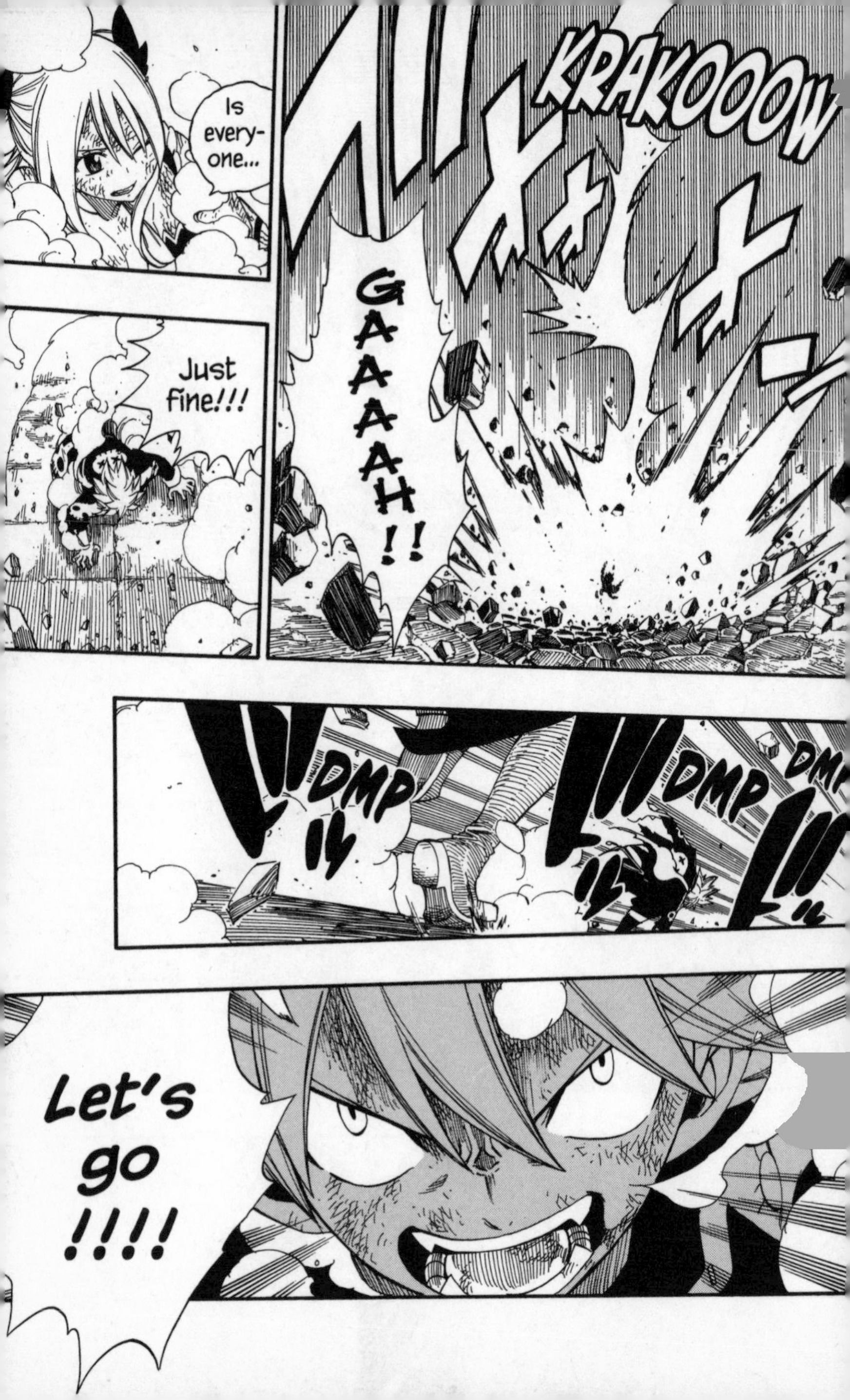
KRAKOOOW
GAAAAAH!!
Is everyone...
Just fine!!!
DMP
DMP
Let's go!!!!

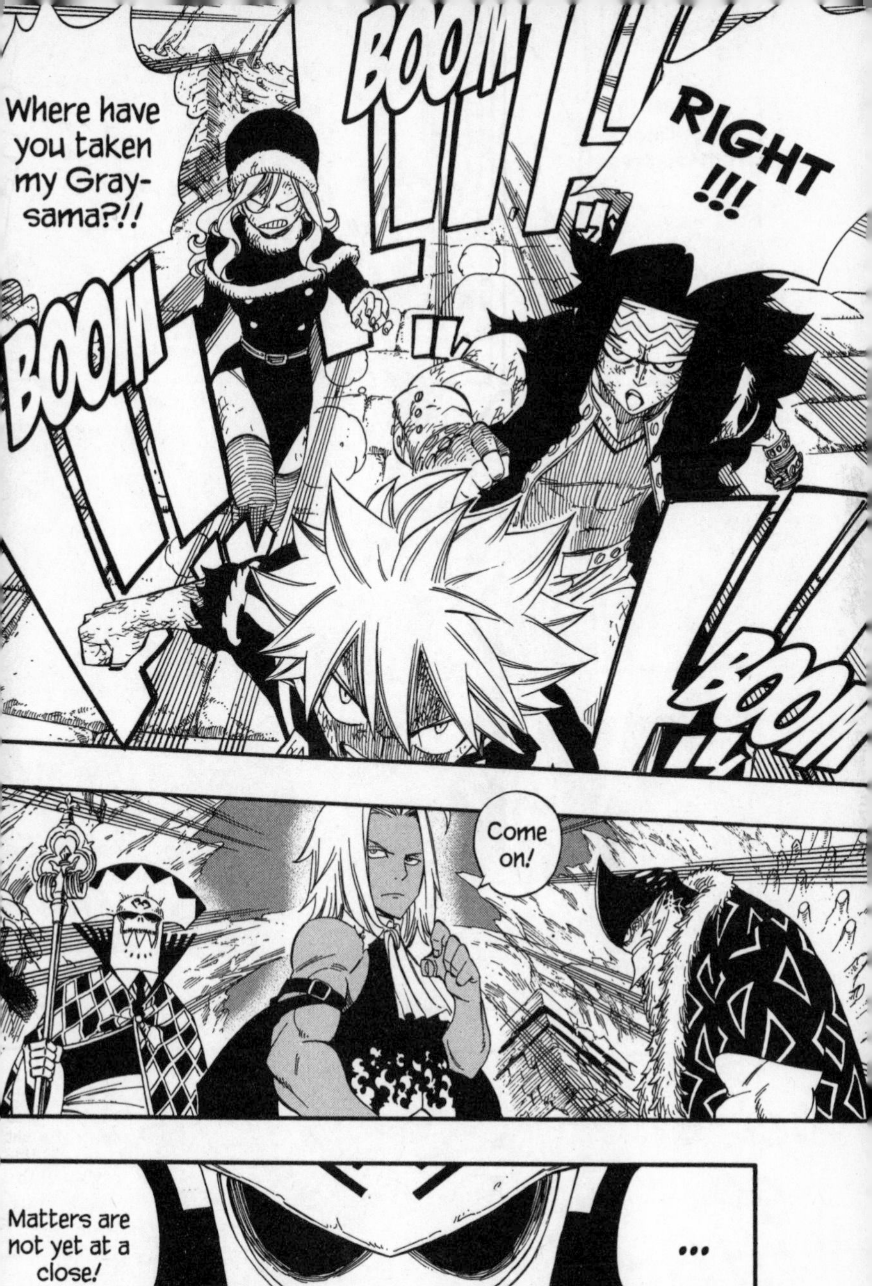
RIGHT !!!
BOOM
Where have you taken my Gray-sama?!!
BOOM
BOOM
Come on!
...
Matters are not yet at a close!

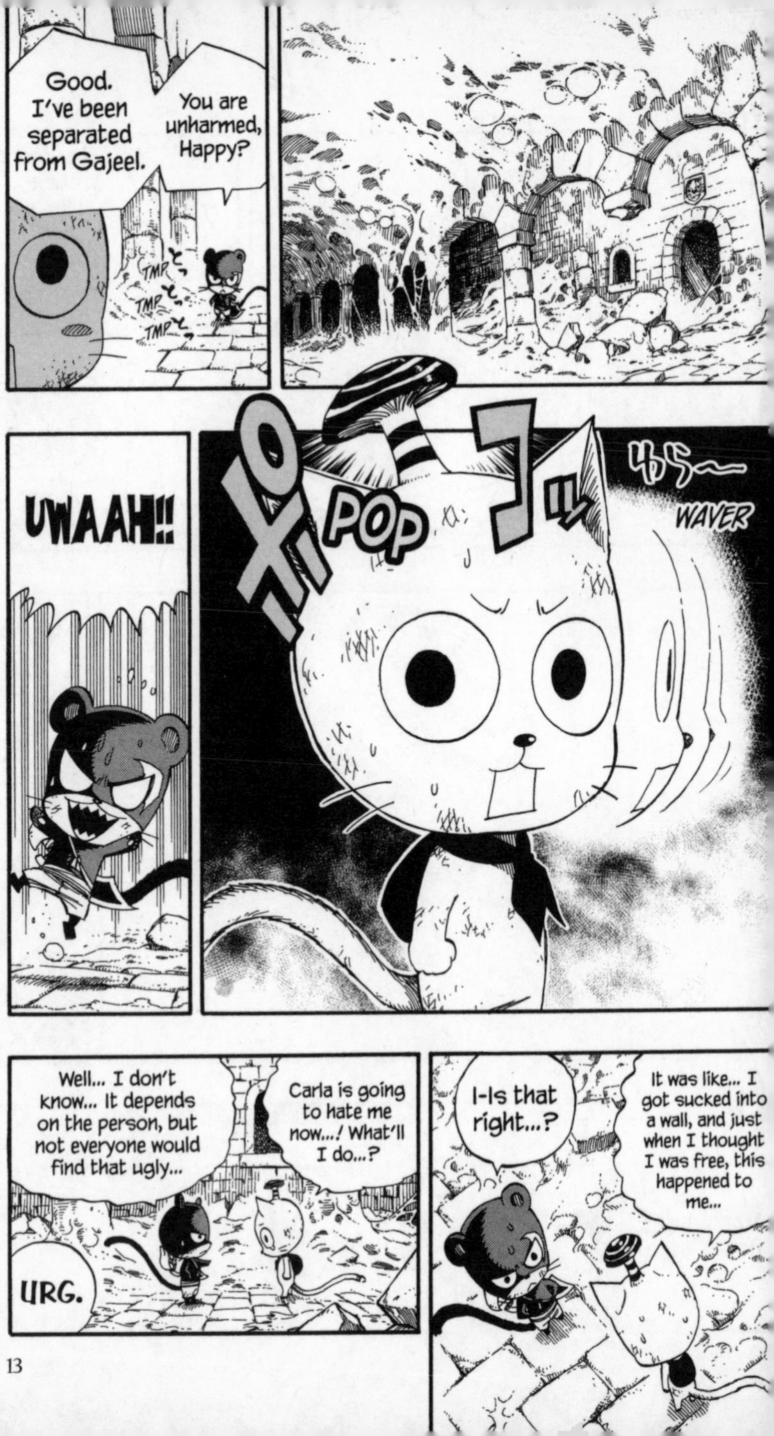
You are unharmed, Happy?
Good. I've been separated from Gajeel.
TMP TMP TMP
WAVER
POP
UWAAH!!
It was like... I got sucked into a wall, and just when I thought I was free, this happened to me...
I-Is that right...?
Carla is going to hate me now...! What'll I do...?
Well... I don't know... It depends on the person, but not everyone would find that ugly...
URG.

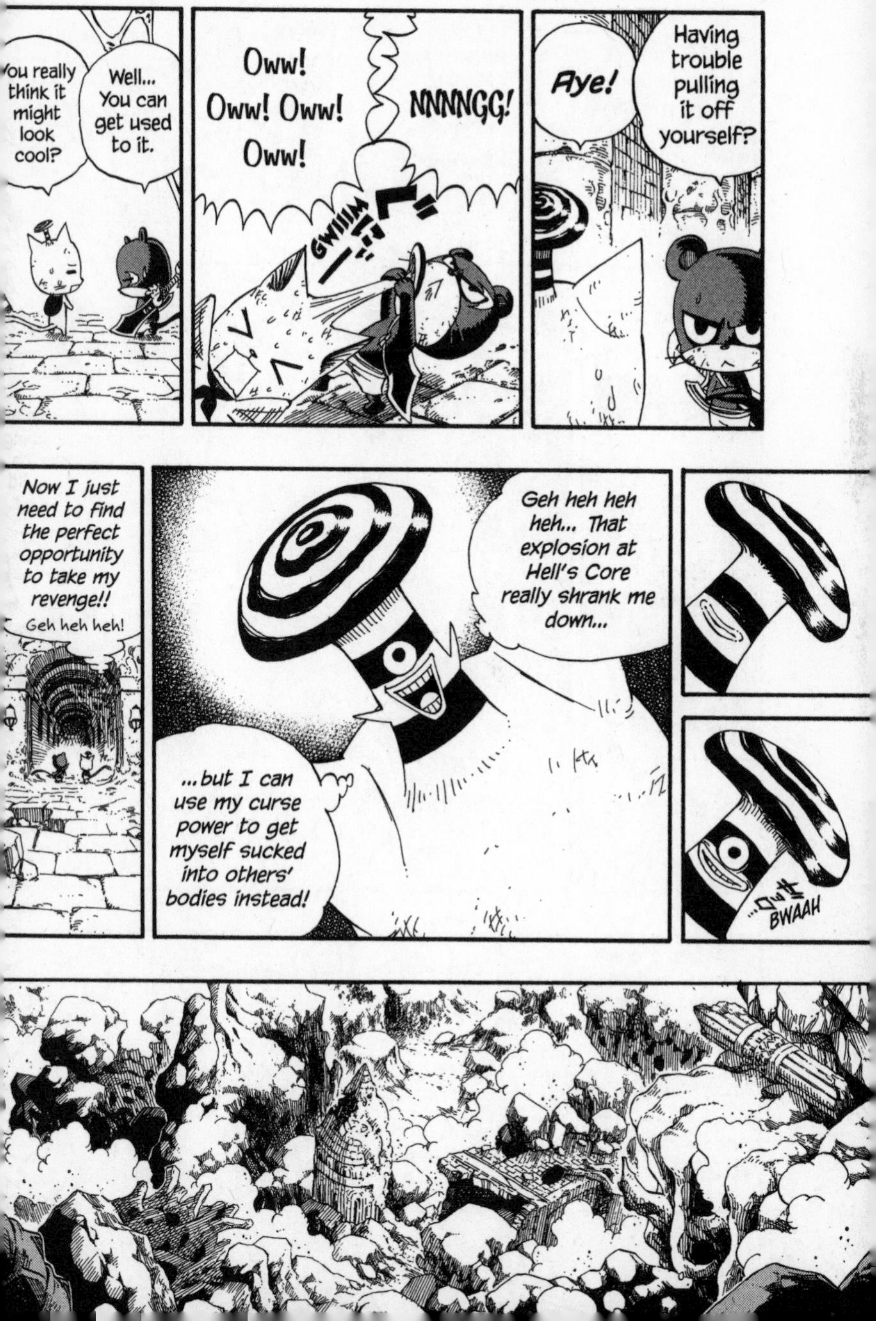
Having trouble pulling it off yourself?
Aye!
NNNNGG!
Oww! Oww! Oww! Oww!
Well... You can get used to it.
ou really think it might look cool?
...BWAAH
Geh heh heh heh... That explosion at Hell's Core really shrank me down...
...but I can use my curse power to get myself sucked into others' bodies instead!
Now I just need to find the perfect opportunity to take my revenge!!
Geh heh heh!

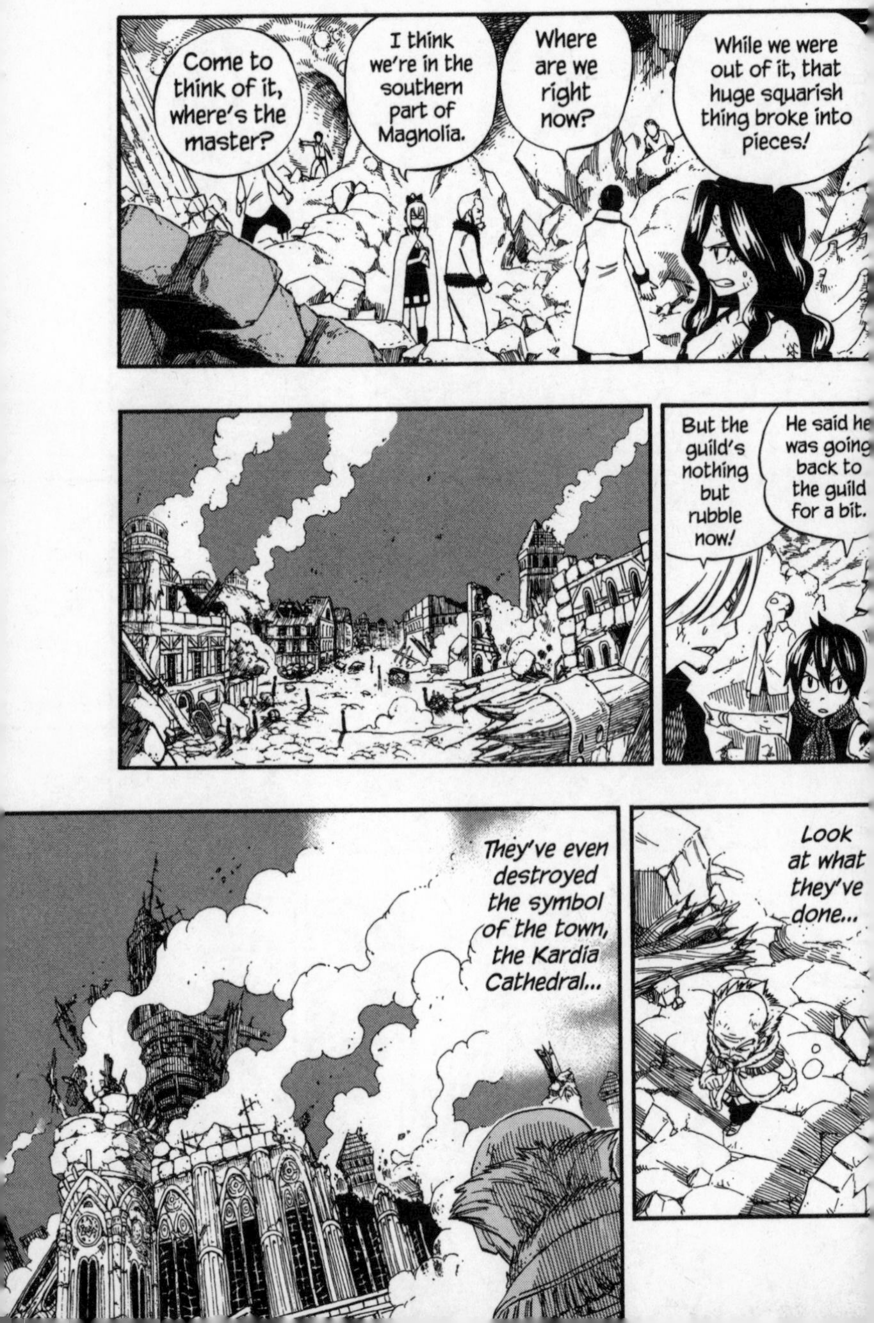
While we were out of it, that huge squarish thing broke into pieces!
Where are we right now?
I think we're in the southern part of Magnolia.
Come to think of it, where's the master?
He said he was going back to the guild for a bit.
But the guild's nothing but rubble now!
Look at what they've done...
They've even destroyed the symbol of the town, the Kardia Cathedral...

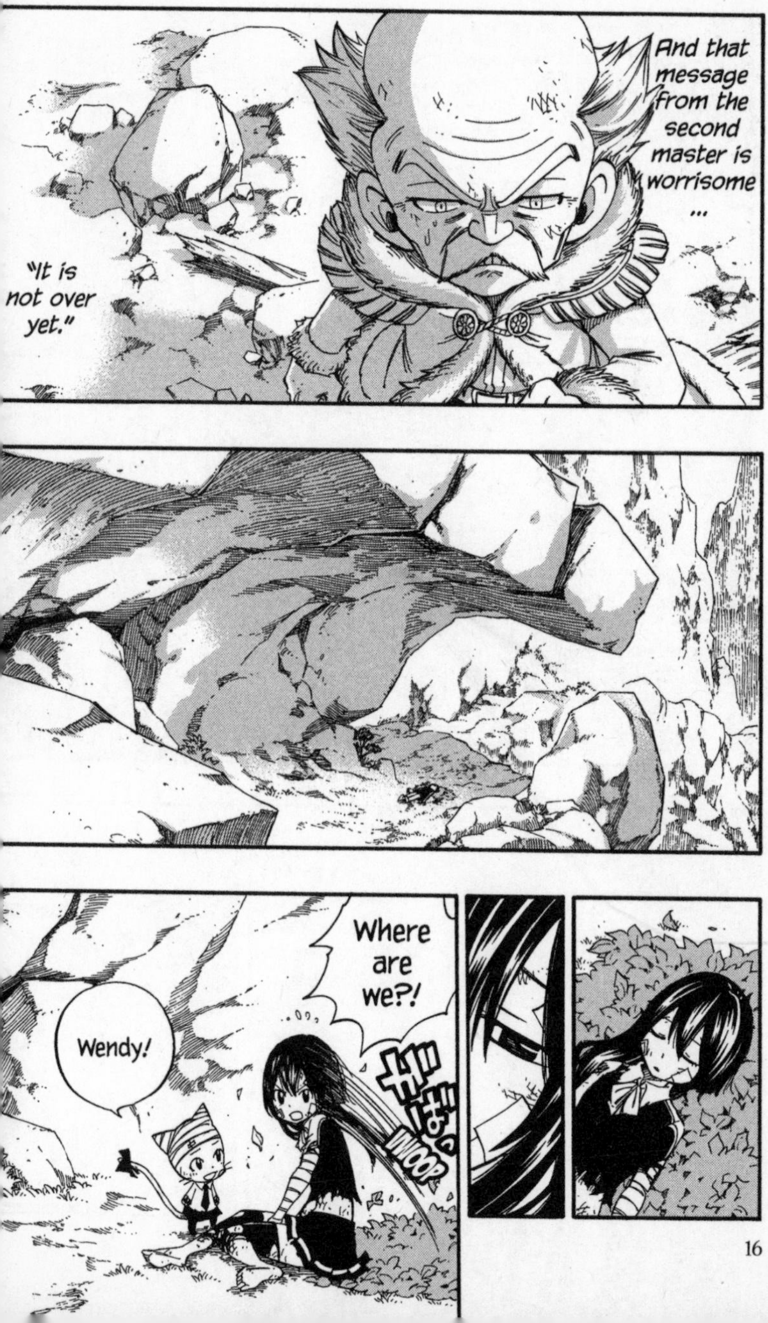
And that message from the second master is worrisome ...
"It is not over yet."
Where are we?!
WOOP
Wendy!

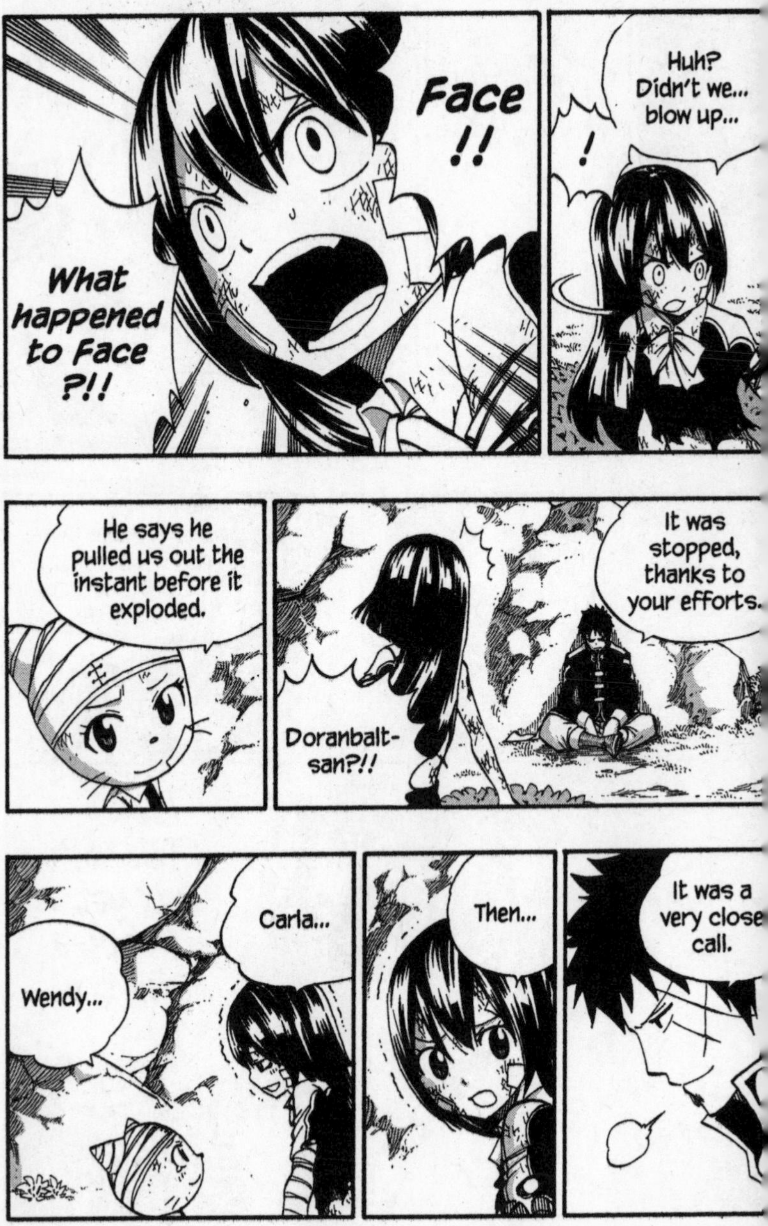
!
Huh? Didn't we... blow up...
Face !!
What happened to Face ?!!
It was stopped, thanks to your efforts.
Doranbalt-san?!!
He says he pulled us out the instant before it exploded.
It was a very close call.
Then...
Carla...
Wendy...

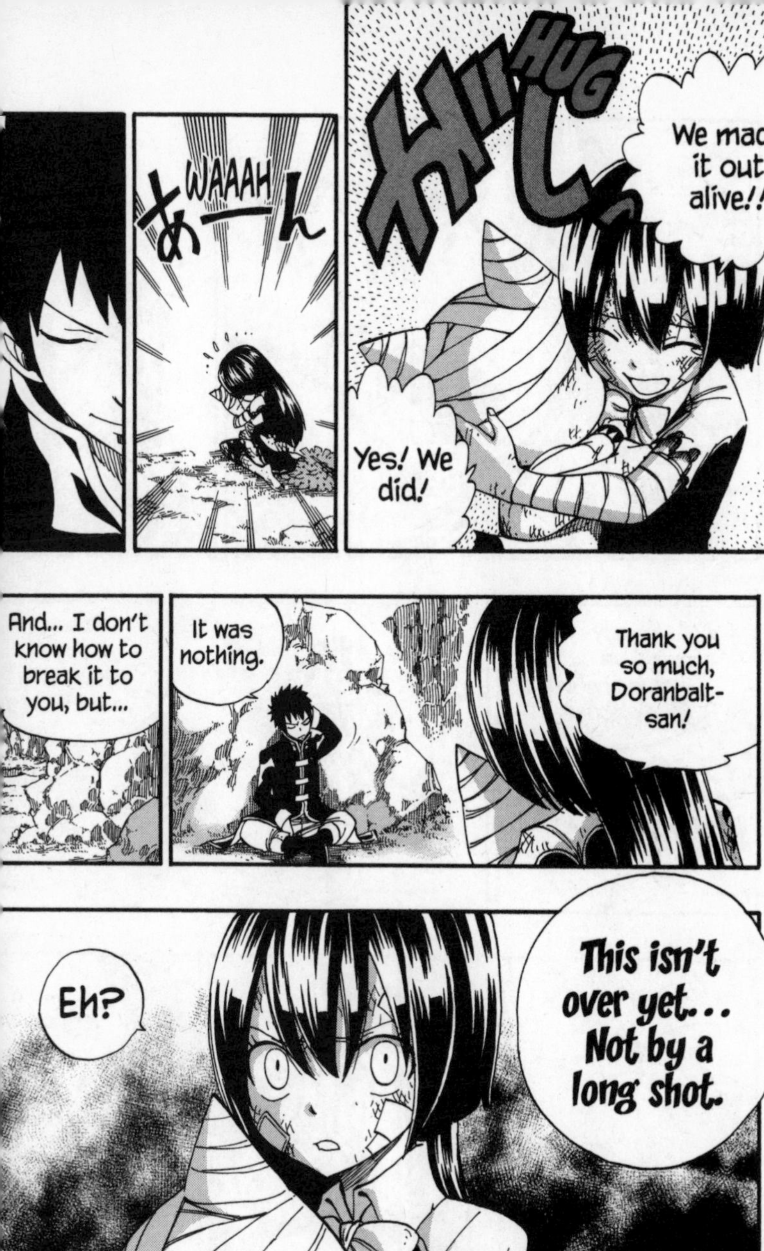
HUG
We made it out alive!!
Yes! We did!
WAAAH
あーん
Thank you so much, Doranbalt-san!
It was nothing.
And... I don't know how to break it to you, but...
This isn't over yet... Not by a long shot.
Eh?

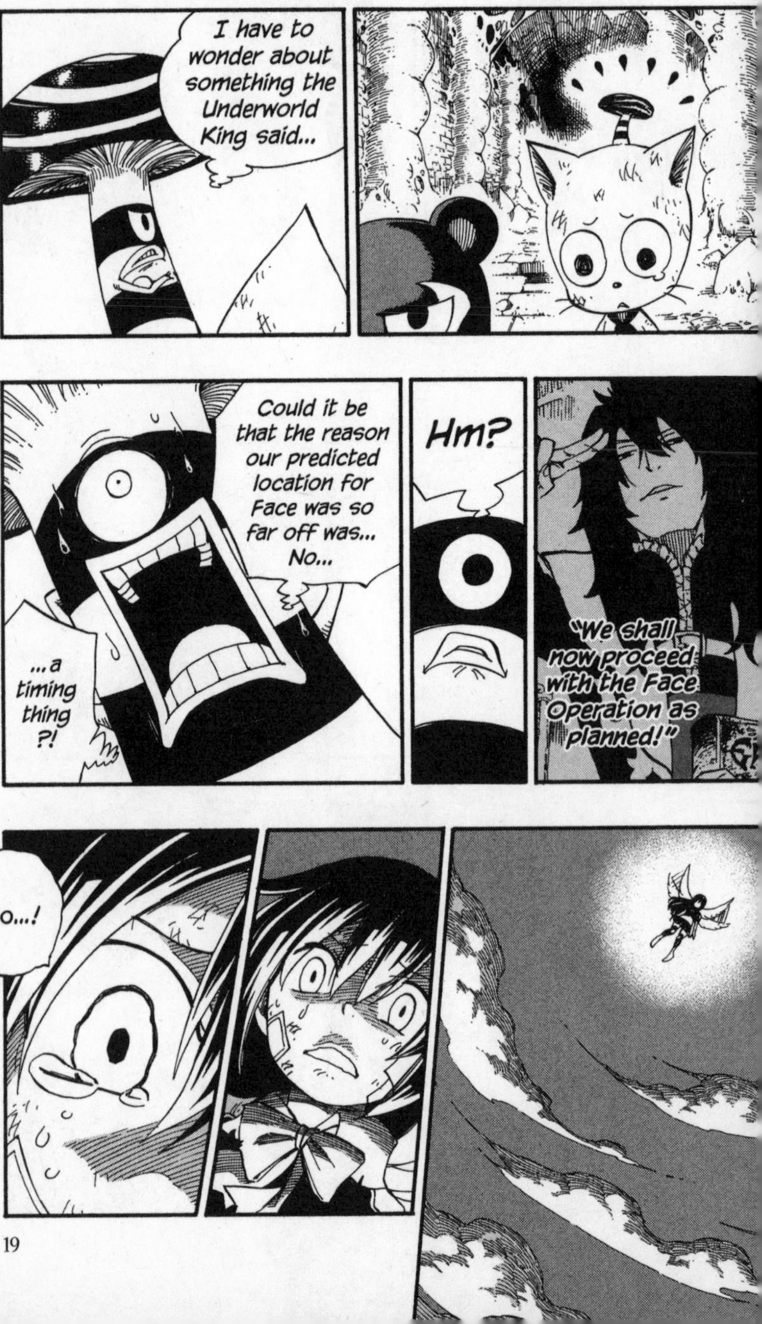
I have to wonder about something the Underworld King said...
"We shall now proceed with the Face Operation as planned!"
Hm?
Could it be that the reason our predicted location for Face was so far off was... No...
...a timing thing?!
No...!

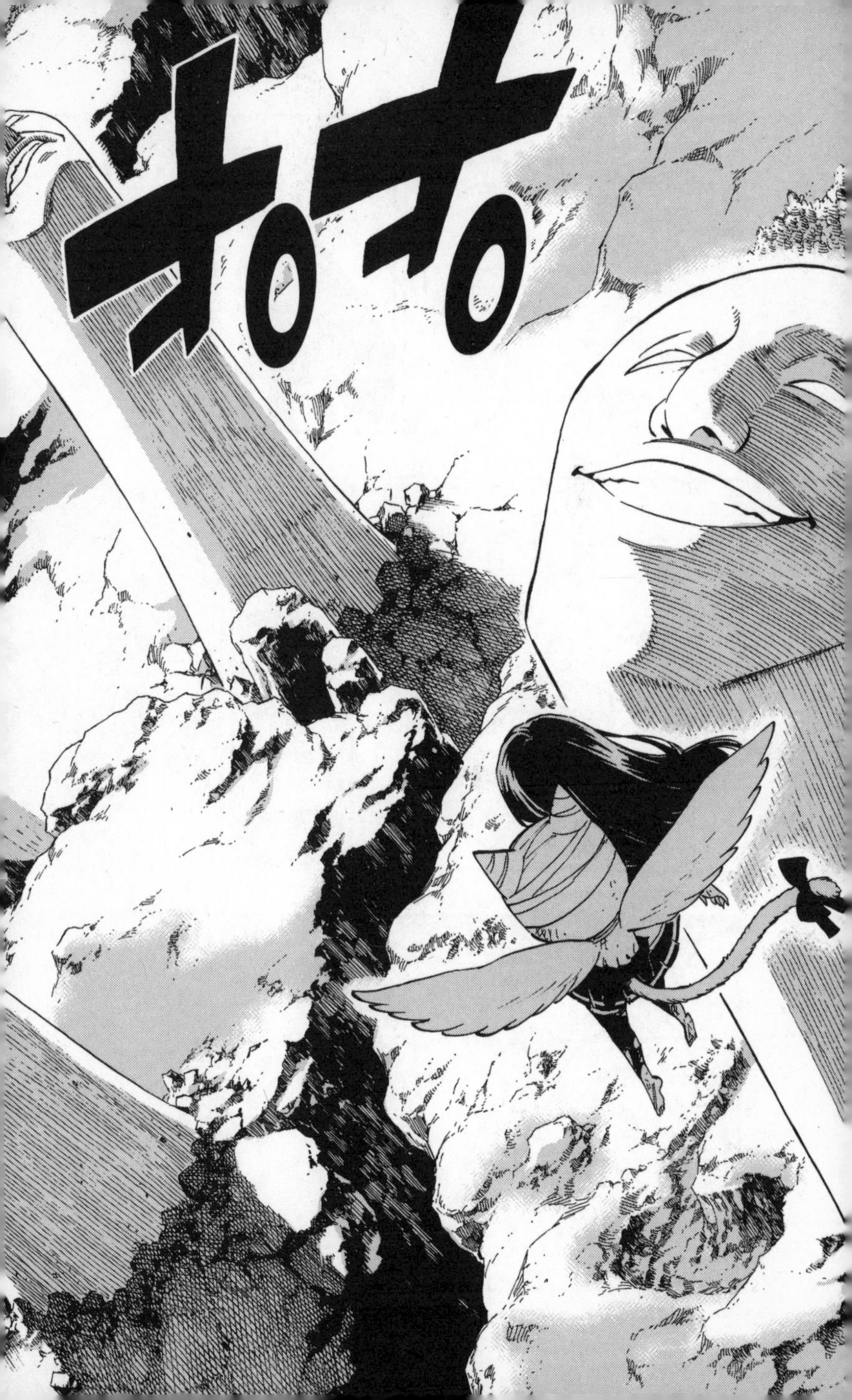

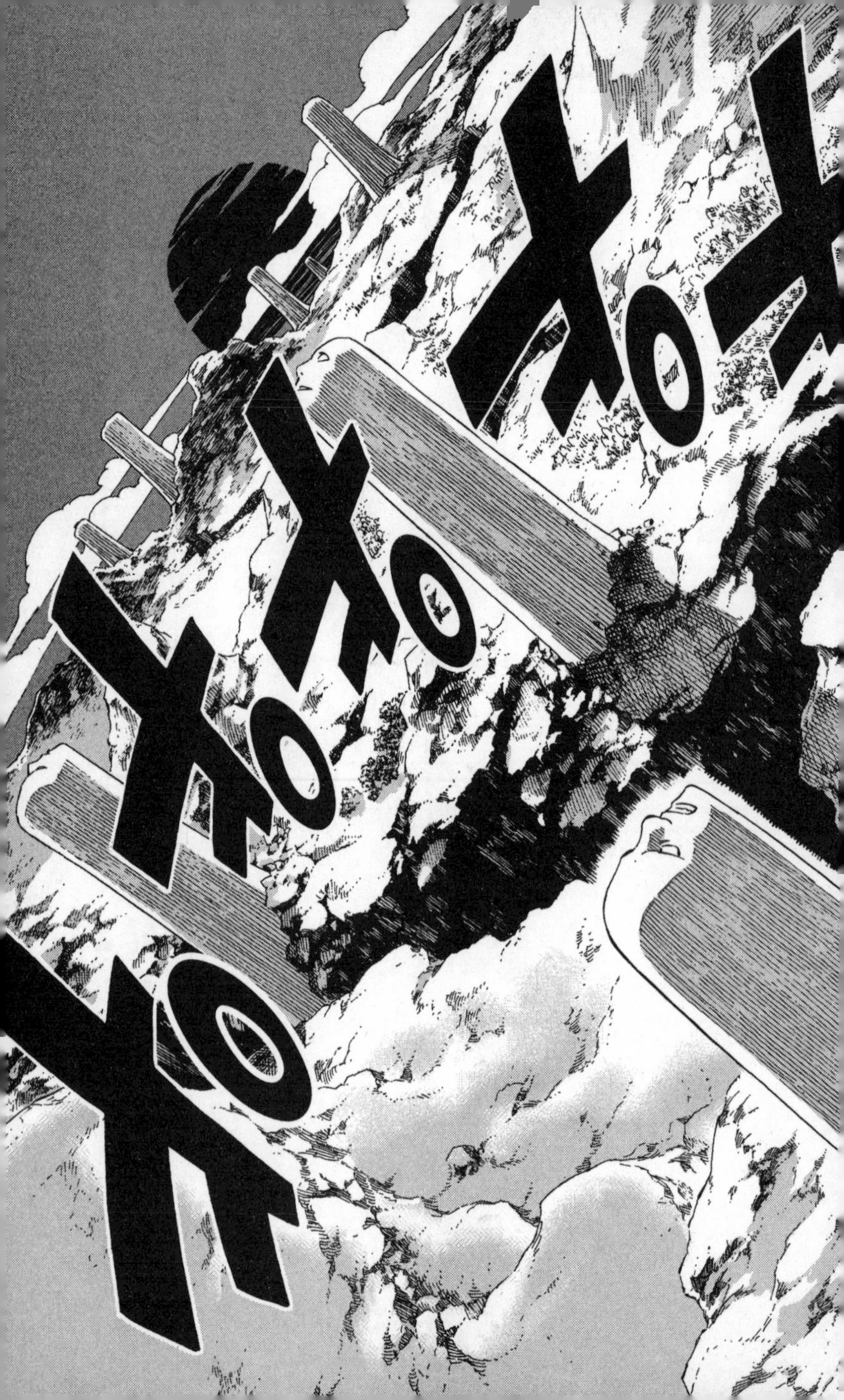

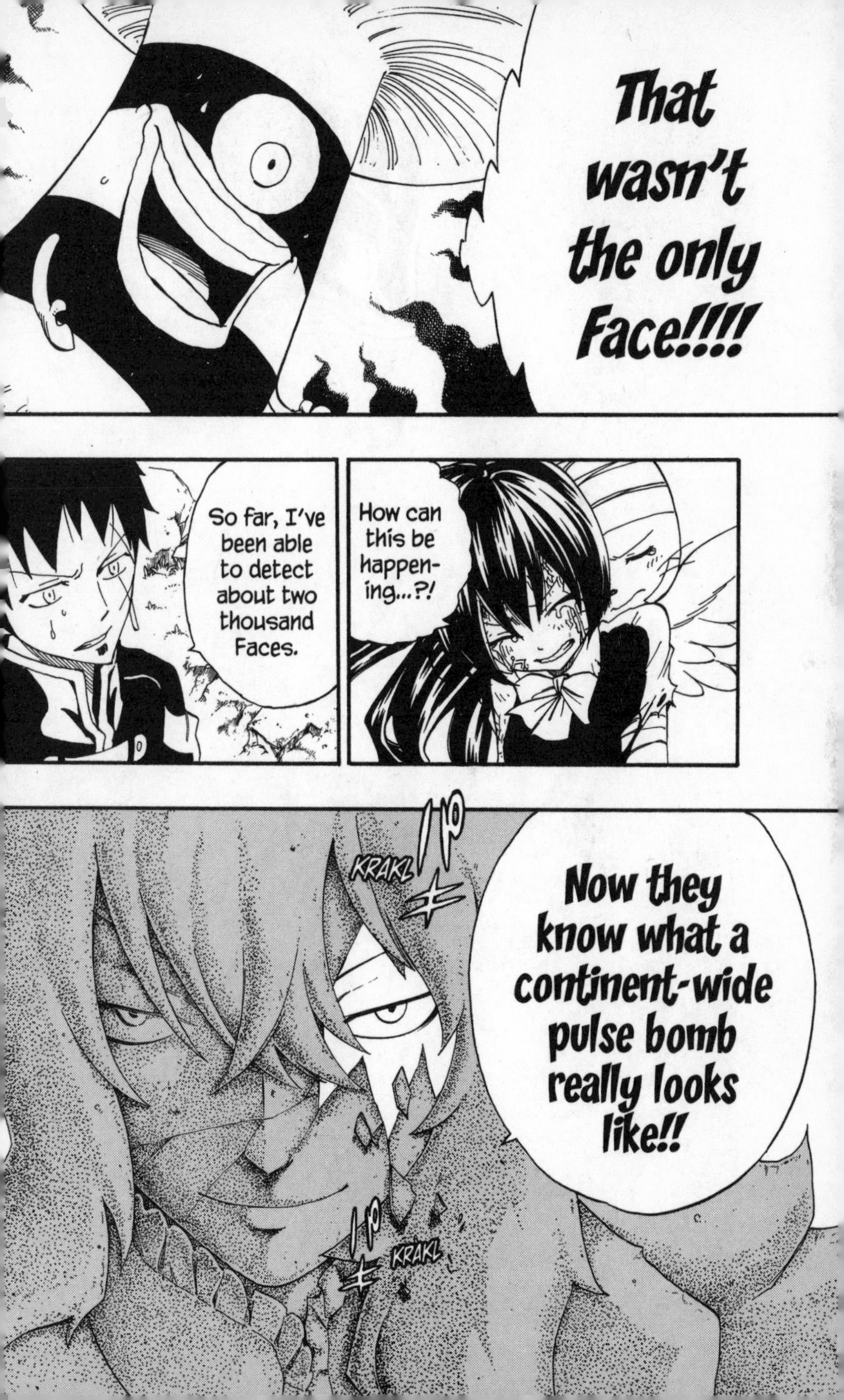
That wasn't the only Face!!!!
How can this be happen-ing...?!
So far, I've been able to detect about two thousand Faces.
Now they know what a continent-wide pulse bomb really looks like!!
KRAKL
KRAKL

FAIRY TAIL
フェアリーテイル

Chapter 388: Erza vs. Minerva

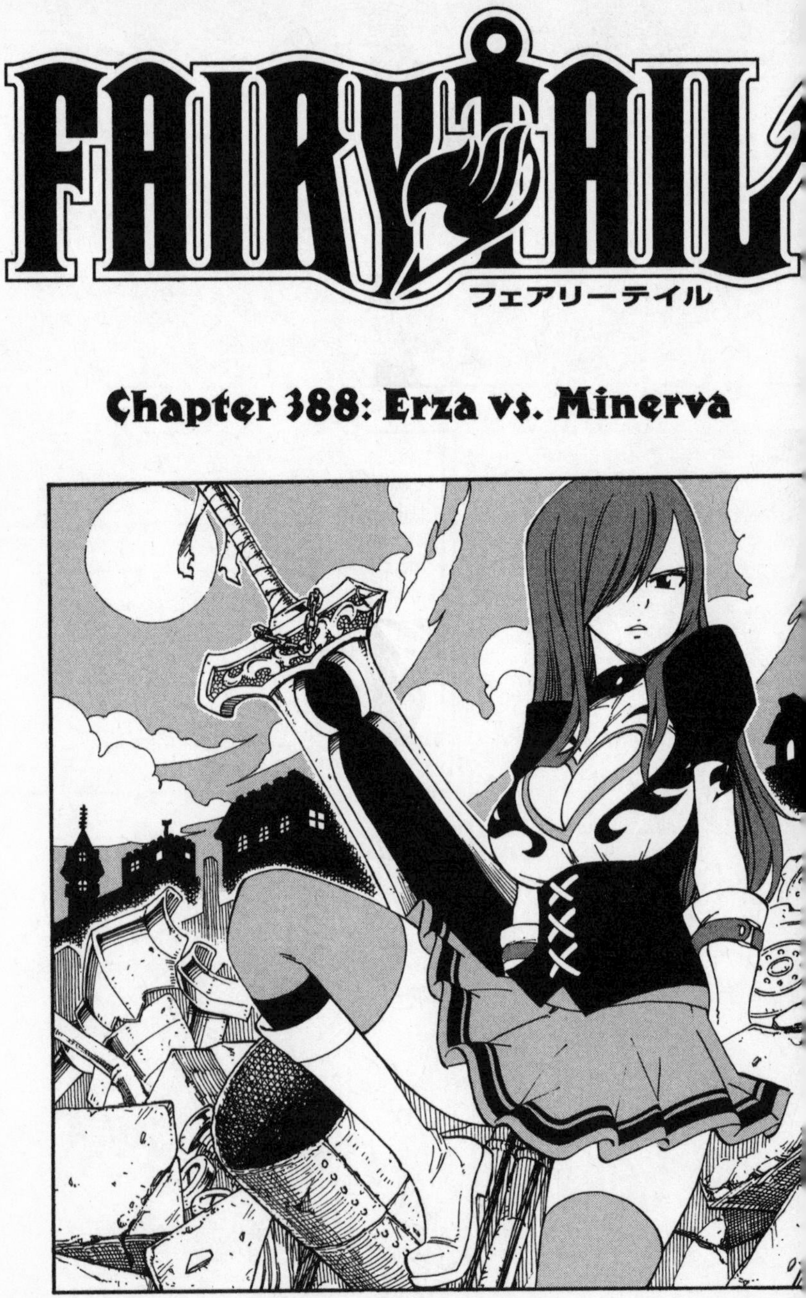

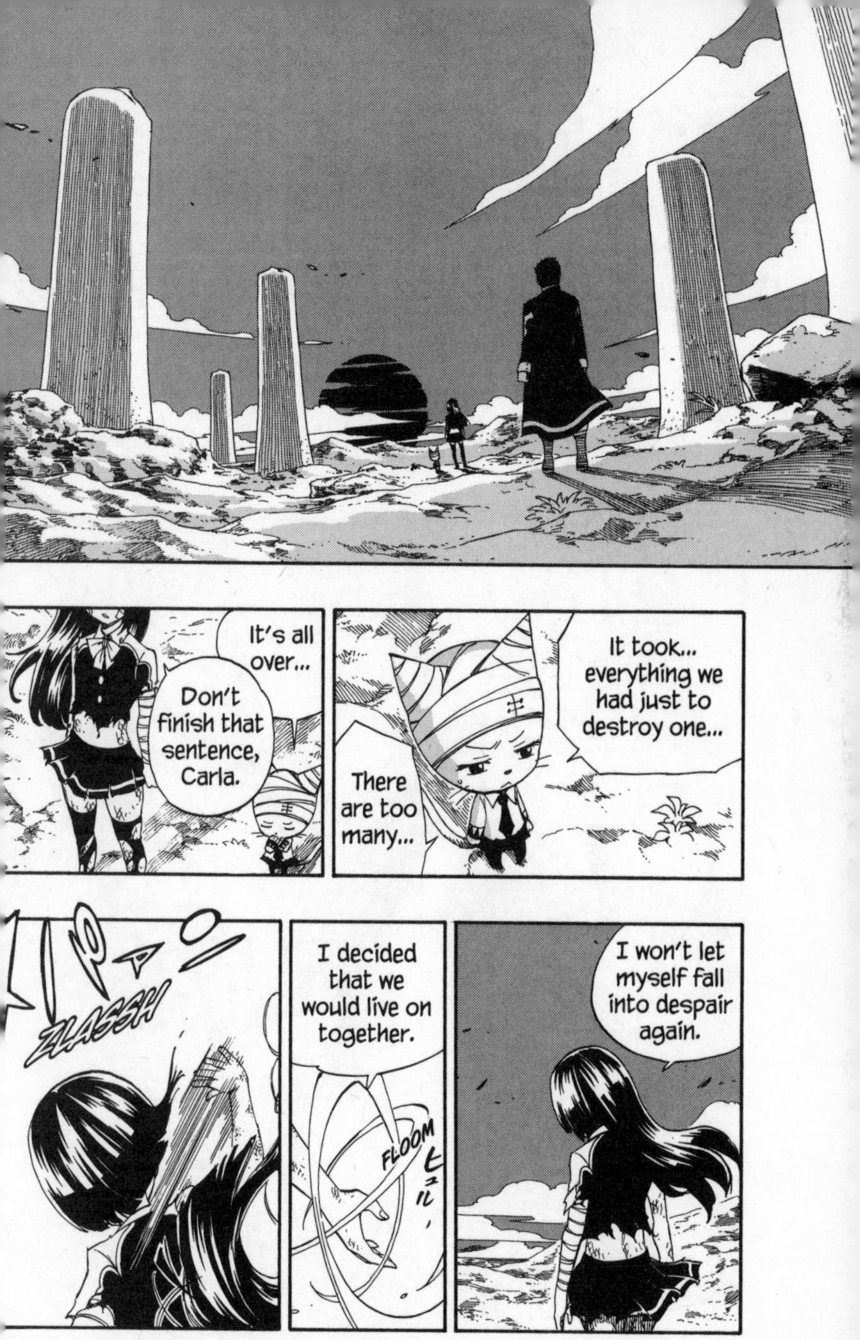
It took... everything we had just to destroy one...
There are too many...
It's all over...
Don't finish that sentence, Carla.
I won't let myself fall into despair again.
I decided that we would live on together.
FLOOM
ヒュル
ZLASSH

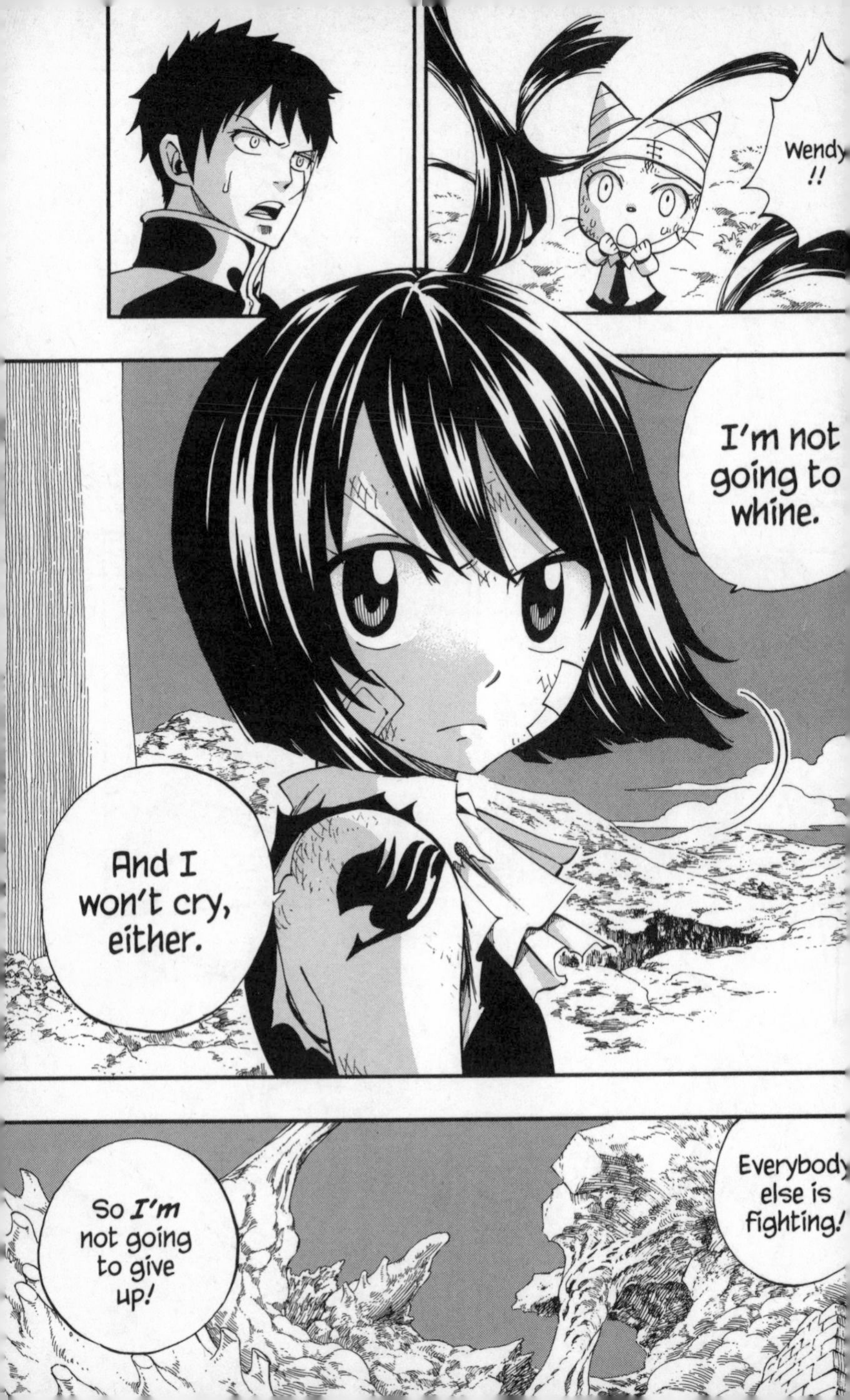
Wendy!!
I'm not going to whine.
And I won't cry, either.
Everybody else is fighting!
So I'm not going to give up!

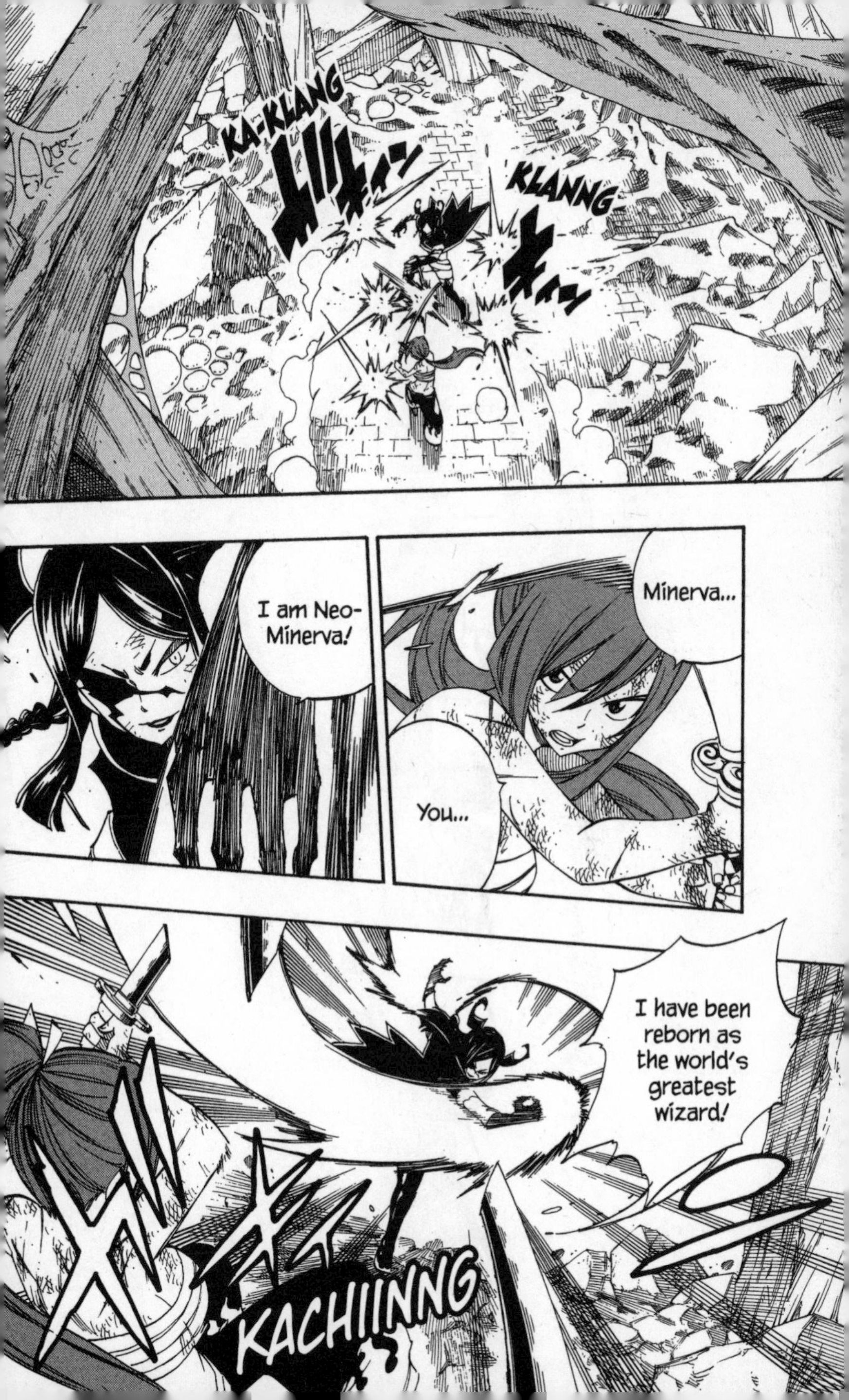
KA-KLANG
KLANNG
Minerva...
You...
I am Neo-Minerva!
I have been reborn as the world's greatest wizard!
KACHIINNG

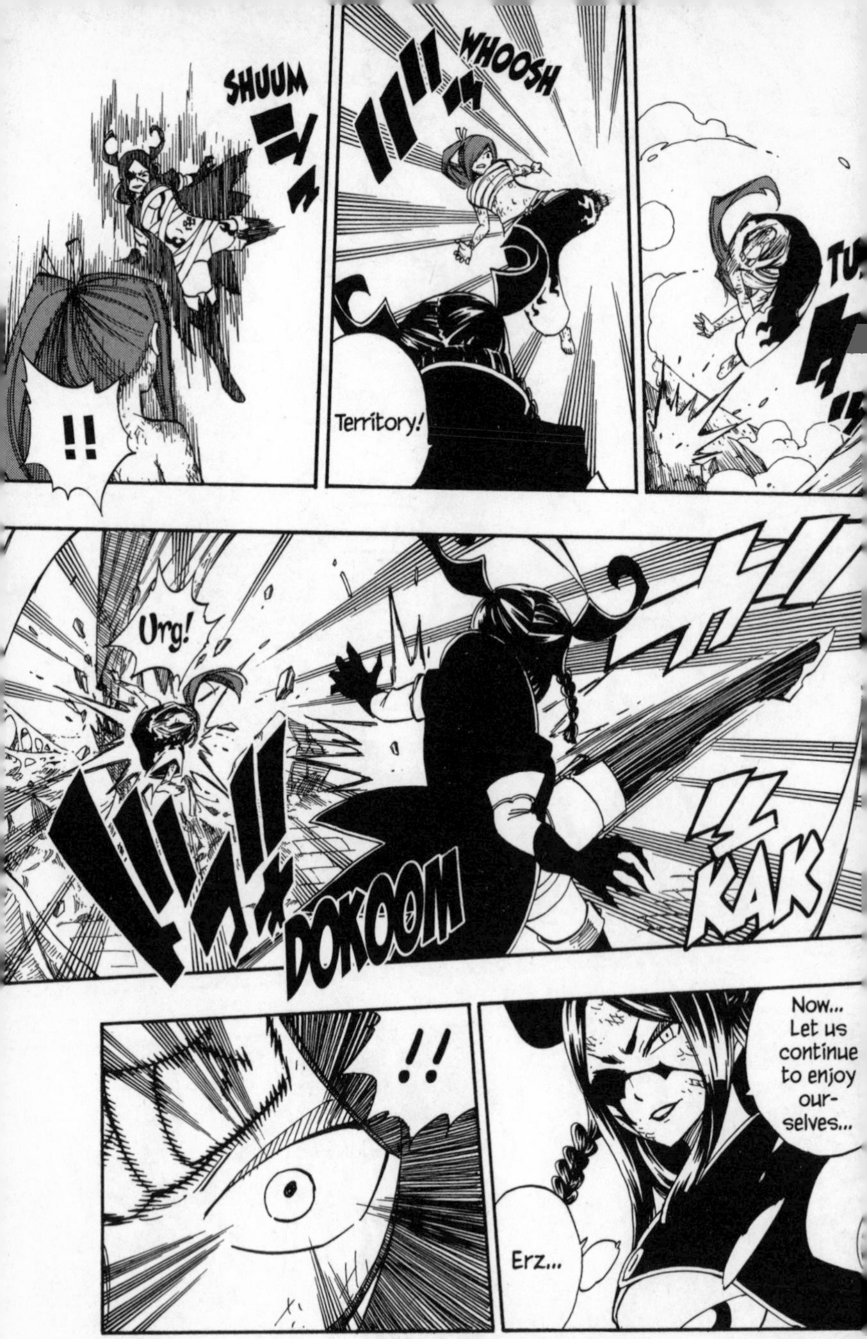
WHOOSH
Territory!
SHUUM
!!
KAK
DOKOOM
Urg!
Now... Let us continue to enjoy our-selves...
Erz...
!!

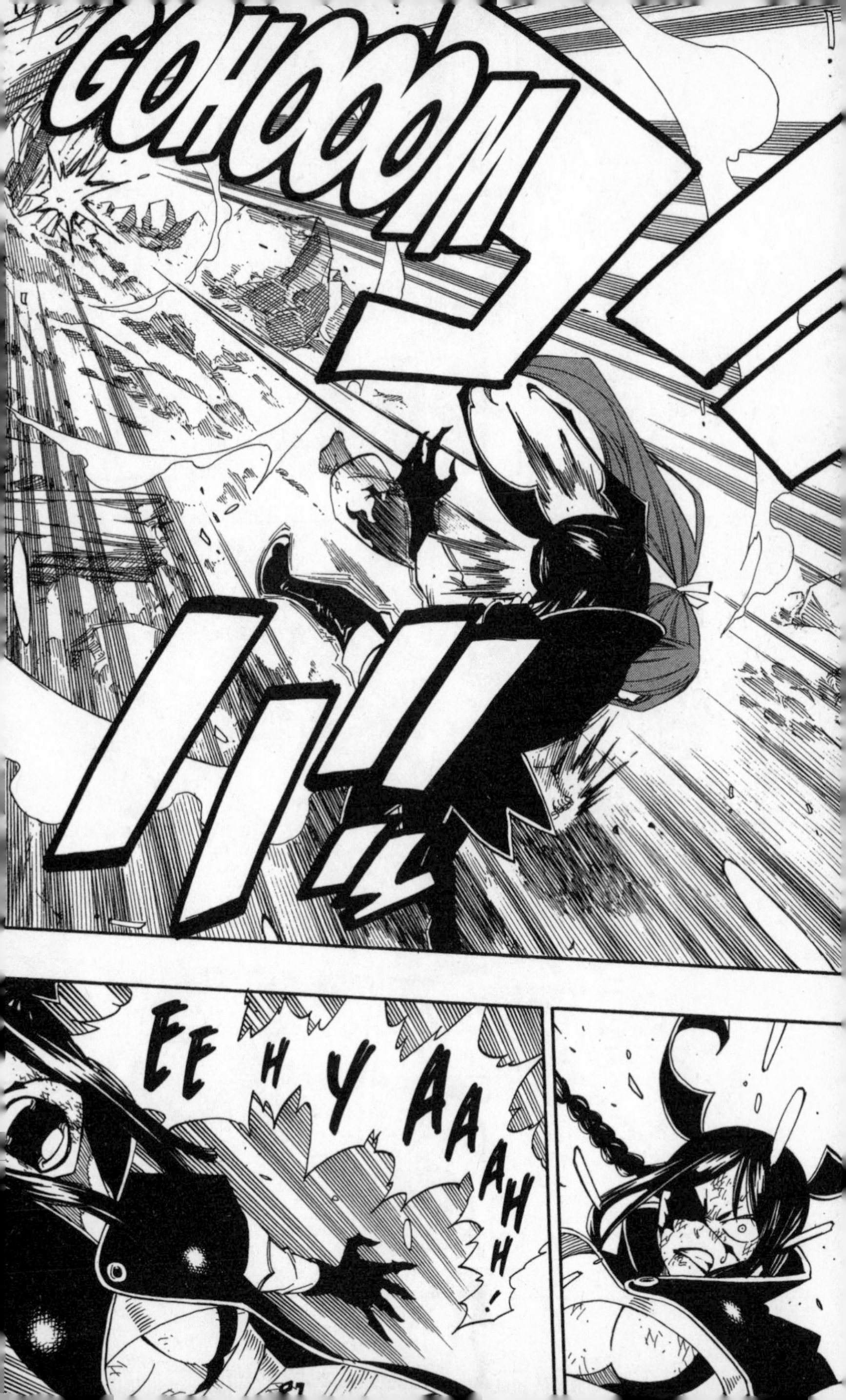
GOHOOOM
EEHYAAAHH!

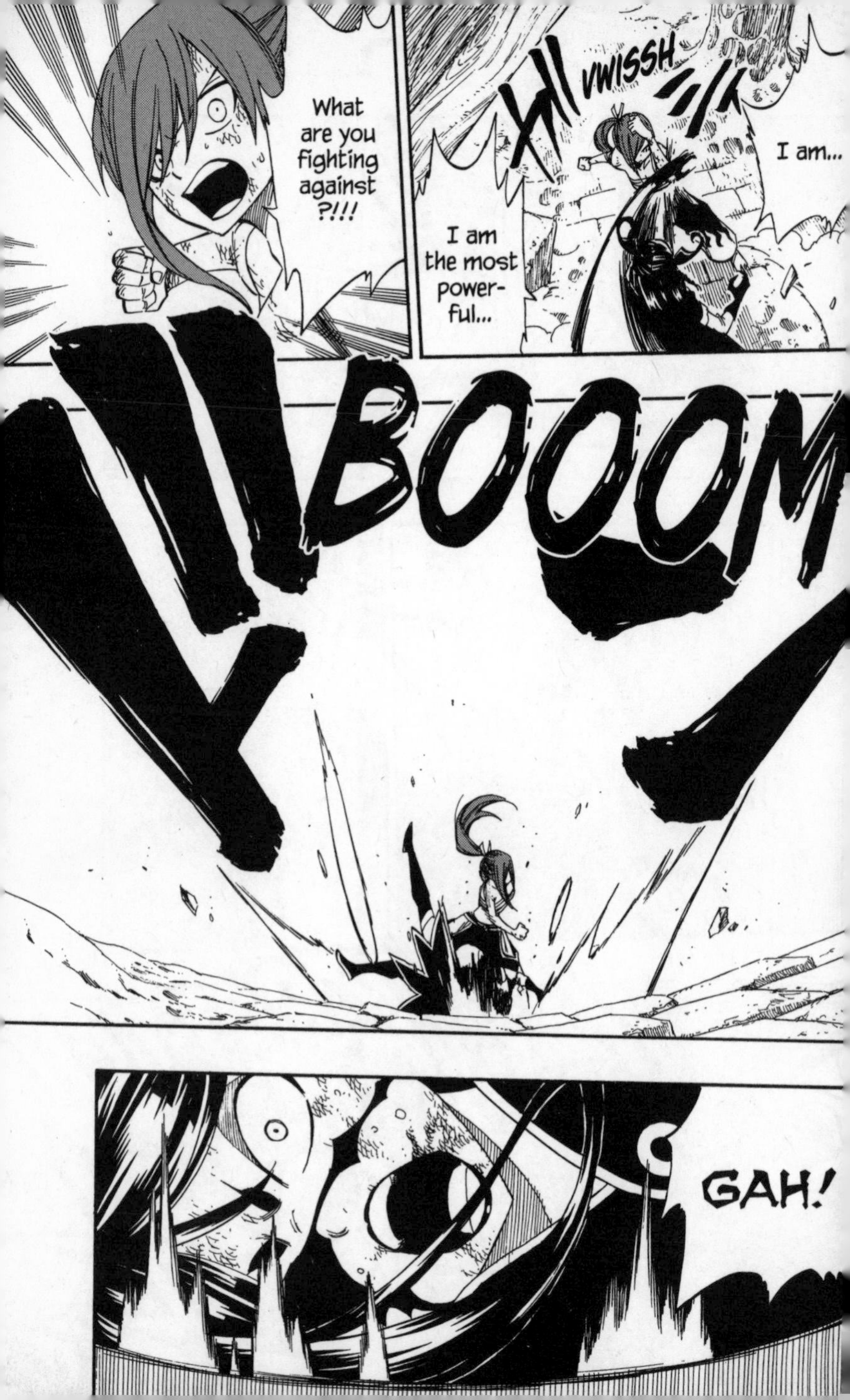
VWISSH
I am...
I am the most power-ful...
What are you fighting against ?!!!
BOOOM
GAH!

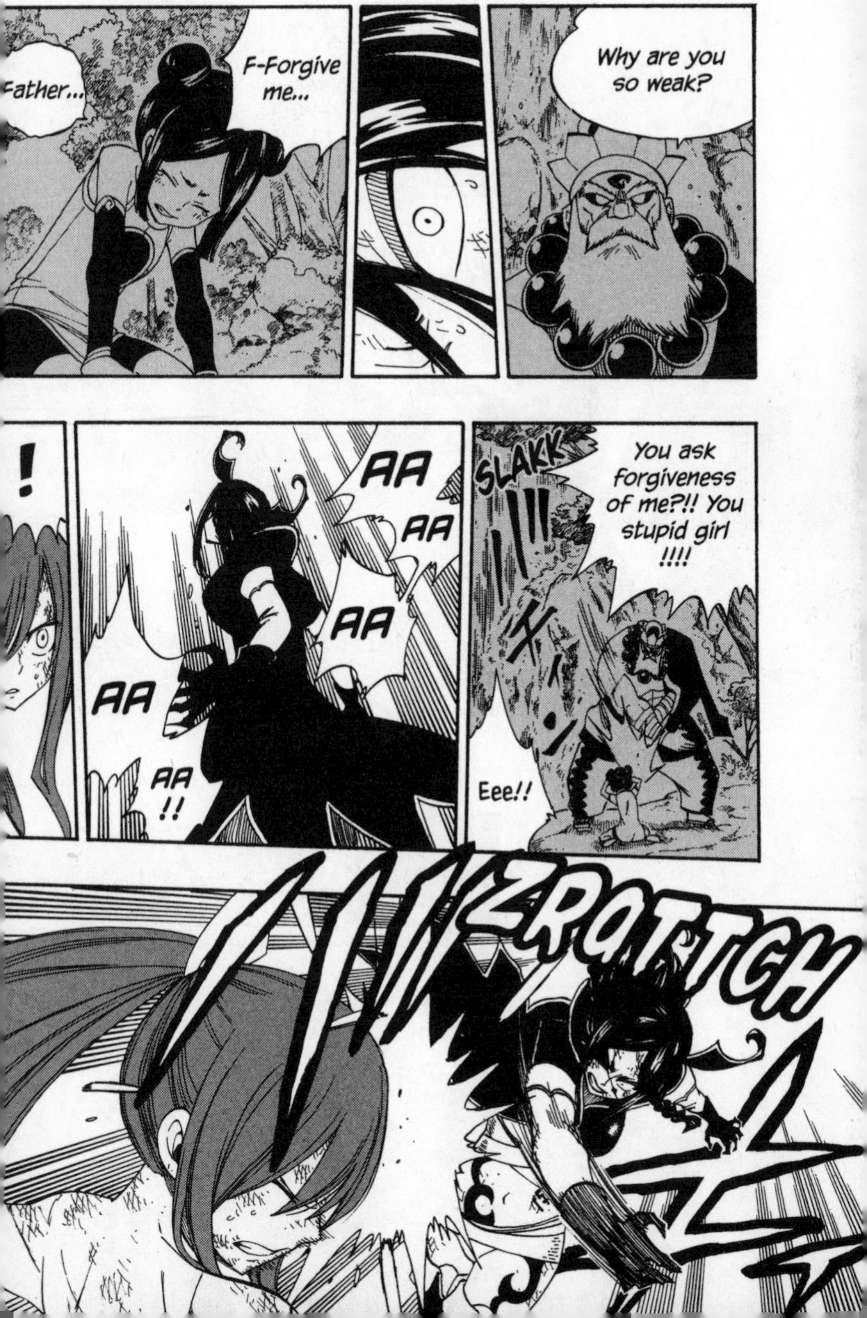
Why are you so weak?
F-Forgive me...
Father...
You ask forgiveness of me?!! You stupid girl !!!!
SLAKK
Eee!!
AA
AA
AA
AA
AA !!
!
ZRATTCH

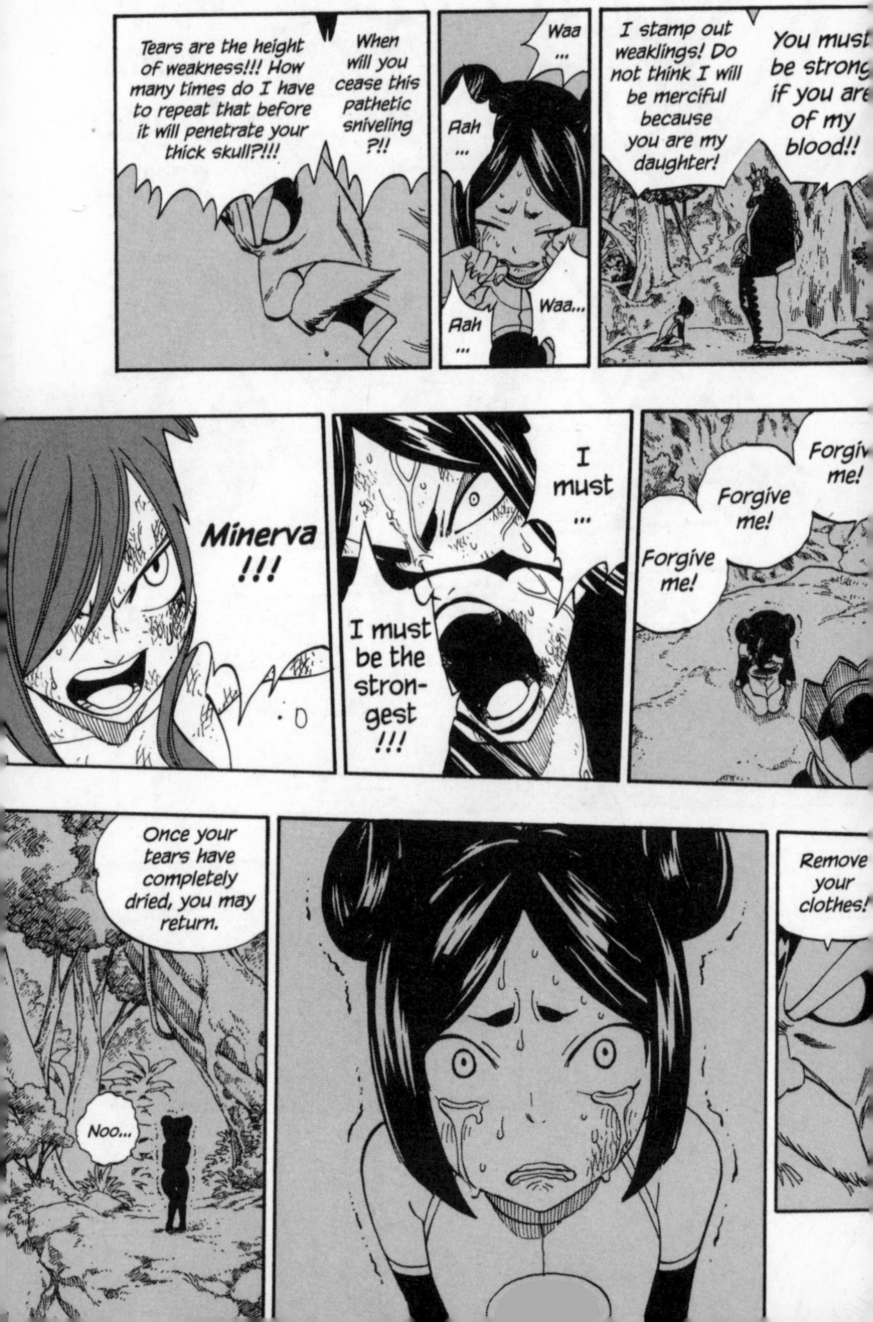
You must be strong if you are of my blood!!
I stamp out weaklings! Do not think I will be merciful because you are my daughter!
Waa ...
Aah ...
Waa...
Aah ...
When will you cease this pathetic sniveling ?!!
Tears are the height of weakness!!! How many times do I have to repeat that before it will penetrate your thick skull?!!!
Forgive me!
Forgive me!
Forgive me!
I must ...
I must be the strongest !!!
Minerva !!!
Remove your clothes!
Once your tears have completely dried, you may return.
Noo...

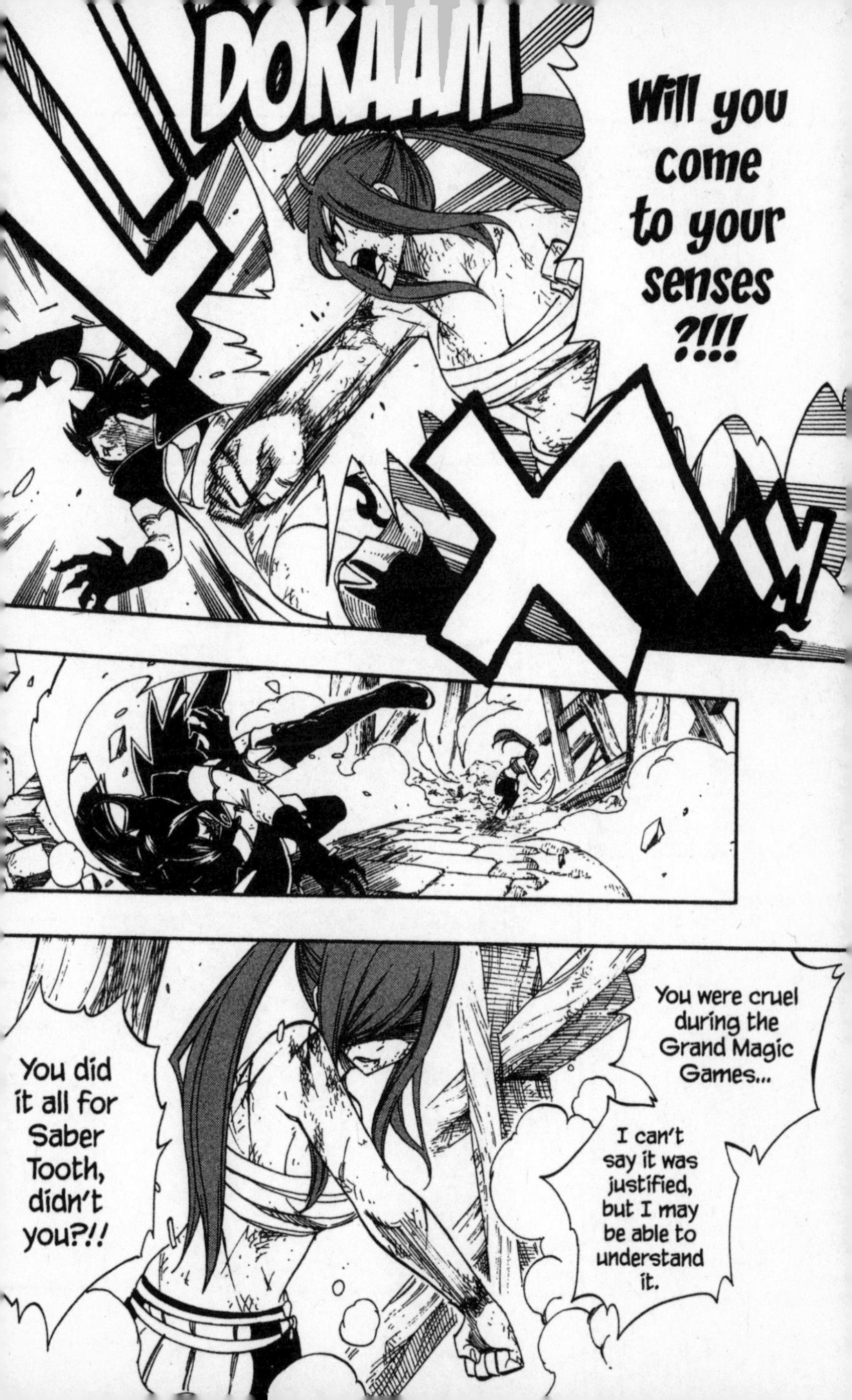
DOKAAM
Will you come to your senses ?!!!
You were cruel during the Grand Magic Games...
I can't say it was justified, but I may be able to understand it.
You did it all for Saber Tooth, didn't you?!!

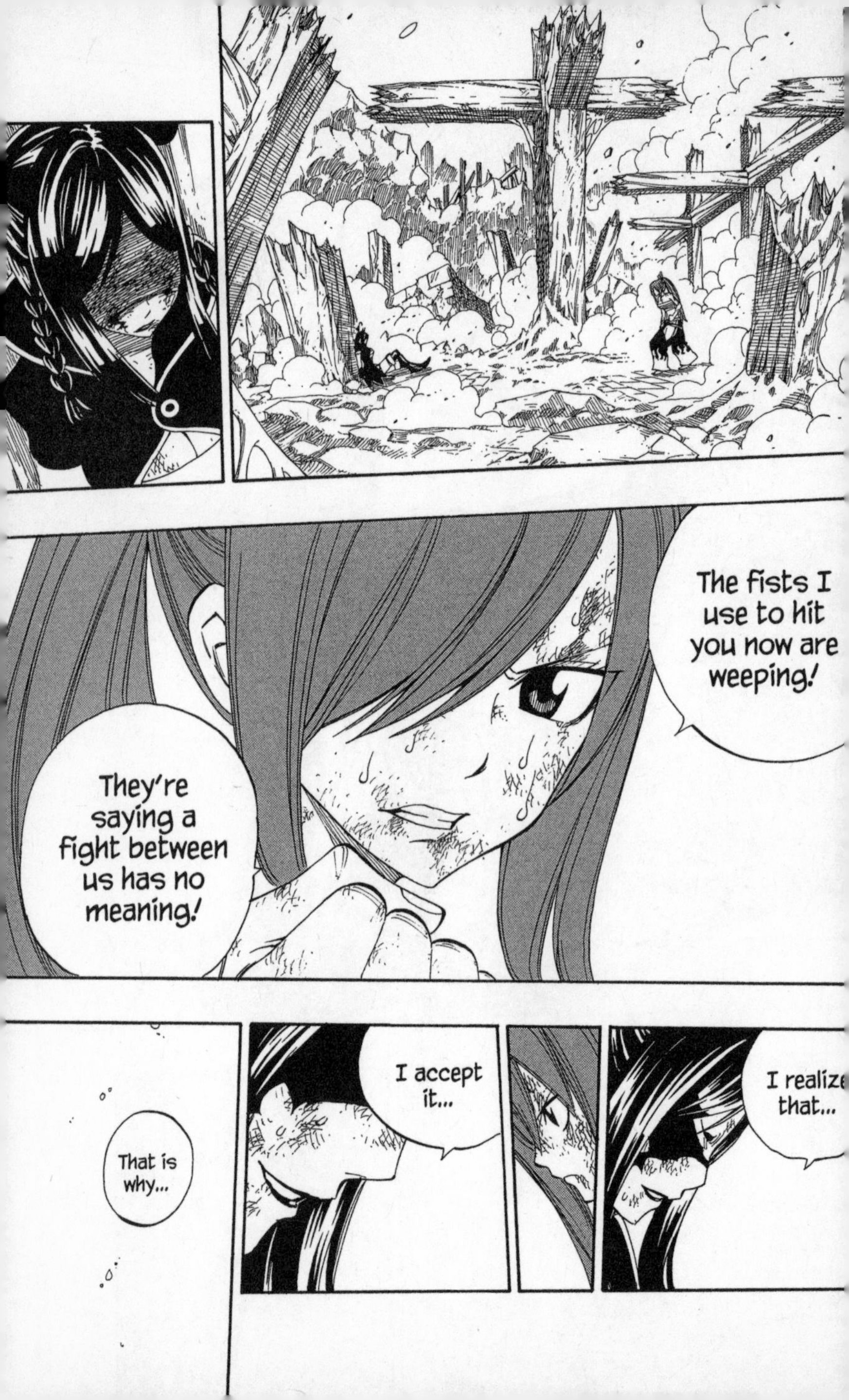
The fists I use to hit you now are weeping!
They're saying a fight between us has no meaning!
I realize that...
I accept it...
That is why...

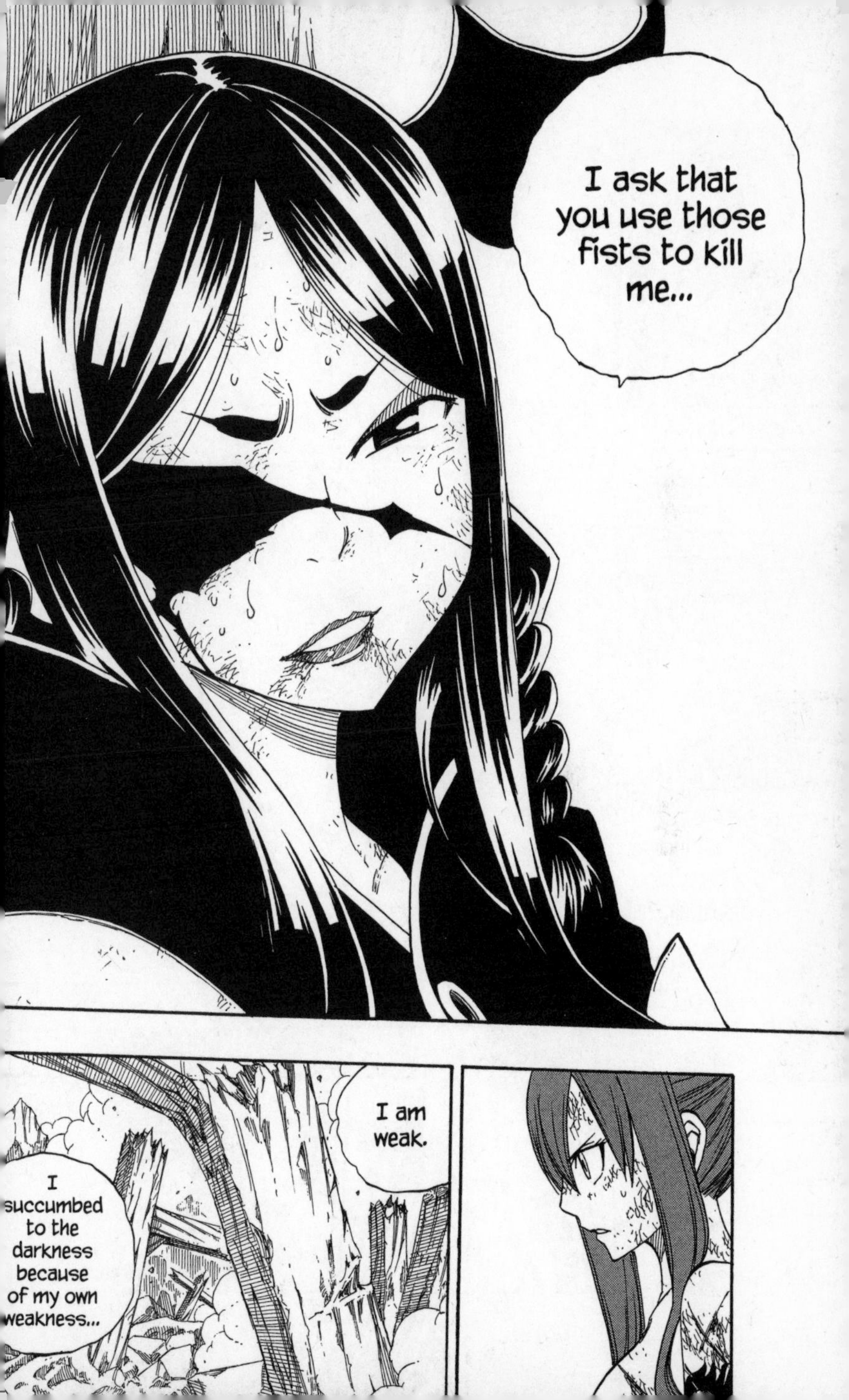
I ask that you use those fists to kill me...
I am weak.
I succumbed to the darkness because of my own weakness...

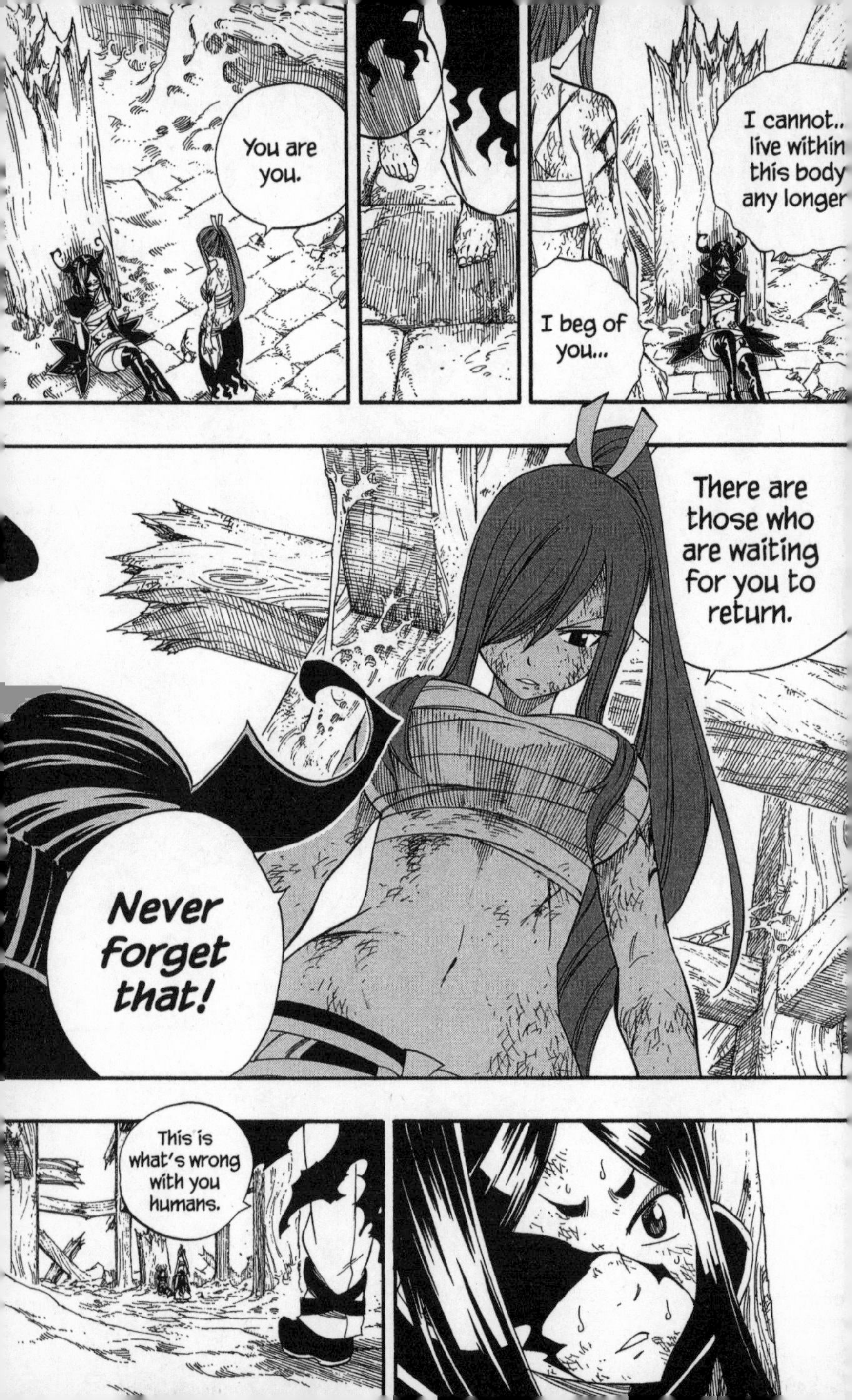
I cannot.. live within this body any longer
I beg of you...
You are you.
There are those who are waiting for you to return.
Never forget that!
This is what's wrong with you humans.

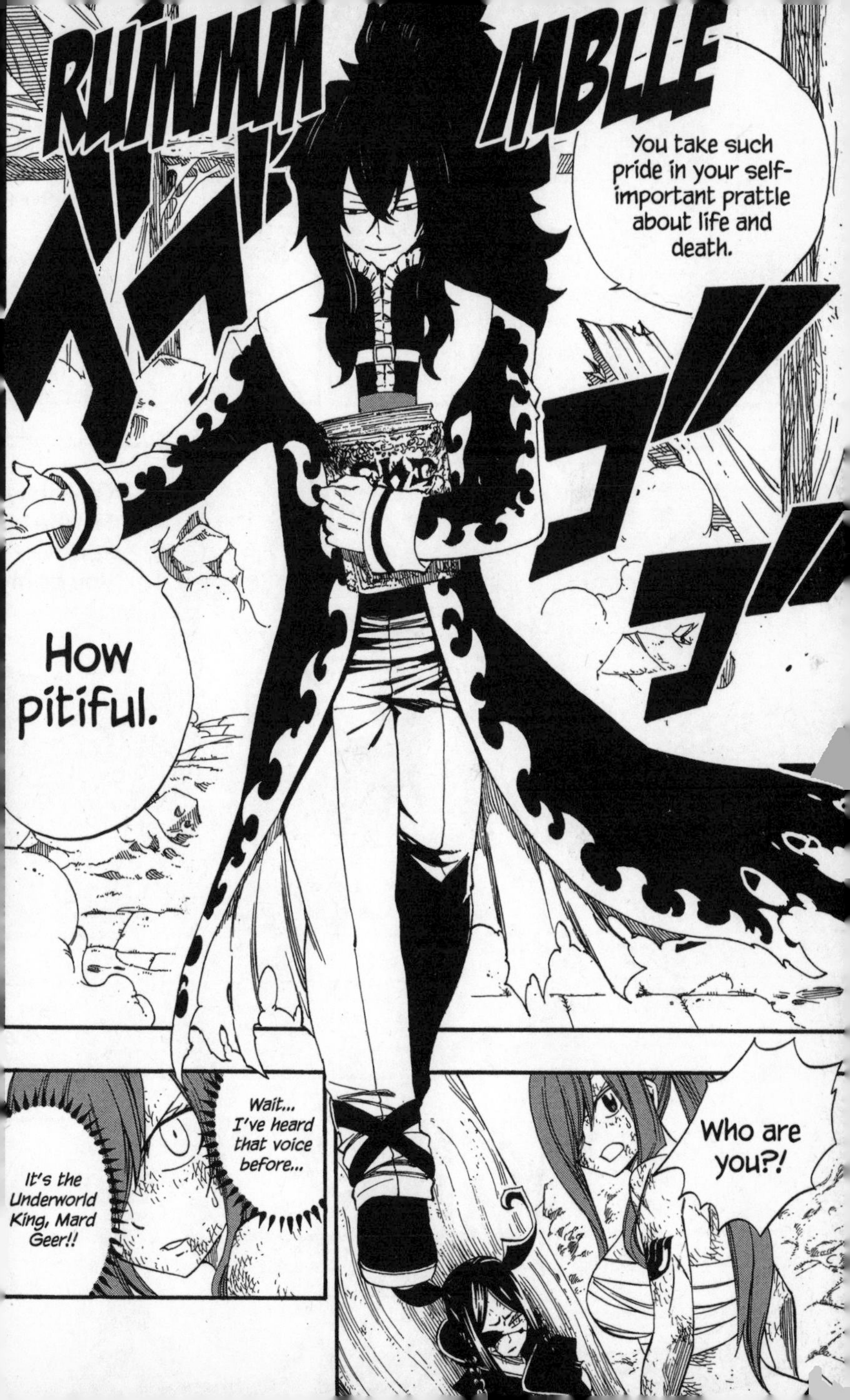
RUMMM MBLLE
You take such pride in your self-important prattle about life and death.
How pitiful.
Who are you?!
Wait... I've heard that voice before...
It's the Underworld King, Mard Geer!!

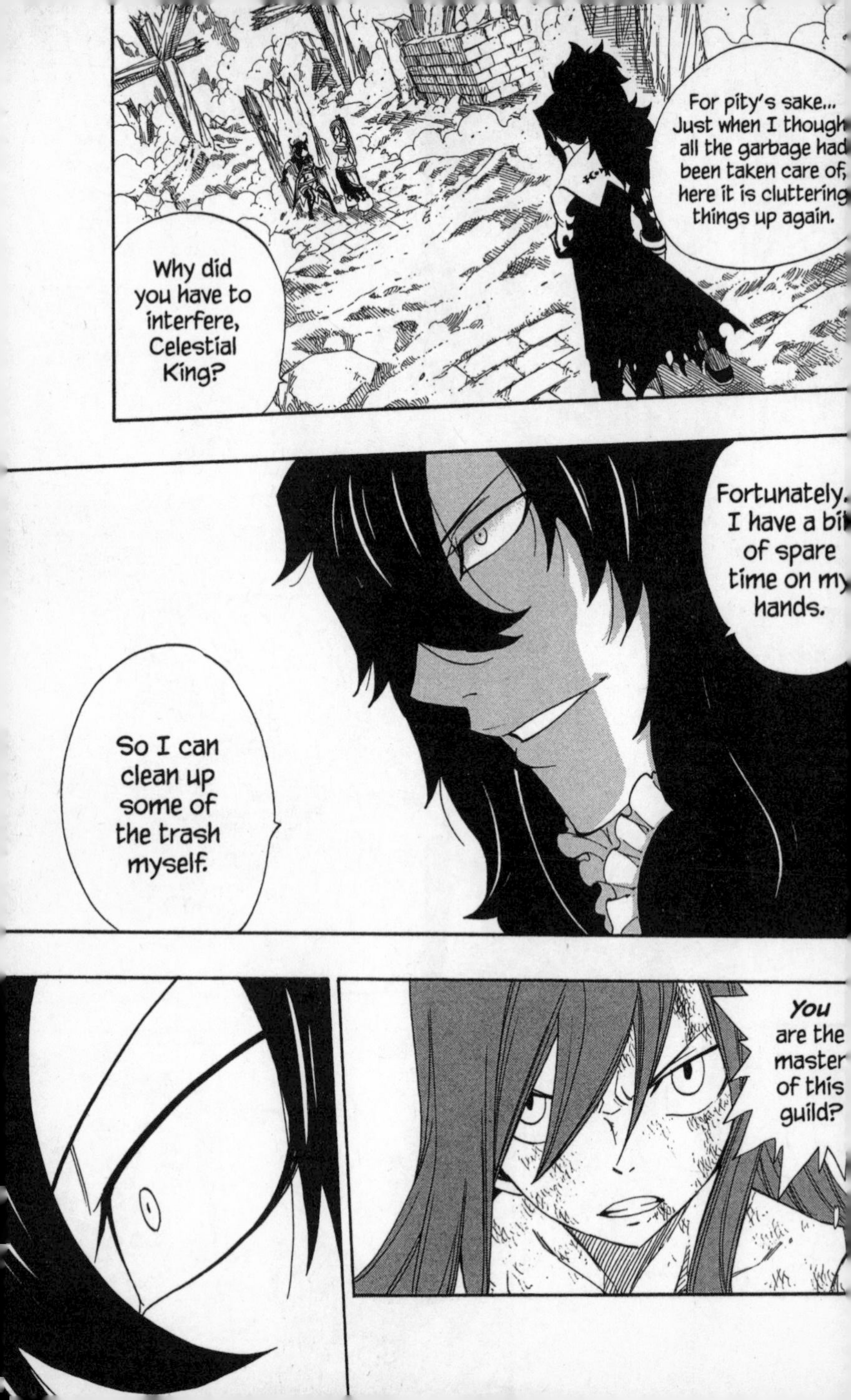
For pity's sake... Just when I though all the garbage had been taken care of, here it is cluttering things up again.
Why did you have to interfere, Celestial King?
Fortunately. I have a bi of spare time on my hands.
So I can clean up some of the trash myself.
You are the master of this guild?

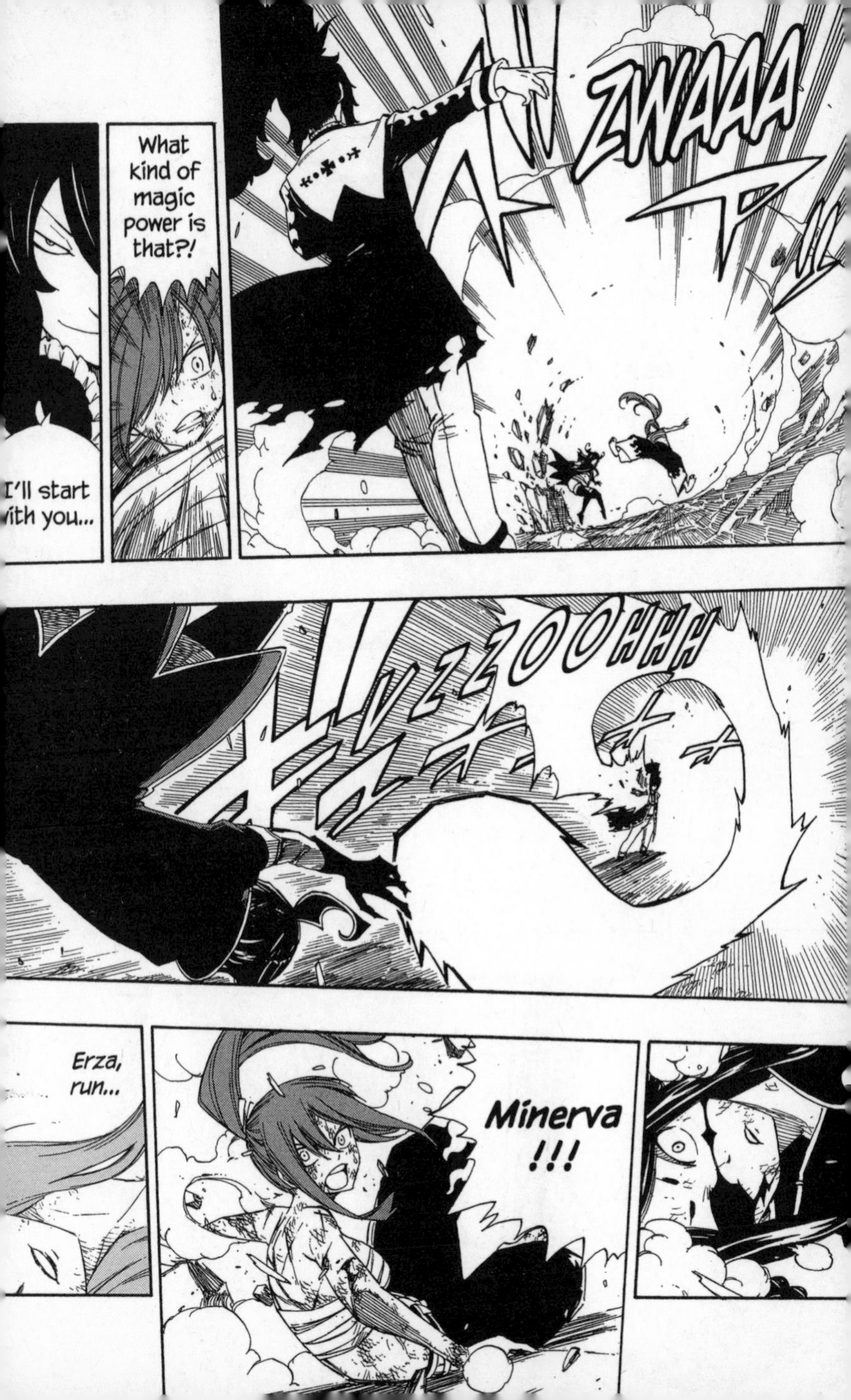
ZWAAA
What kind of magic power is that?!
I'll start ith you...
VZZOOHHH
Minerva !!!
Erza, run...

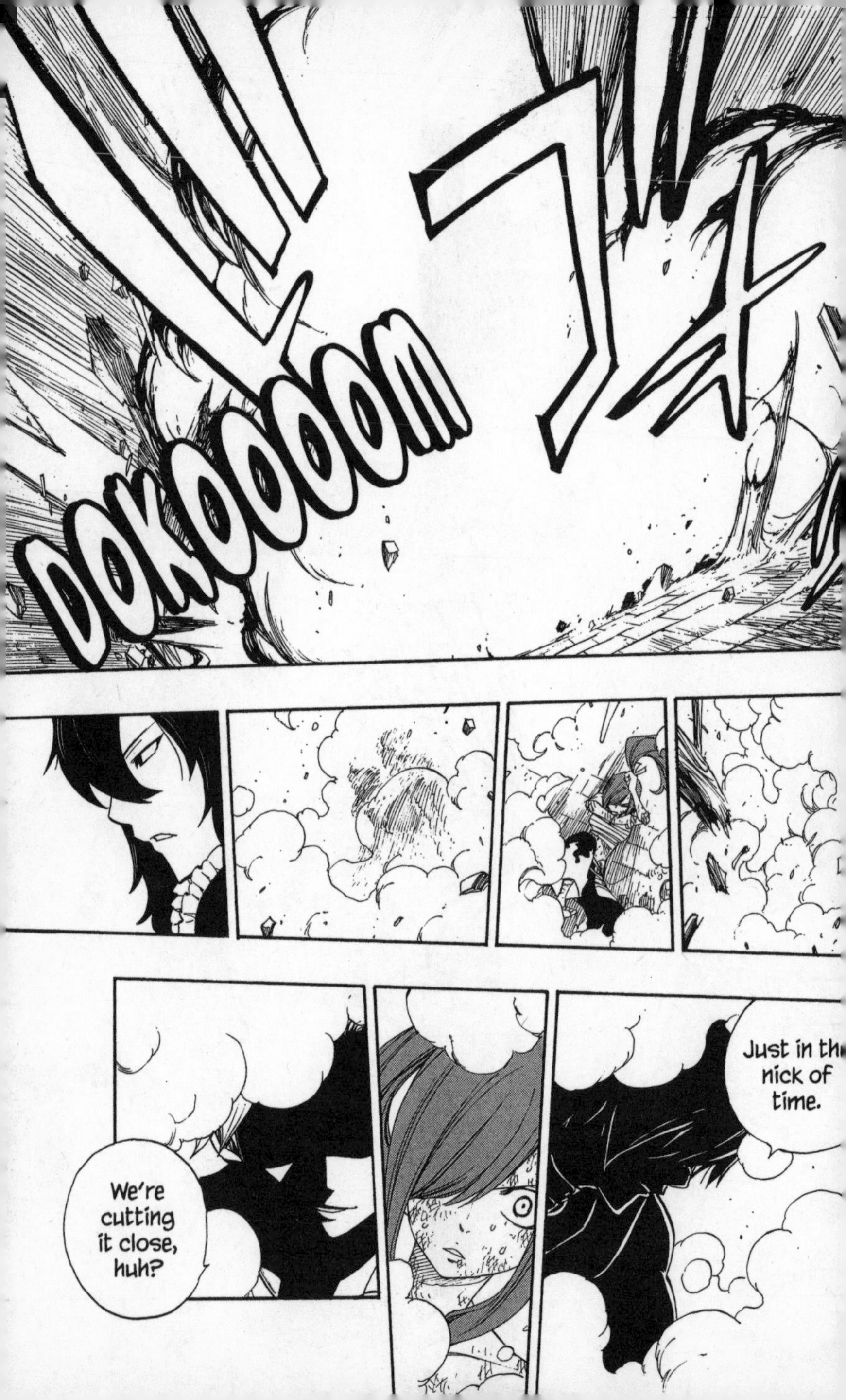
DOKOOOOM
Just in the nick of time.
We're cutting it close, huh?

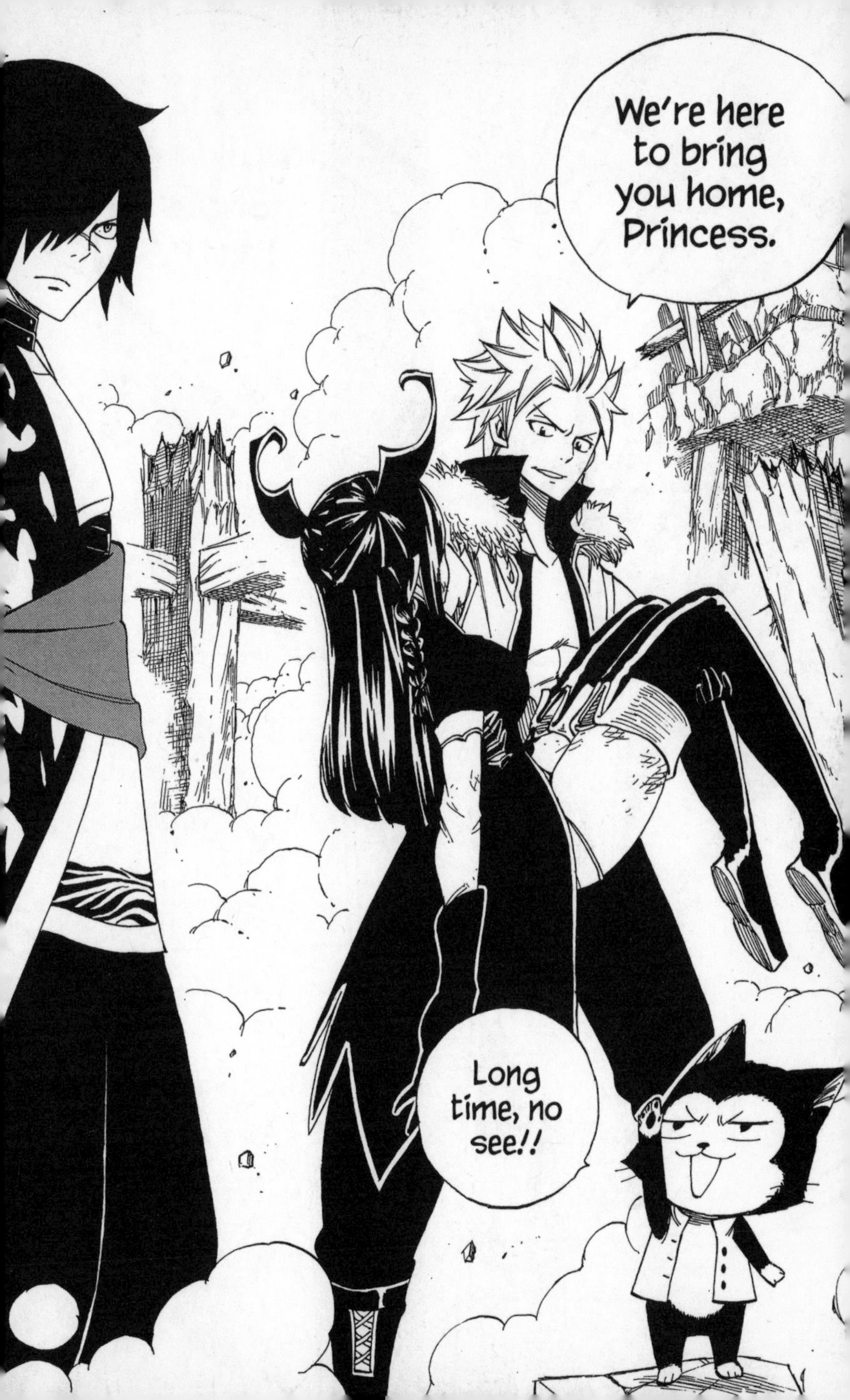
We're here to bring you home, Princess.
Long time, no see!!

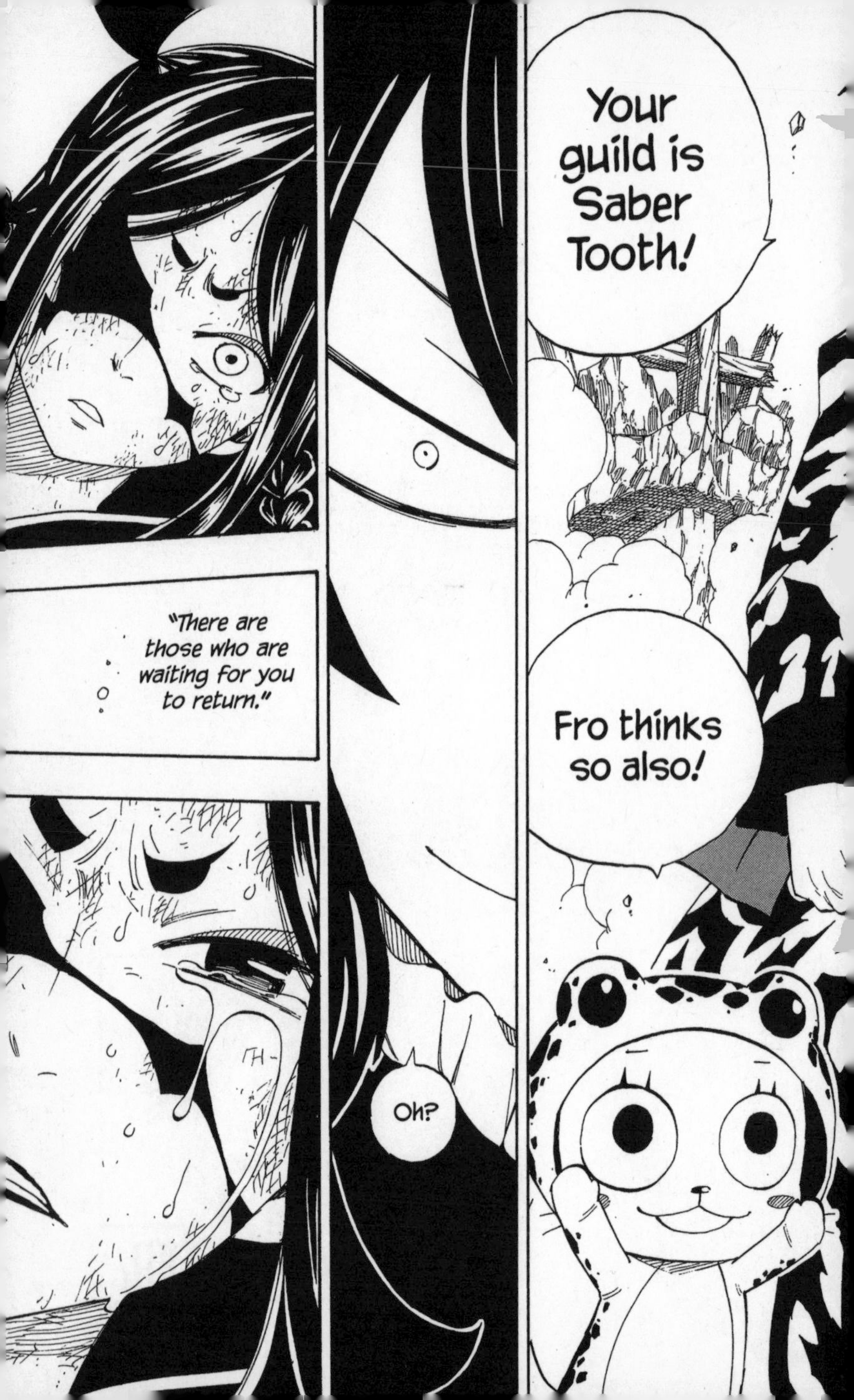
Your guild is Saber Tooth!
Fro thinks so also!
Oh?
"There are those who are waiting for you to return."

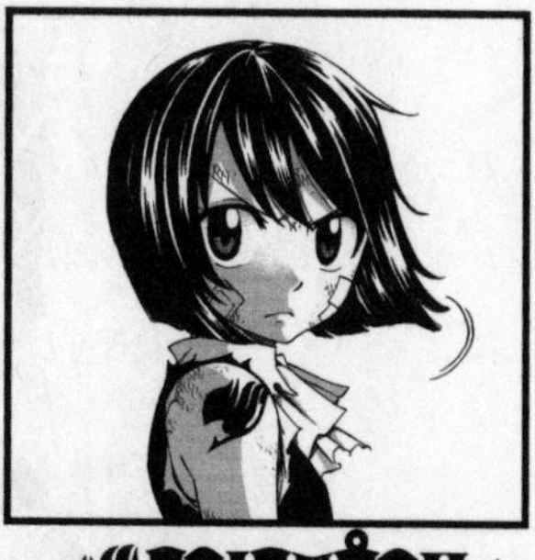

FAIRY TAIL

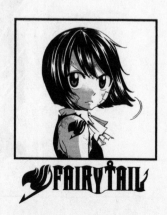

FAIRY TAIL

フェアリーテイル

Chapter 389: The Twin Dragons vs. the Underworld King

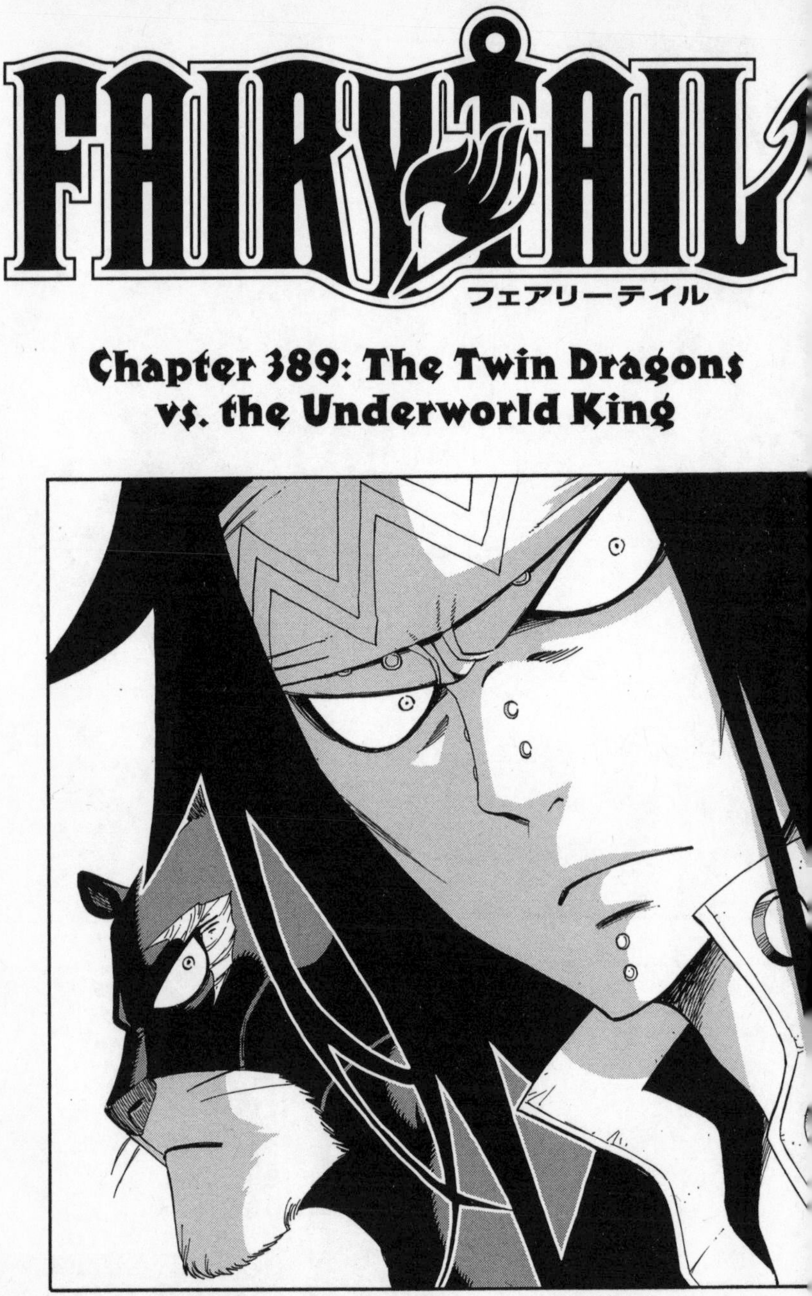

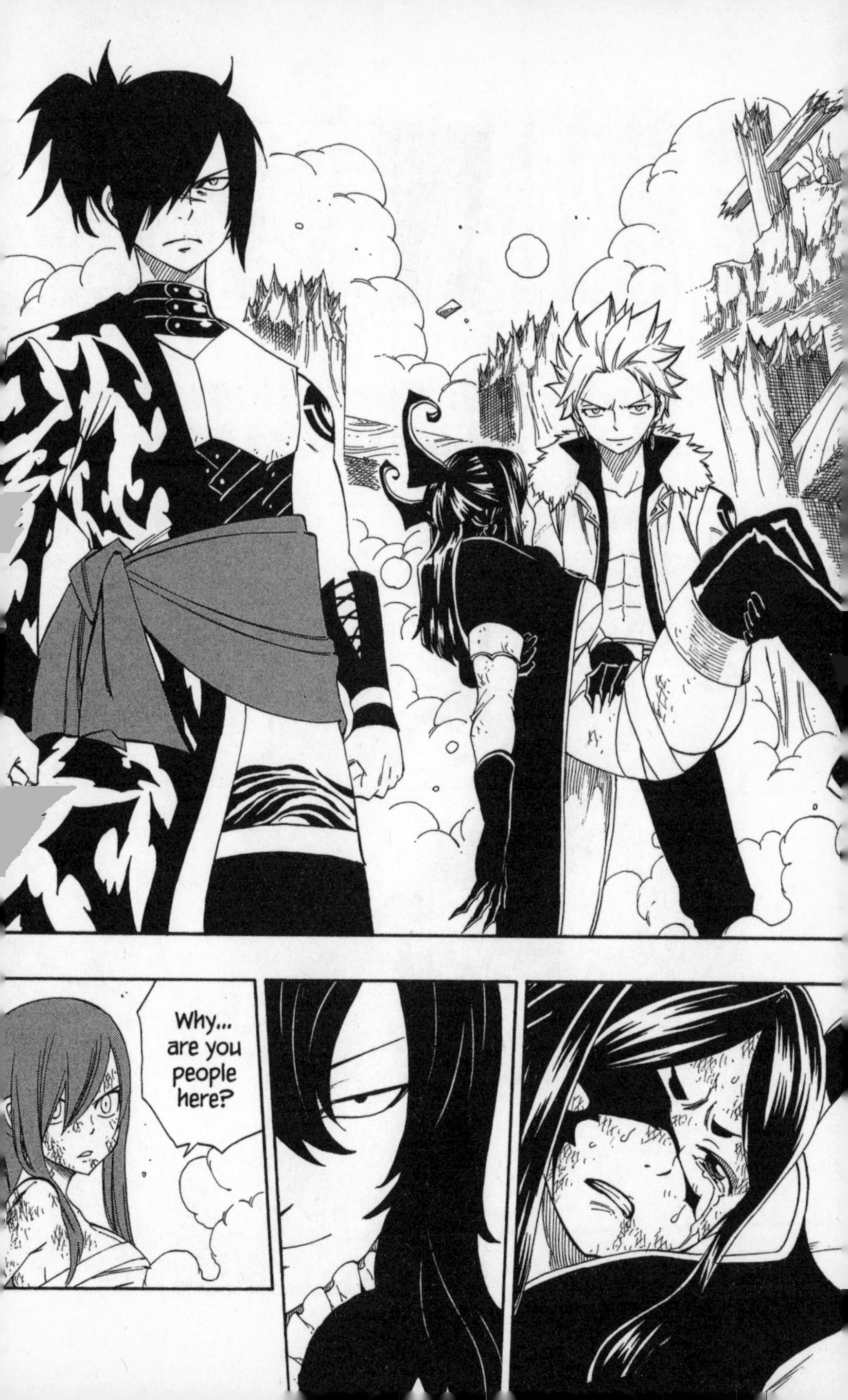
Why... are you people here?

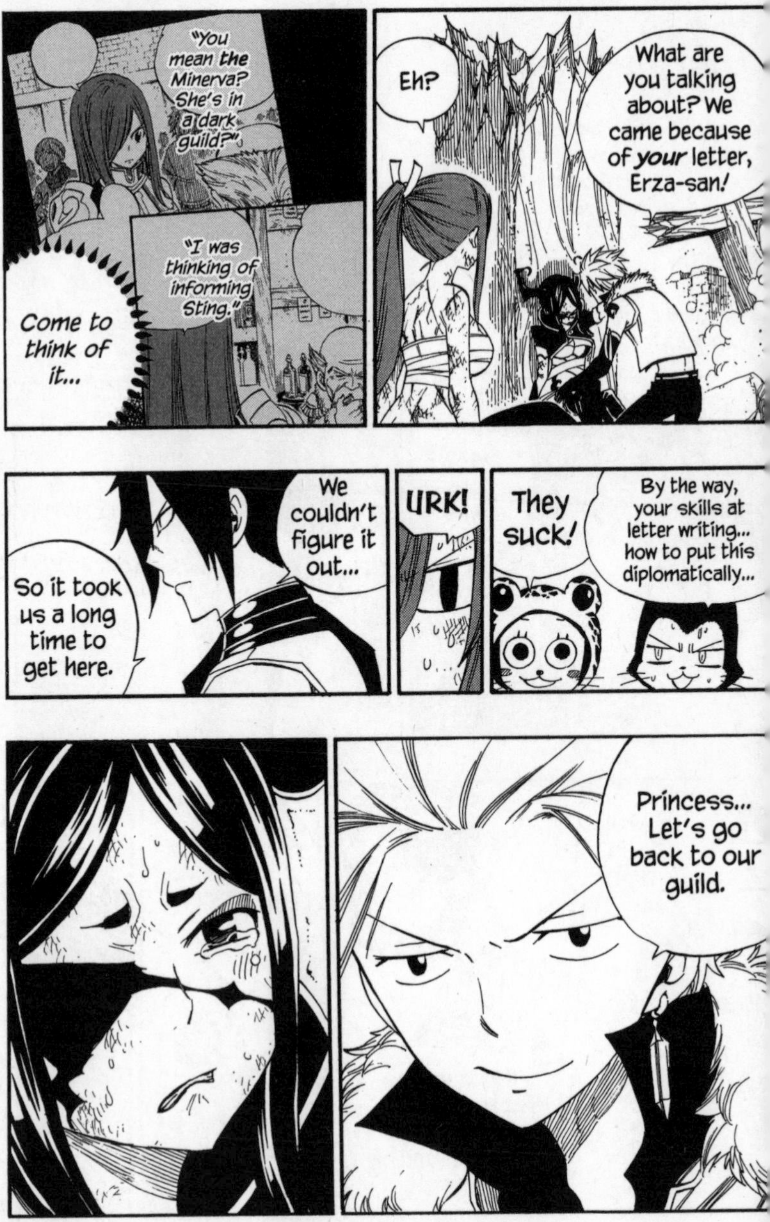
What are you talking about? We came because of *your* letter, Erza-san!
Eh?
"You mean **the** Minerva? She's in a dark guild?"
"I was thinking of informing Sting."
Come to think of it...
By the way, your skills at letter writing... how to put this diplomatically...
They suck!
URK!
We couldn't figure it out...
So it took us a long time to get here.
Princess... Let's go back to our guild.

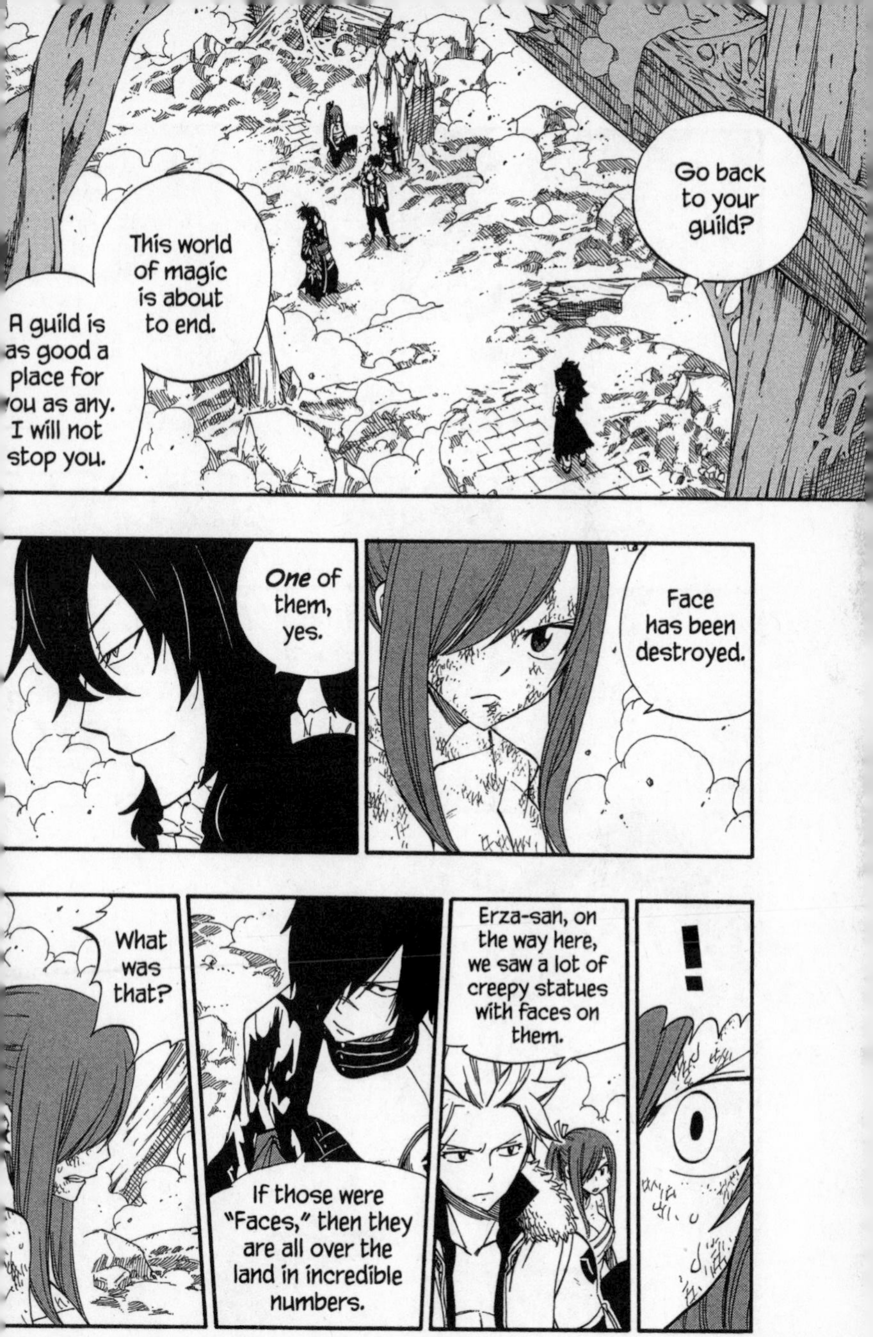

Go back to your guild?
This world of magic is about to end.
A guild is as good a place for you as any. I will not stop you.
Face has been destroyed.
One of them, yes.
!
Erza-san, on the way here, we saw a lot of creepy statues with faces on them.
If those were "Faces," then they are all over the land in incredible numbers.
What was that?

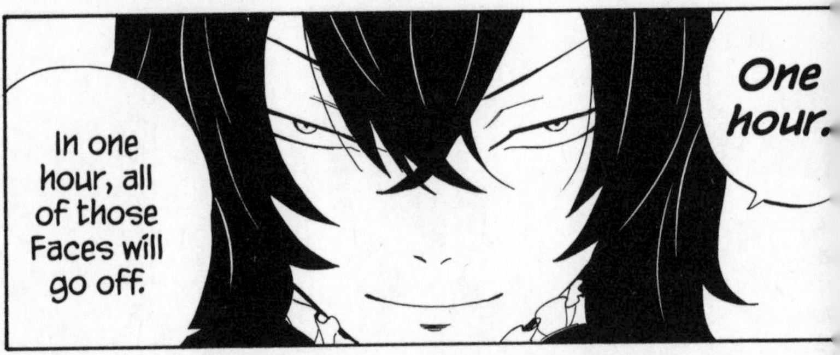
One hour.
In one hour, all of those Faces will go off.
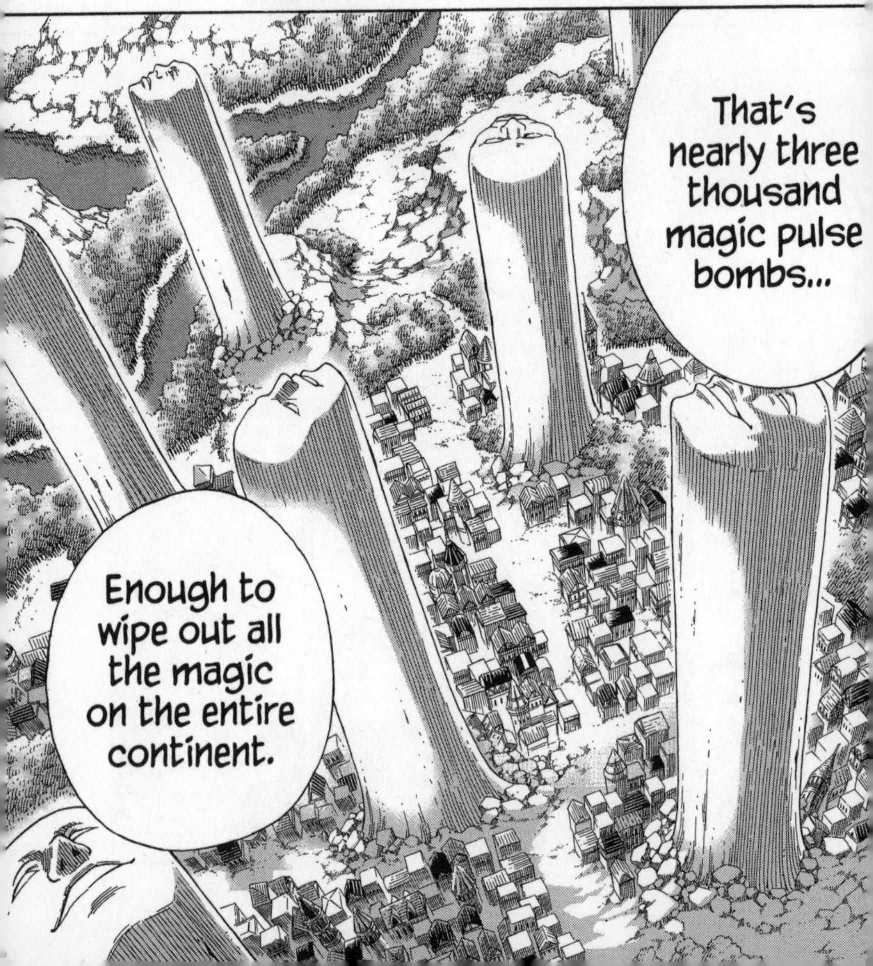
That's nearly three thousand magic pulse bombs...
Enough to wipe out all the magic on the entire continent.

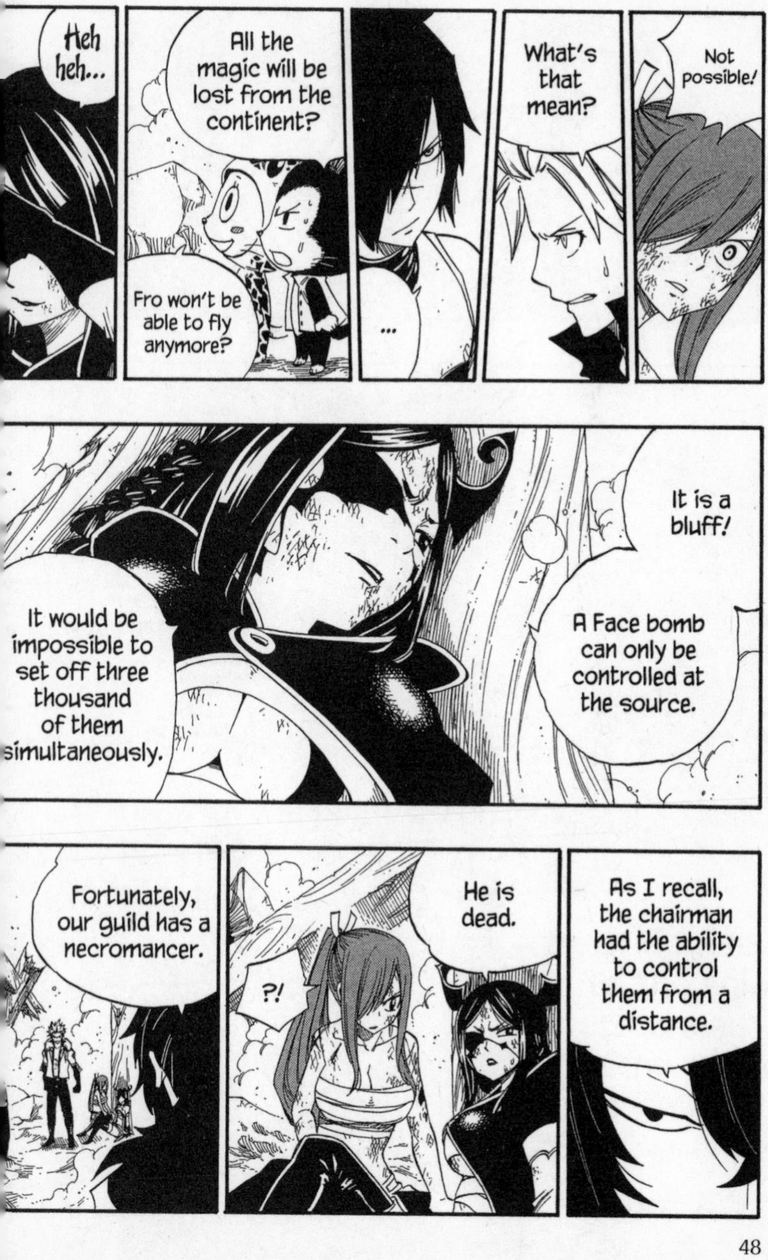
Not possible!
What's that mean?
...
All the magic will be lost from the continent?
Fro won't be able to fly anymore?
Heh heh...
It is a bluff!
A Face bomb can only be controlled at the source.
It would be impossible to set off three thousand of them simultaneously.
As I recall, the chairman had the ability to control them from a distance.
He is dead.
?!
Fortunately, our guild has a necromancer.

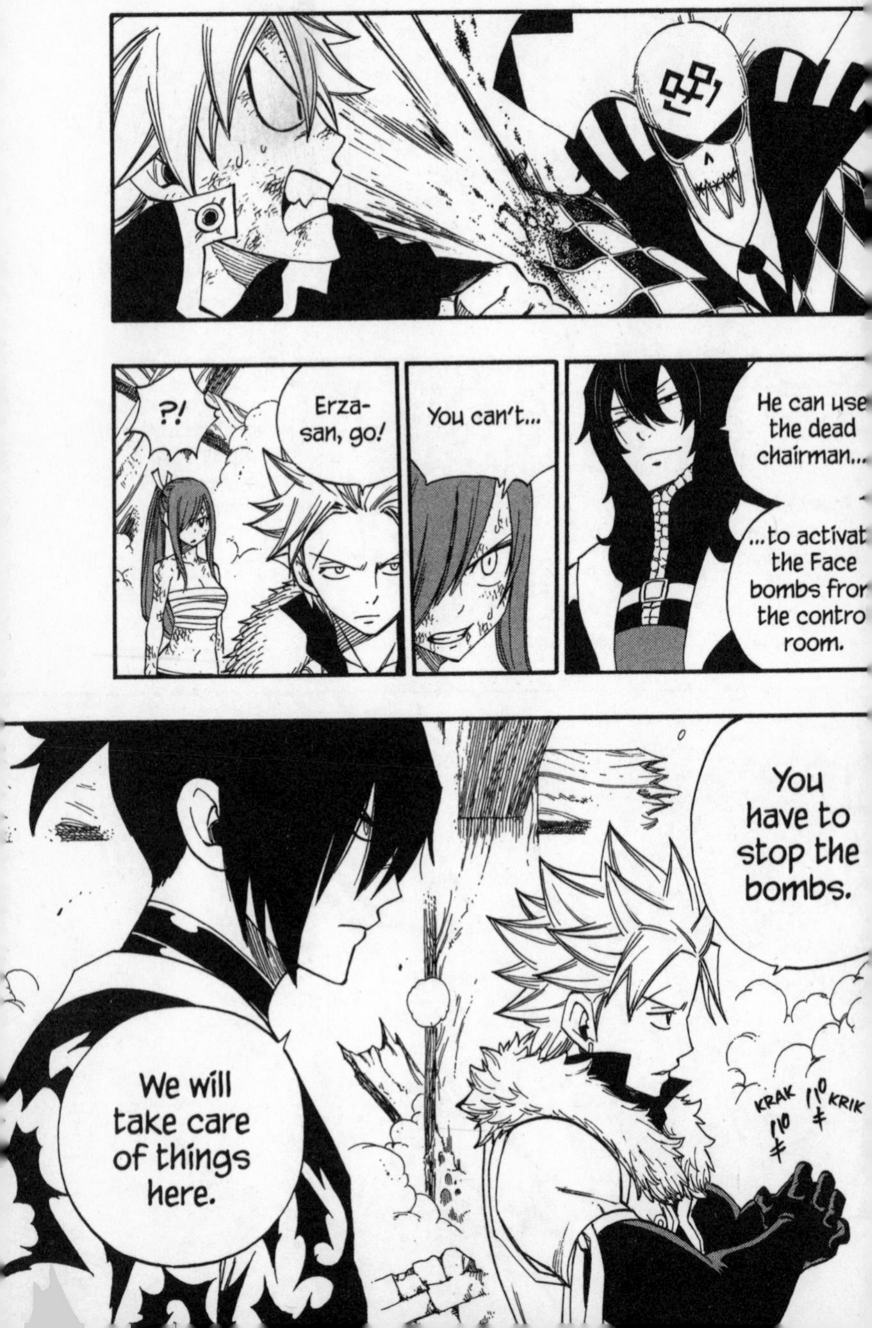
He can use the dead chairman...
...to activat the Face bombs fror the contro room.
You can't...
Erza-san, go!
?!
You have to stop the bombs.
KRIK
KRAK
We will take care of things here.

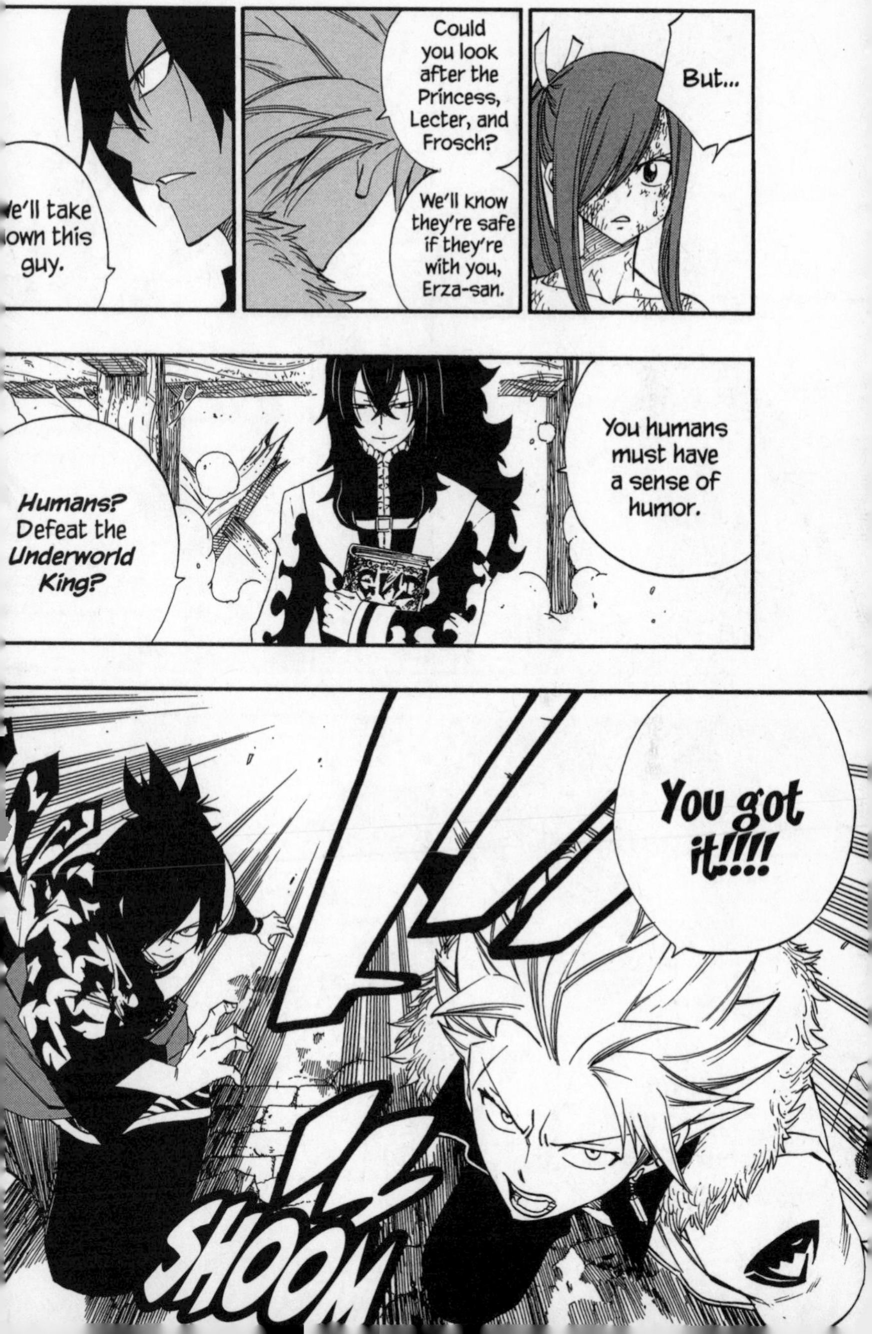
But...
Could you look after the Princess, Lecter, and Frosch?
We'll know they're safe if they're with you, Erza-san.
e'll take own this guy.
You humans must have a sense of humor.
Humans? Defeat the *Underworld* King?
You got it!!!!
SHOOM

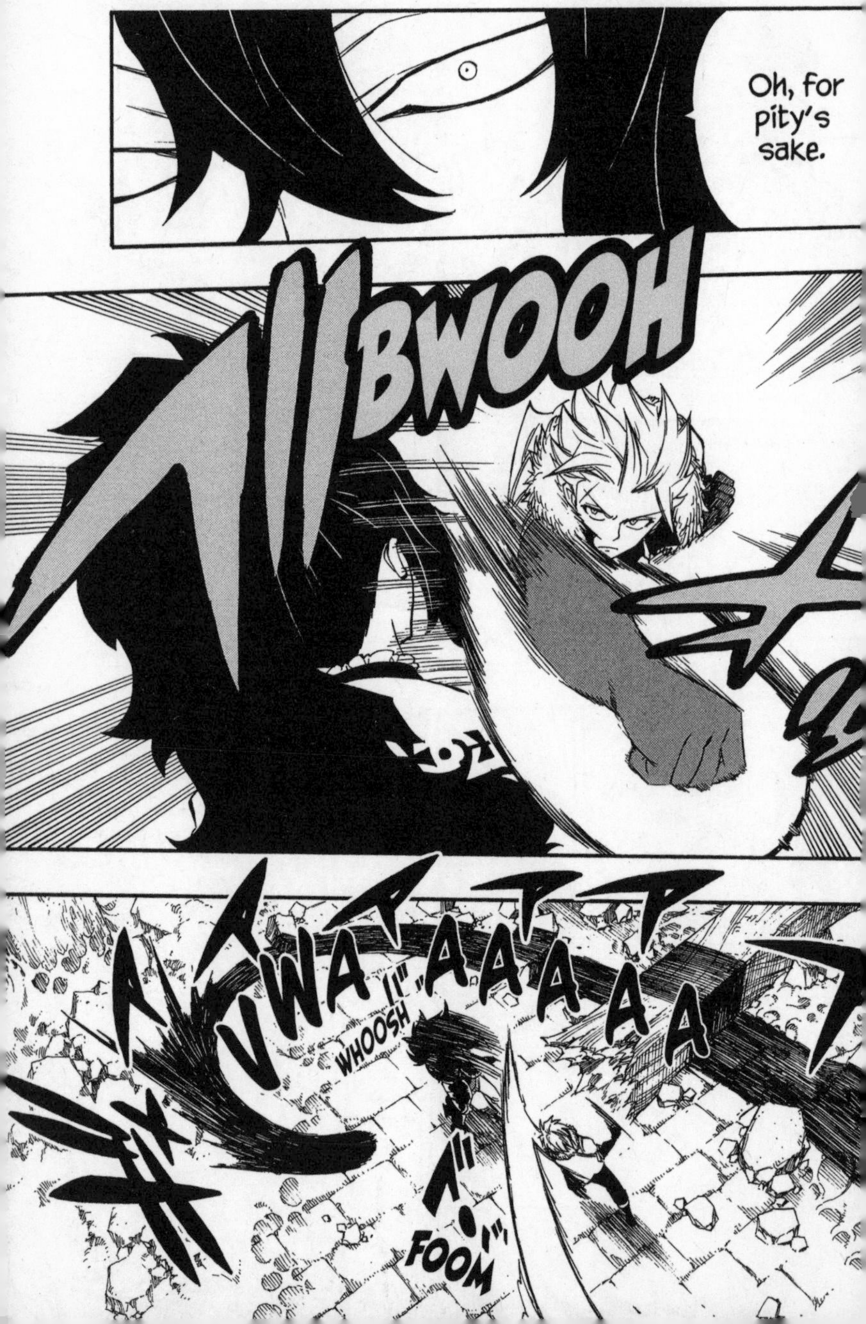

Oh, for pity's sake.
BWOOH
VWAAAAAA
WHOOSH
FOOM

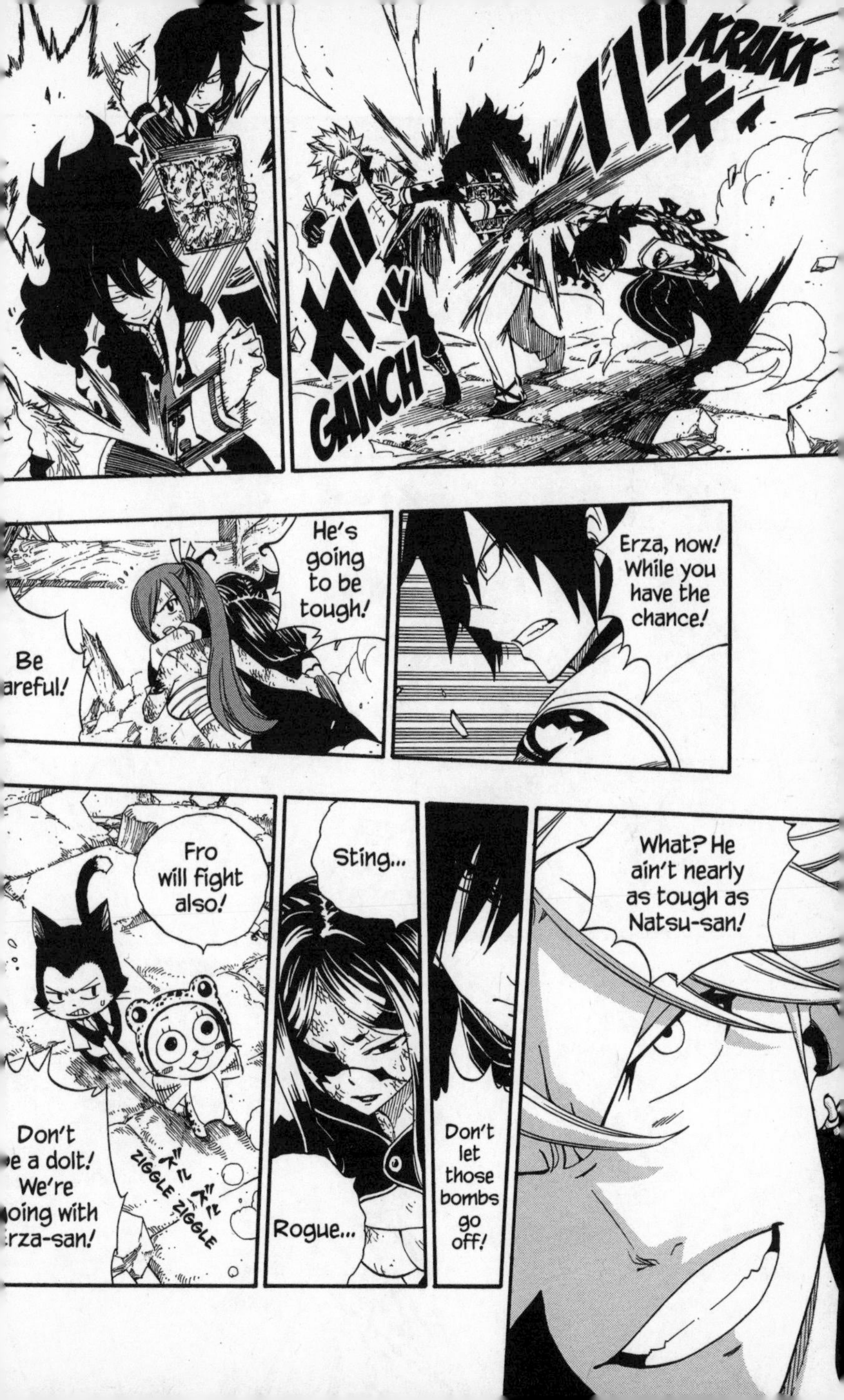
KRAKK
GANCH
Erza, now! While you have the chance!
He's going to be tough!
Be
areful!
What? He ain't nearly as tough as Natsu-san!
Don't let those bombs go off!
Sting...
Rogue...
Fro will fight also!
Don't
e a dolt! We're
oing with
rza-san!
ZIGGLE ZIGGLE

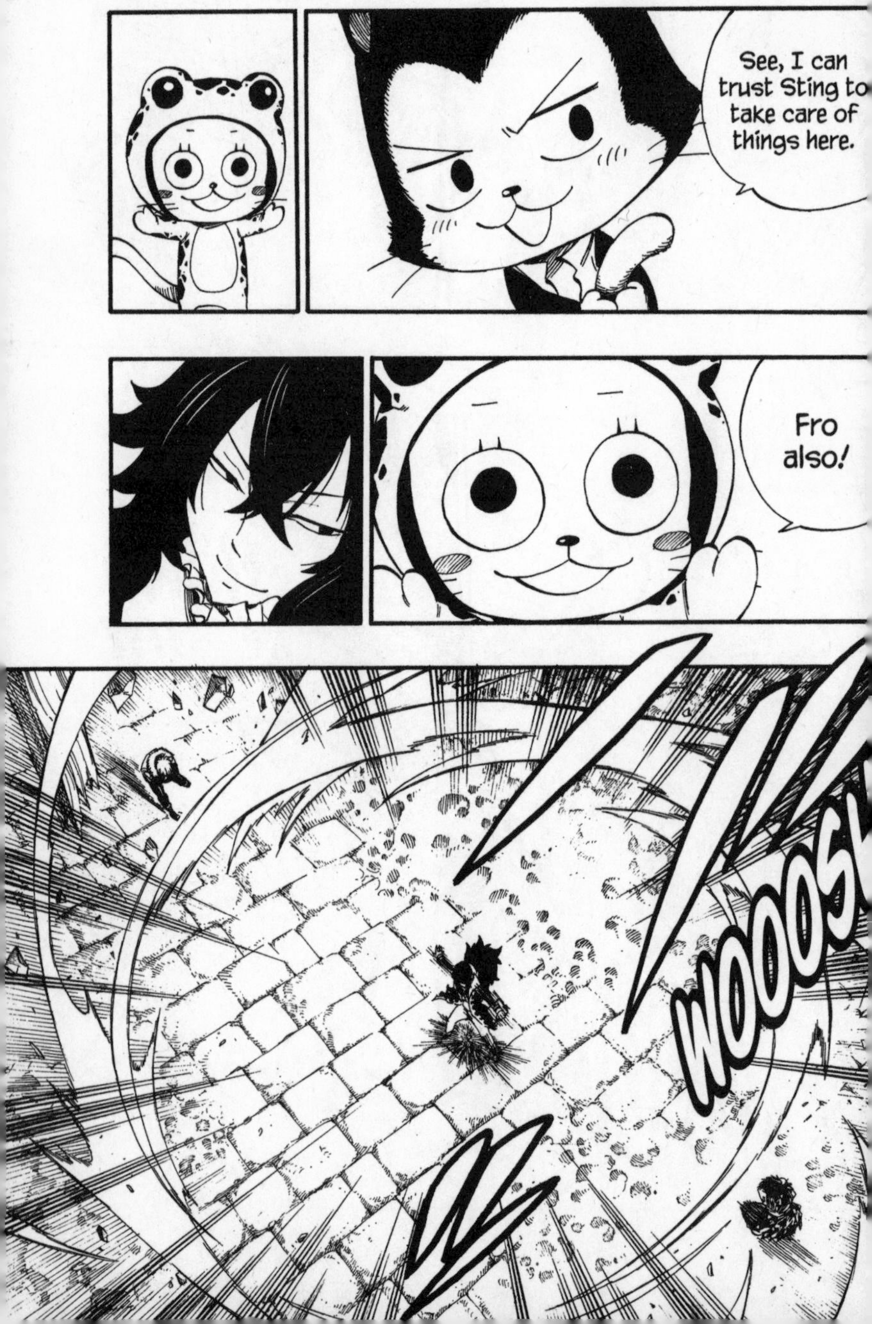
See, I can trust Sting to take care of things here.
Fro also!
WOOOS

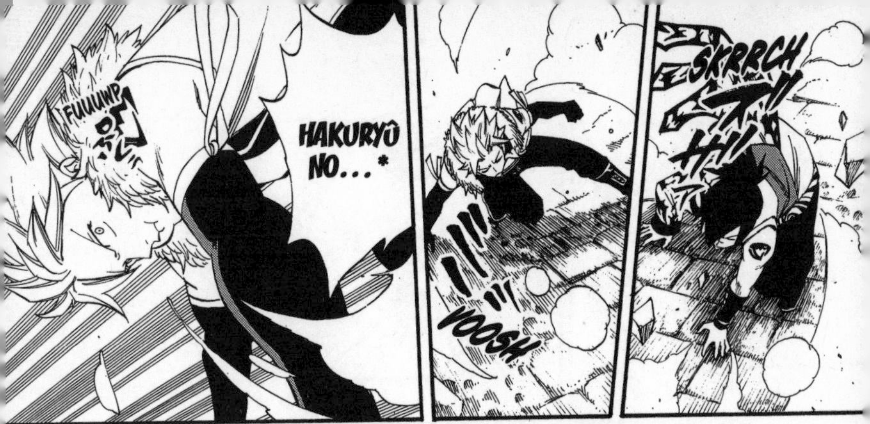
SKRRCH
VOOSH
HAKURYÔ NO...*
FUUUMP

*White Dragon's...

**...Roar

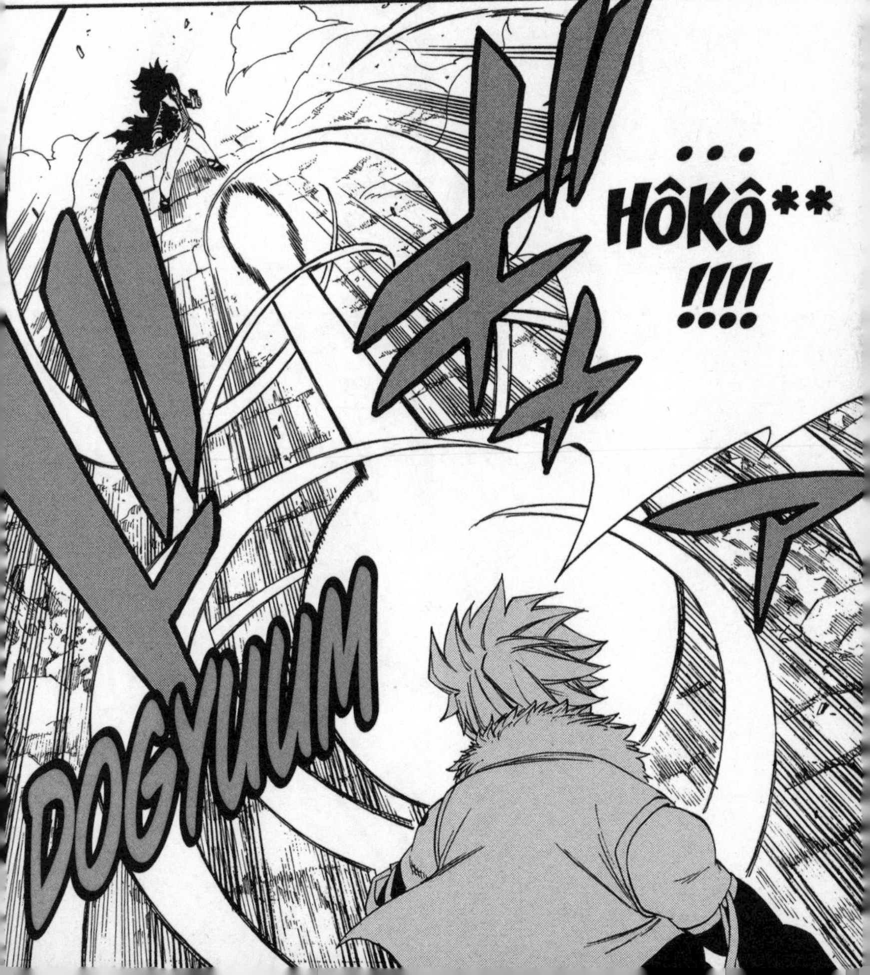
...HÔKÔ** !!!!
DOGYUUM

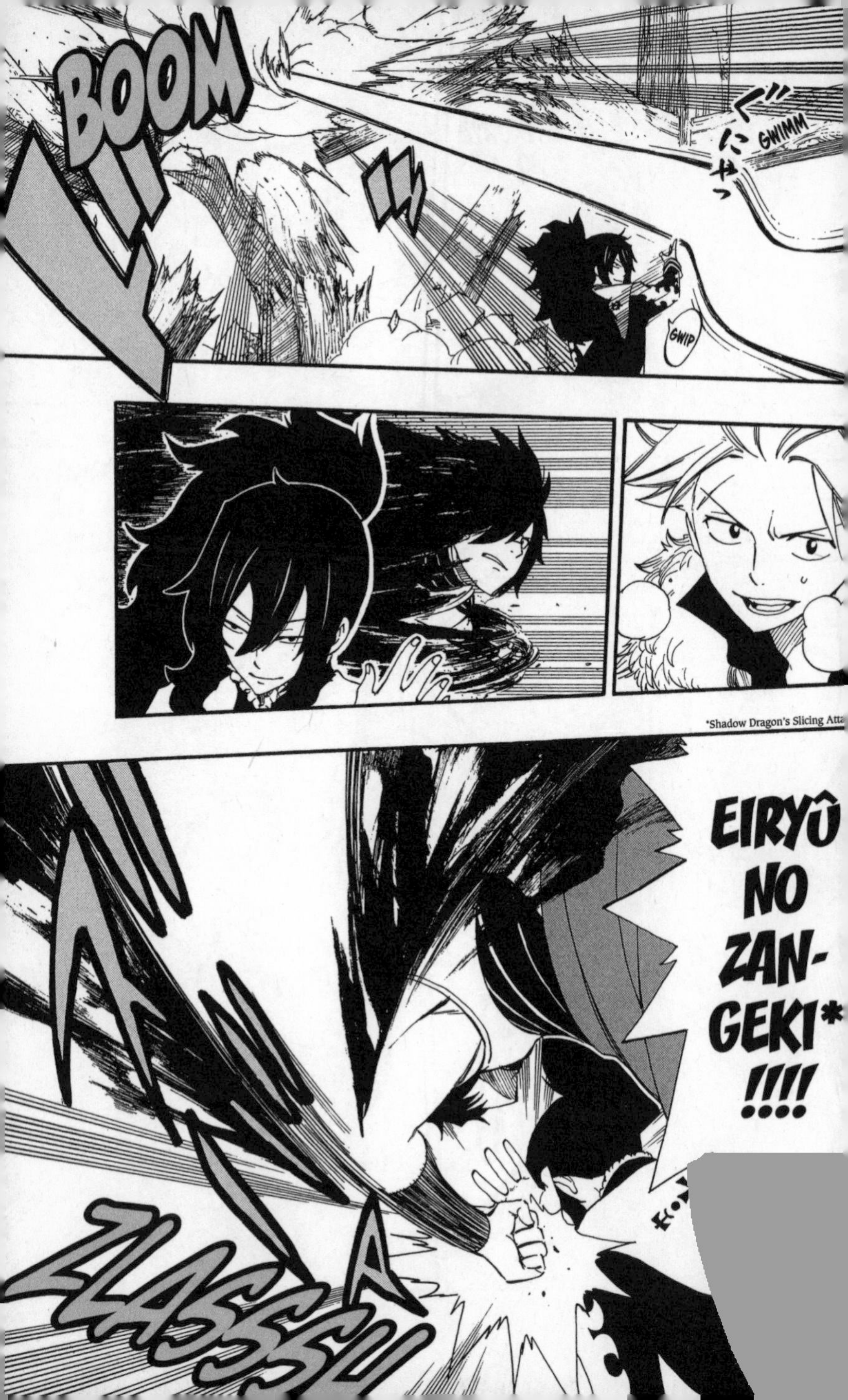
BOOM
ぐにゃっ
GWIMM
GWIP
EIRYÛ NO ZAN-GEKI*!!!!
ZLASSH

*Shadow Dragon's Slicing Atta

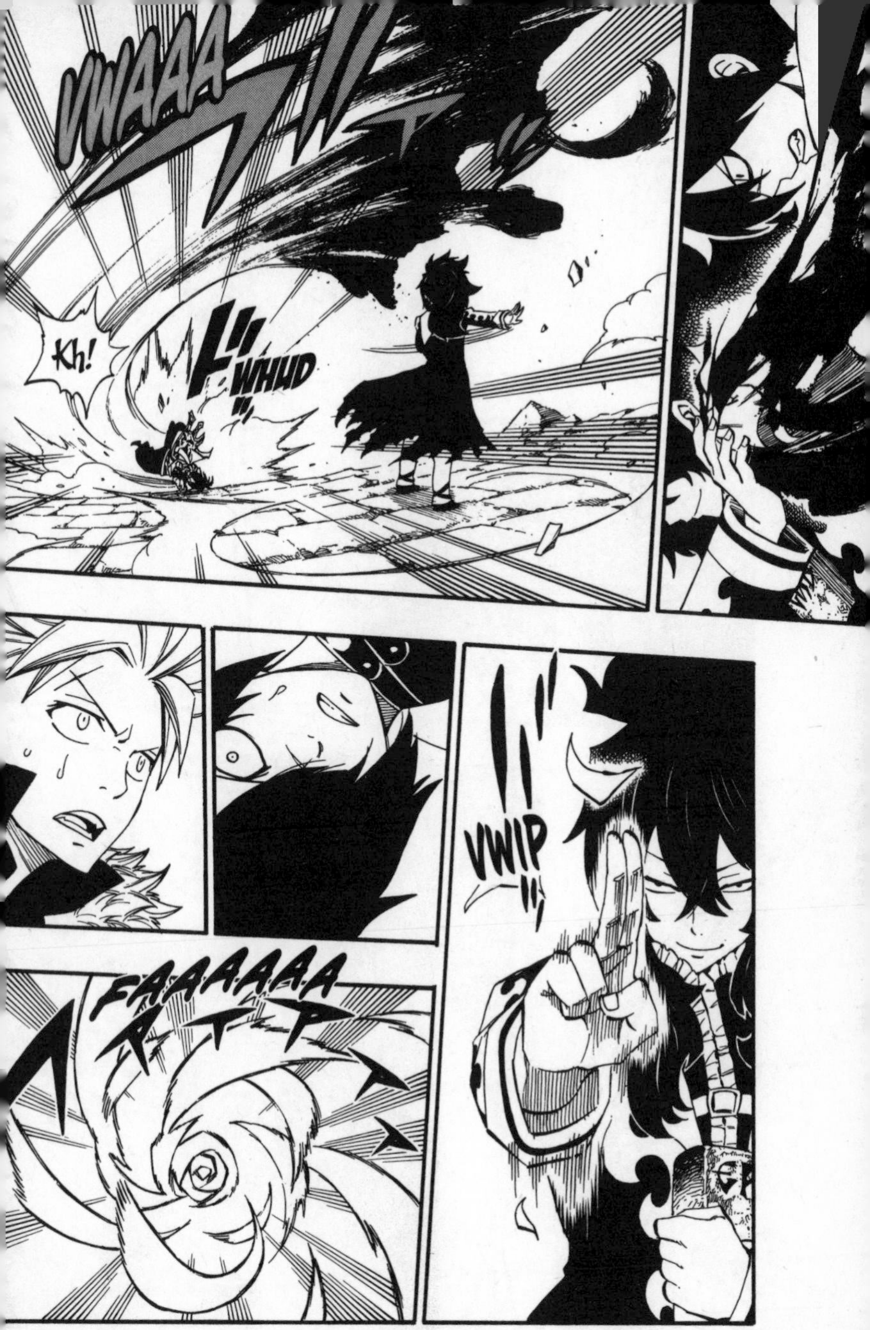
VWAAA
Kh!
WHUD
VWIP
FAAAAAAA

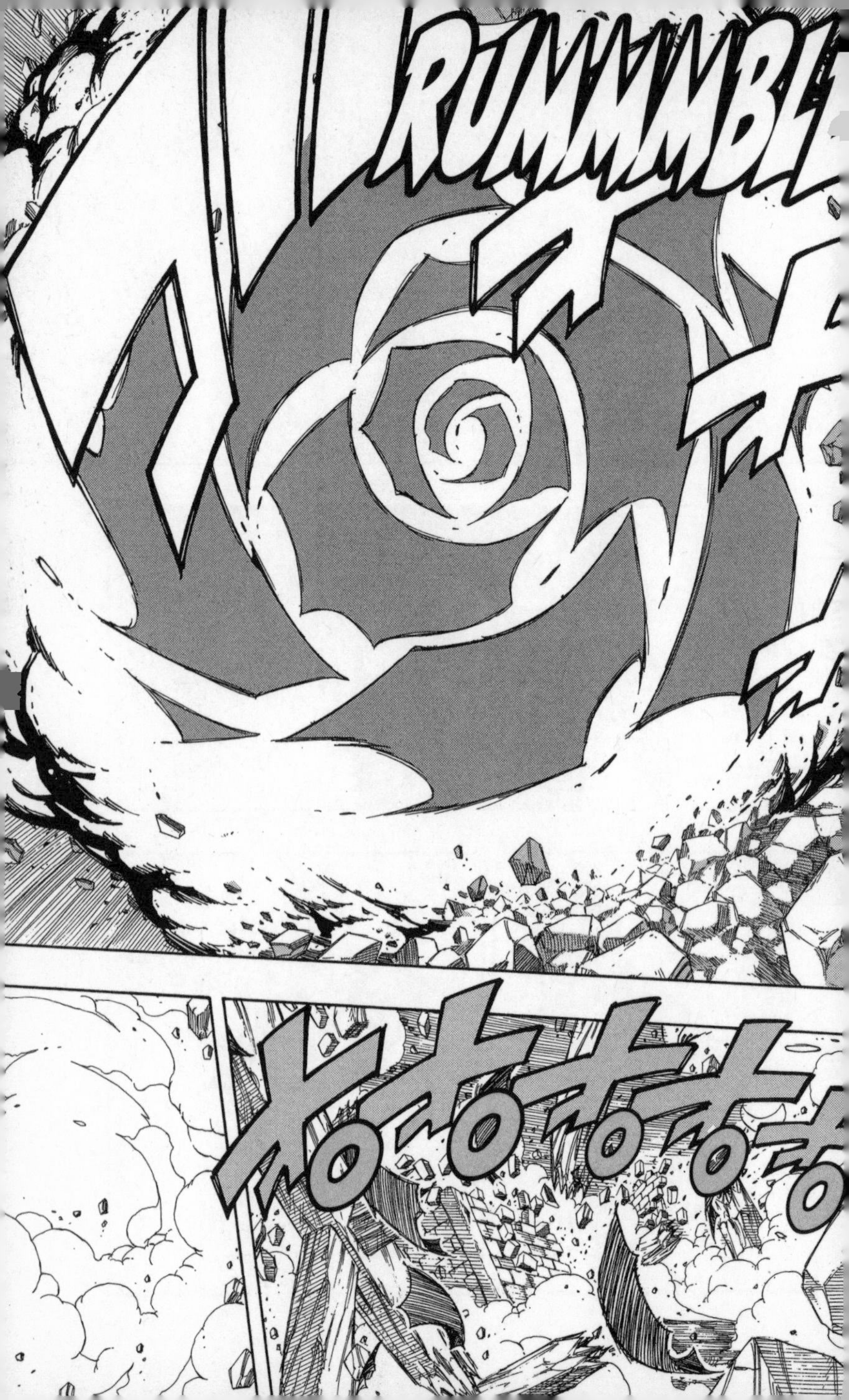
RUMMMBL

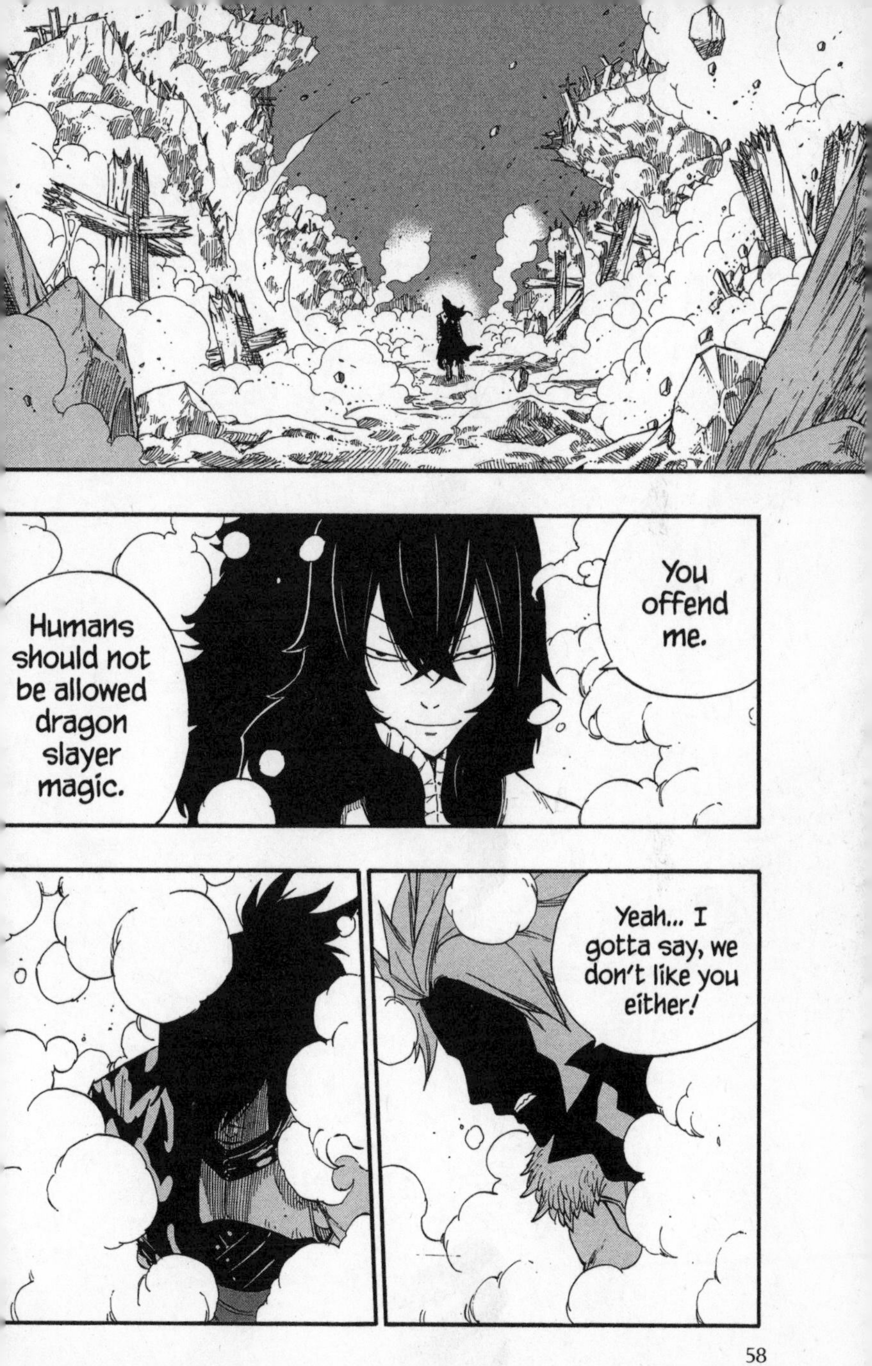
You offend me.
Humans should not be allowed dragon slayer magic.
Yeah... I gotta say, we don't like you either!

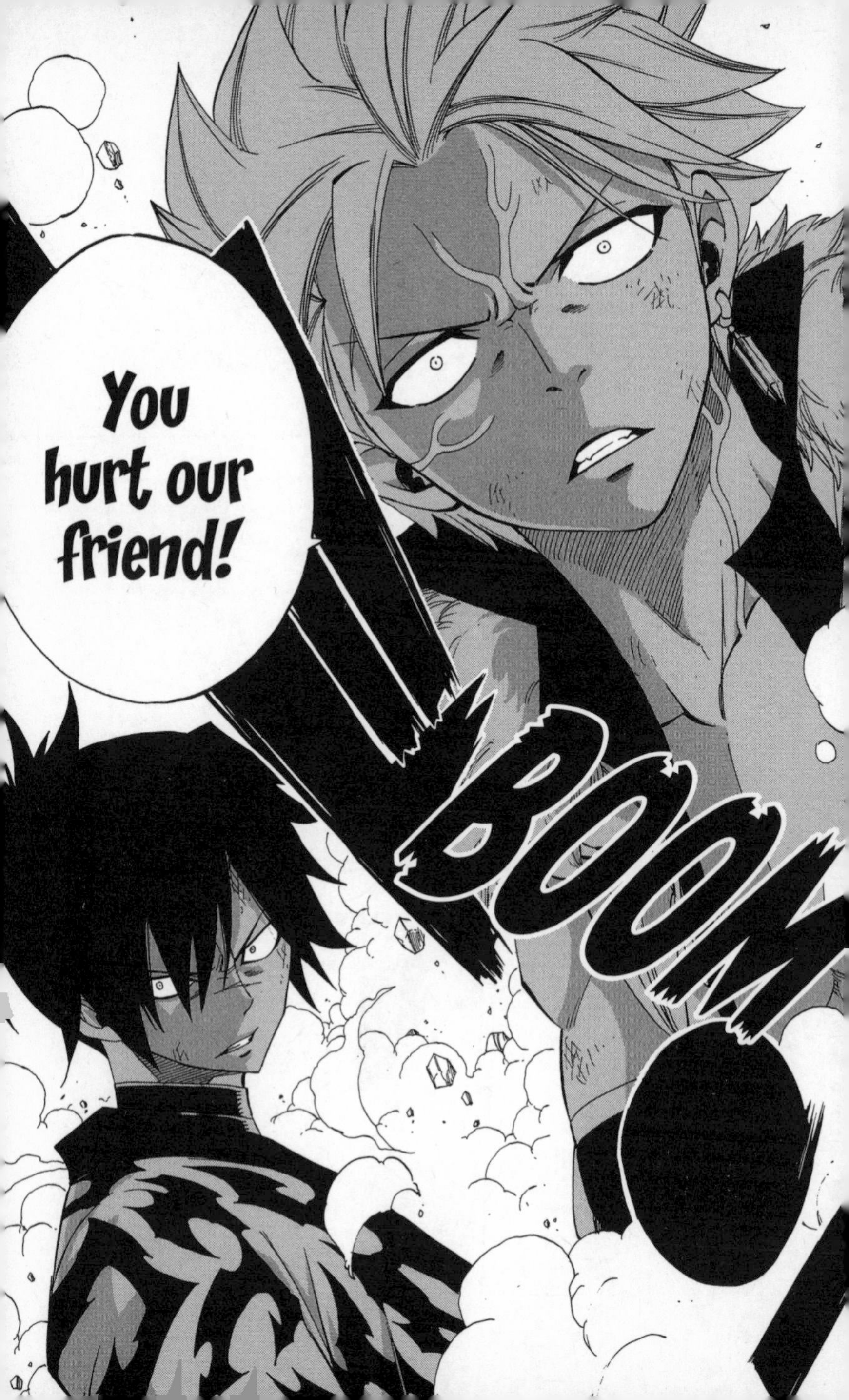
You hurt our friend!
BOOM

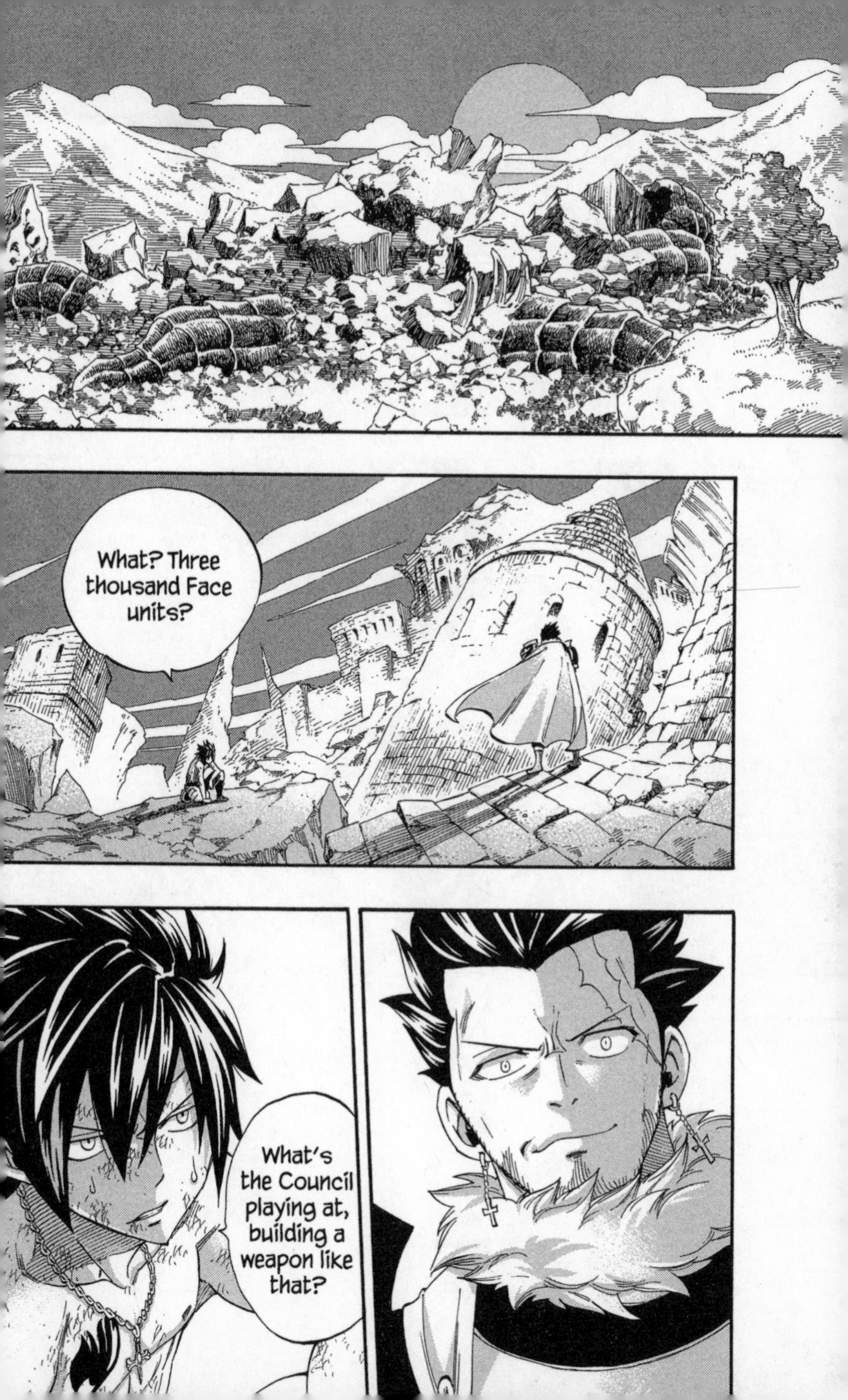
What? Three thousand Face units?
What's the Council playing at, building a weapon like that?

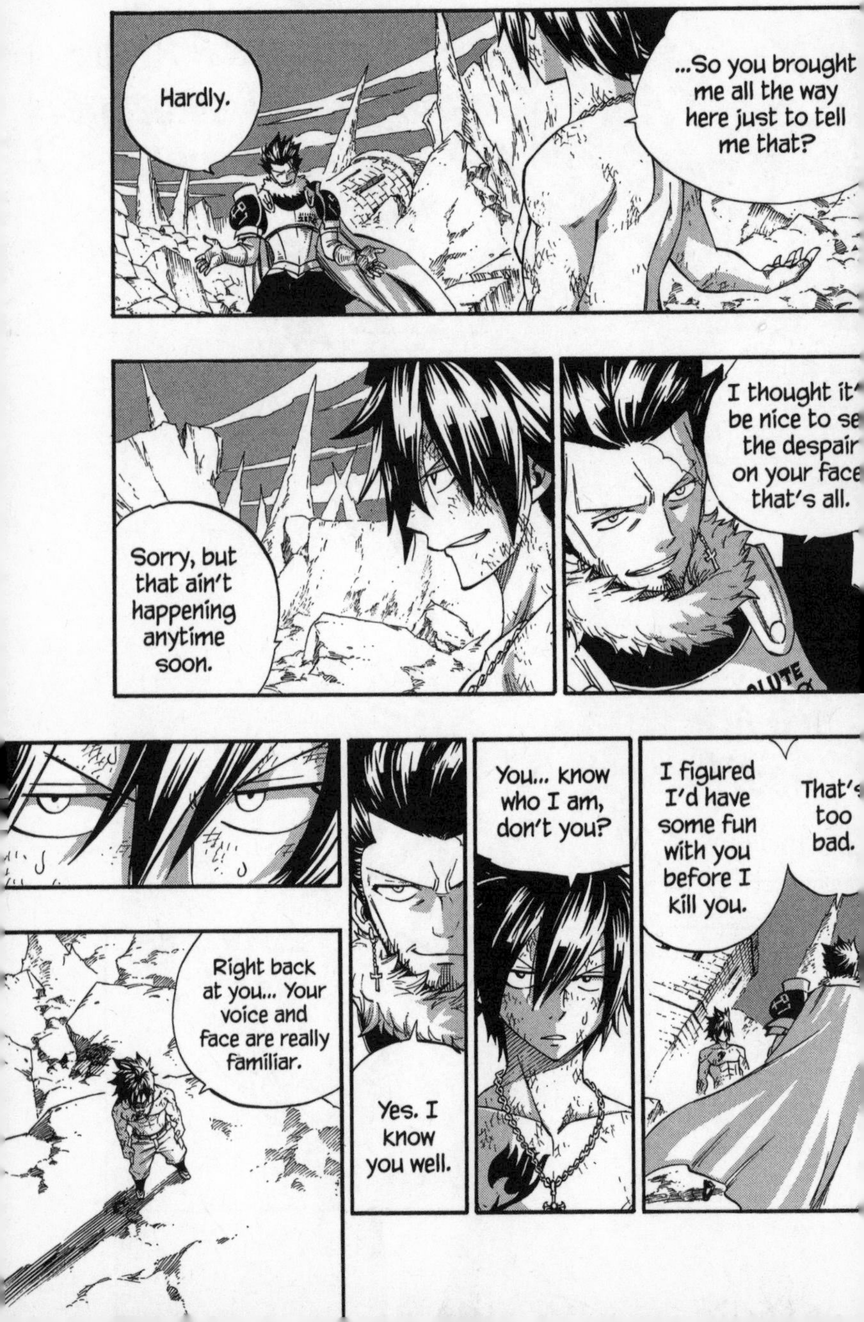
...So you brought me all the way here just to tell me that?
Hardly.
I thought it' be nice to se the despair on your face that's all.
Sorry, but that ain't happening anytime soon.
That's too bad.
I figured I'd have some fun with you before I kill you.
You... know who I am, don't you?
Yes. I know you well.
Right back at you... Your voice and face are really familiar.

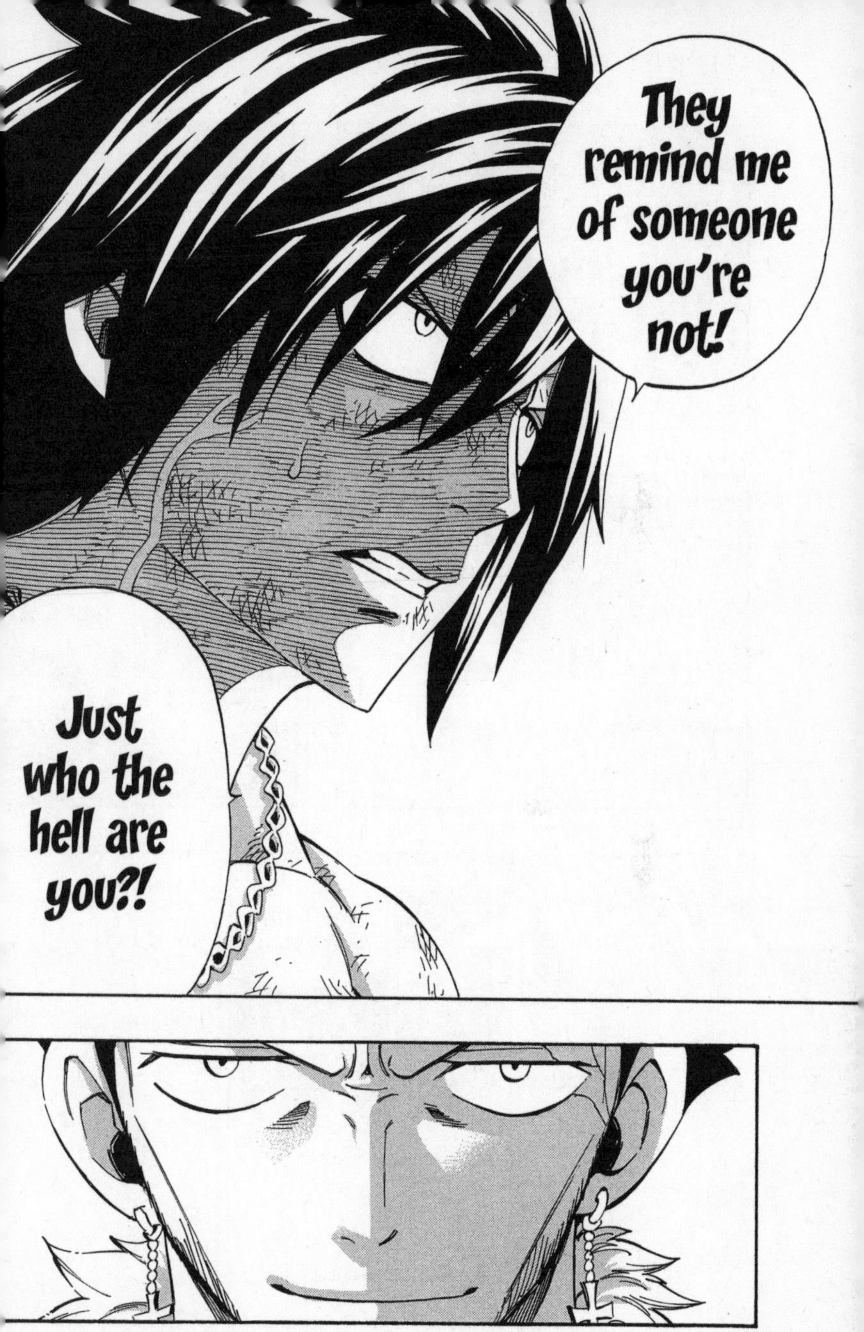
They remind me of someone you're not!
Just who the hell are you?!

FAIRY TAIL

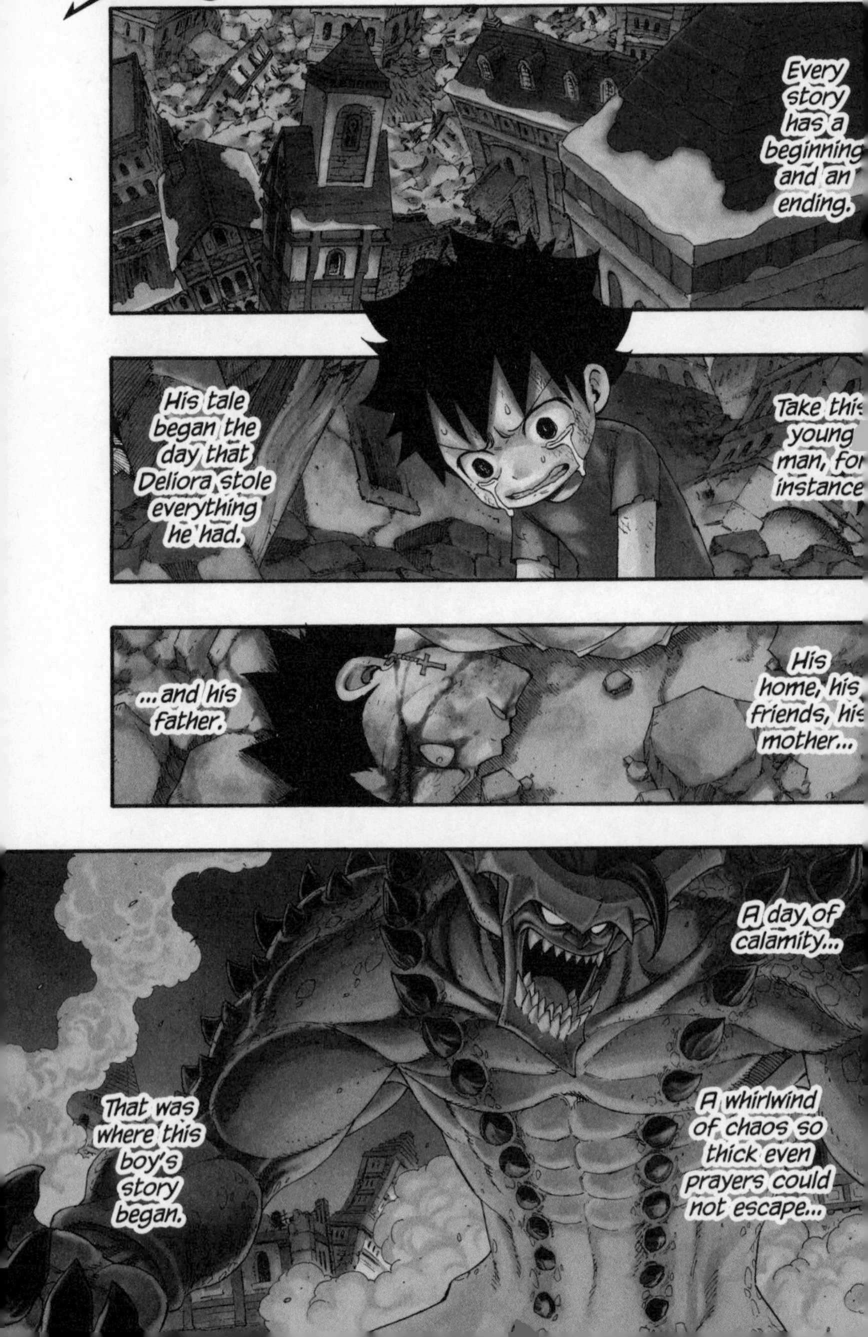
Every story has a beginning and an ending.
Take this young man, for instance.
His tale began the day that Deliora stole everything he had.
His home, his friends, his mother...
...and his father.
A day of calamity...
A whirlwind of chaos so thick even prayers could not escape...
That was where this boy's story began.

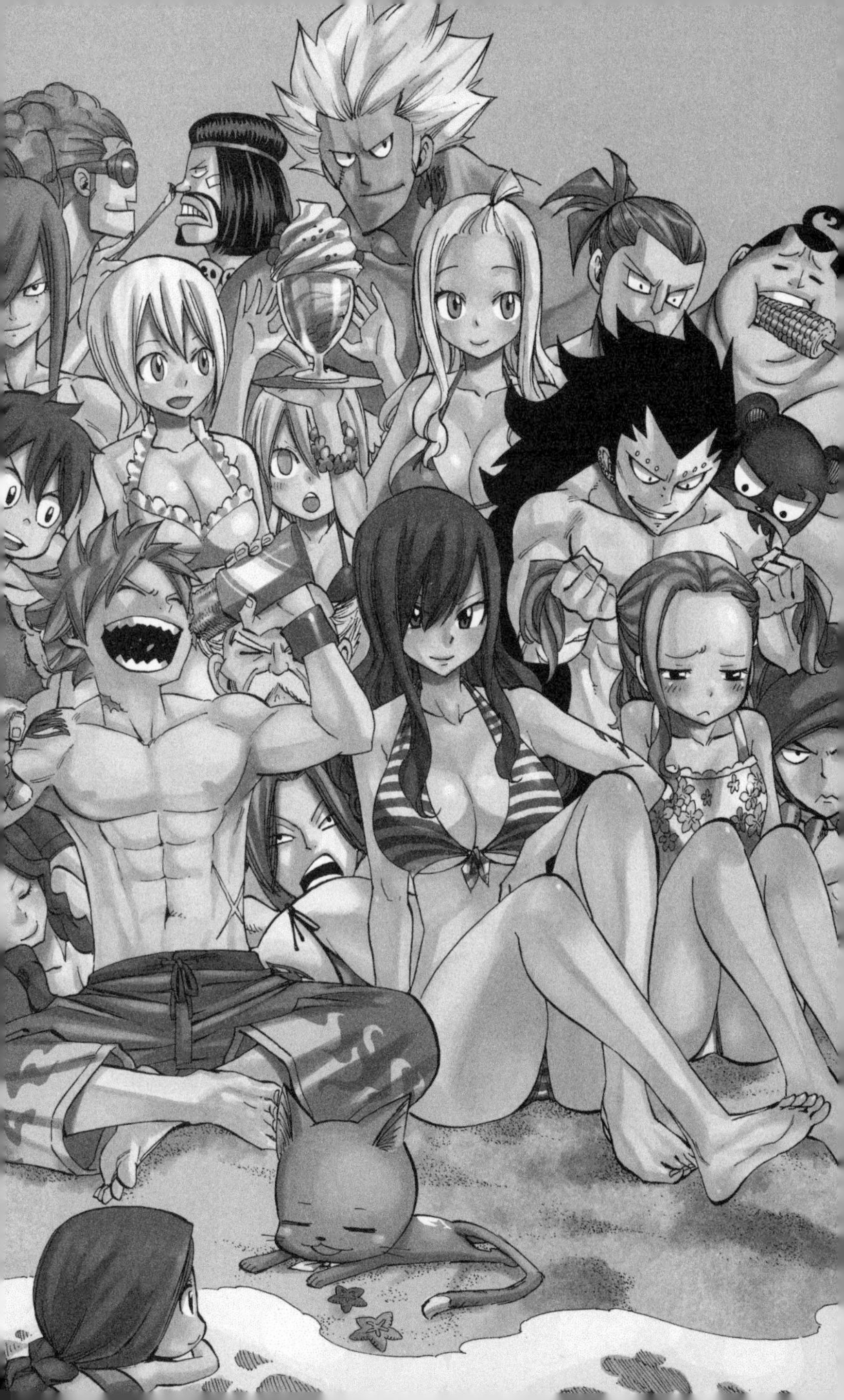

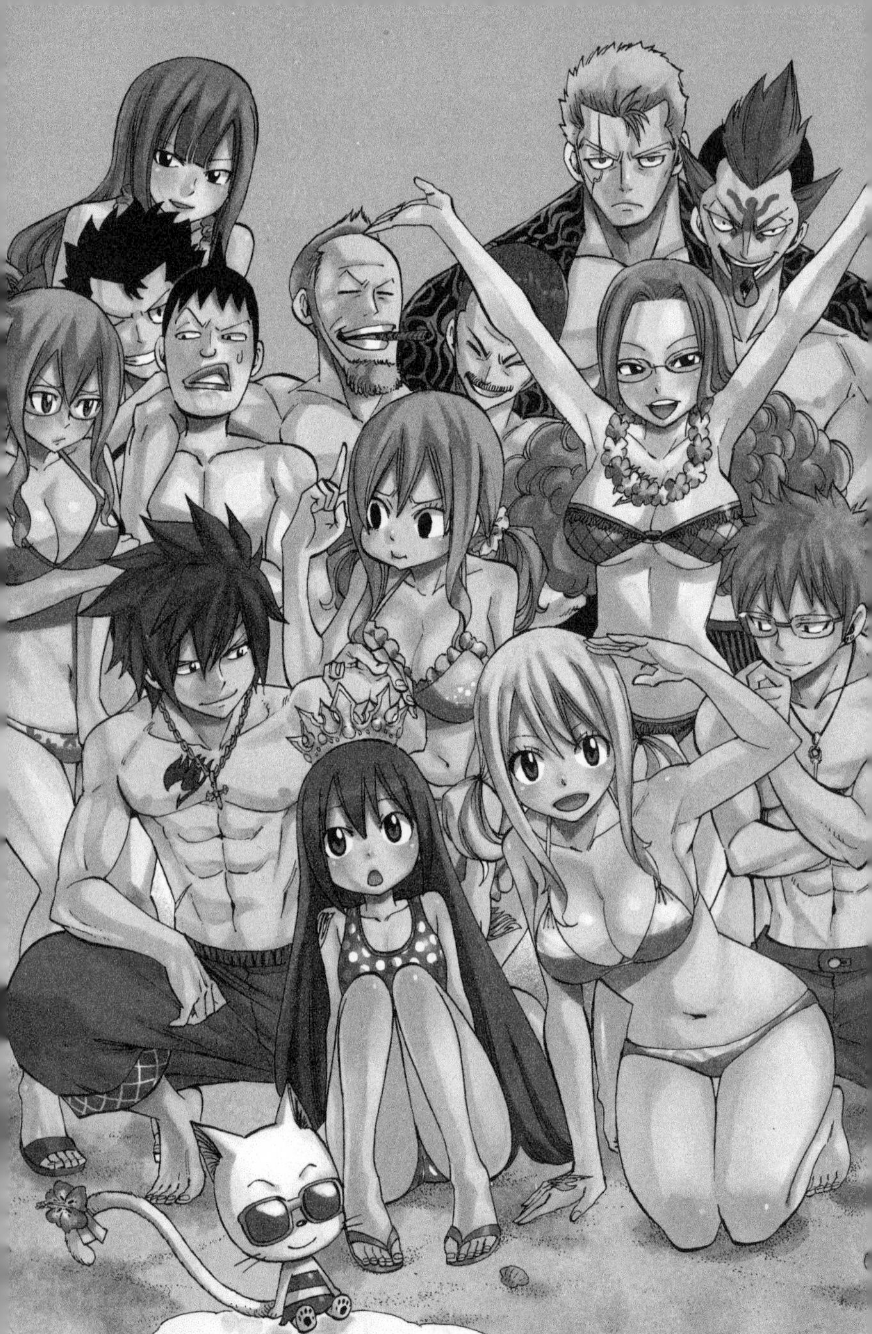

Chapter 390: A Young Boy's Story

FAIRY TAIL
フェアリーテイル

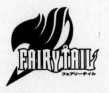

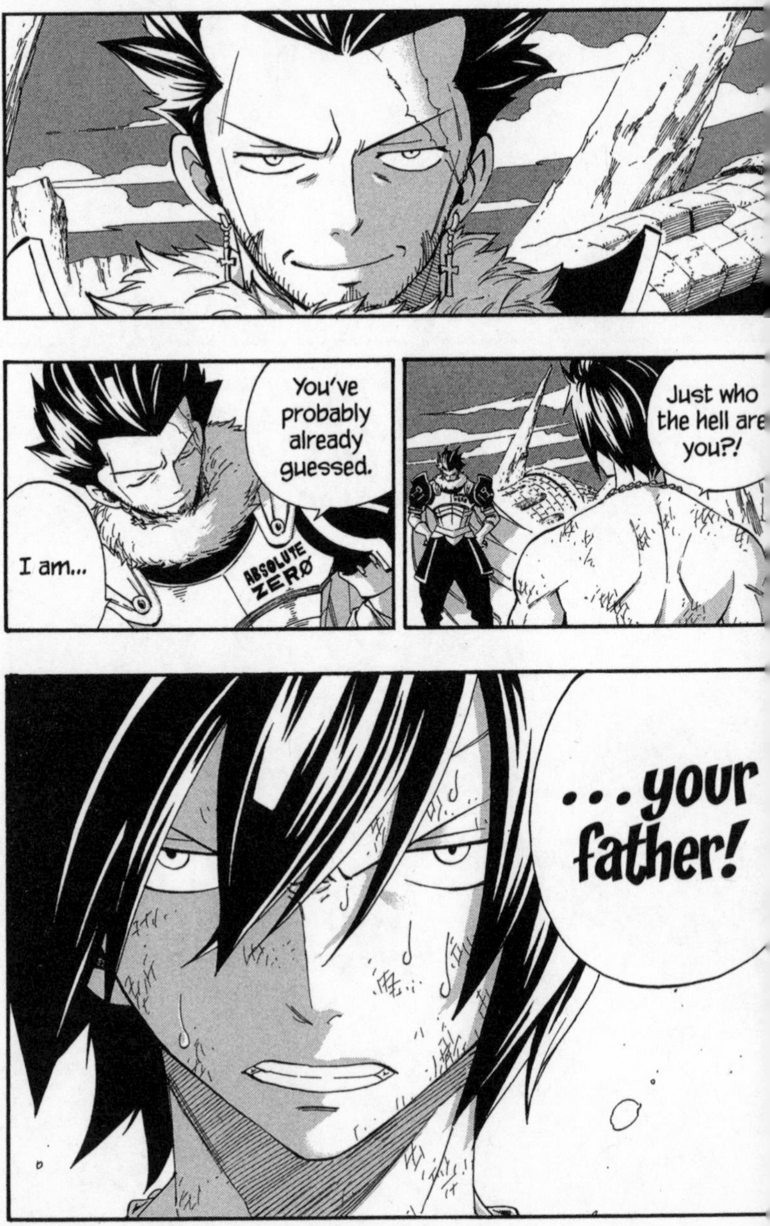
Just who the hell are you?!
You've probably already guessed.
I am...
ABSOLUTE ZERØ
...your father!

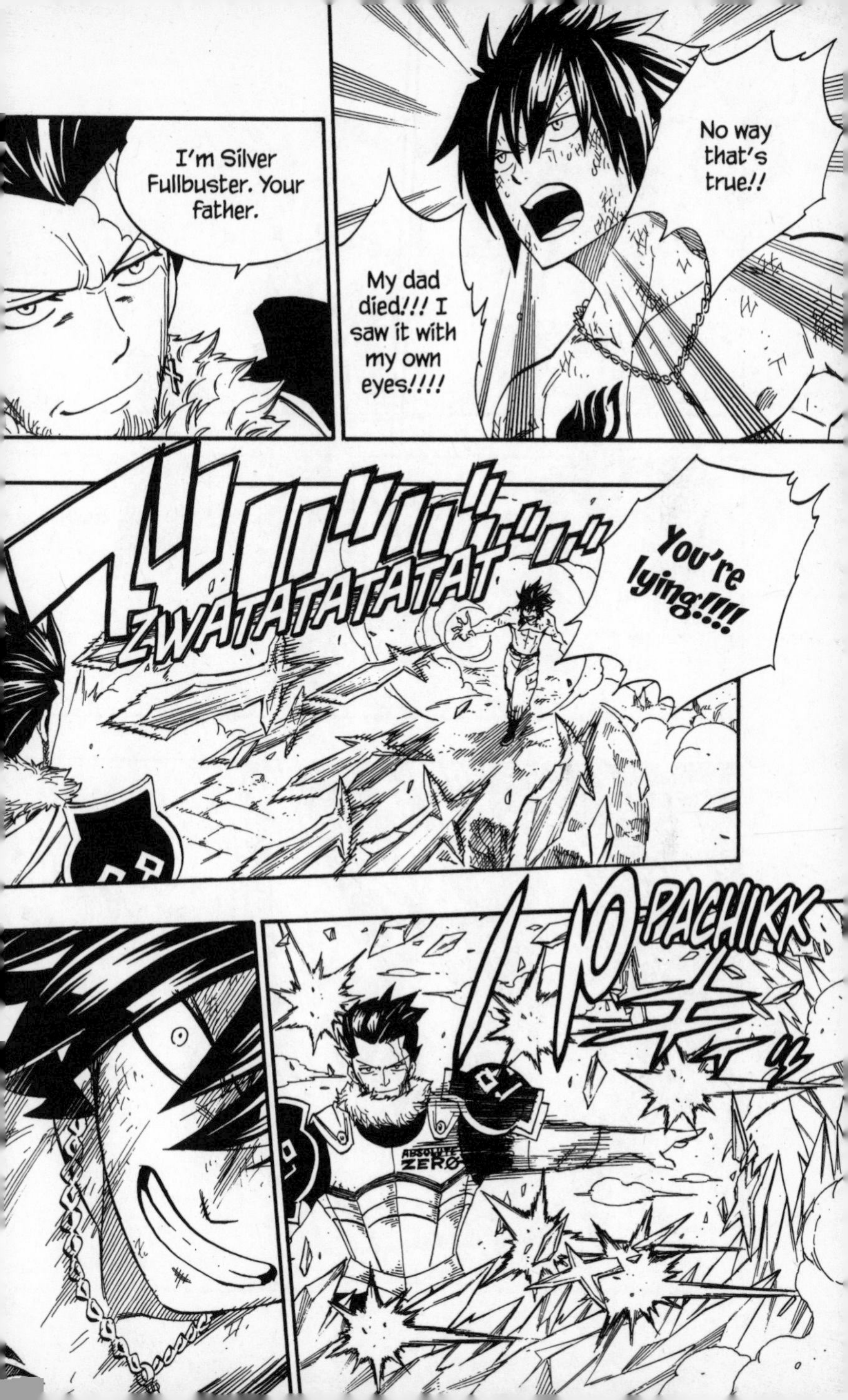
No way that's true!!
My dad died!!! I saw it with my own eyes!!!!
I'm Silver Fullbuster. Your father.
You're lying!!!!
ZWATATATATAT
PACHIKK
ABSOLUTE ZERO

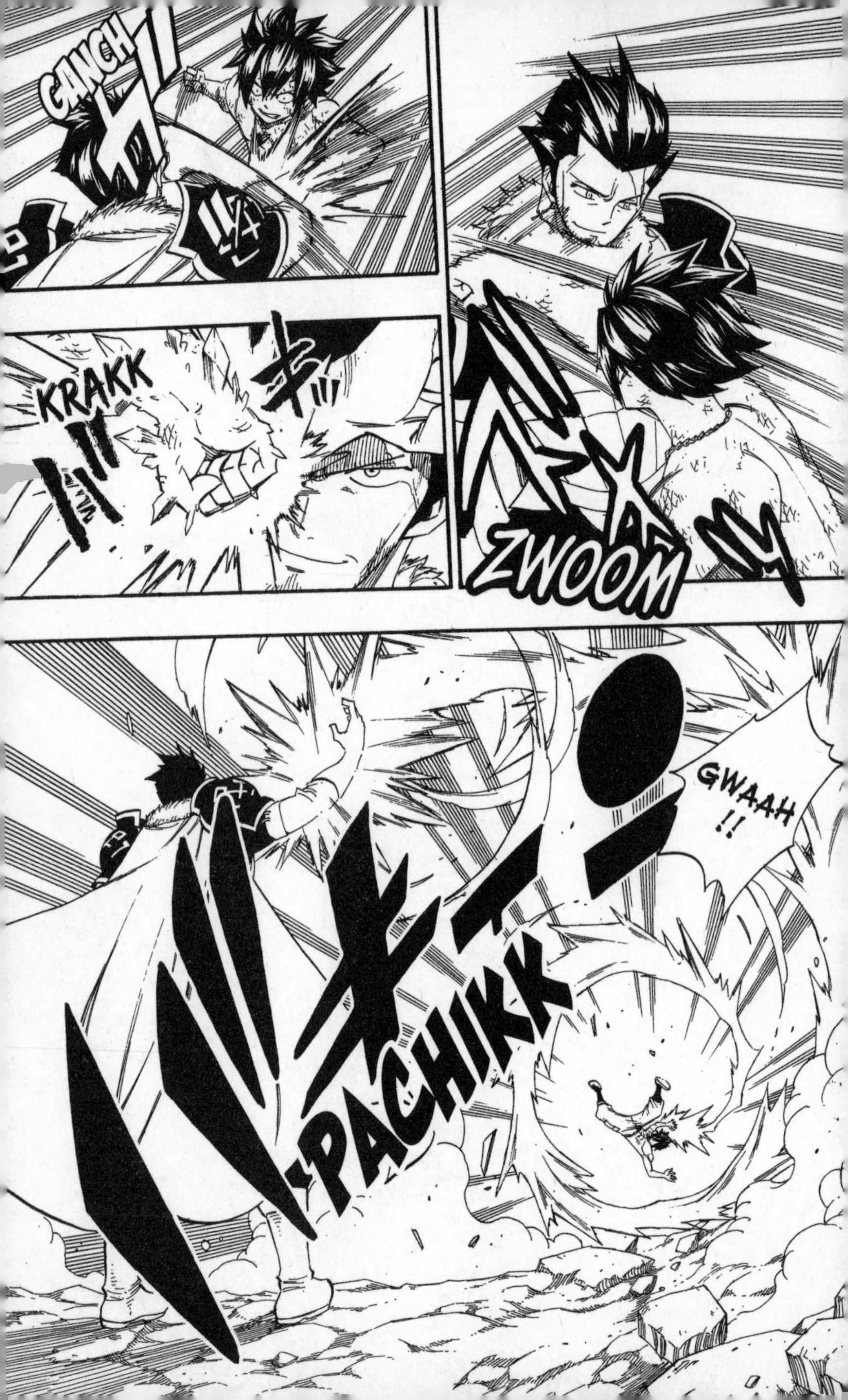
ZWOOM
GANCH
KRAKK
GWAAH !!
PACHIKK

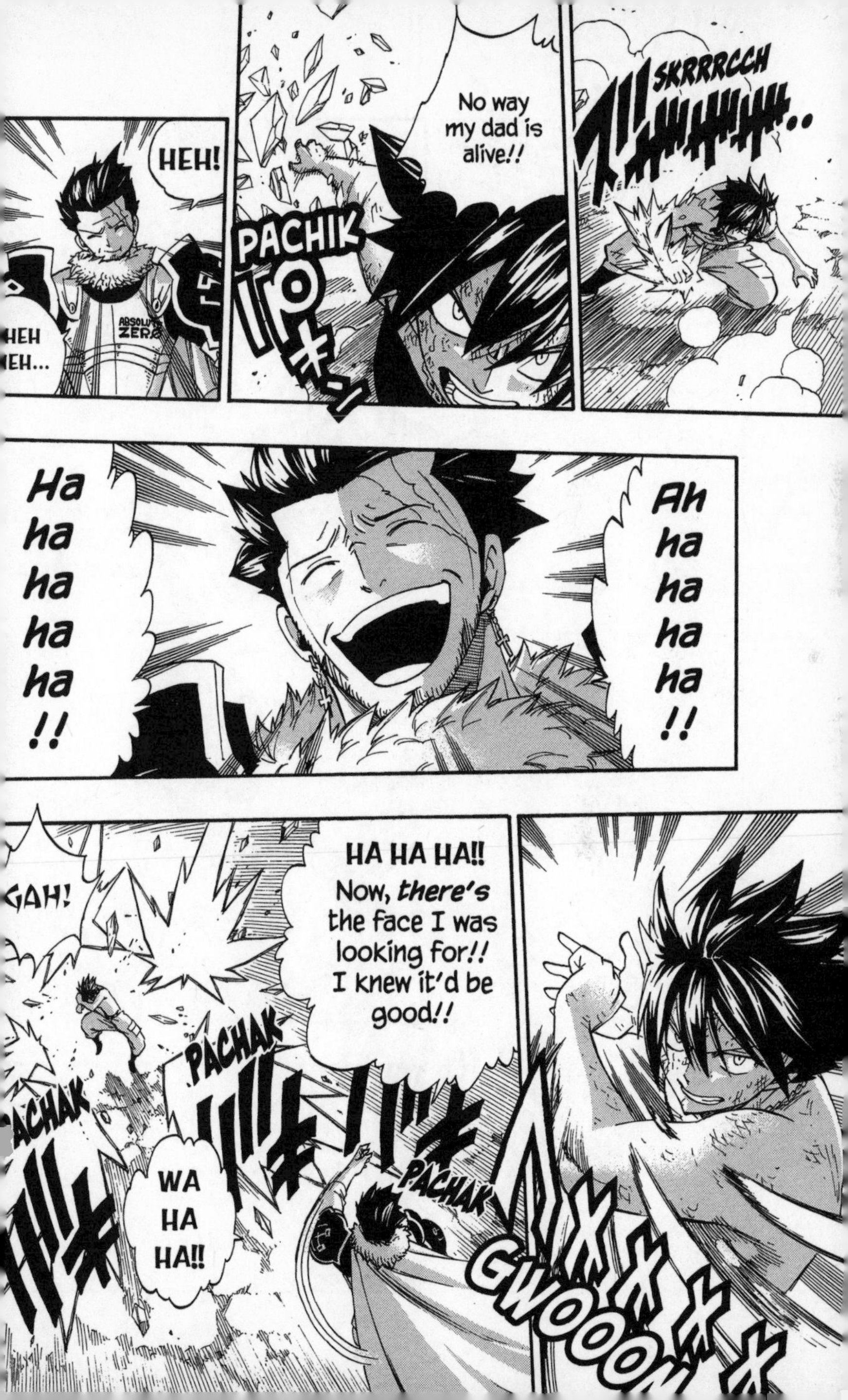
SKRRRCCH
No way my dad is alive!!
PACHIK
HEH!
HEH
EH...
Ah ha ha ha ha!!
Ha ha ha ha ha!!
GWOOO
HA HA HA!! Now, *there's* the face I was looking for!! I knew it'd be good!!
GAH!
PACHAK
PACHAK
WA HA HA!!
PACHAK

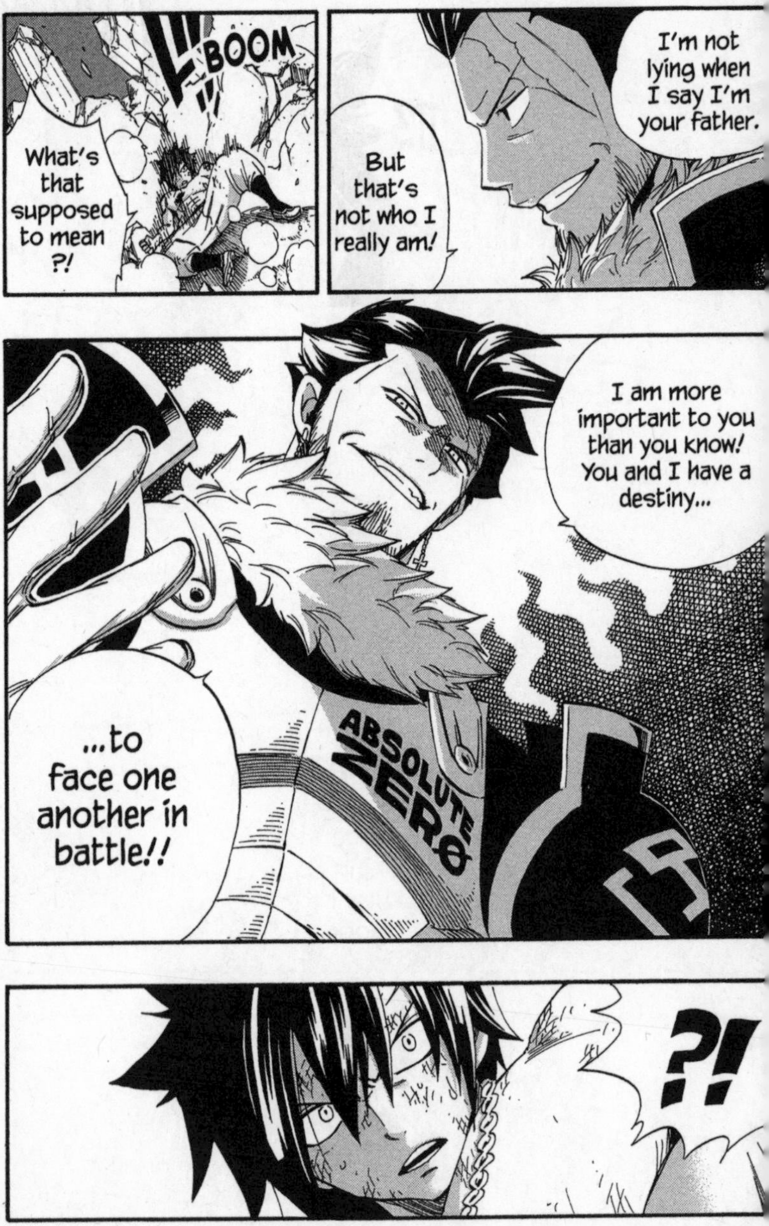
I'm not lying when I say I'm your father.
But that's not who I really am!
BOOM
What's that supposed to mean ?!
I am more important to you than you know! You and I have a destiny...
ABSOLUTE ZERO
...to face one another in battle!!
?!

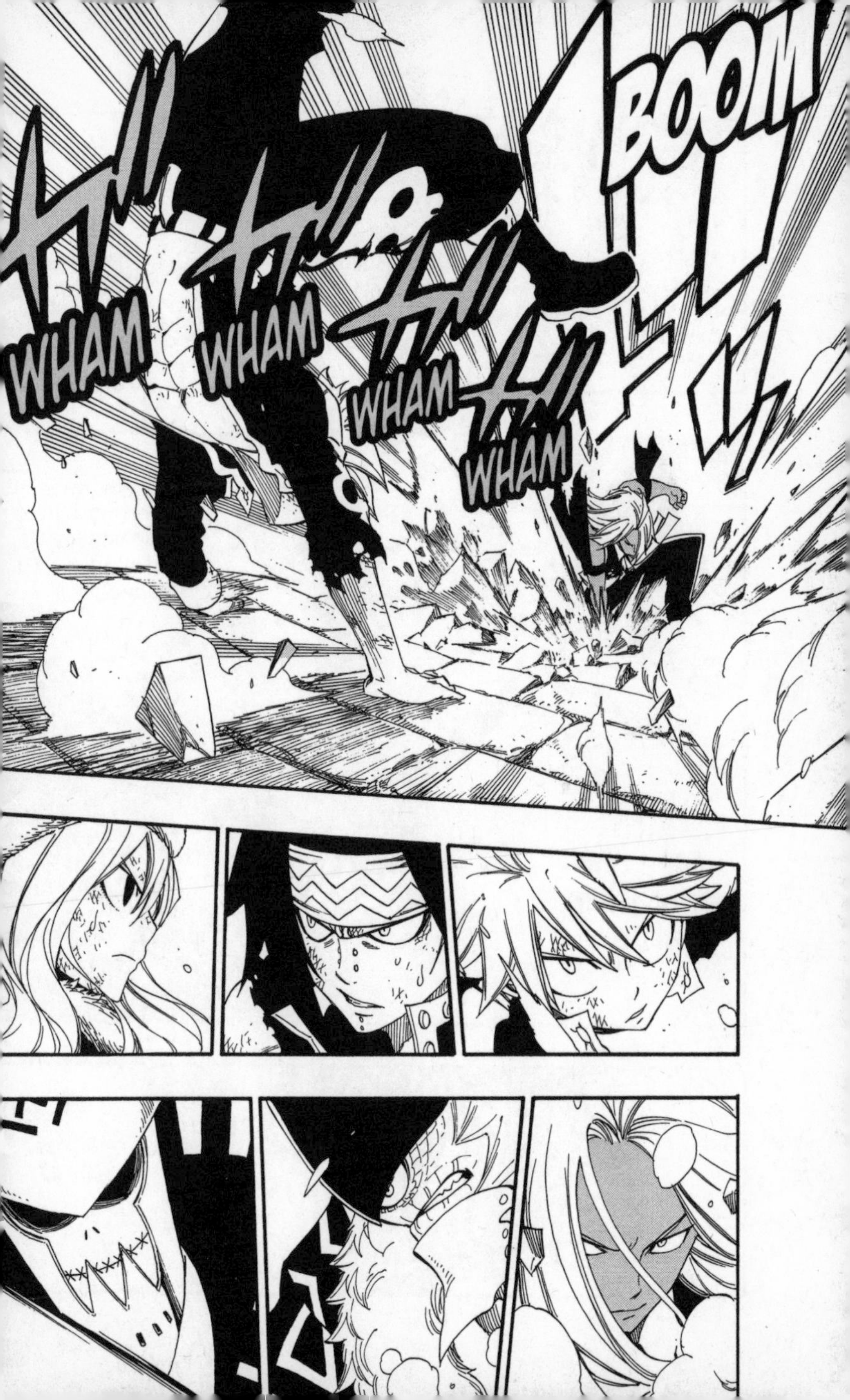
BOOM
WHAM
WHAM
WHAM
WHAM

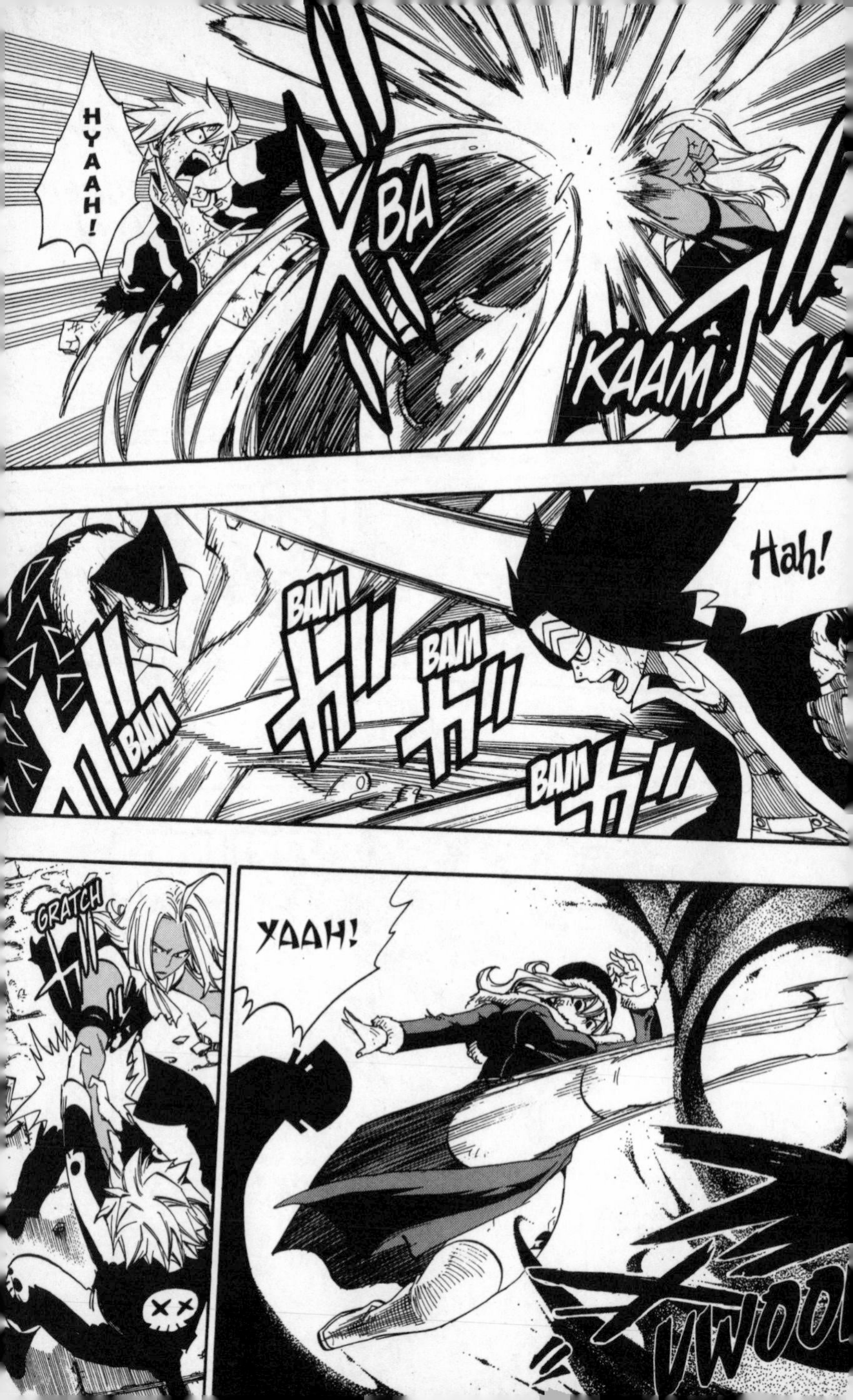
BA
KAAM
HYAAAH!
Hah!
BAM
BAM
BAM
BAM
YAAH!
GRATCH

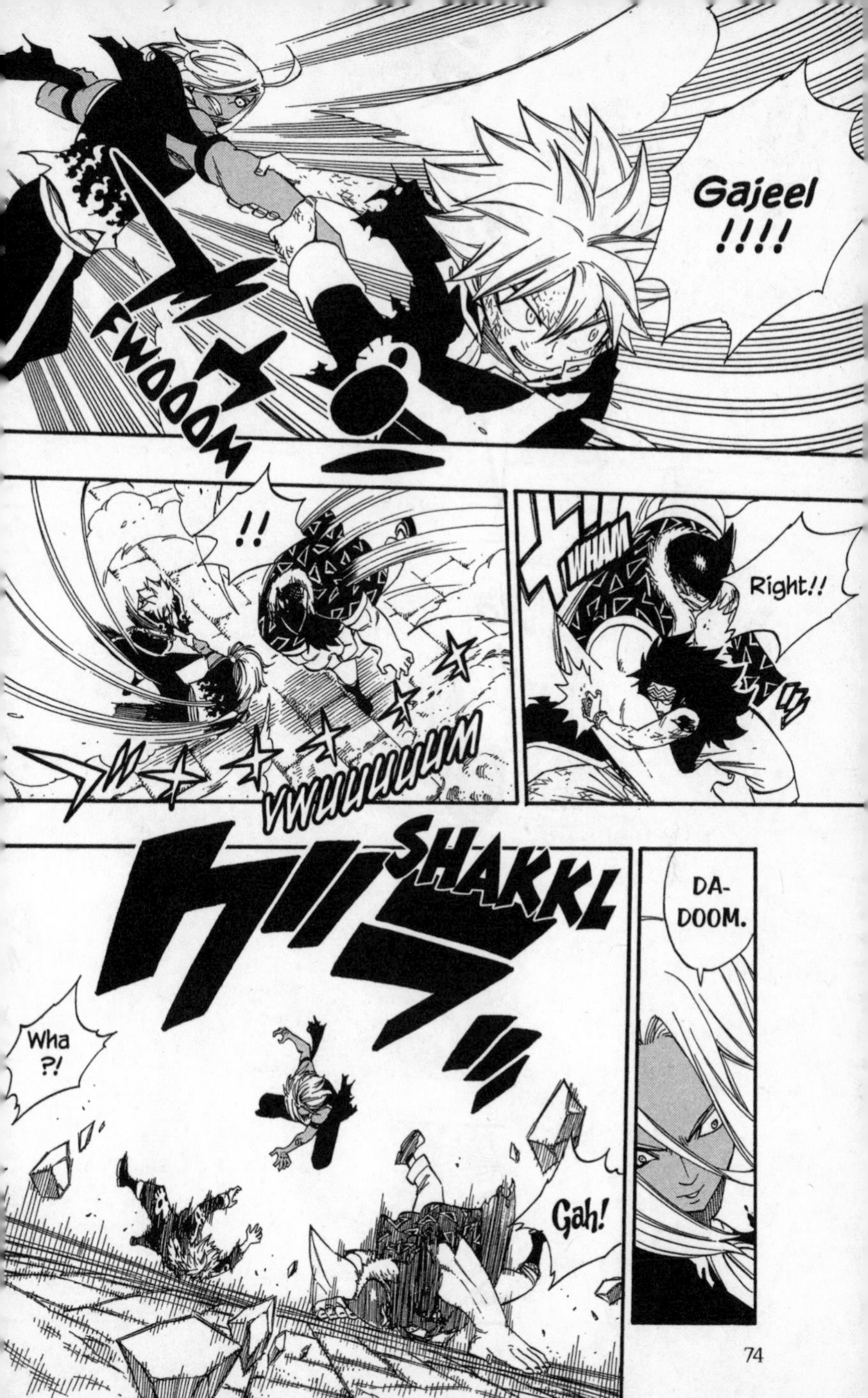
Gajeel !!!!
FWOOOM
WHAM
Right!!
!!
VWUUUUUM
DA-DOOM.
SHAKKL
Wha ?!
Gah!

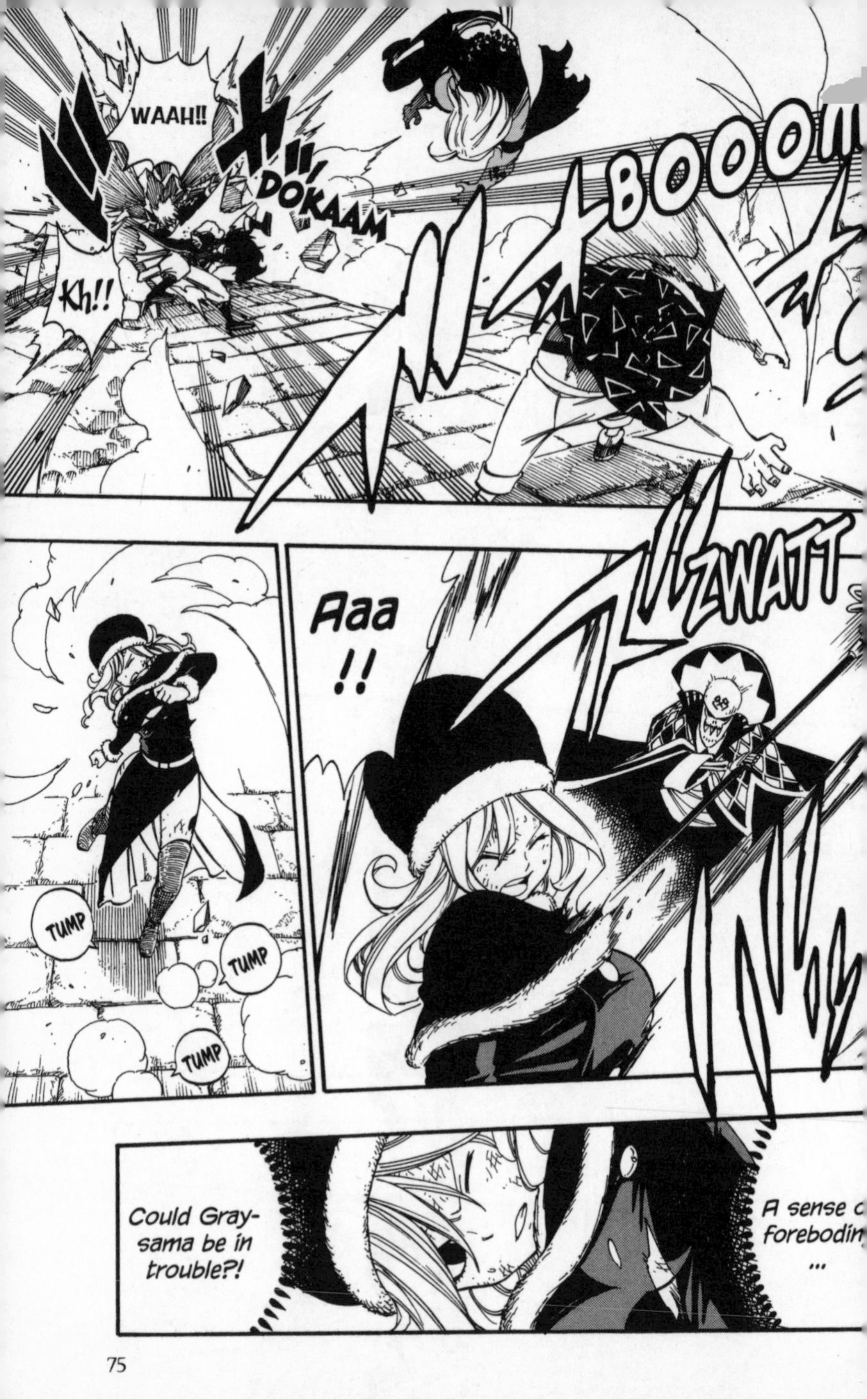
BOOOOM
WAAH!!
DOKAAM
Kh!!
ZWATT
Aaa !!
TUMP
TUMP
TUMP
A sense o forebodin ...
Could Gray-sama be in trouble?!

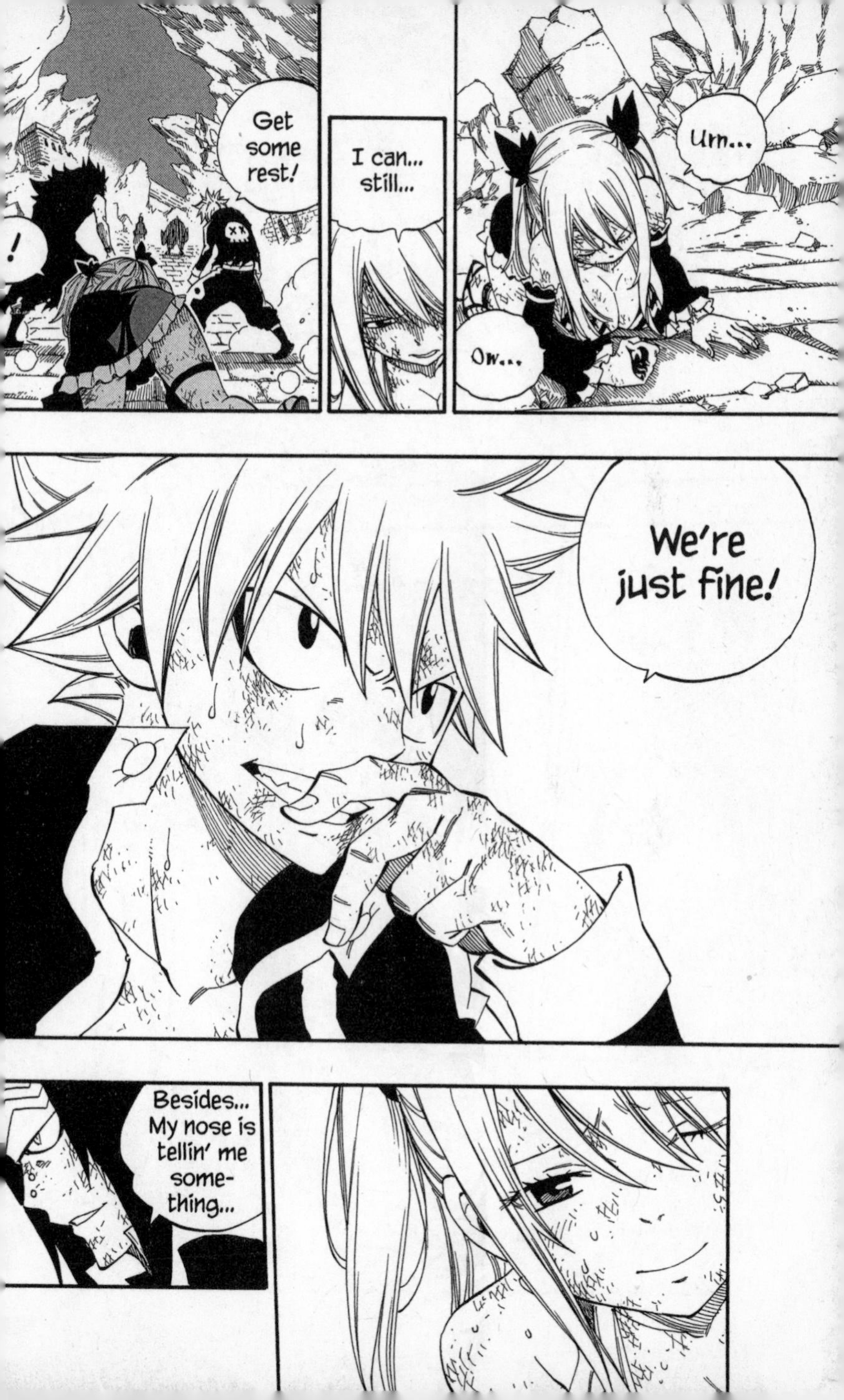
Um...
Ow...
I can... still...
Get some rest!
!
We're just fine!
Besides... My nose is tellin' me some-thing...

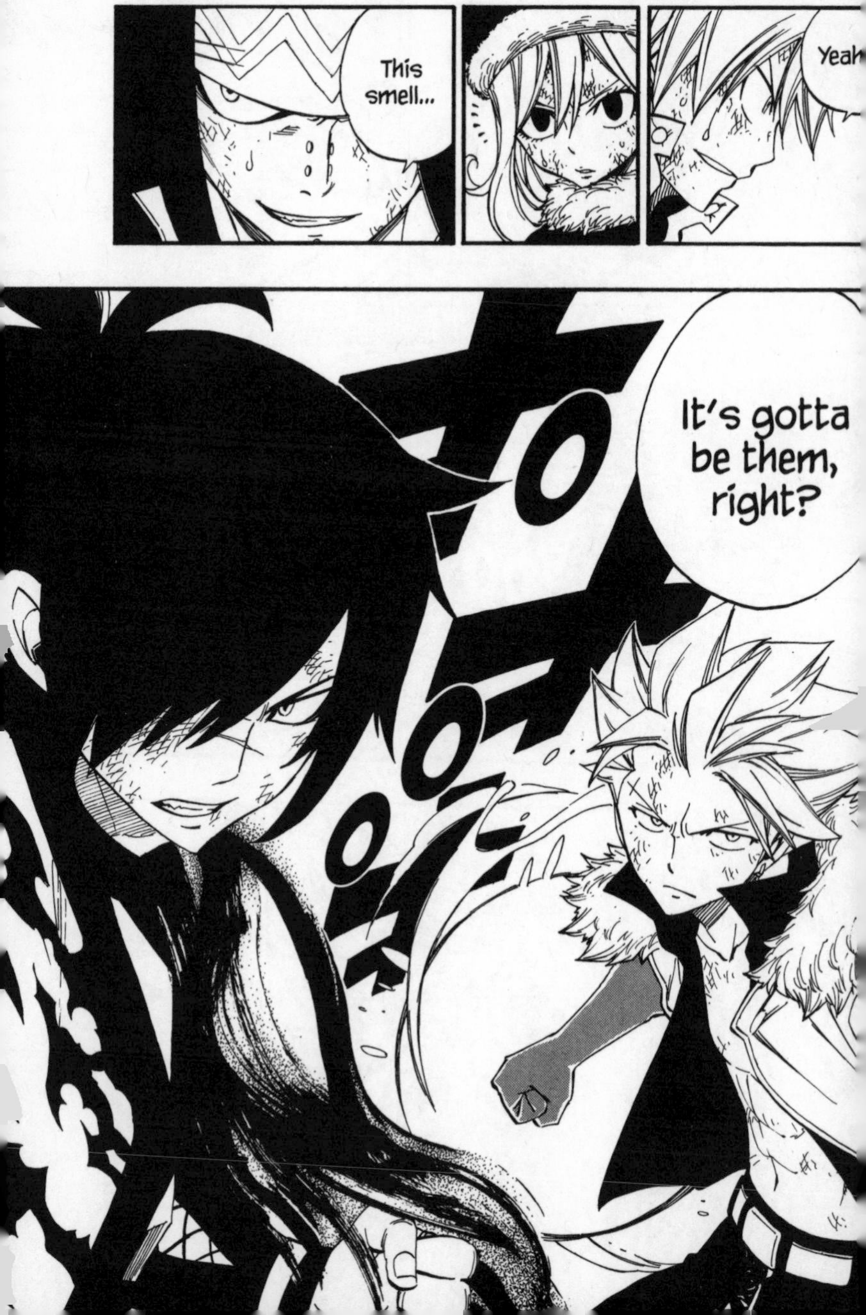
Yeah
This smell...
It's gotta be them, right?

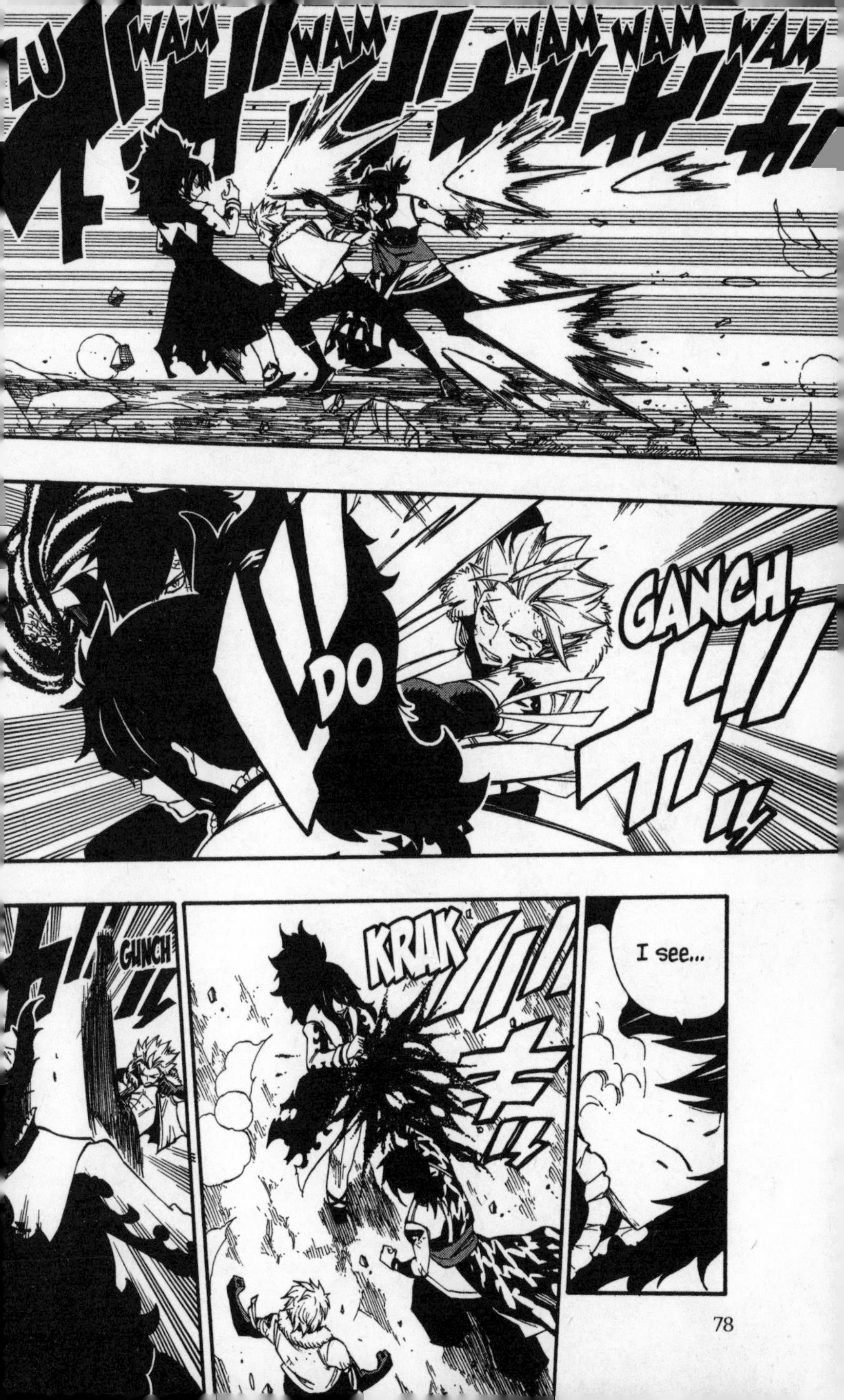
LU
WAM
WAM
WAM
WAM
WAM
GANCH
DO
I see...
KRAK
GUNCH

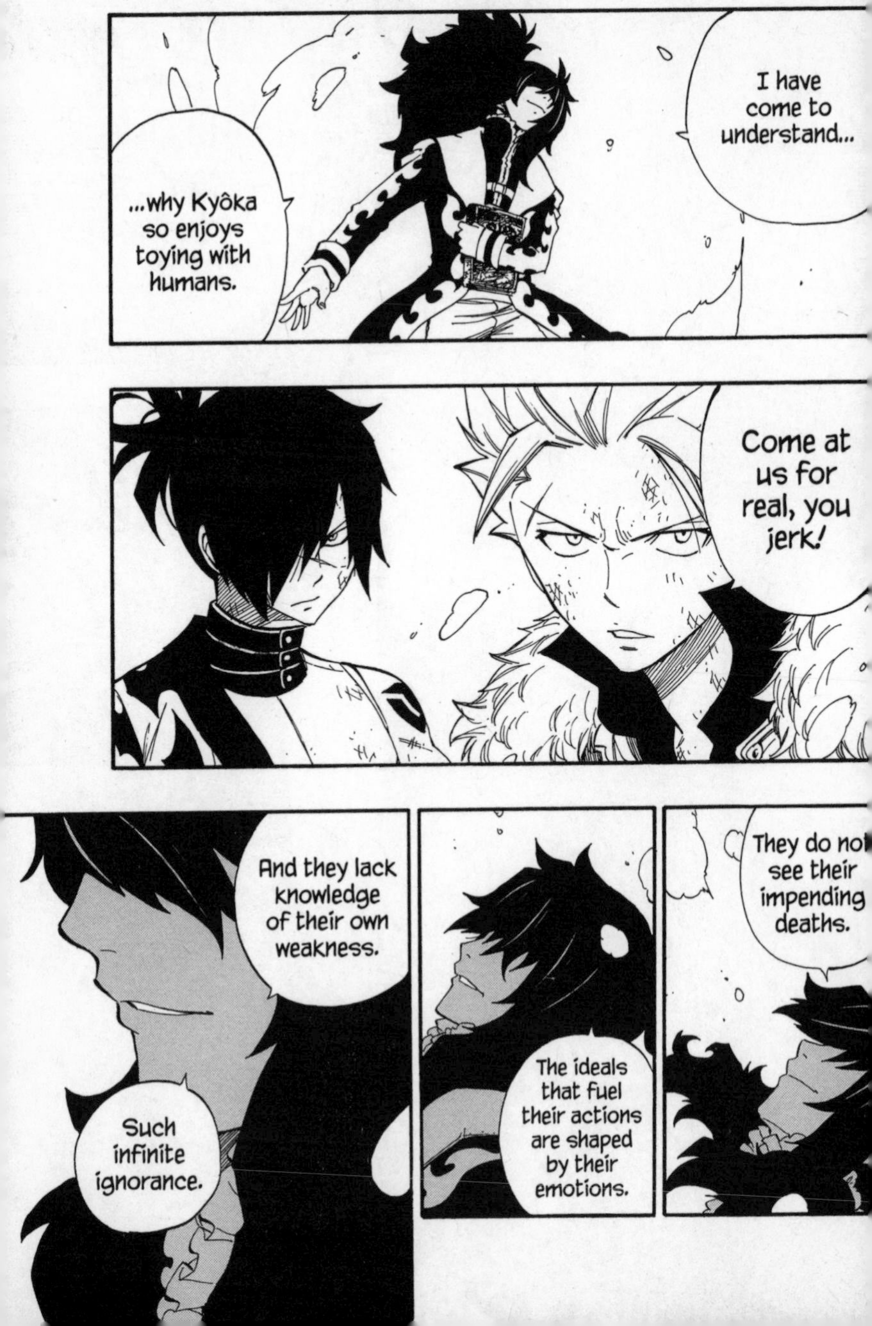
I have come to understand...
...why Kyôka so enjoys toying with humans.
Come at us for real, you jerk!
They do not see their impending deaths.
The ideals that fuel their actions are shaped by their emotions.
And they lack knowledge of their own weakness.
Such infinite ignorance.

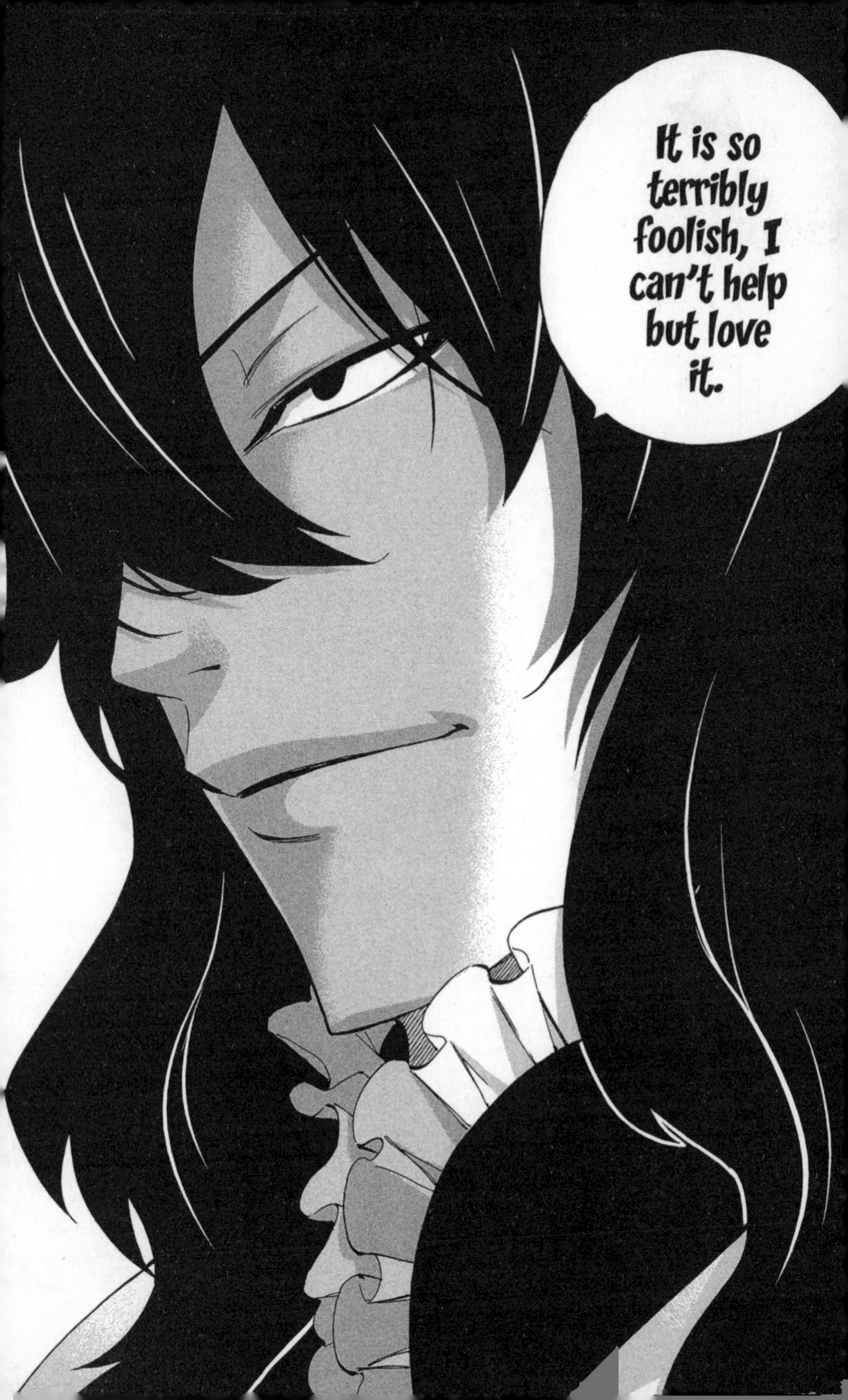
It is so terribly foolish, I can't help but love it.

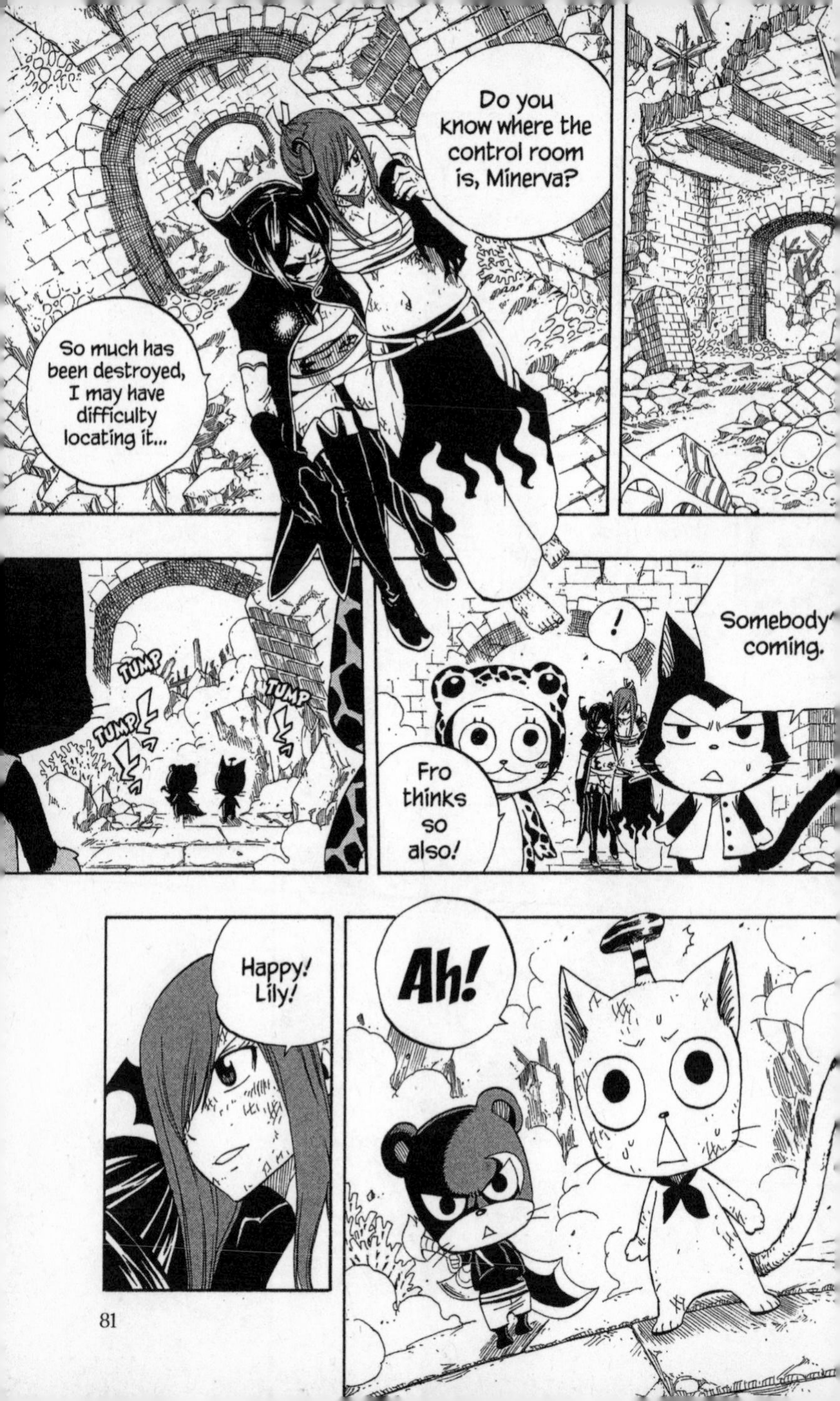
Do you know where the control room is, Minerva?
So much has been destroyed, I may have difficulty locating it...
!
Somebody' coming.
Fro thinks so also!
TUMP
TUMP
TUMP
Ah!
Happy! Lily!

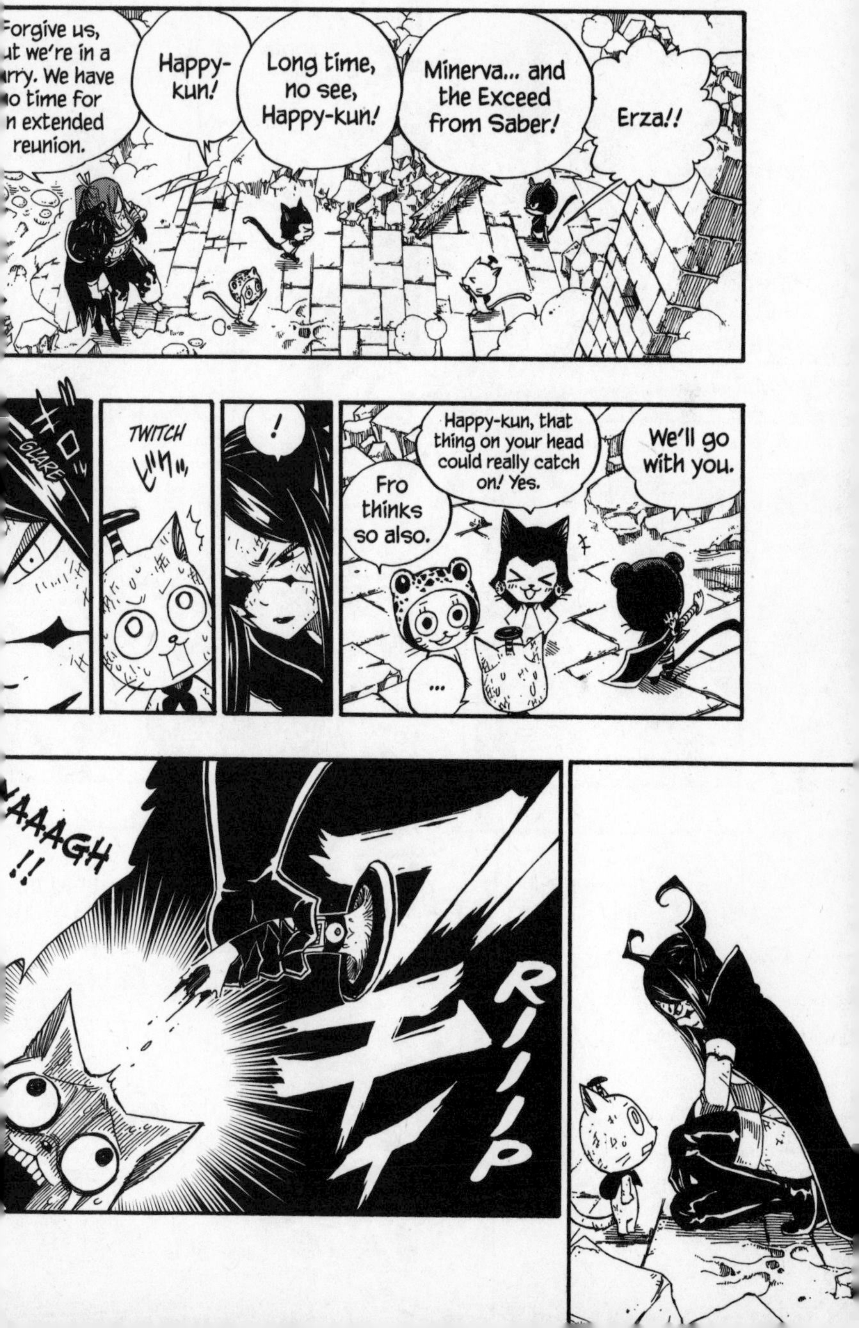
Erza!!
Minerva... and the Exceed from Saber!
Long time, no see, Happy-kun!
Happy-kun!
orgive us, ut we're in a rry. We have o time for n extended reunion.
We'll go with you.
Happy-kun, that thing on your head could really catch on! Yes.
Fro thinks so also.
...
!
TWITCH
GLARE
RIIIP
AAAGH !!

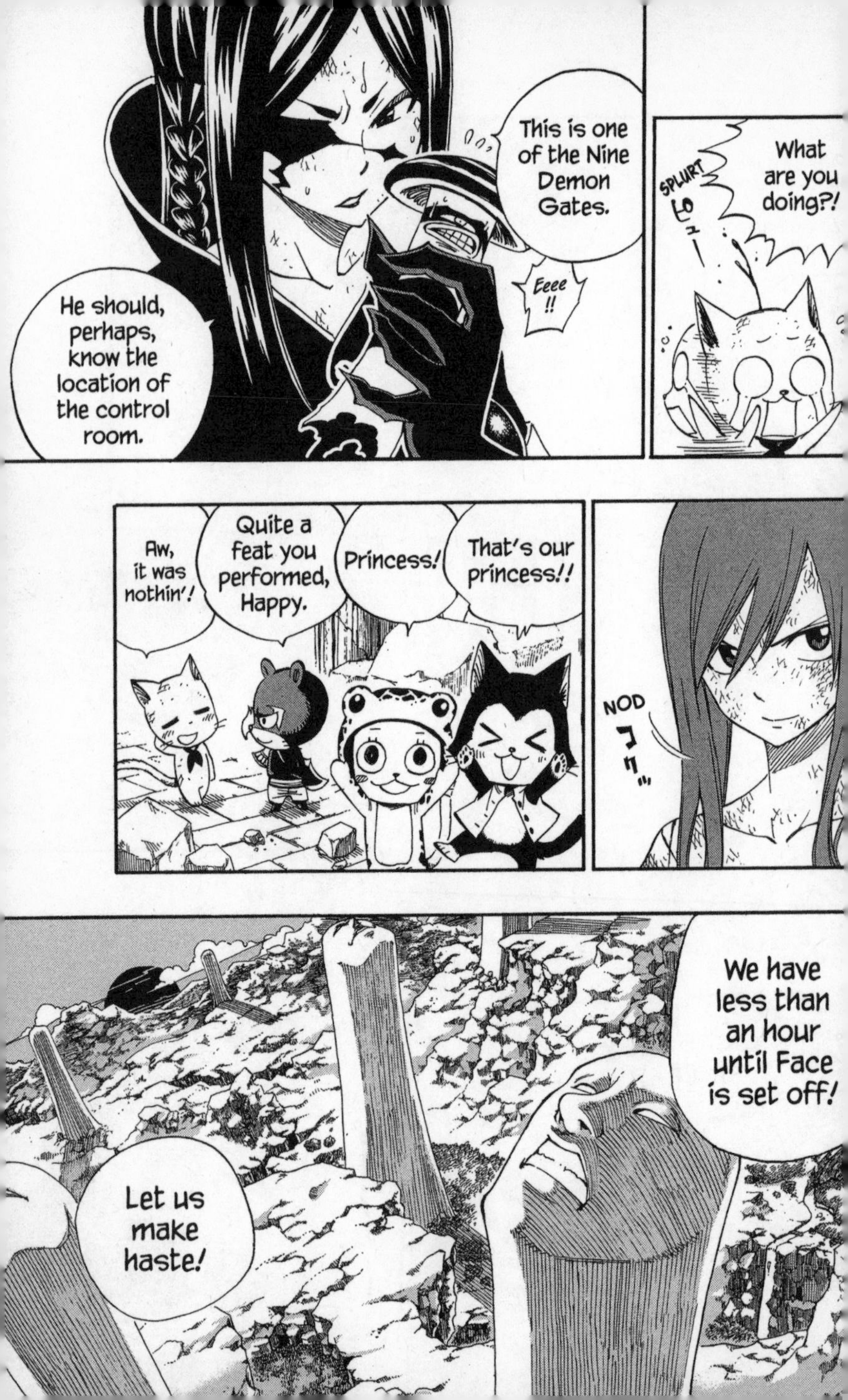
What are you doing?!
SPLURT
This is one of the Nine Demon Gates.
Eeee!!
He should, perhaps, know the location of the control room.
NOD
That's our princess!!
Princess!
Quite a feat you performed, Happy.
Aw, it was nothin'!
We have less than an hour until Face is set off!
Let us make haste!

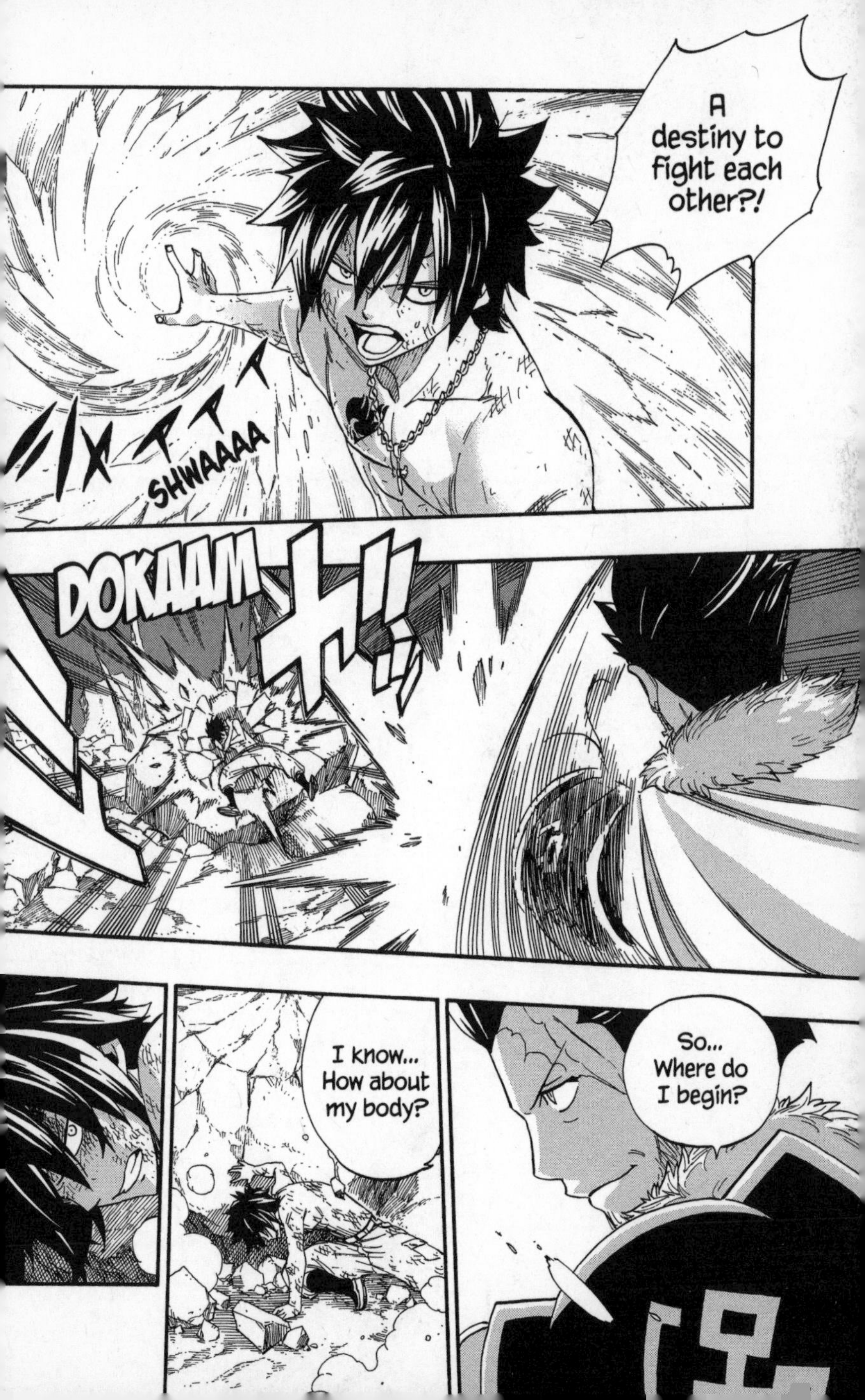
A destiny to fight each other?!
SHWAAAA
DOKAAM
So... Where do I begin?
I know... How about my body?

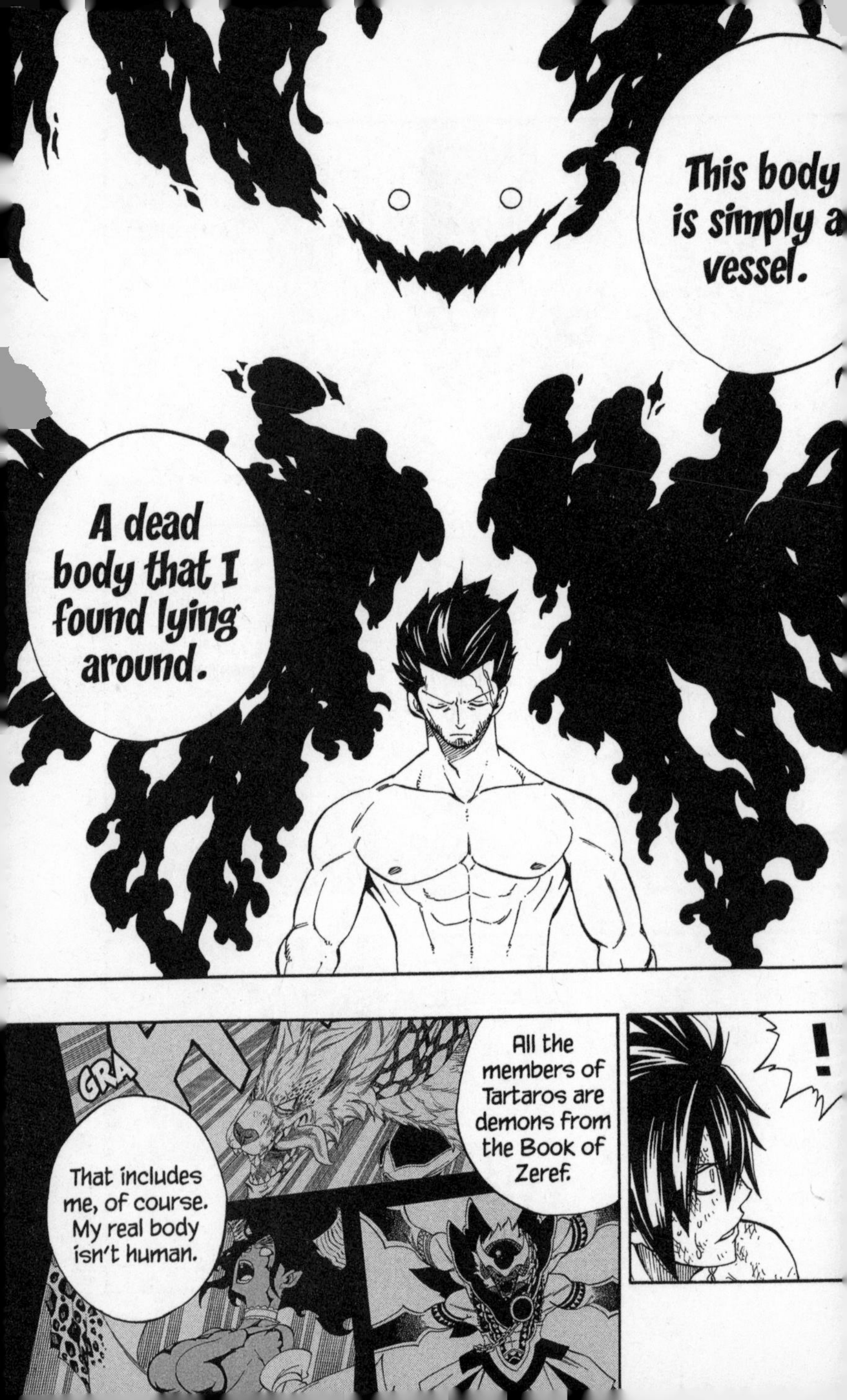
This body is simply a vessel.
A dead body that I found lying around.
!
All the members of Tartaros are demons from the Book of Zeref.
GRA
That includes me, of course. My real body isn't human.

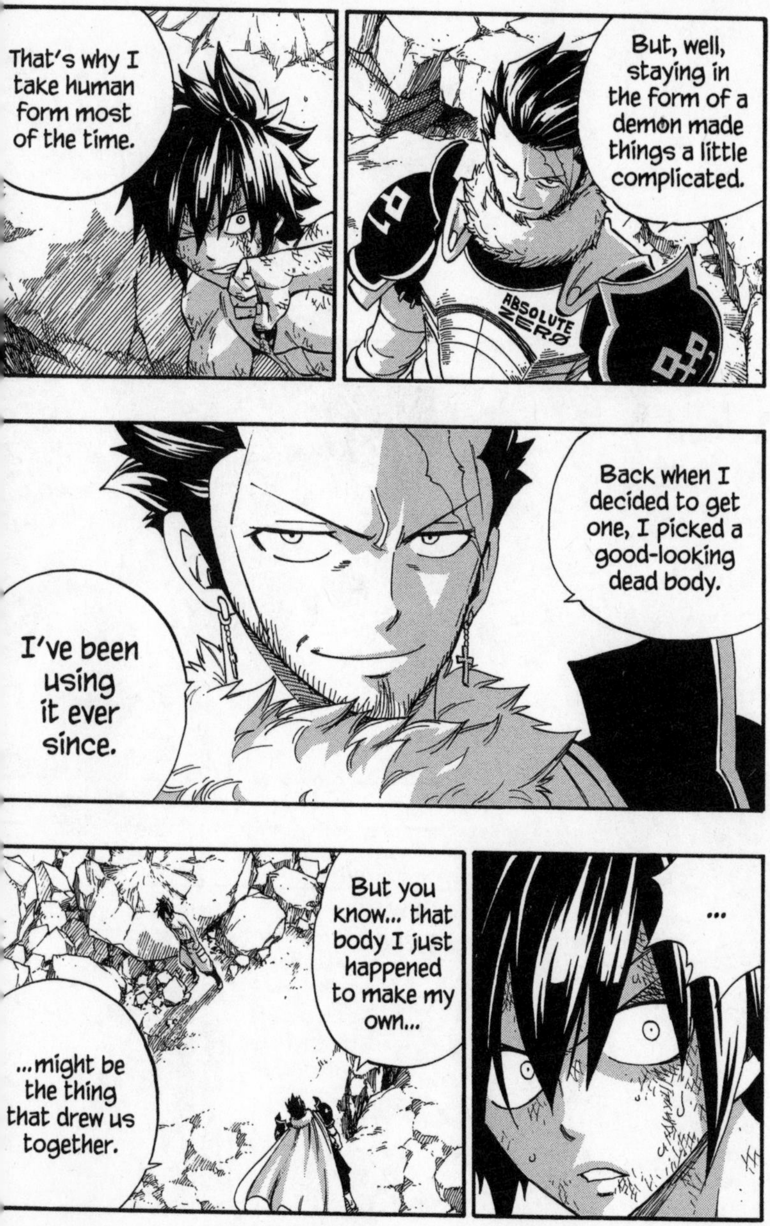
But, well, staying in the form of a demon made things a little complicated.
That's why I take human form most of the time.
ABSOLUTE ZERØ
Back when I decided to get one, I picked a good-looking dead body.
I've been using it ever since.
...
But you know... that body I just happened to make my own...
...might be the thing that drew us together.

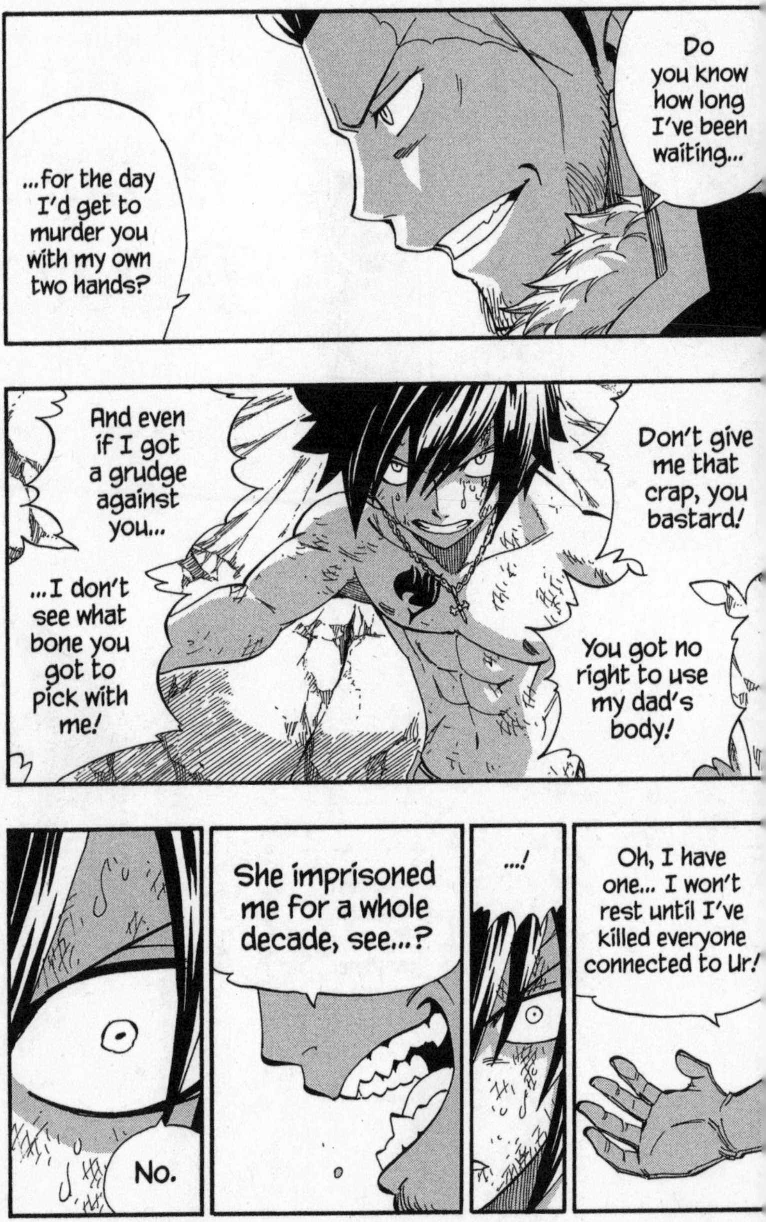
Do you know how long I've been waiting...
...for the day I'd get to murder you with my own two hands?
Don't give me that crap, you bastard!
You got no right to use my dad's body!
And even if I got a grudge against you...
...I don't see what bone you got to pick with me!
Oh, I have one... I won't rest until I've killed everyone connected to Ur!
...!
She imprisoned me for a whole decade, see...?
No.

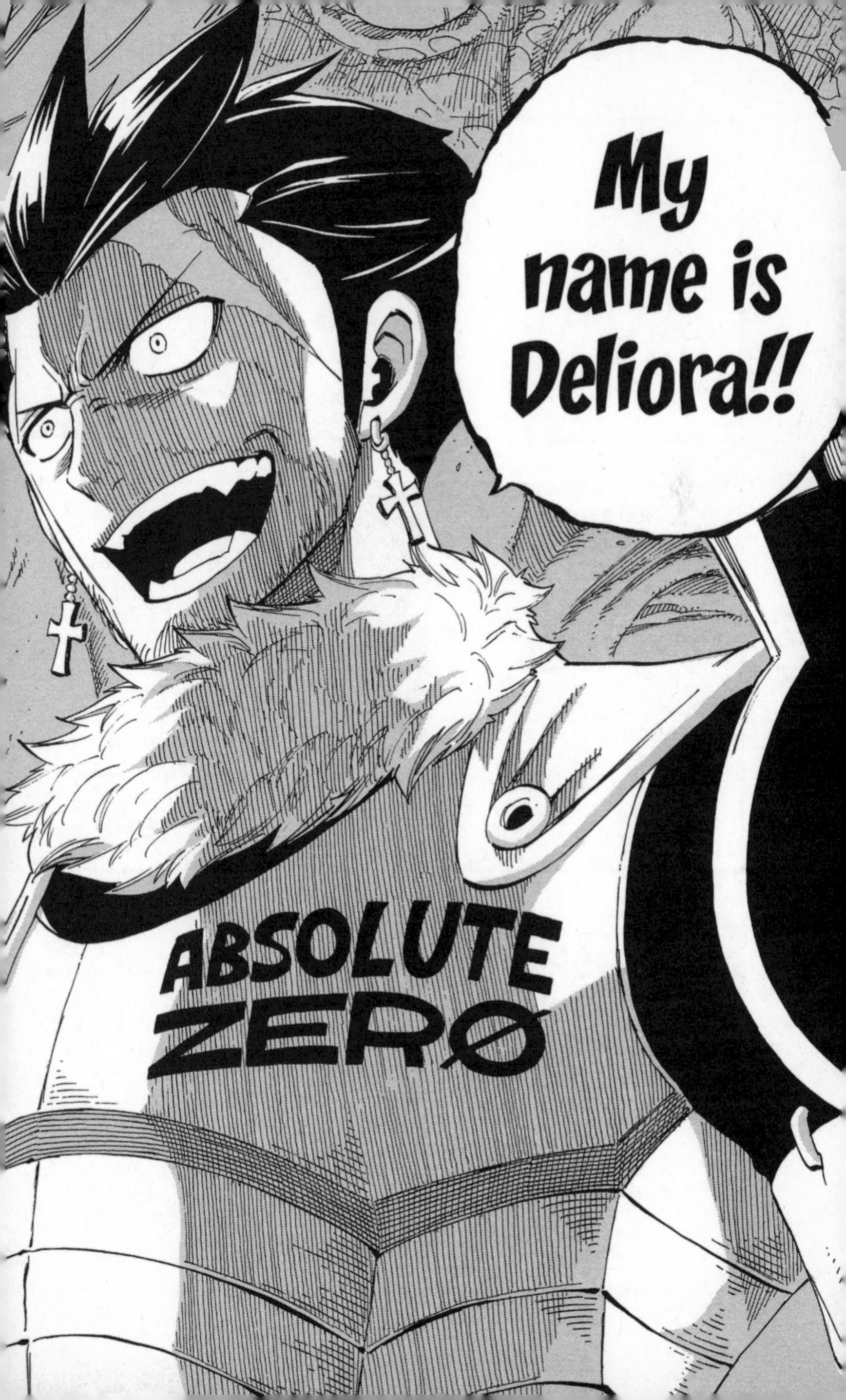
My name is Deliora!!
ABSOLUTE ZERØ

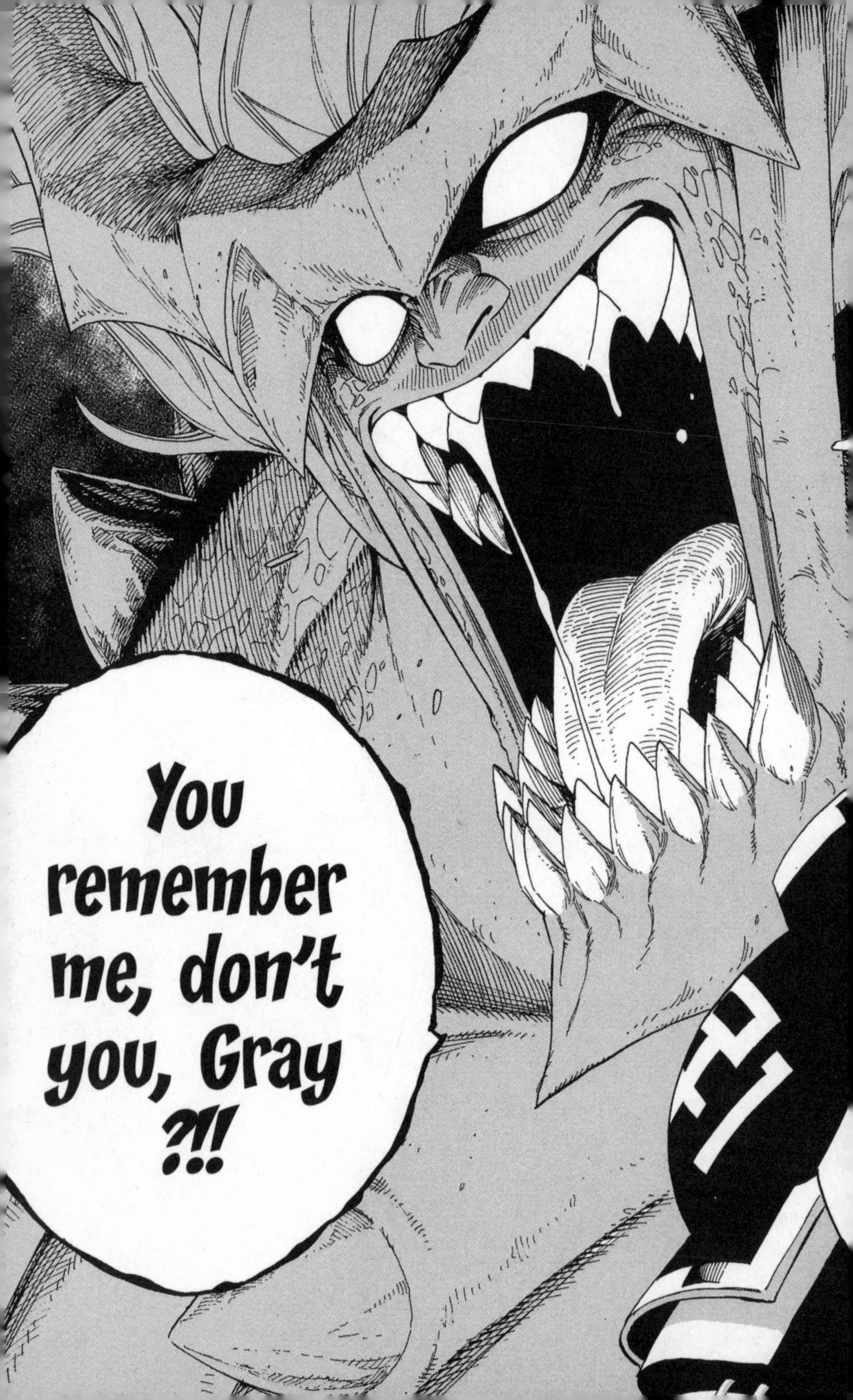
You remember me, don't you, Gray ?!!

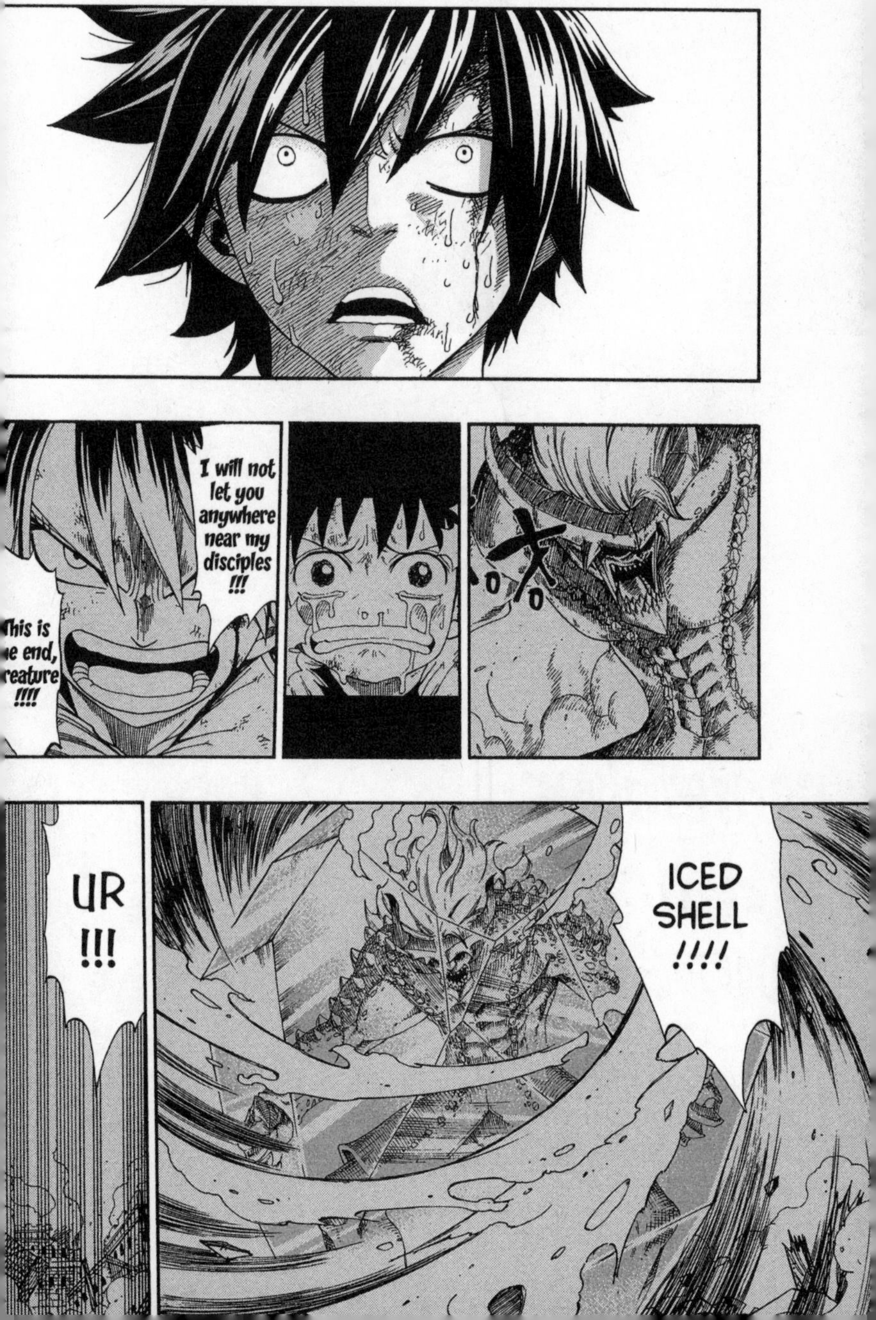
I will not let you anywhere near my disciples !!!
his is e end, reature !!!!
ICED SHELL !!!!
UR !!!

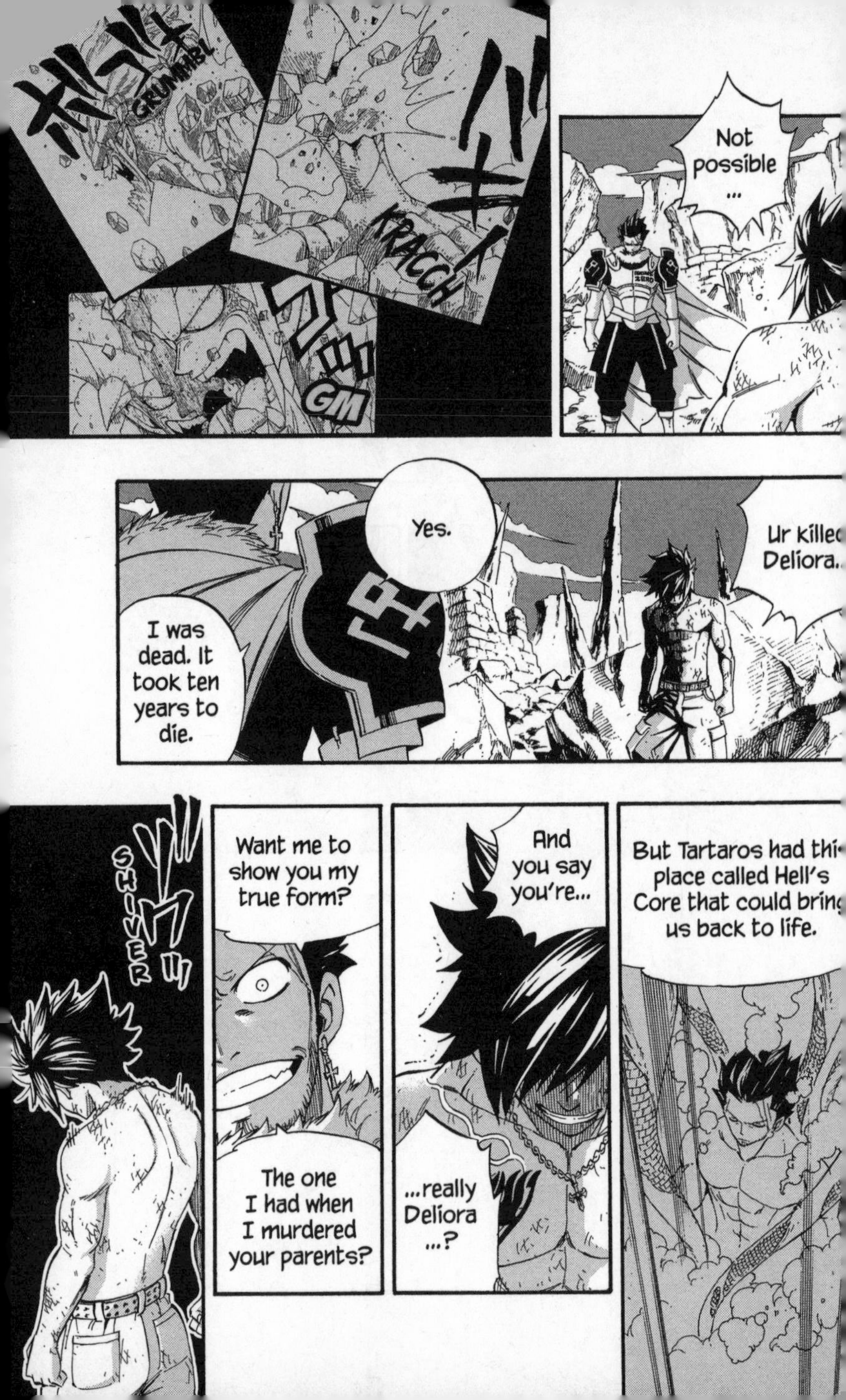
Not possible ...
KRACCH
GRUMMBL
GM
Ur killed Deliora...
Yes.
I was dead. It took ten years to die.
But Tartaros had thi place called Hell's Core that could brin us back to life.
And you say you're...
...really Deliora ...?
Want me to show you my true form?
The one I had when I murdered your parents?
SHIVER

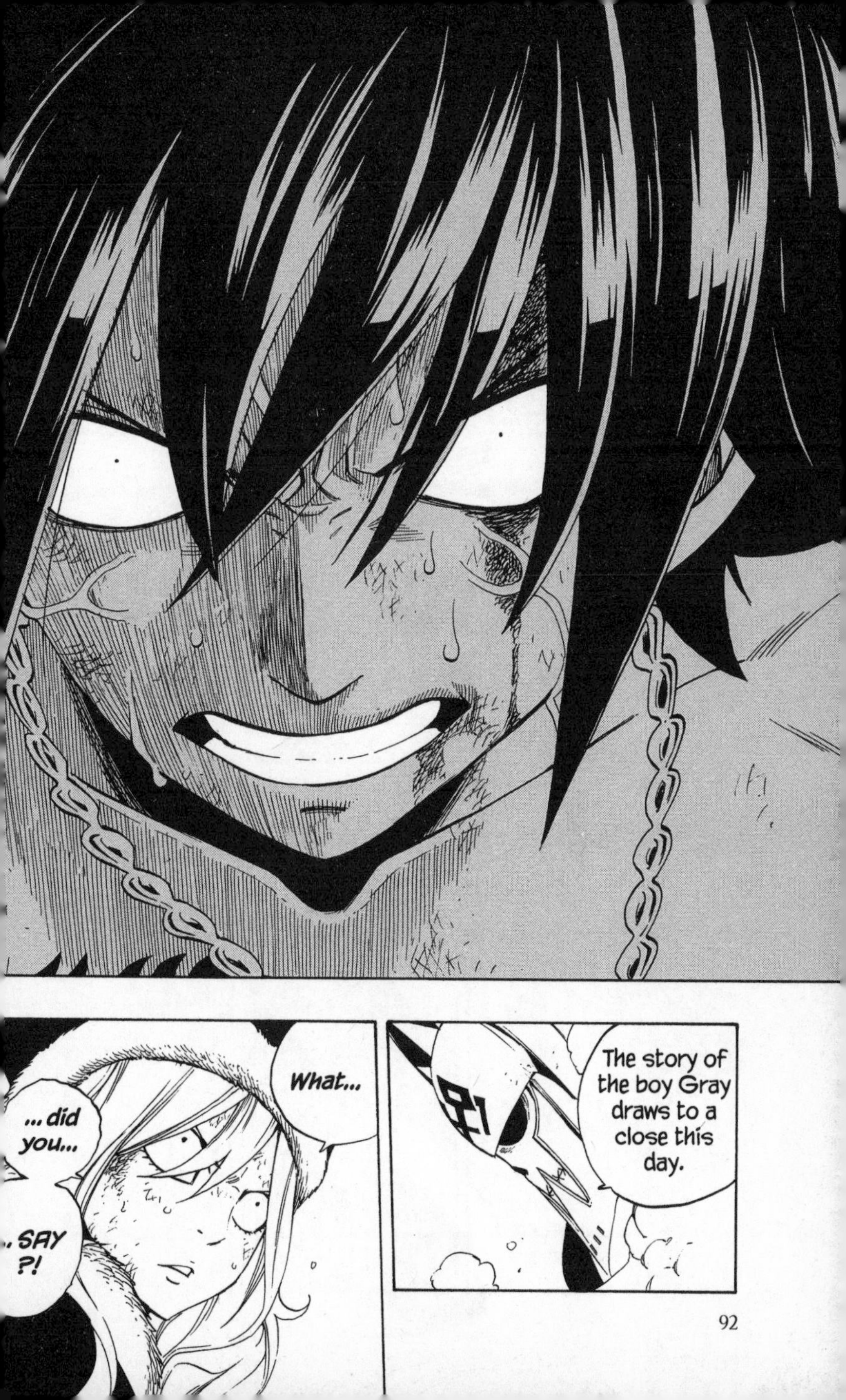

The story of the boy Gray draws to a close this day.
What...
...did you...
. SAY ?!

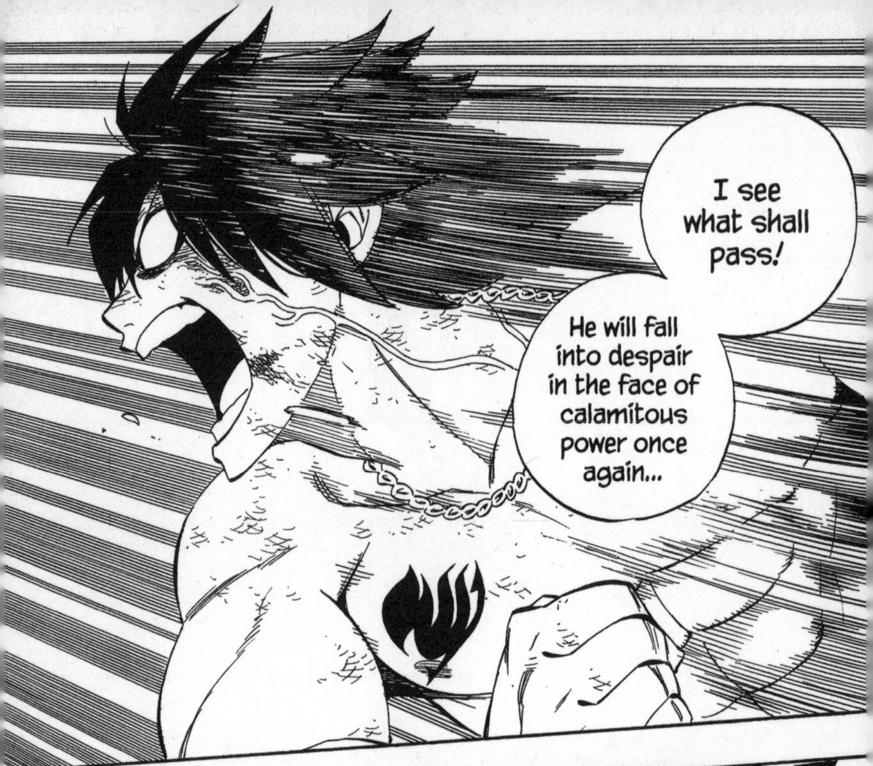
I see what shall pass!
He will fall into despair in the face of calamitous power once again...

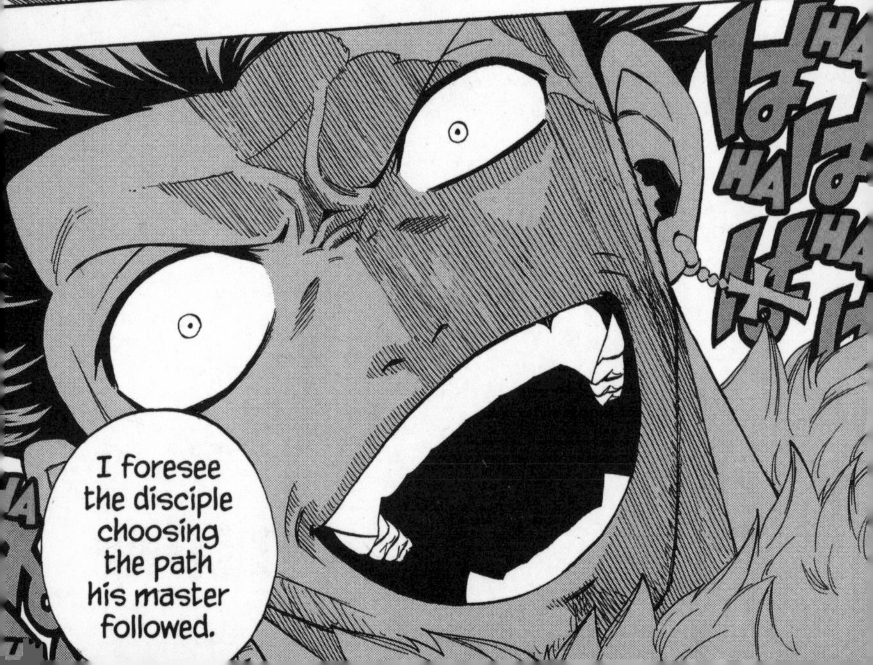
HA
I foresee the disciple choosing the path his master followed.

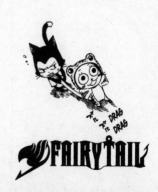

ズル ズル
ZI   ZI   DRAG
      DRAG

FAIRYTAIL

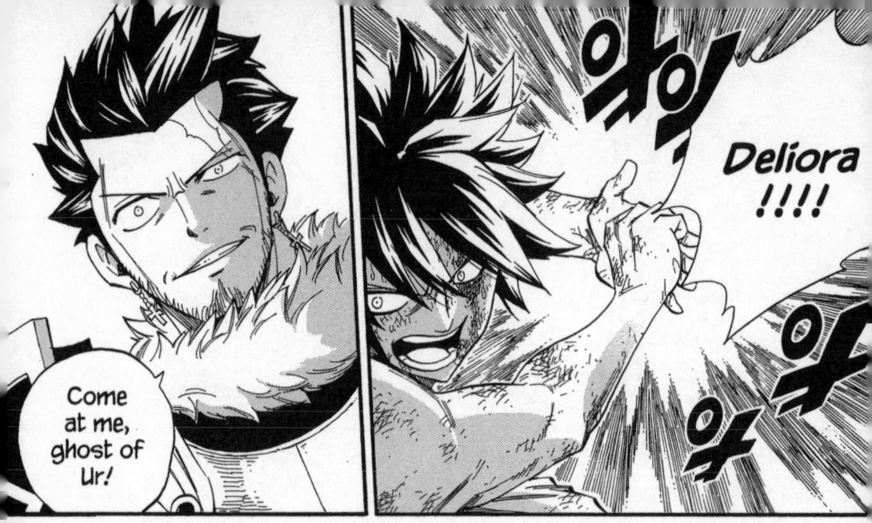
Deliora !!!!
Come at me, ghost of Ur!

Chapter 391: Gray vs. Silver

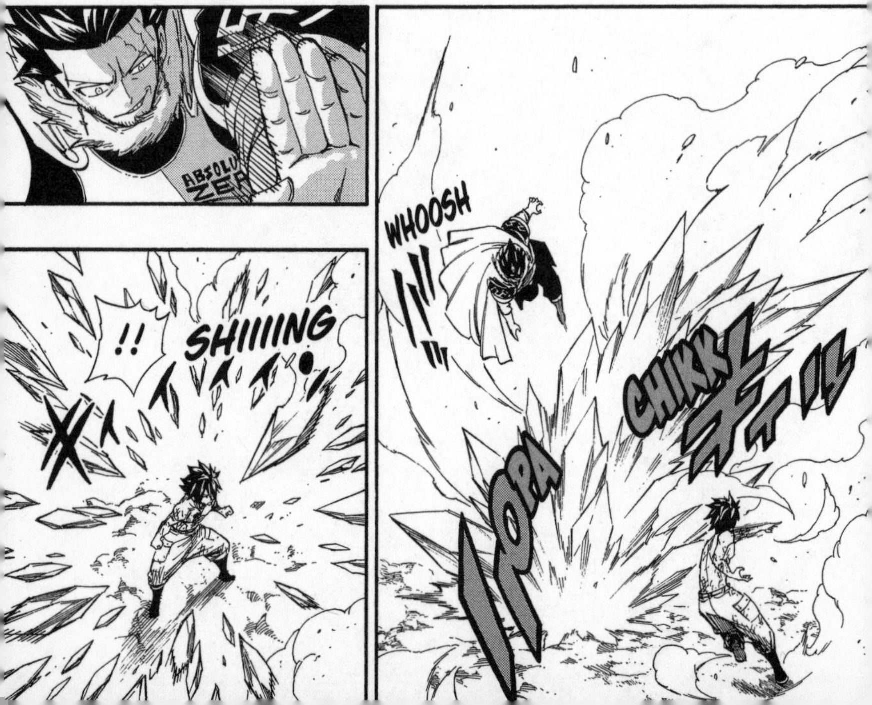
WHOOSH
CHIKK
POPA
ABSOLU ZER
!!
SHIIIING

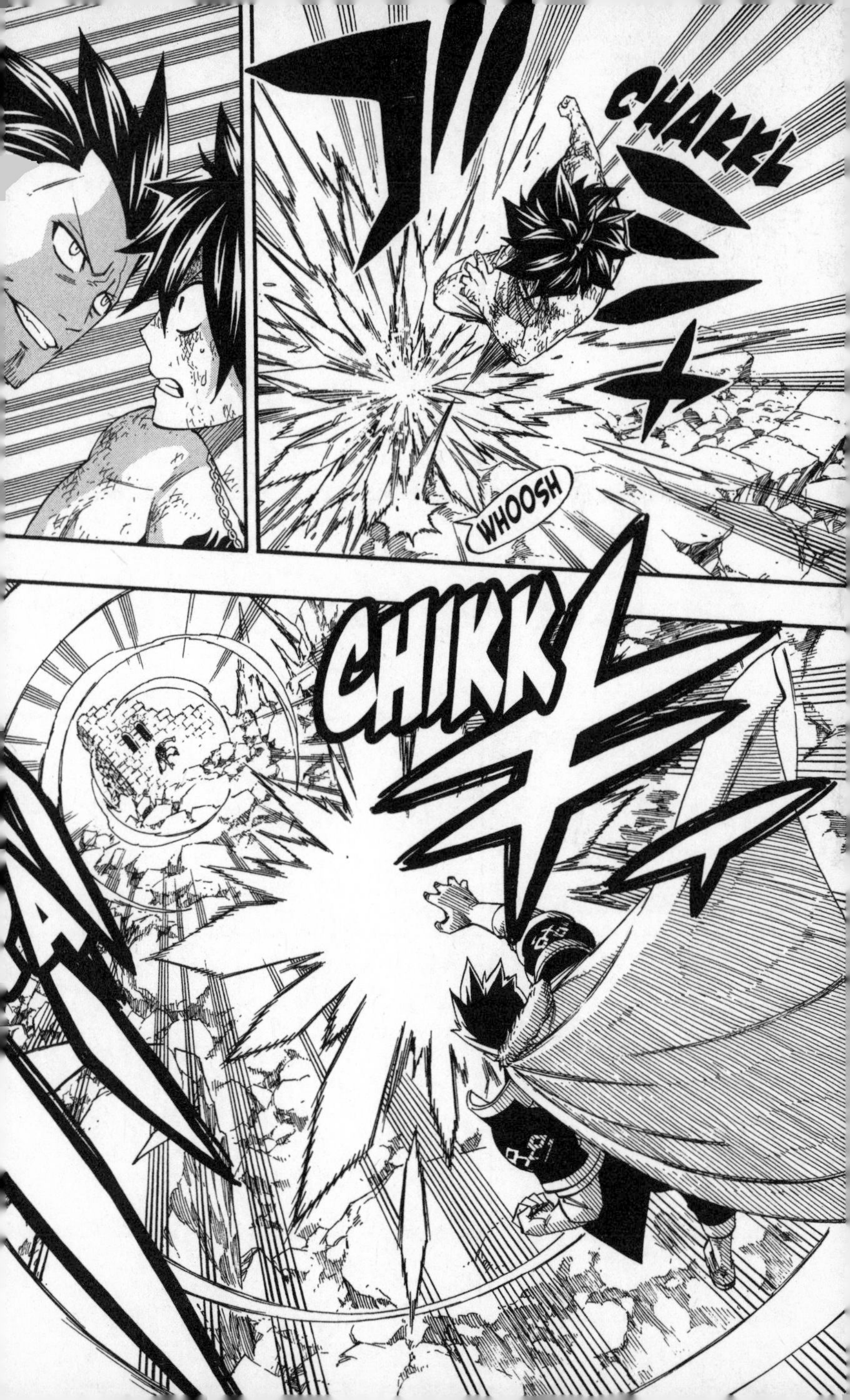
CHAKKI
WHOOSH
CHIKK

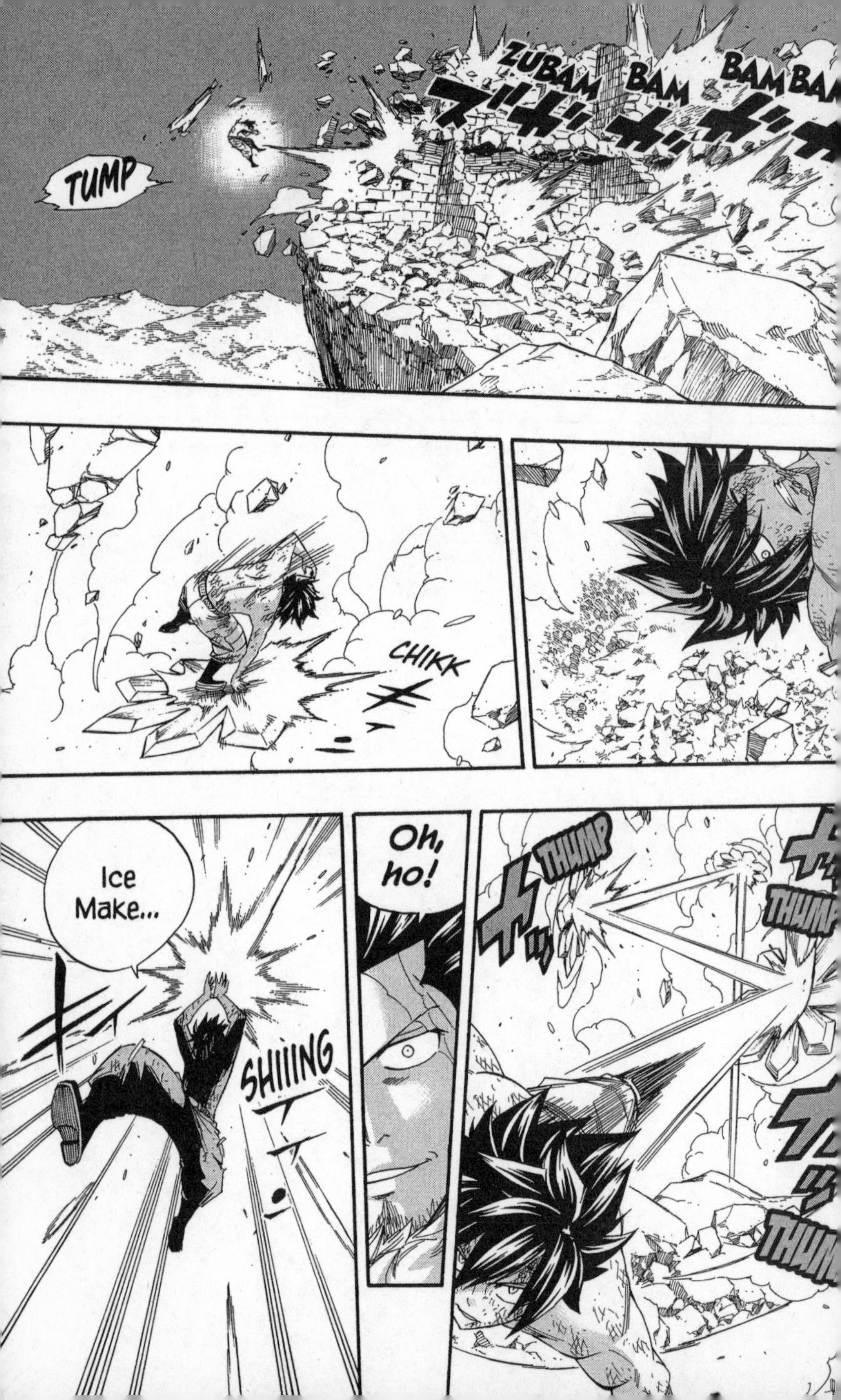
ZUBAM BAM BAMBAM
TUMP
CHIKK
THUMP
THUMP
THUM
Oh, ho!
Ice Make...
SHIIING

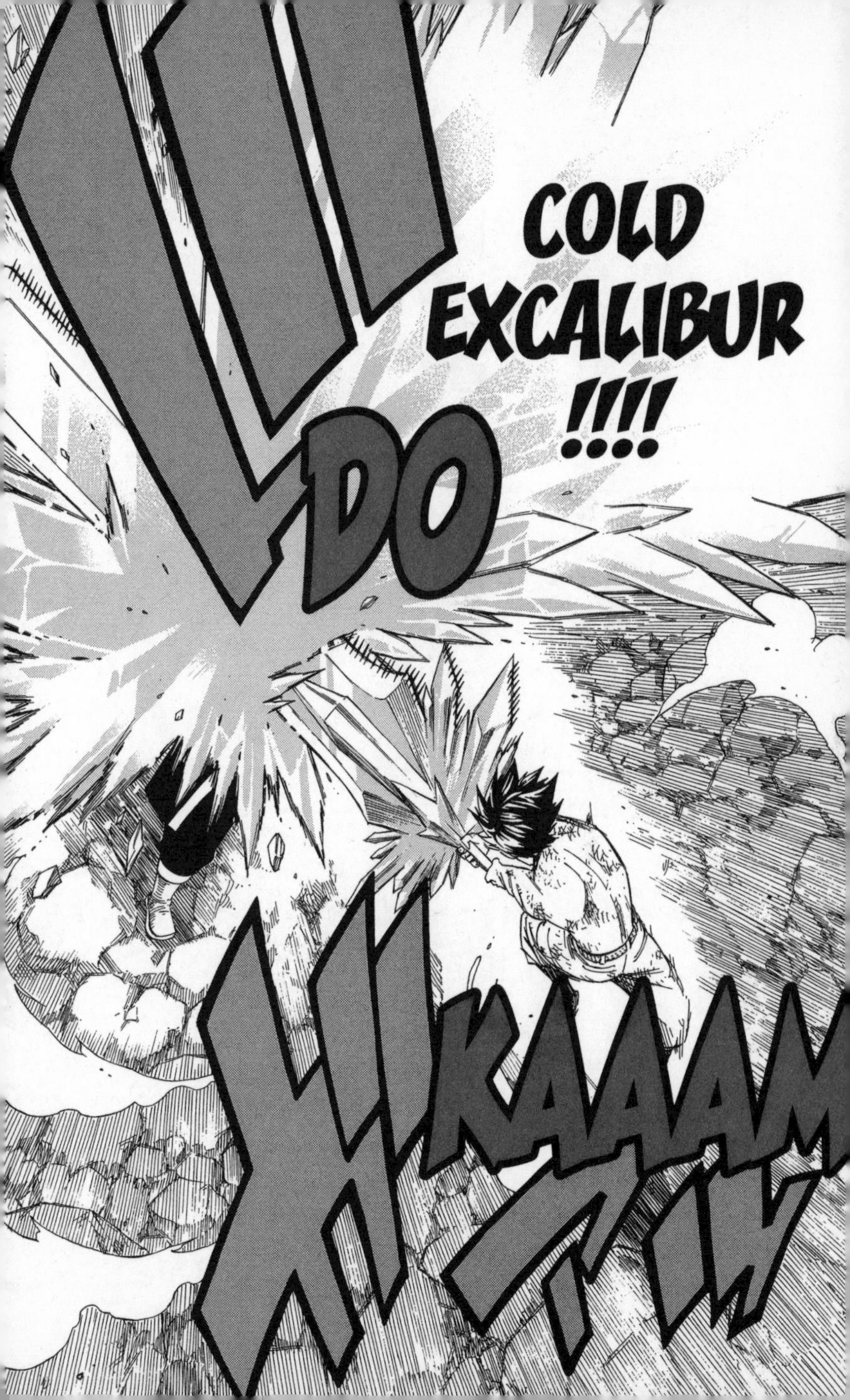
COLD EXCALIBUR!!!!
DO
KAAAM

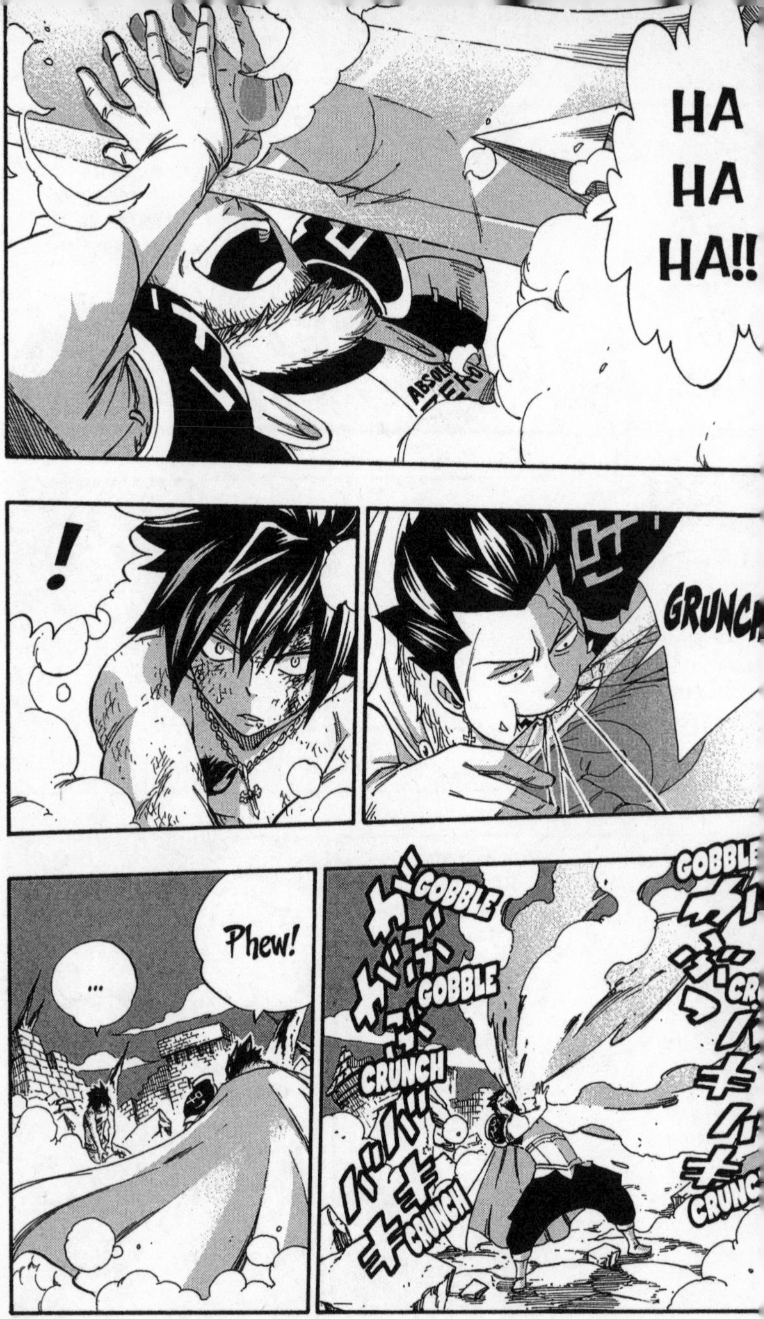
HA
HA
HA!!
GRUNC
!
GOBBLE
CRUNC
GOBBLE
GOBBLE
CRUNCH
CRUNCH
Phew!
...

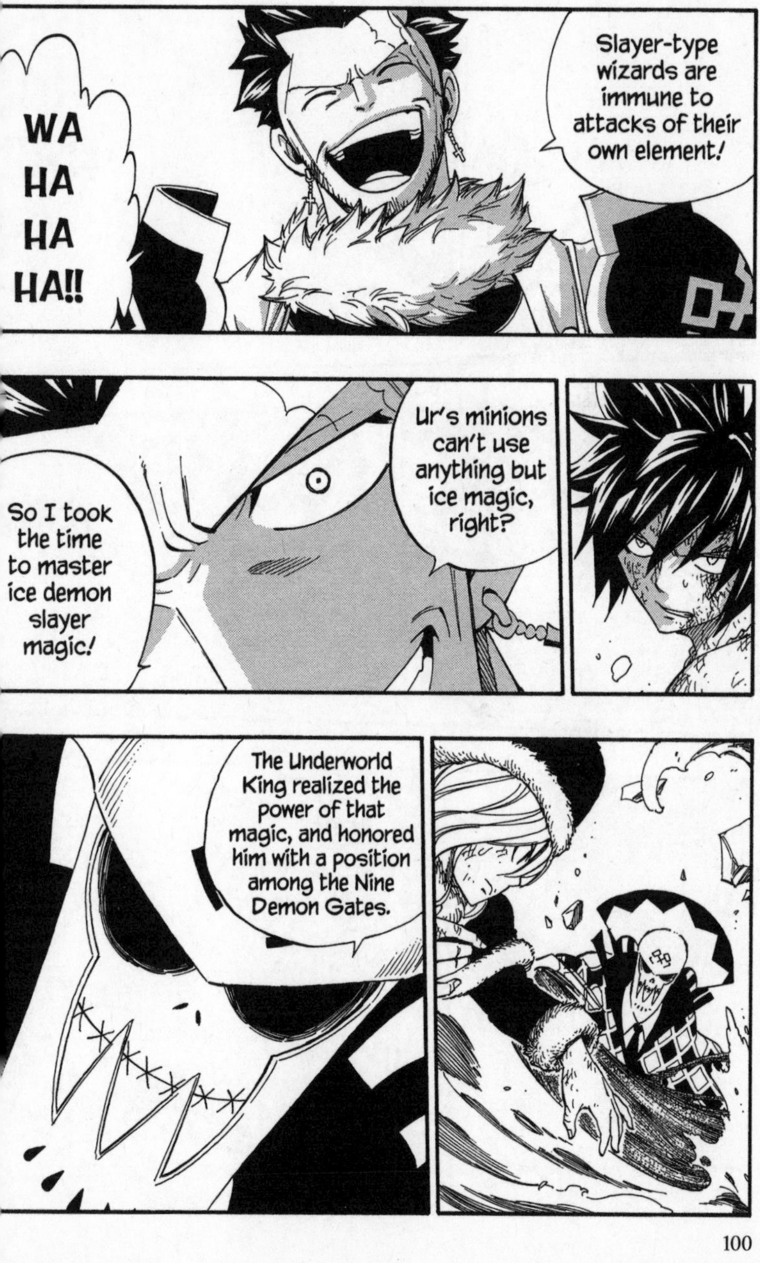
Slayer-type wizards are immune to attacks of their own element!
WA HA HA HA!!
Ur's minions can't use anything but ice magic, right?
So I took the time to master ice demon slayer magic!
The Underworld King realized the power of that magic, and honored him with a position among the Nine Demon Gates.

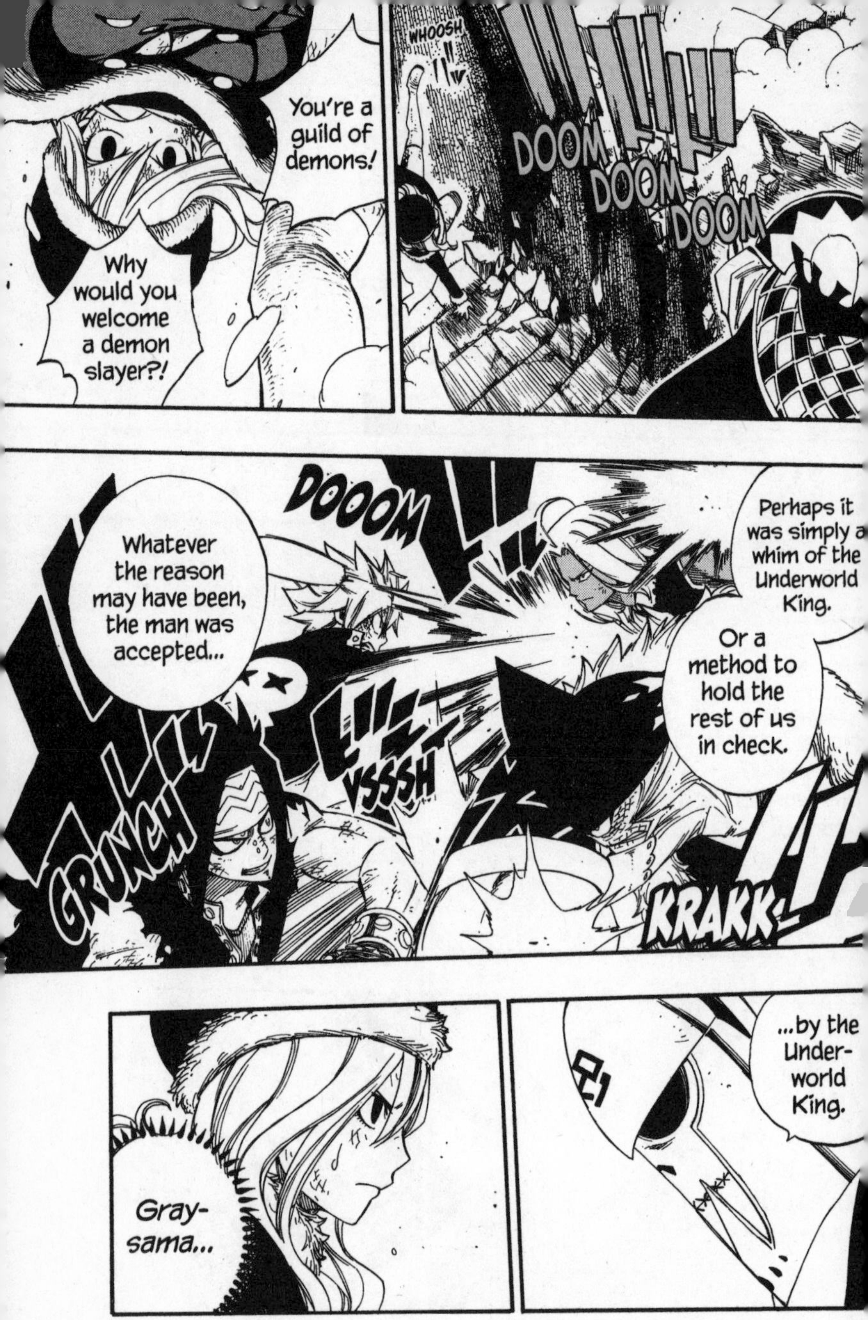
DOOM DOOM DOOM
WHOOSH
You're a guild of demons!
Why would you welcome a demon slayer?!
Perhaps it was simply a whim of the Underworld King.
Or a method to hold the rest of us in check.
DOOOM
Whatever the reason may have been, the man was accepted...
KRAKK
VSSSH
CRUNCH
...by the Under-world King.
Gray-sama...

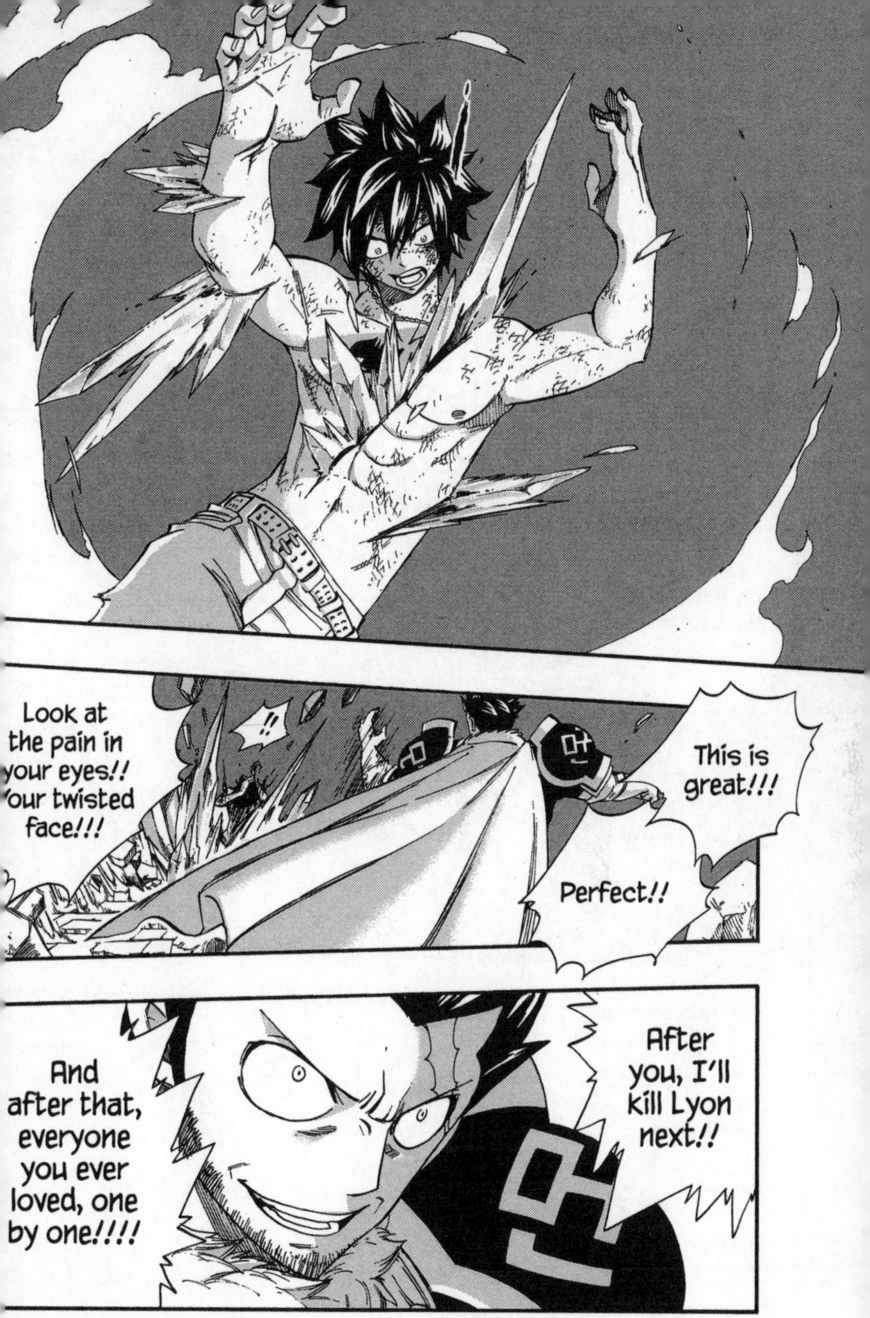
This is great!!!
Perfect!!
!!
Look at the pain in your eyes!! Your twisted face!!!
After you, I'll kill Lyon next!!
And after that, everyone you ever loved, one by one!!!!

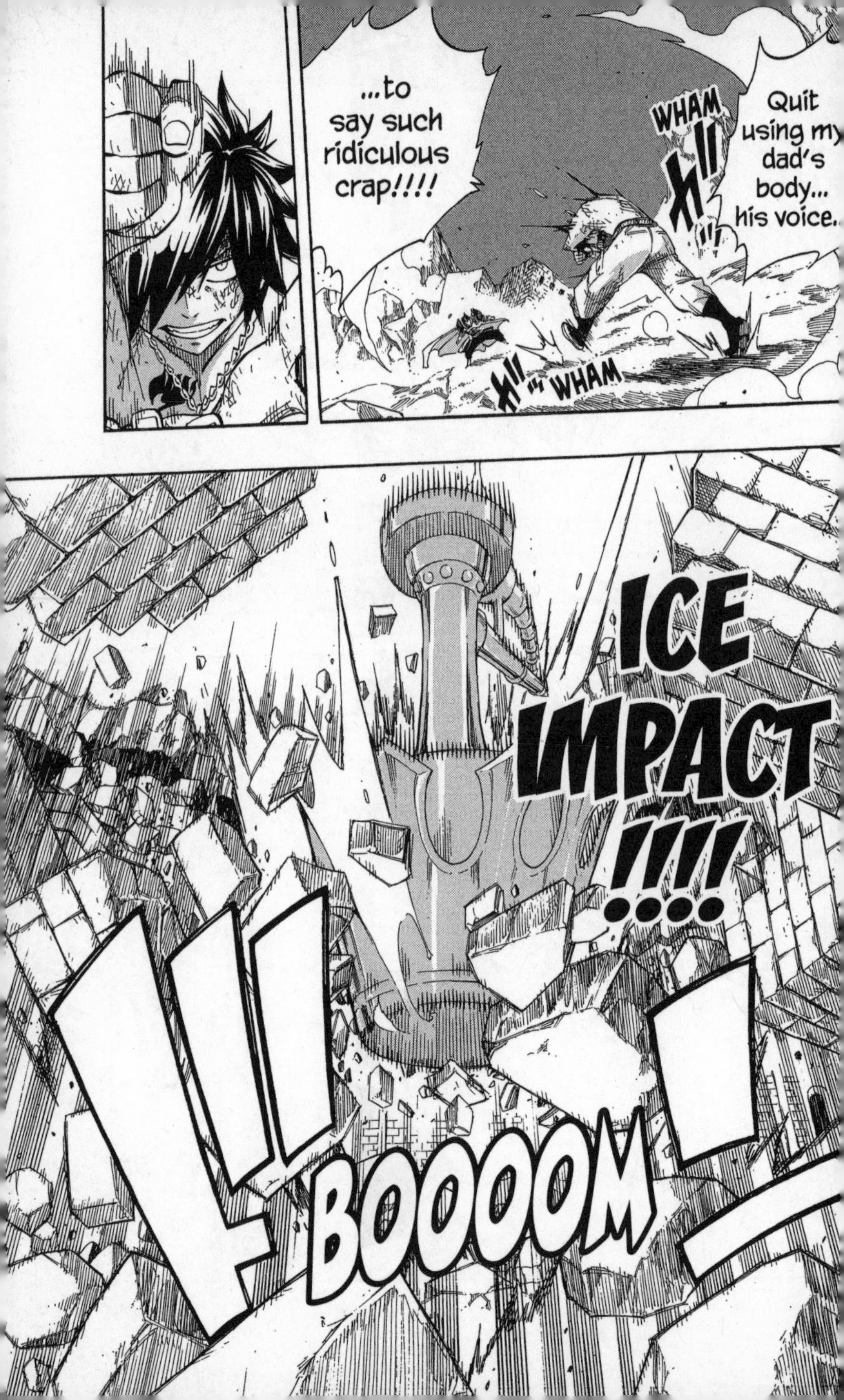
Quit using my dad's body... his voice.
WHAM
WHAM
...to say such ridiculous crap!!!!
ICE IMPACT!!!!
BOOOOM

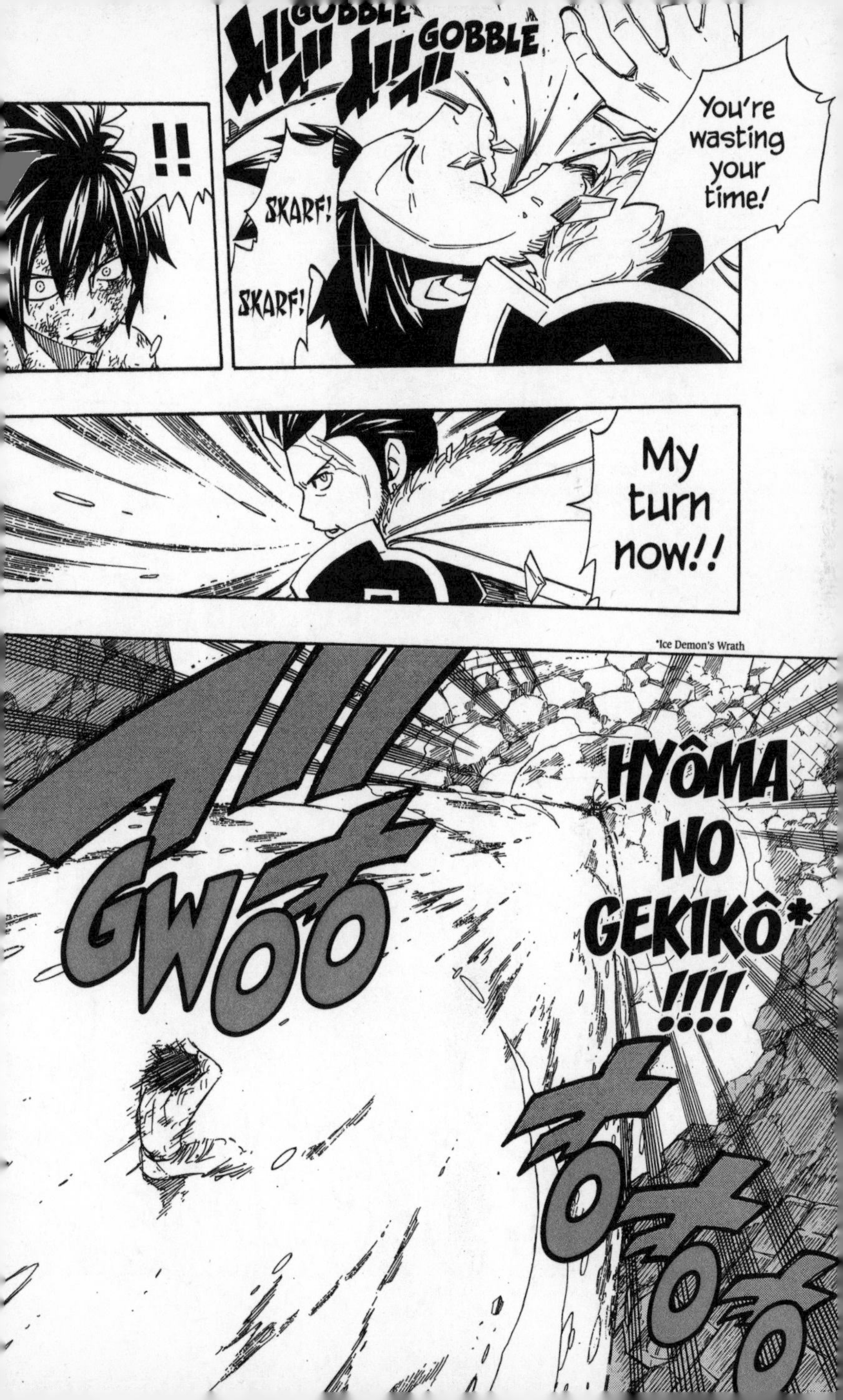
You're wasting your time!
GOBBLE
GOBBLE
SKARF!
SKARF!
!!
My turn now!!
HYÔMA NO GEKIKÔ* !!!!
GWOOO
*Ice Demon's Wrath

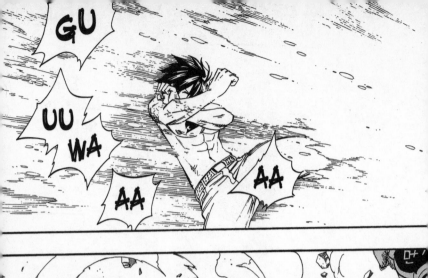

GU

UU
WA

AA

AA

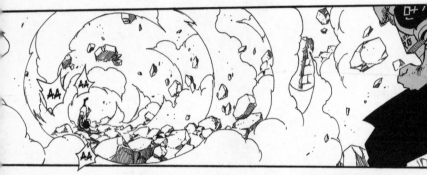

AA AA

AA

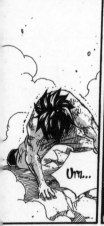

Um...

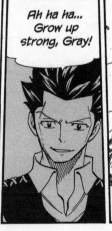

Ah ha ha...
Grow up
strong, Gray!

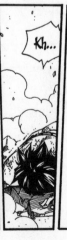

Kh...

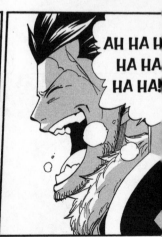

AH HA H
HA HA
HA HA!

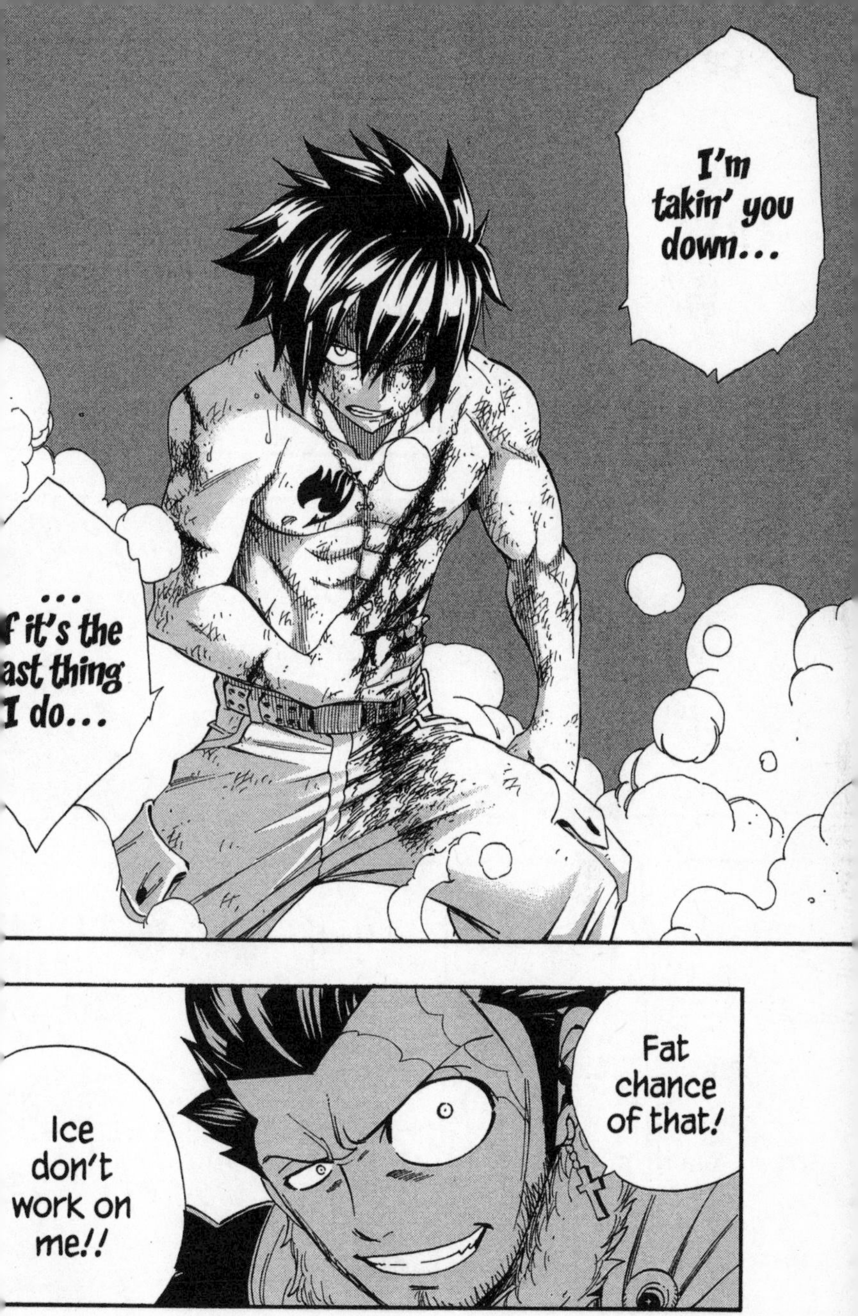
I'm takin' you down...
...
f it's the
ast thing
I do...
Fat chance of that!
Ice don't work on me!!

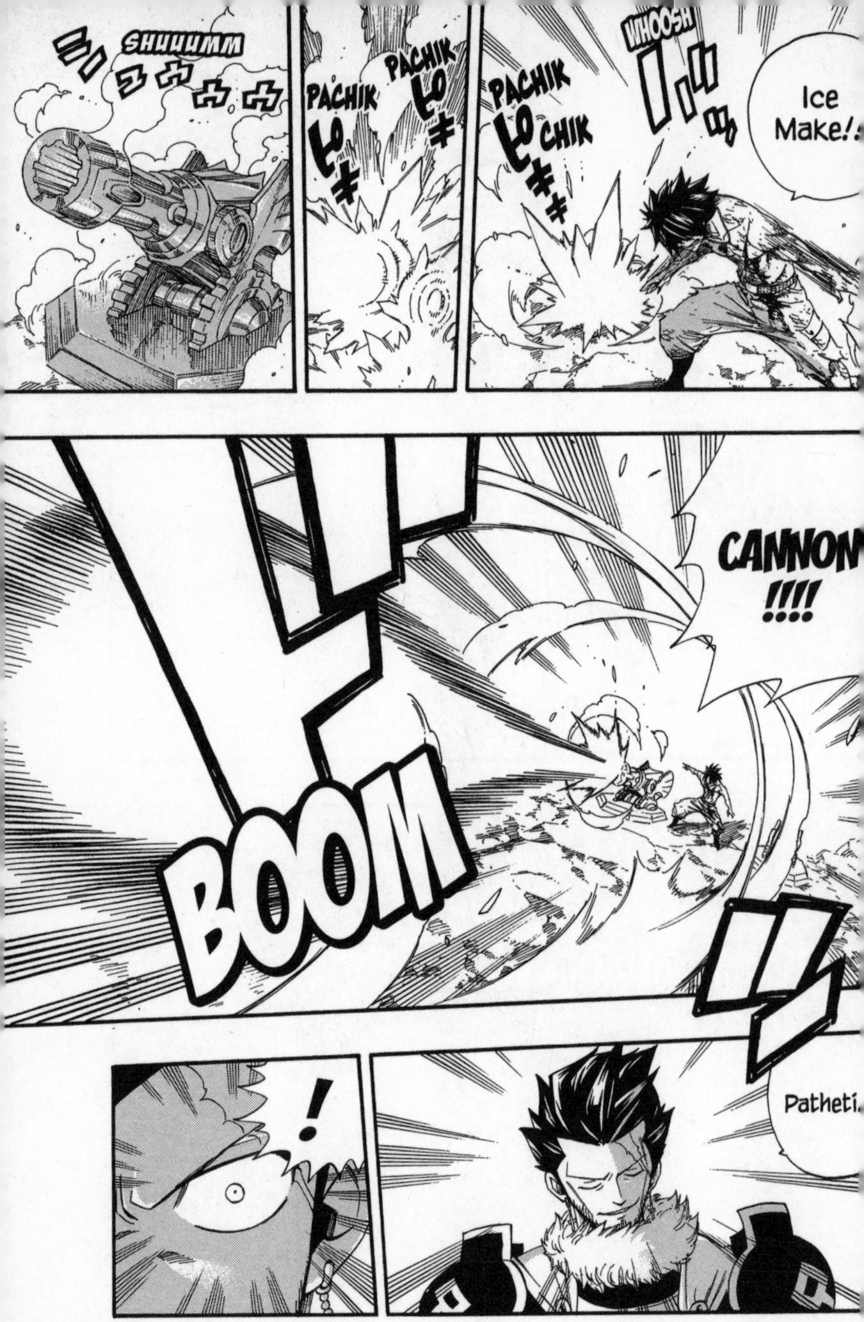
Ice Make!!
WHOOSH
PACHIK
CHIK
PACHIK
PACHIK
SHUUUMM
CANNON!!!!
BOOM
Patheti.
!

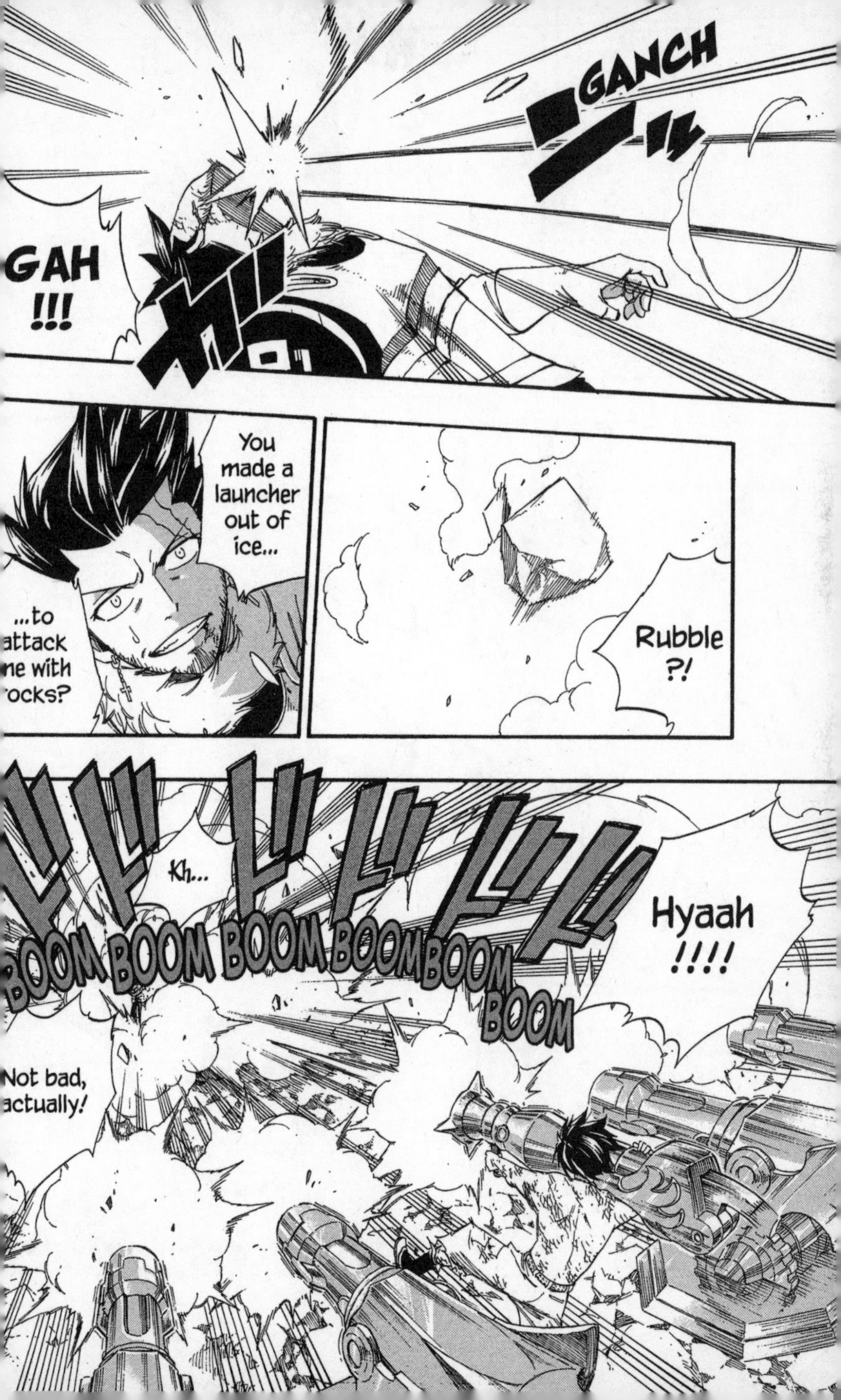

GANCH
GAH!!!
Rubble?!
You made a launcher out of ice...
...to attack ne with ocks?
Hyaah!!!!
BOOM BOOM BOOM BOOM BOOM BOOM
Kh...
Not bad, actually!

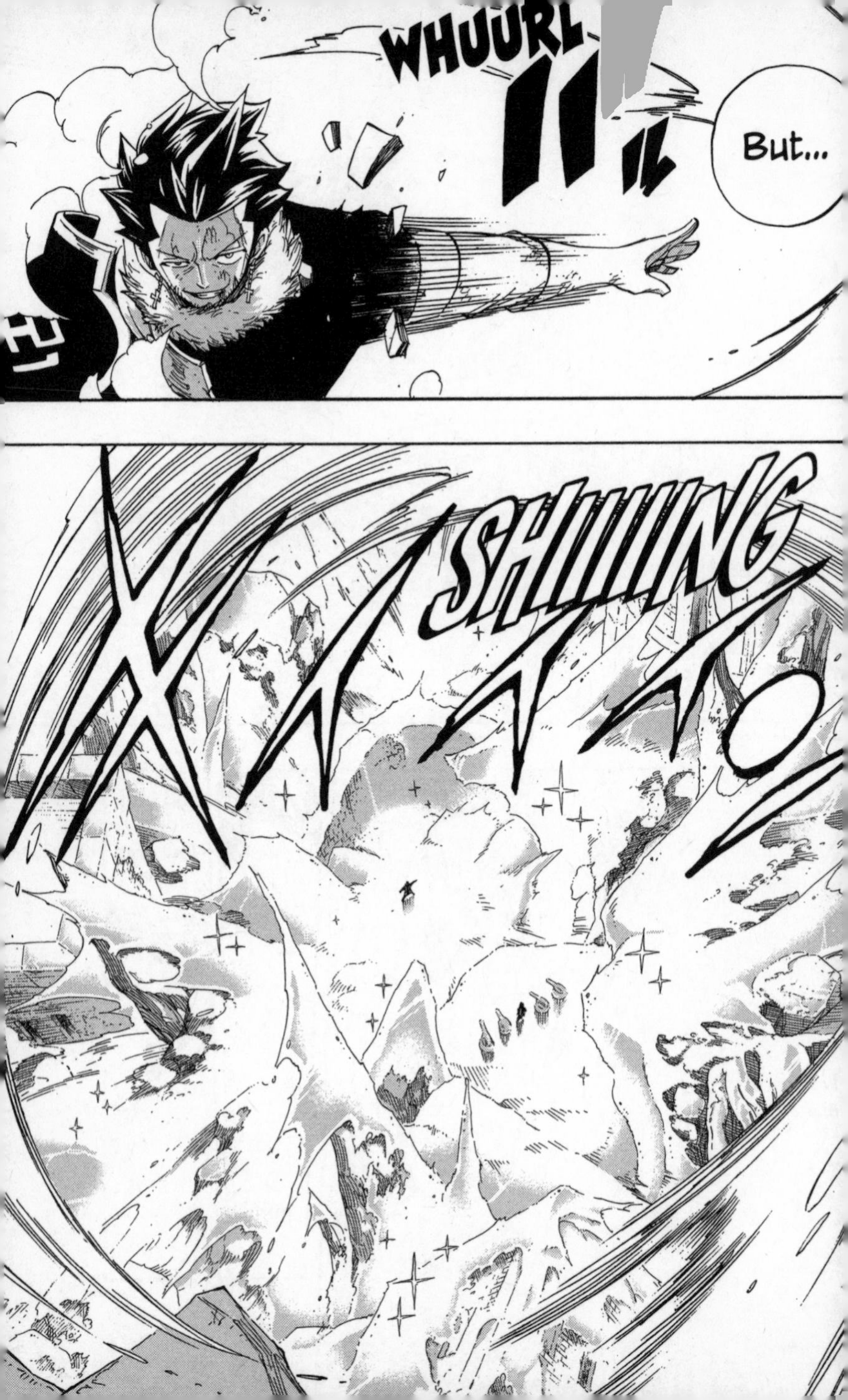
But...
WHUURL
SHIIIING

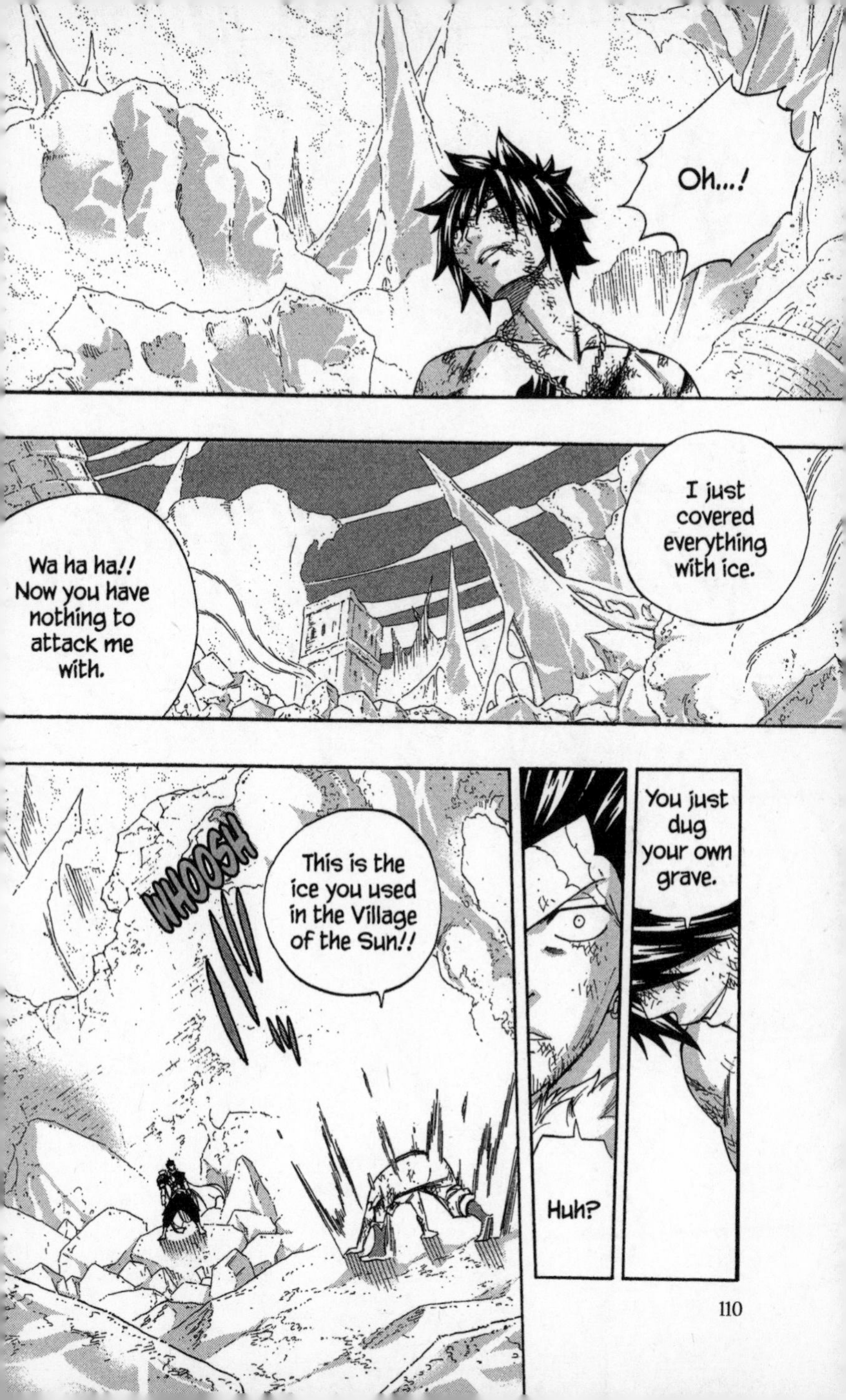
Oh...!
I just covered everything with ice.
Wa ha ha!! Now you have nothing to attack me with.
You just dug your own grave.
Huh?
This is the ice you used in the Village of the Sun!!
WHOOSH

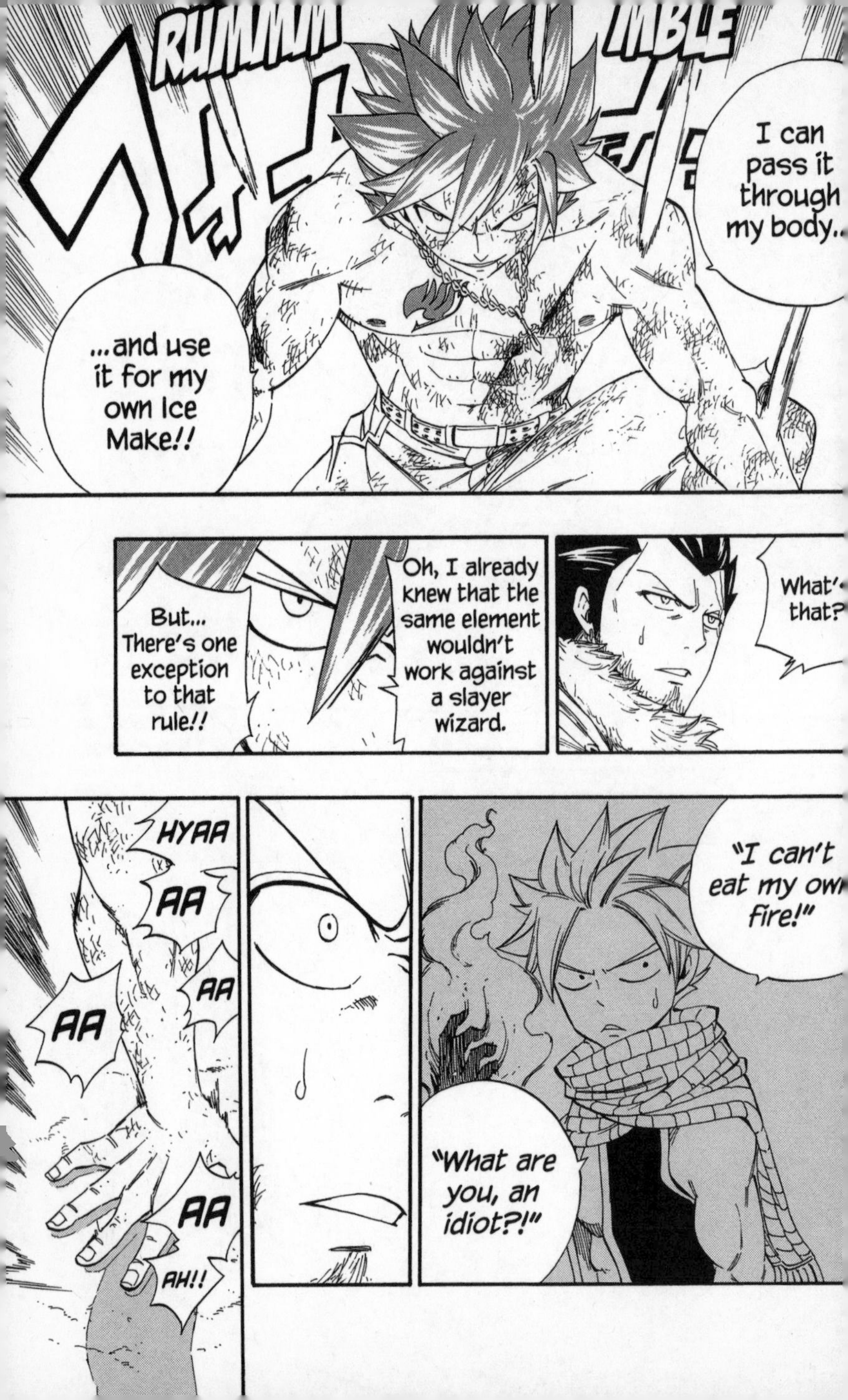

RUMMMM
MBLE
I can pass it through my body..
...and use it for my own Ice Make!!
What' that?
Oh, I already knew that the same element wouldn't work against a slayer wizard.
But... There's one exception to that rule!!
"I can't eat my ow fire!"
"What are you, an idiot?!"
HYAA
AA
AA
AA
AA
AH!!

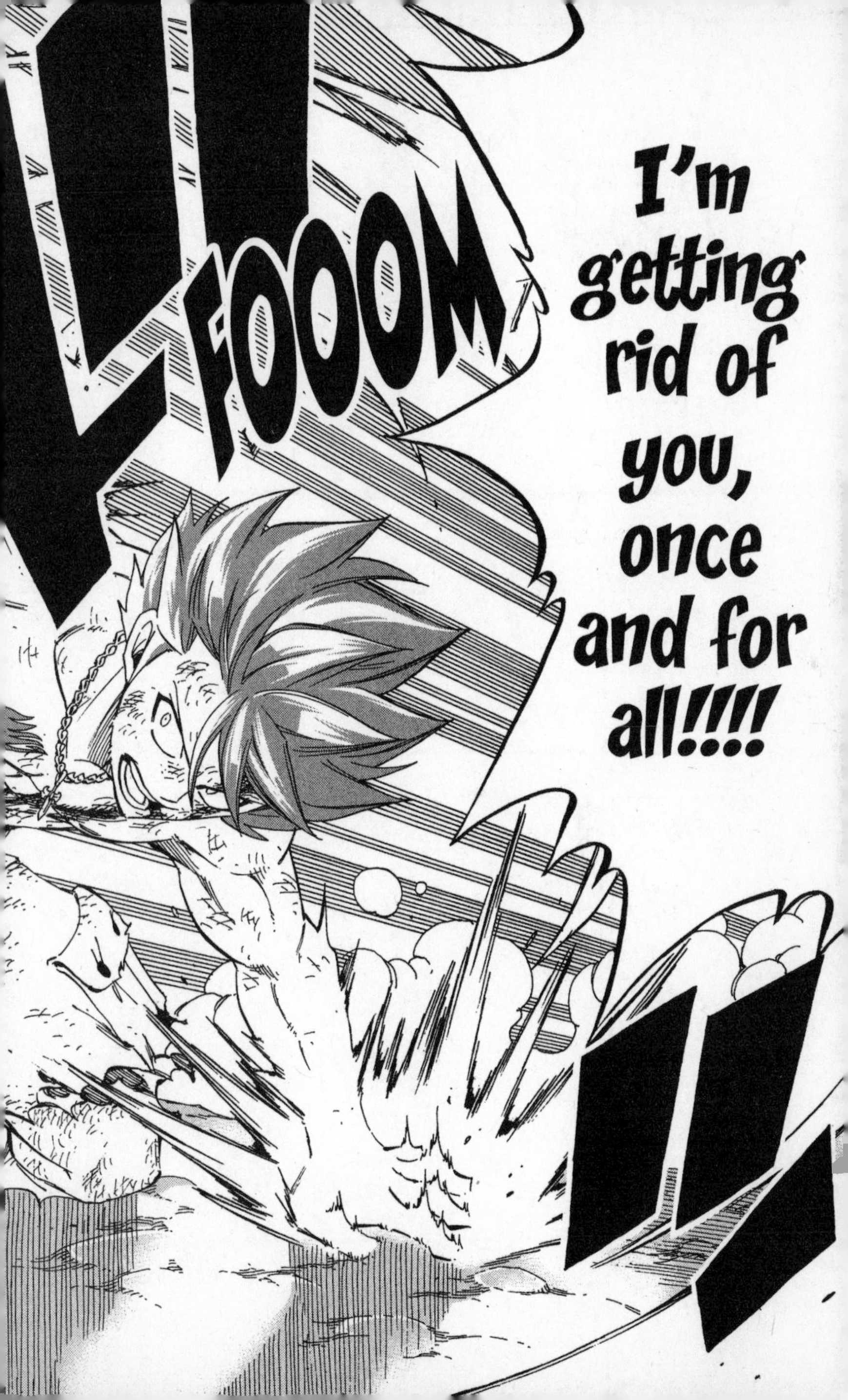
FOOOM
I'm getting rid of you, once and for all!!!!

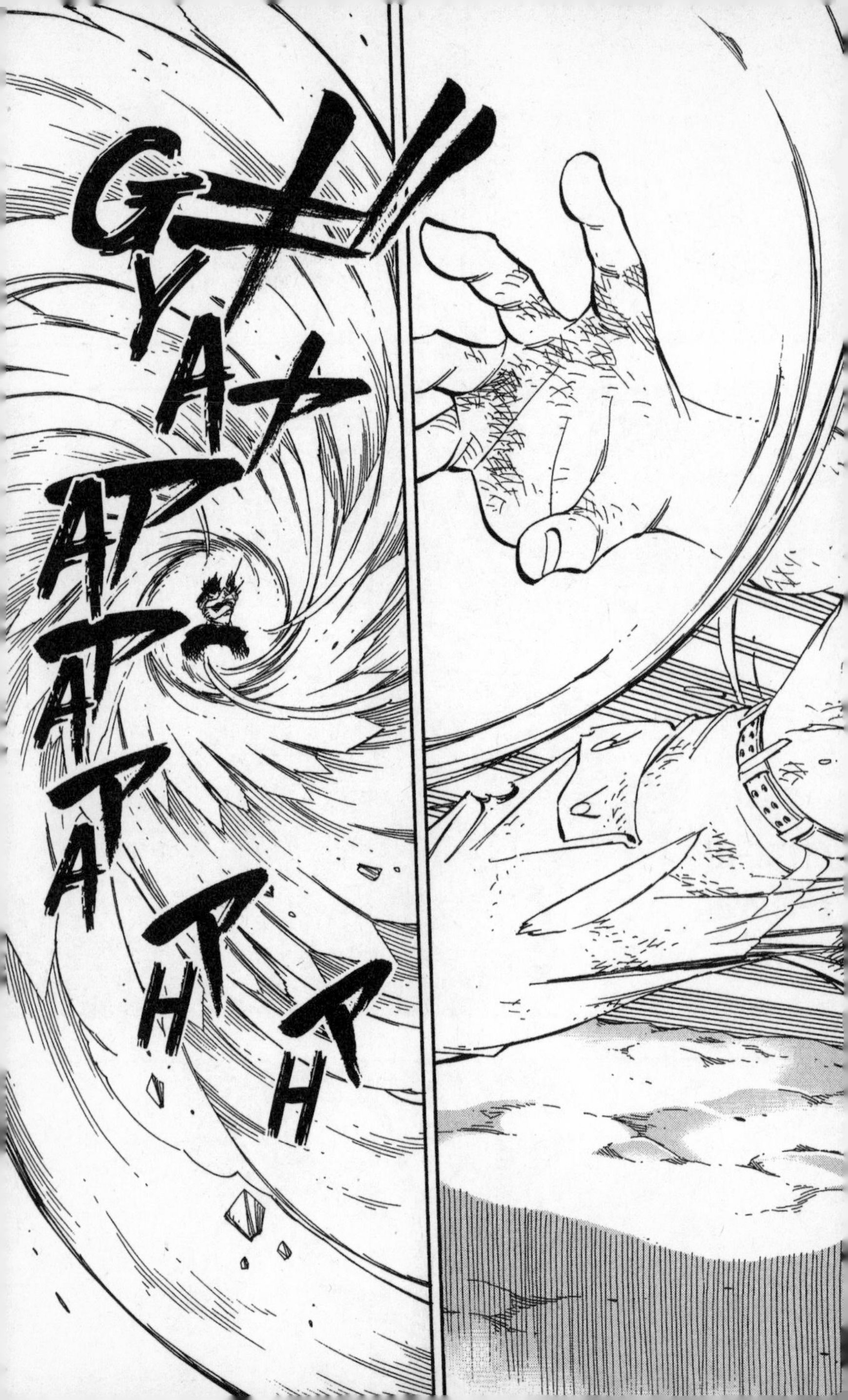
GYAAAAAAAAAHH

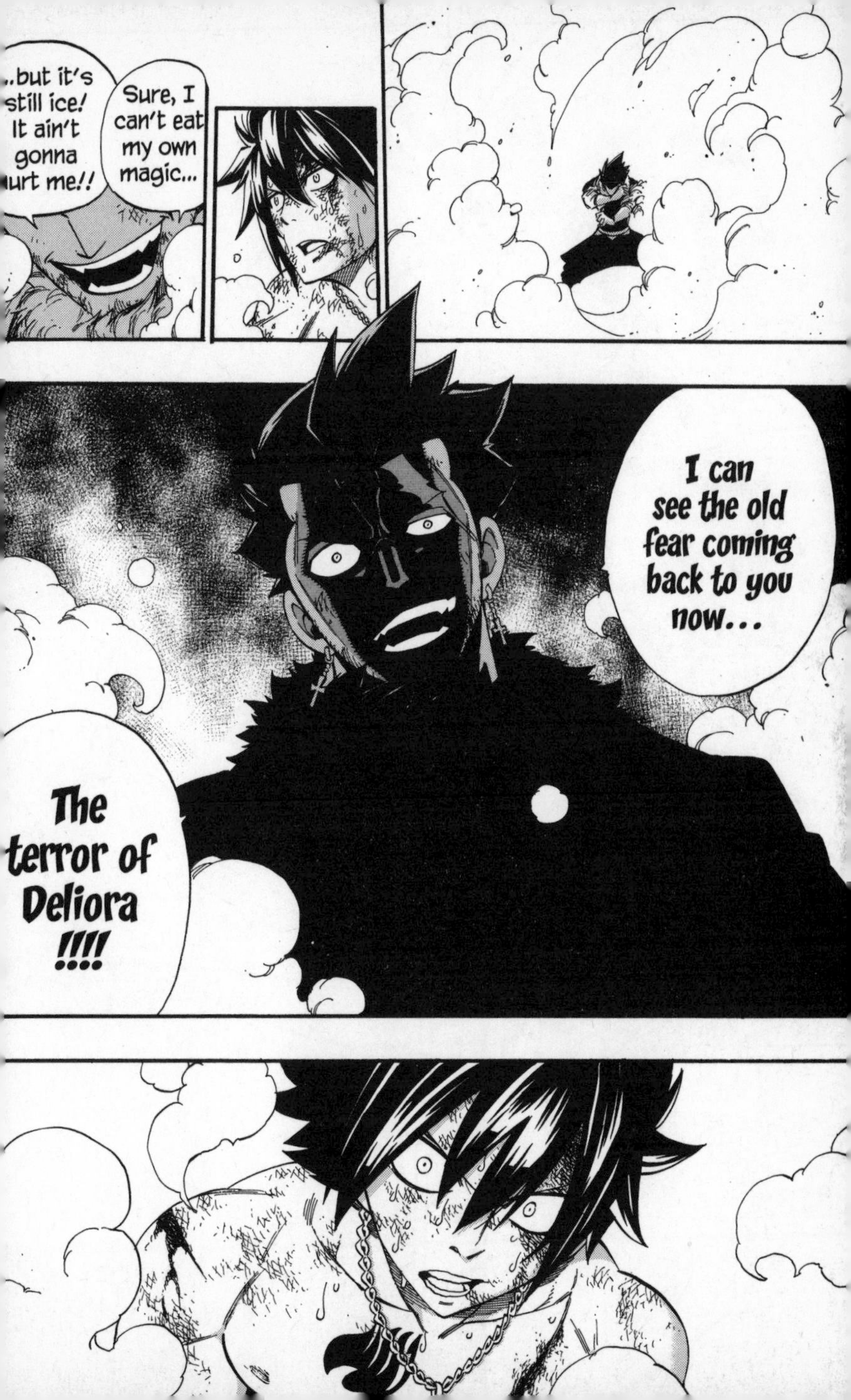

Sure, I can't eat my own magic...
..but it's still ice! It ain't gonna urt me!!
I can see the old fear coming back to you now...
The terror of Deliora!!!!

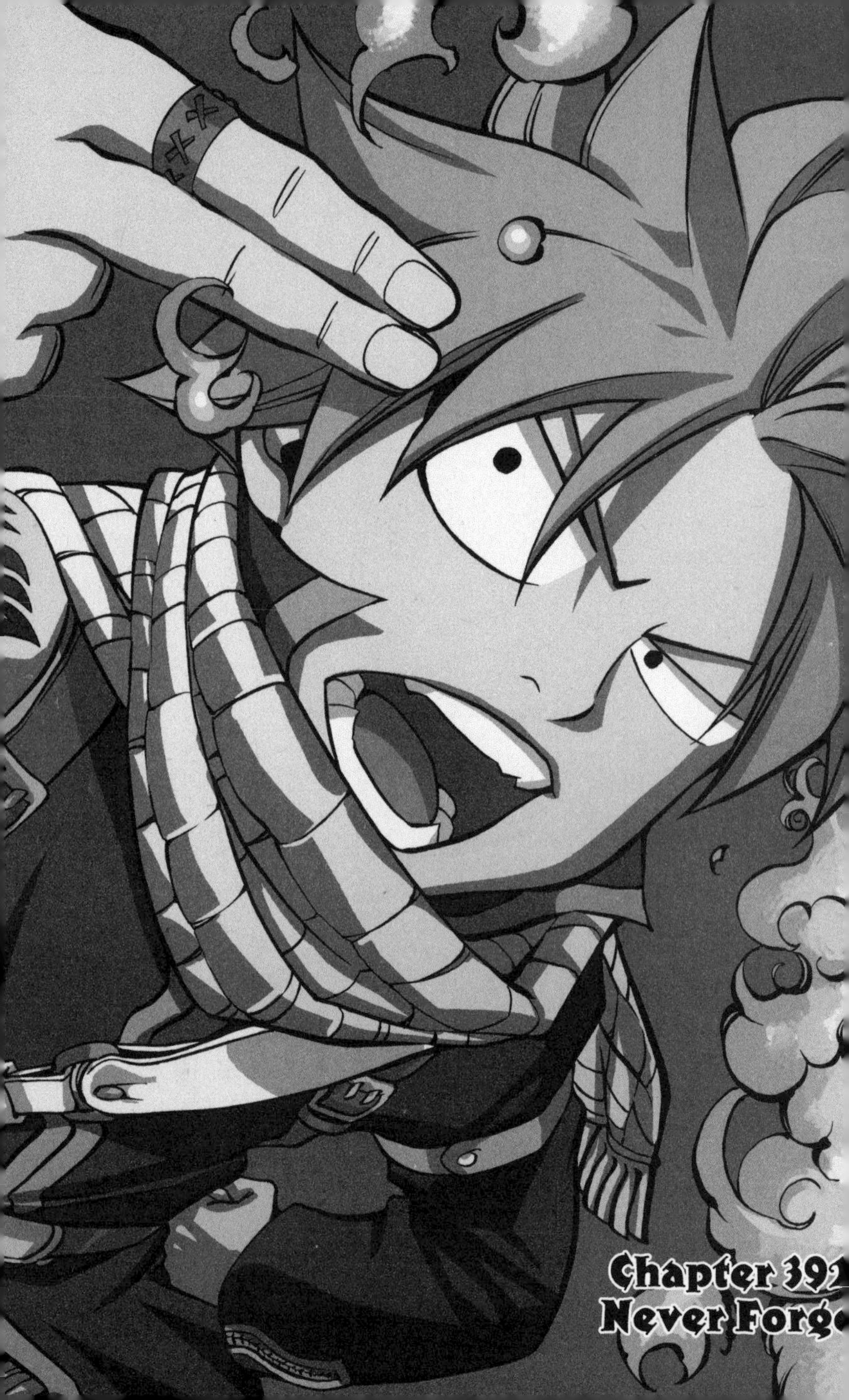

Chapter 39
Never Forg

FAIRY TAIL

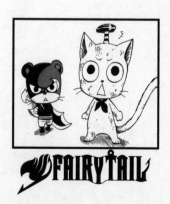

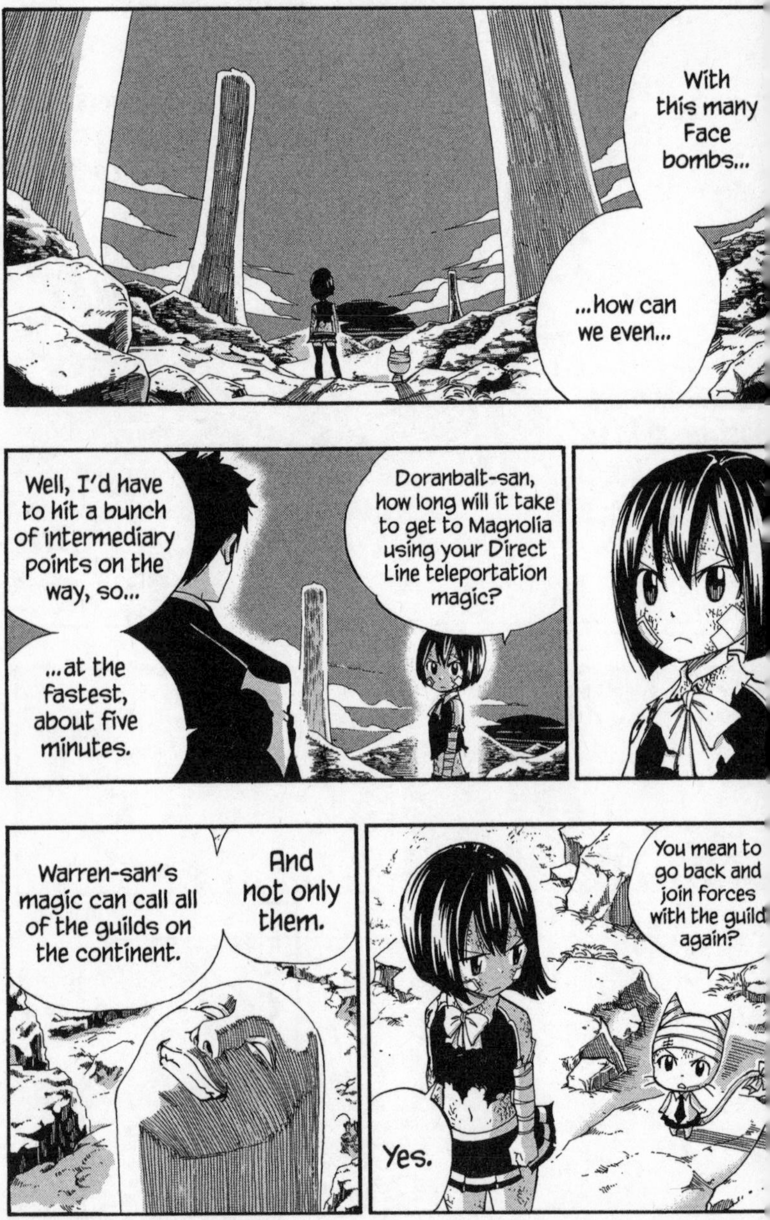
With this many Face bombs...
...how can we even...
Doranbalt-san, how long will it take to get to Magnolia using your Direct Line teleportation magic?
Well, I'd have to hit a bunch of intermediary points on the way, so...
...at the fastest, about five minutes.
You mean to go back and join forces with the guild again?
Yes.
And not only them.
Warren-san's magic can call all of the guilds on the continent.

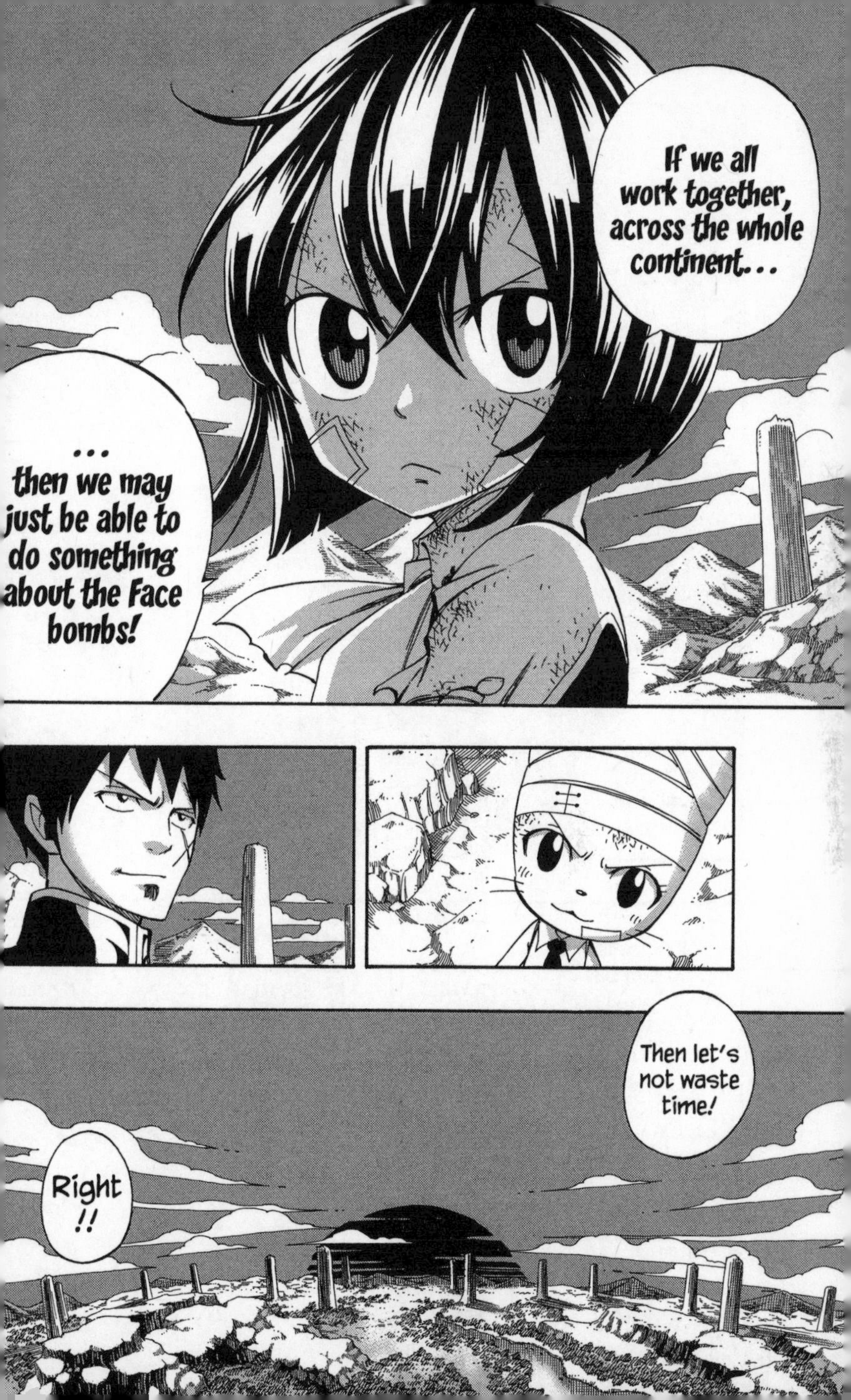
If we all work together, across the whole continent...
...then we may just be able to do something about the Face bombs!
Then let's not waste time!
Right!!

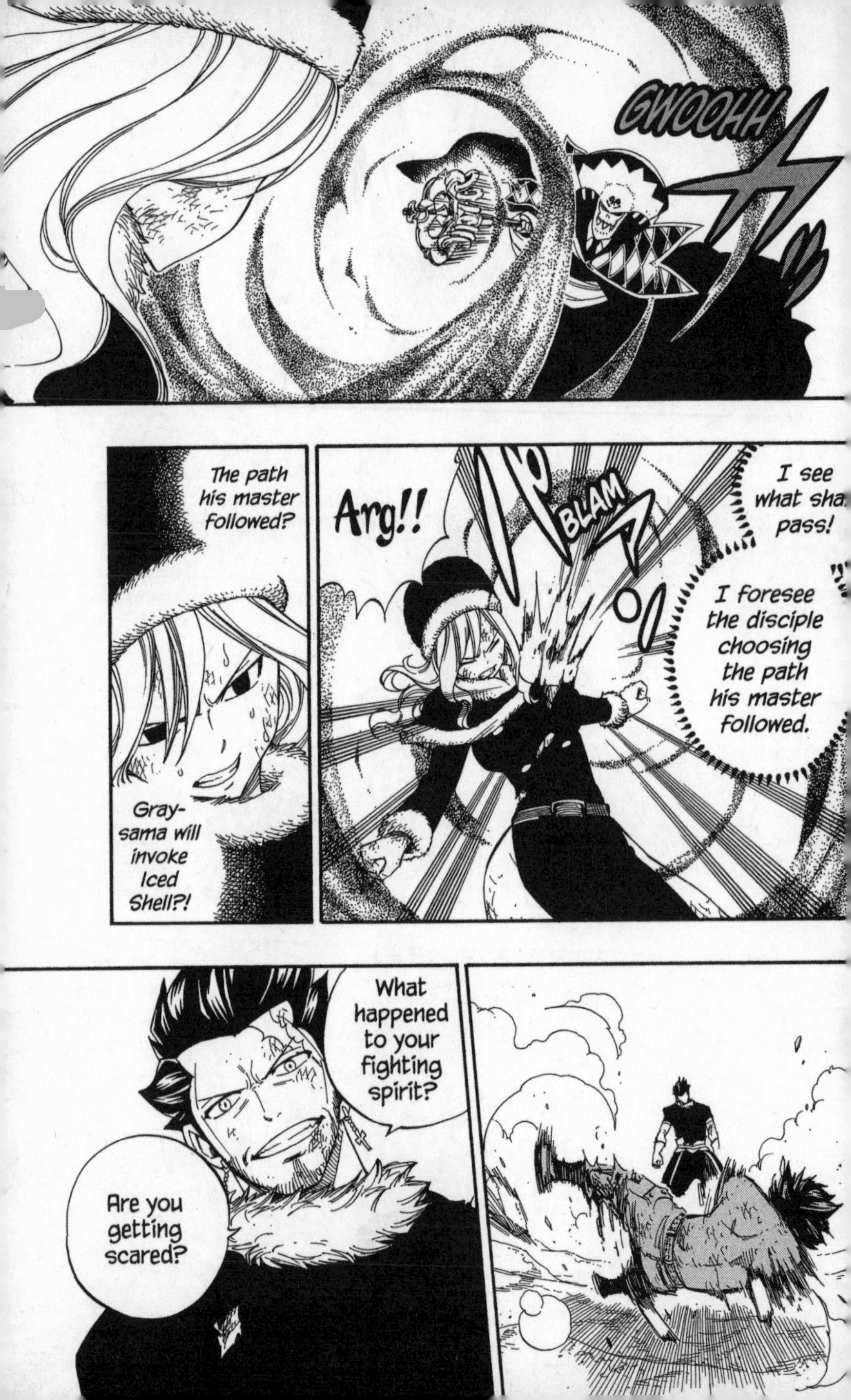
GWOOHH
I see what sha pass!
BLAM
Arg!!
I foresee the disciple choosing the path his master followed.
The path his master followed?
Gray-sama will invoke Iced Shell?!
What happened to your fighting spirit?
Are you getting scared?

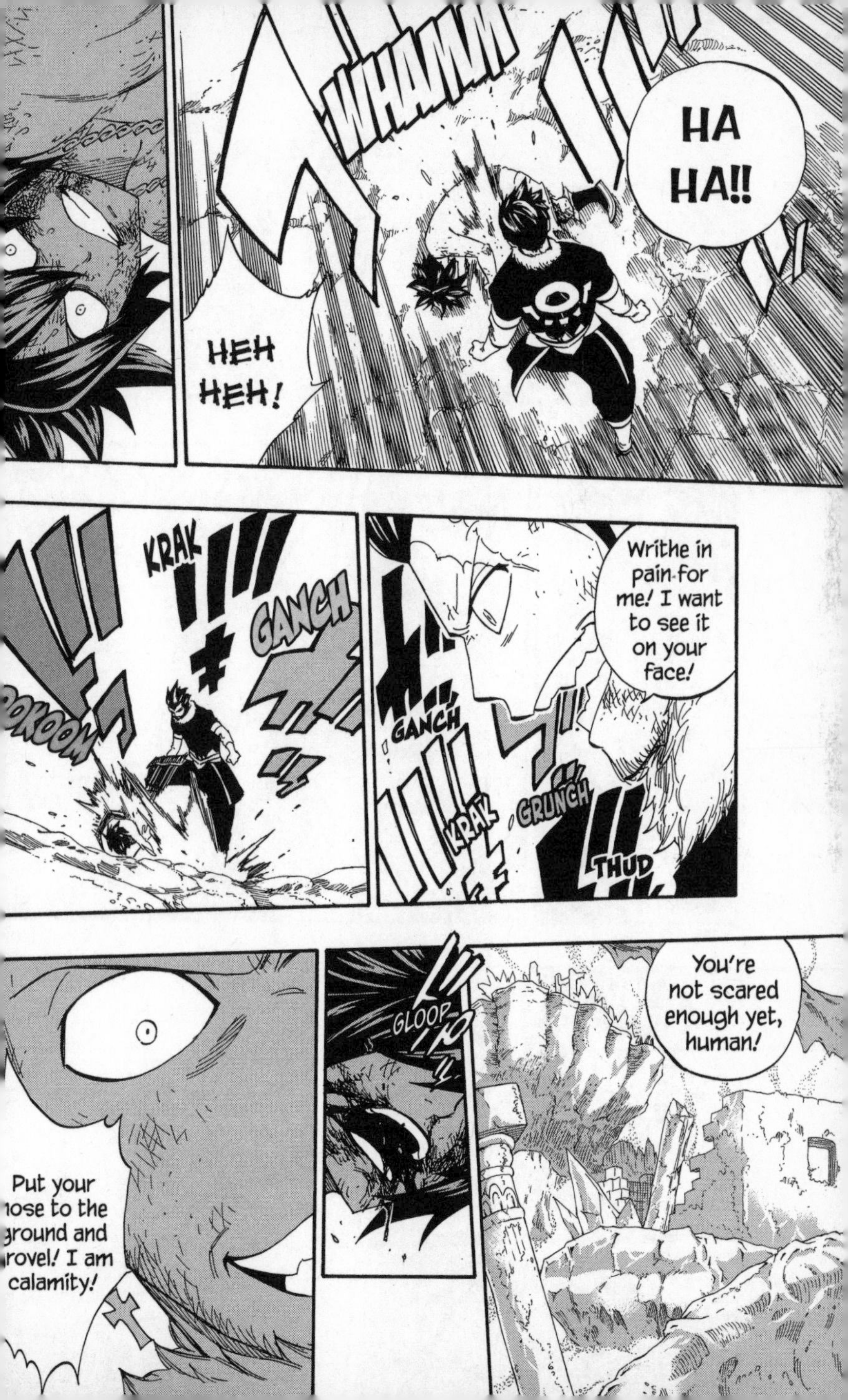

HA HA!!
WHAMM
HEH HEH!
Writhe in pain for me! I want to see it on your face!
GANCH
KRAK
GRUNCH
THUD
KRAK
GANCH
You're not scared enough yet, human!
GLOOP
Put your nose to the ground and grovel! I am calamity!

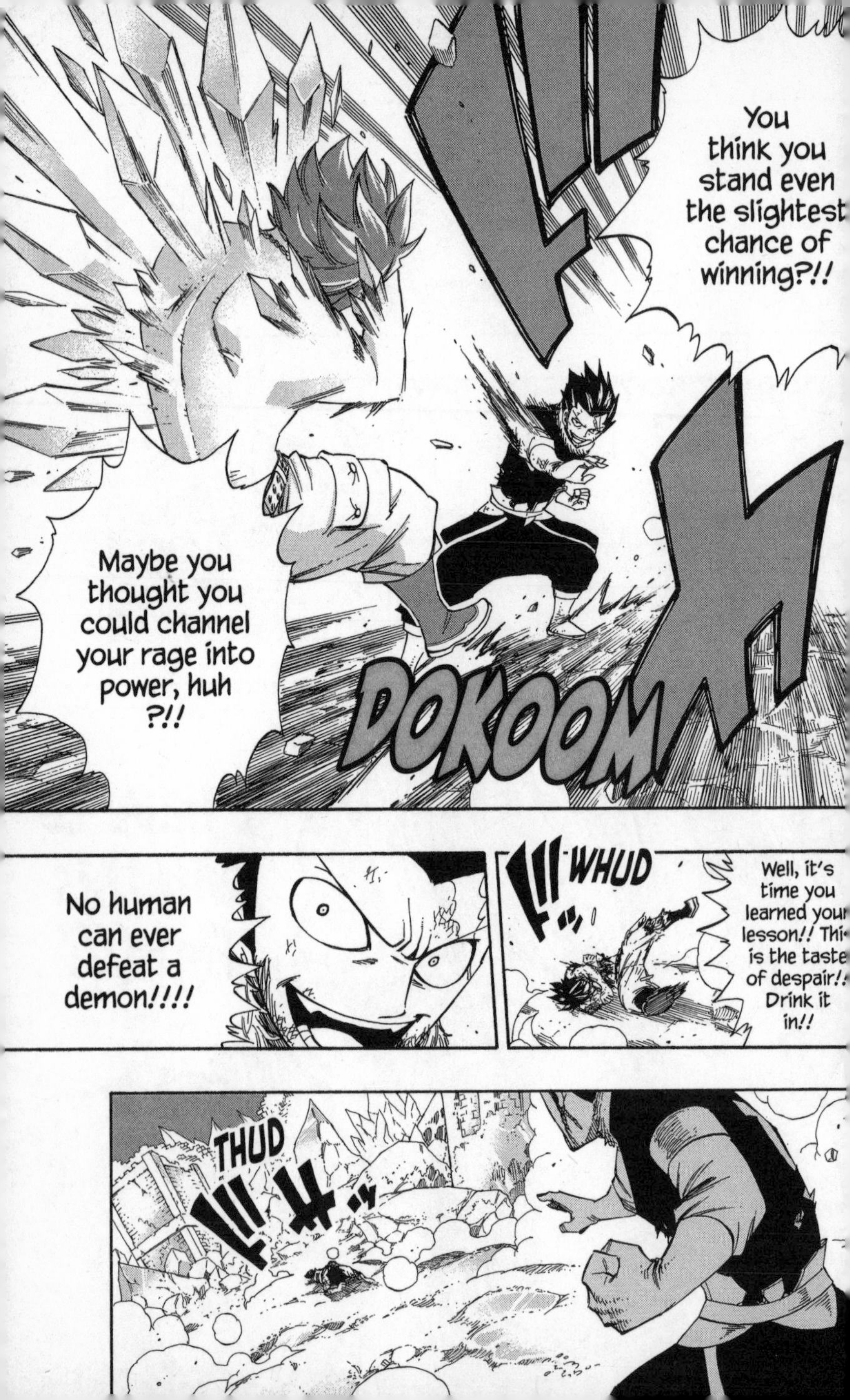
You think you stand even the slightest chance of winning?!!
Maybe you thought you could channel your rage into power, huh?!!
DOKOOM
WHUD
Well, it's time you learned your lesson!! Thi is the taste of despair!! Drink it in!!
No human can ever defeat a demon!!!!
THUD

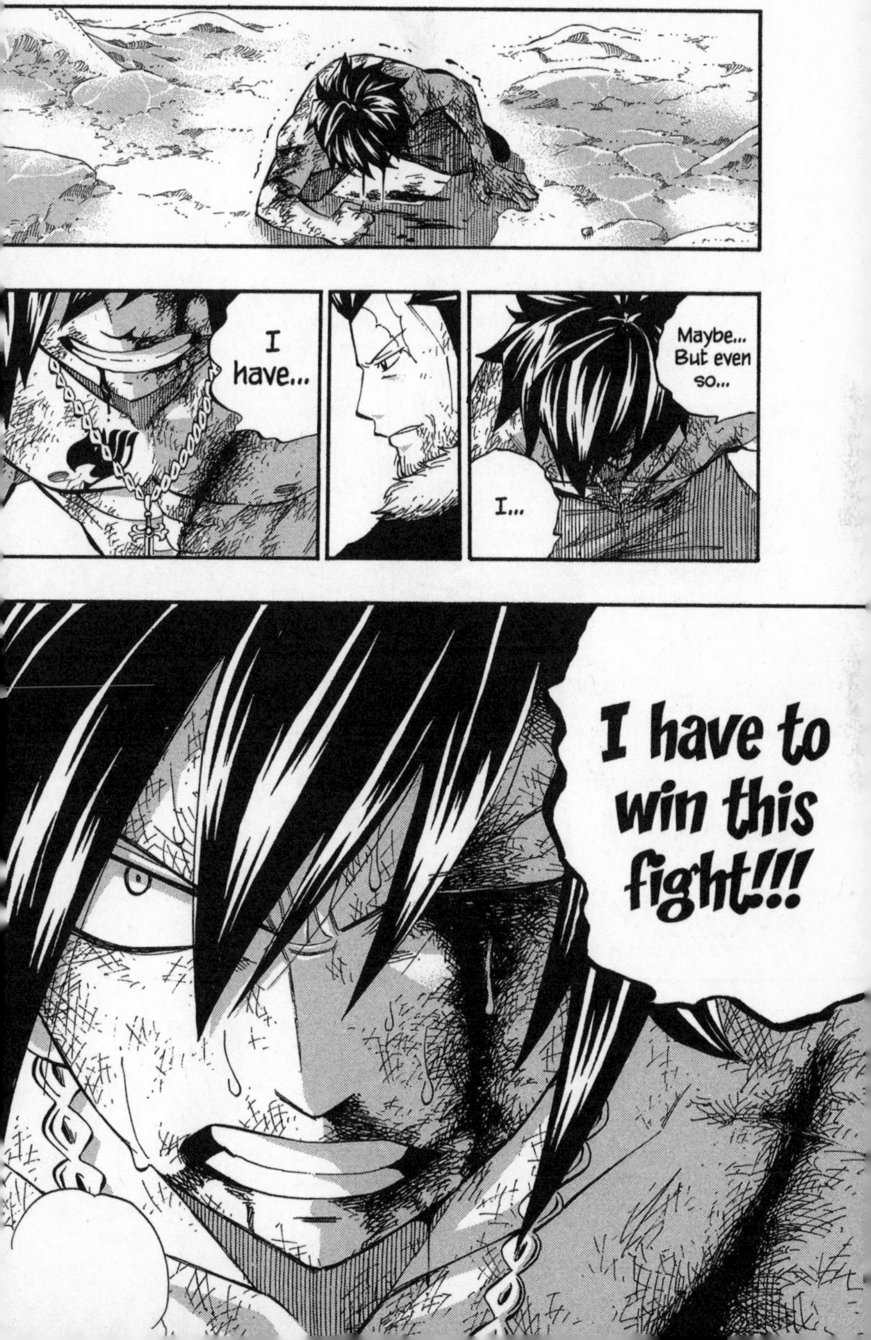
Maybe... But even so...
I...
I have...
I have to win this fight!!!

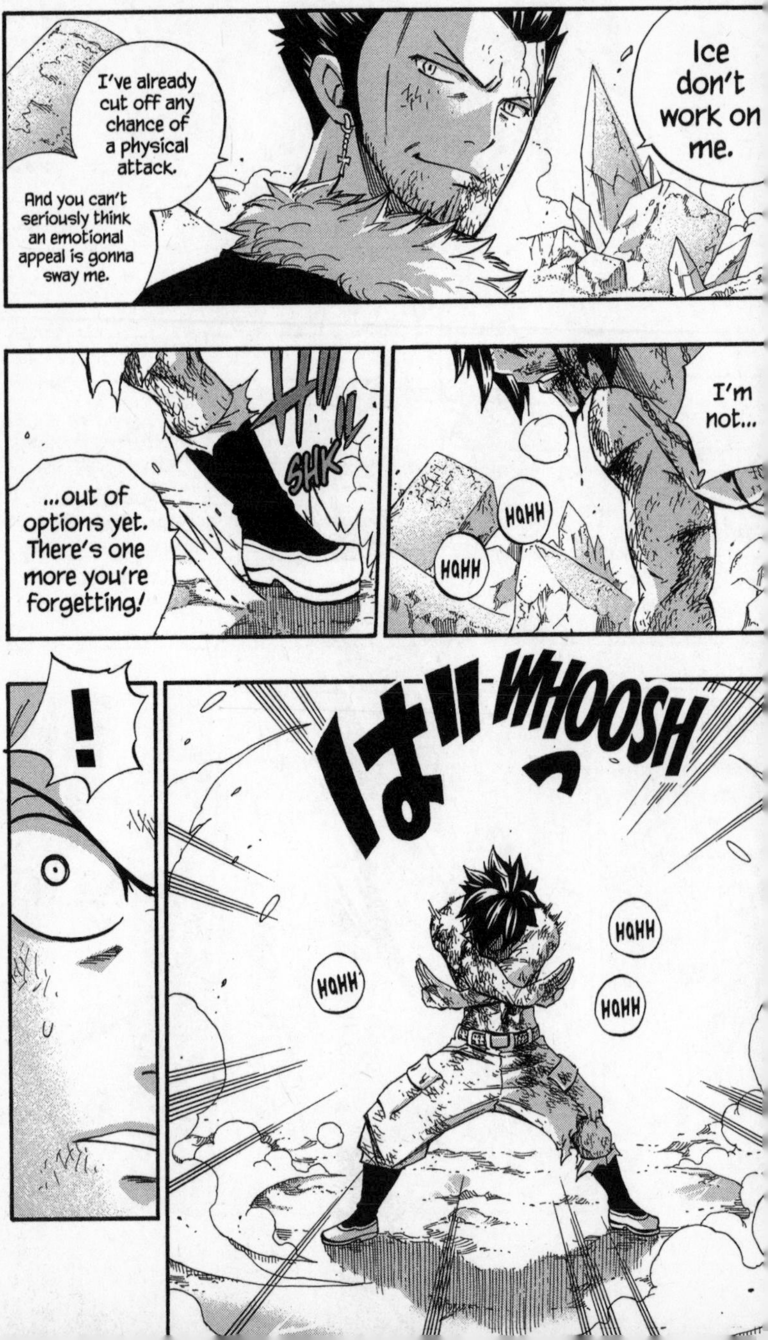
Ice don't work on me.
I've already cut off any chance of a physical attack.
And you can't seriously think an emotional appeal is gonna sway me.
I'm not...
HAHH
HAHH
SHK
...out of options yet. There's one more you're forgetting!
はっ
WHOOSH
HAHH
HAHH
HAHH
!

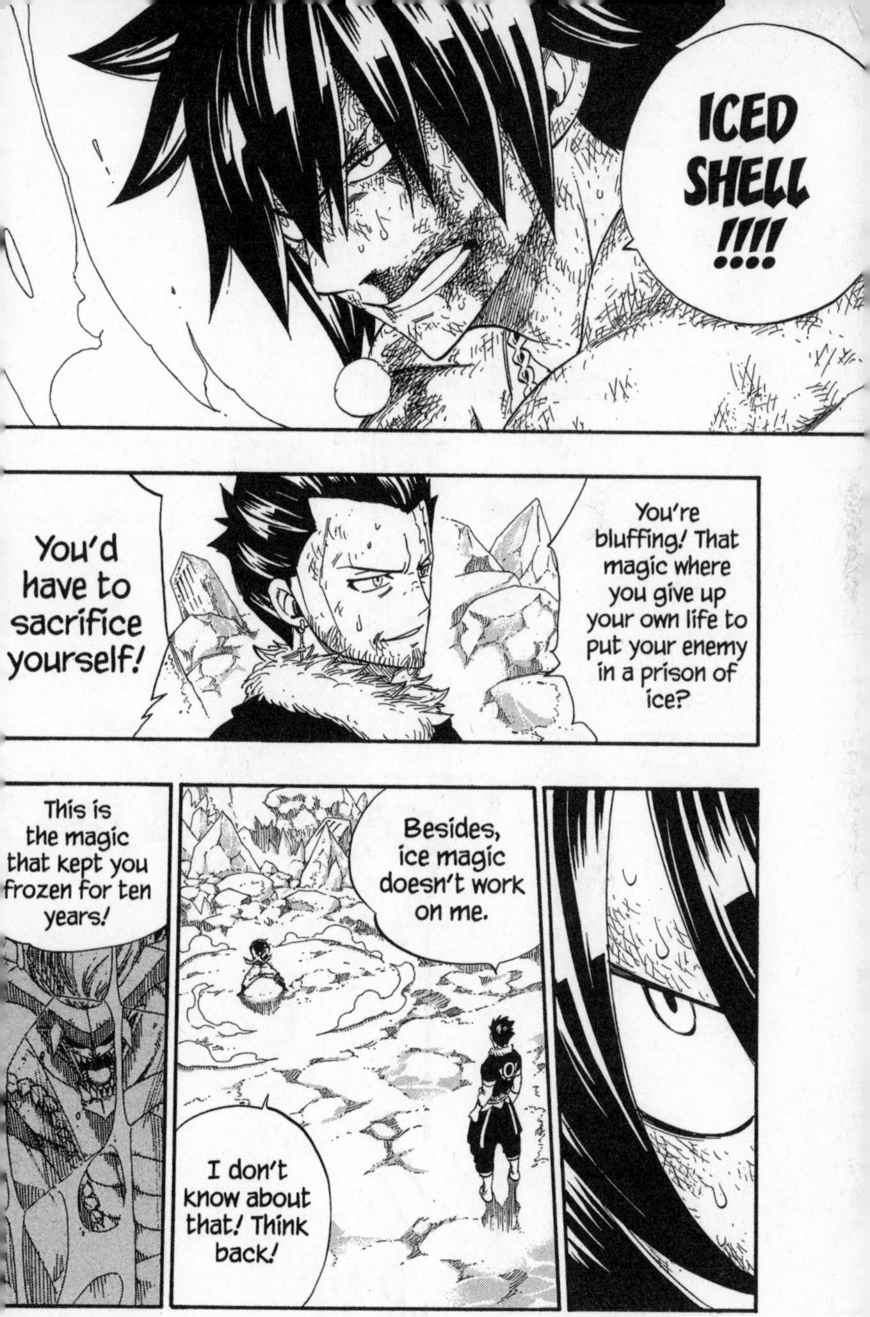
ICED SHELL!!!!
You're bluffing! That magic where you give up your own life to put your enemy in a prison of ice?
You'd have to sacrifice yourself!
Besides, ice magic doesn't work on me.
I don't know about that! Think back!
This is the magic that kept you frozen for ten years!

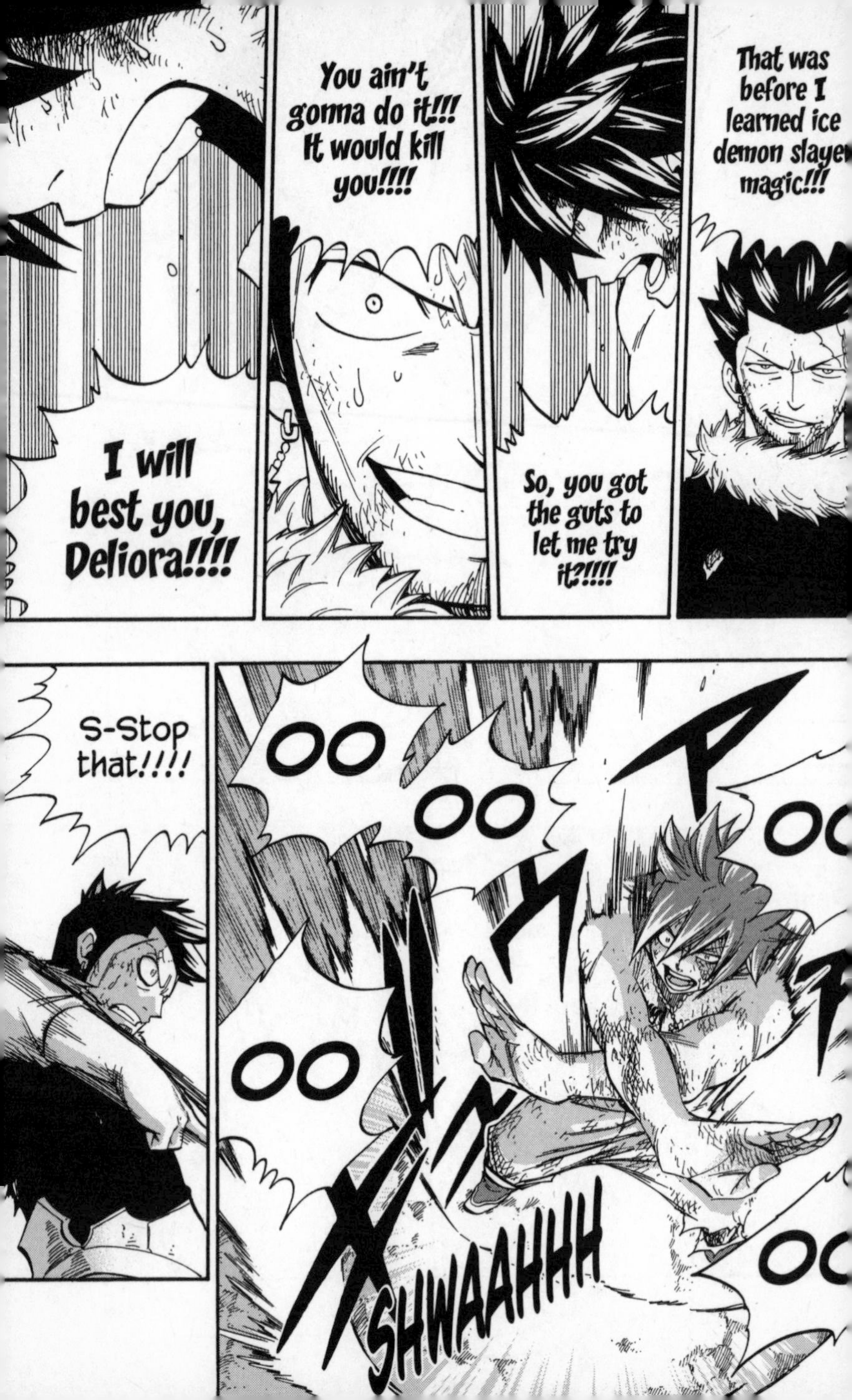
That was before I learned ice demon slayer magic!!!
So, you got the guts to let me try it?!!!!
You ain't gonna do it!!! It would kill you!!!!
I will best you, Deliora!!!!
OO
OO
OO
OO
SHWAAHHH
S-Stop that!!!!

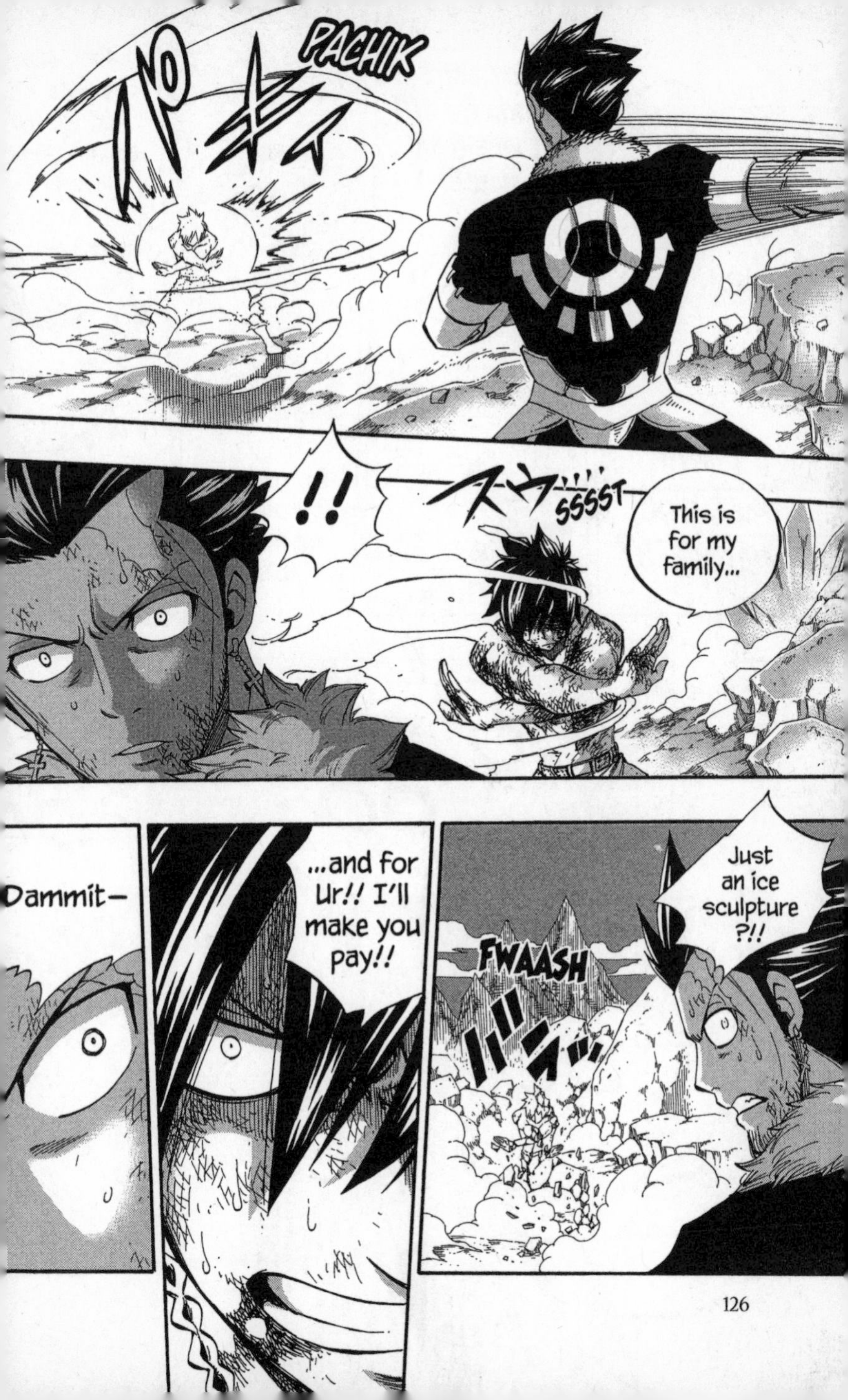
PACHIK
This is for my family...
SSSST
!!
Just an ice sculpture?!!
FWAASH
...and for Ur!! I'll make you pay!!
Dammit—

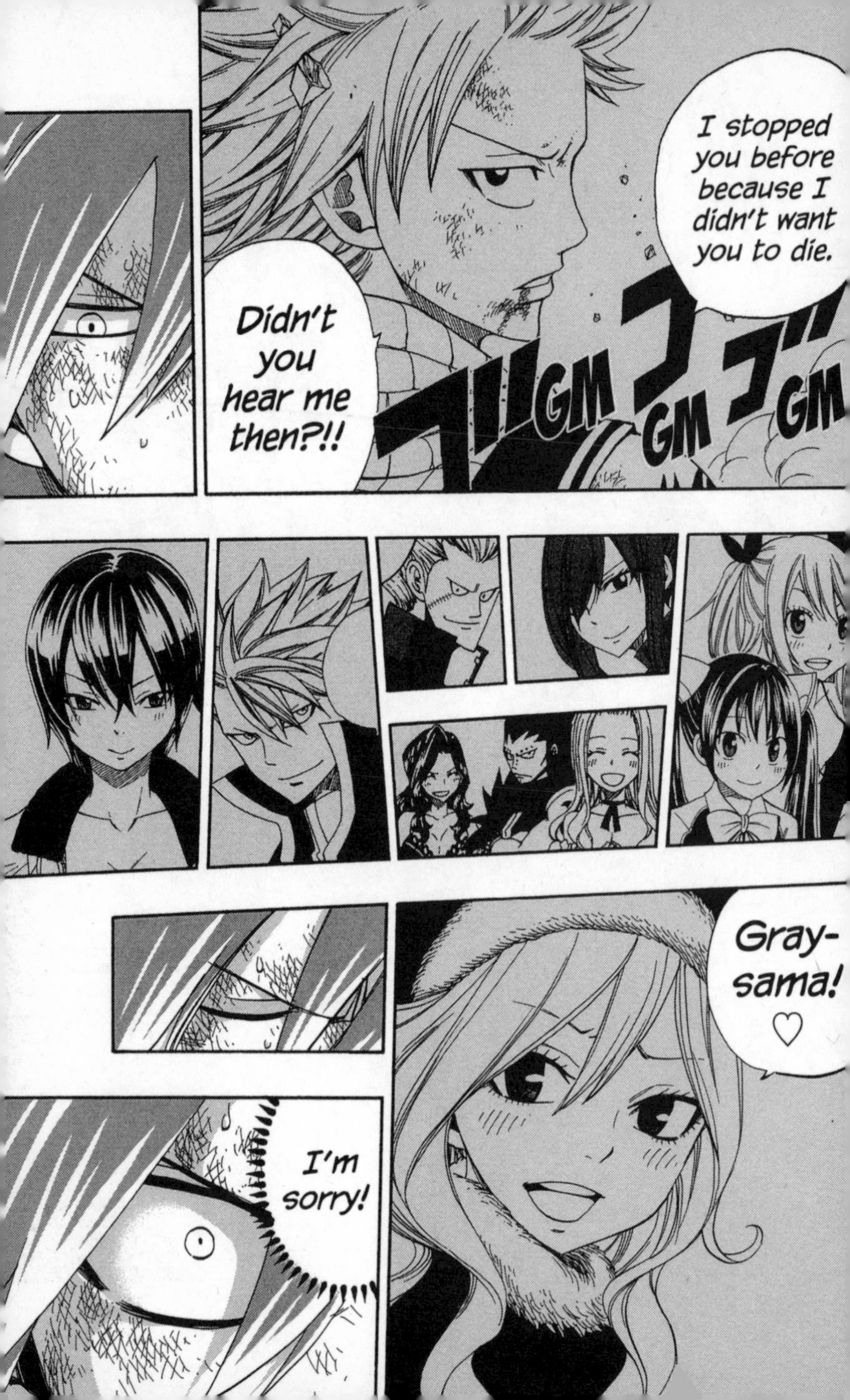
I stopped you before because I didn't want you to die.
Didn't you hear me then?!!
GM GM GM
Gray-sama! ♡
I'm sorry!

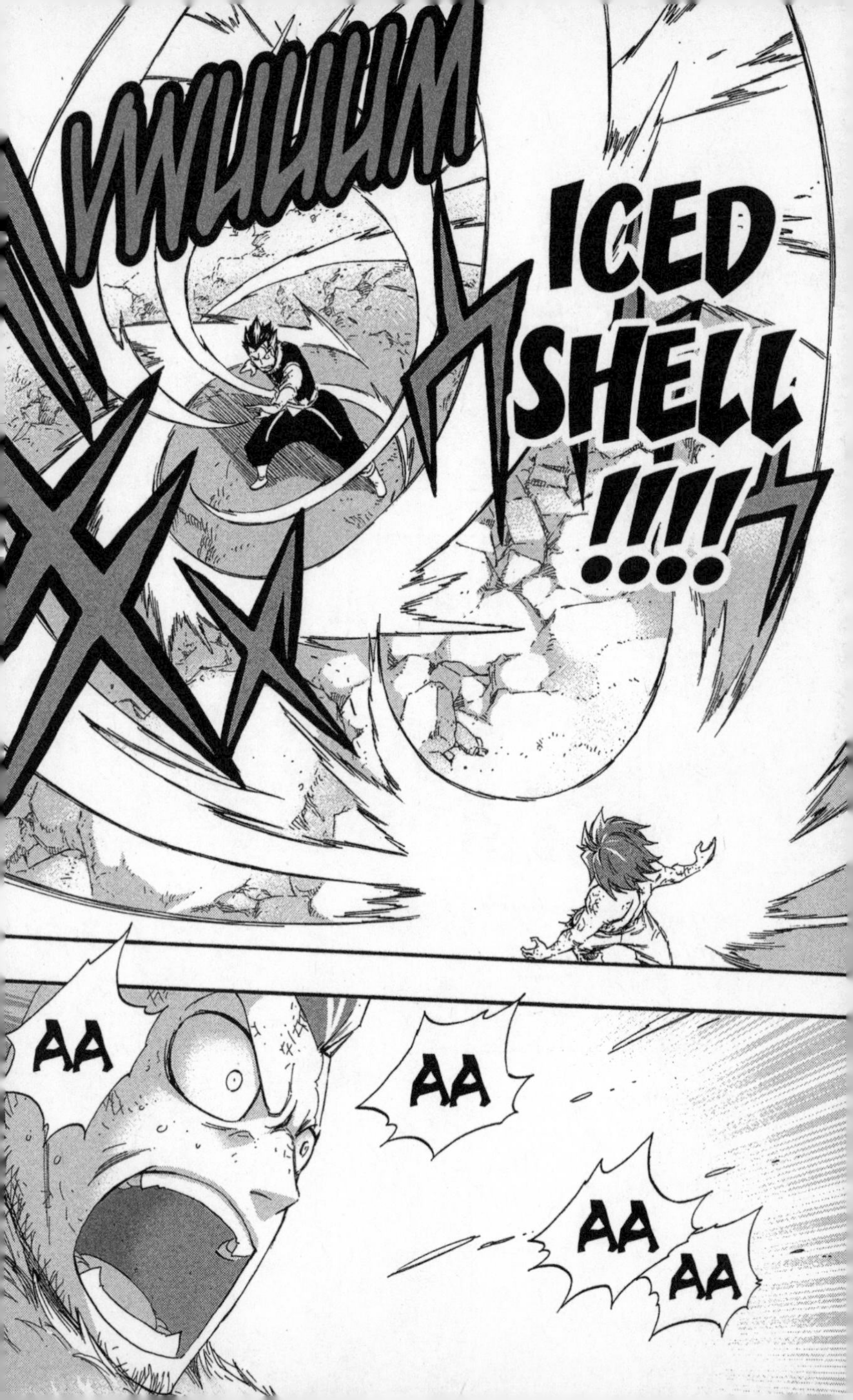
ICED SHELL!!!!
VWUUUM
AA
AA
AA
AA

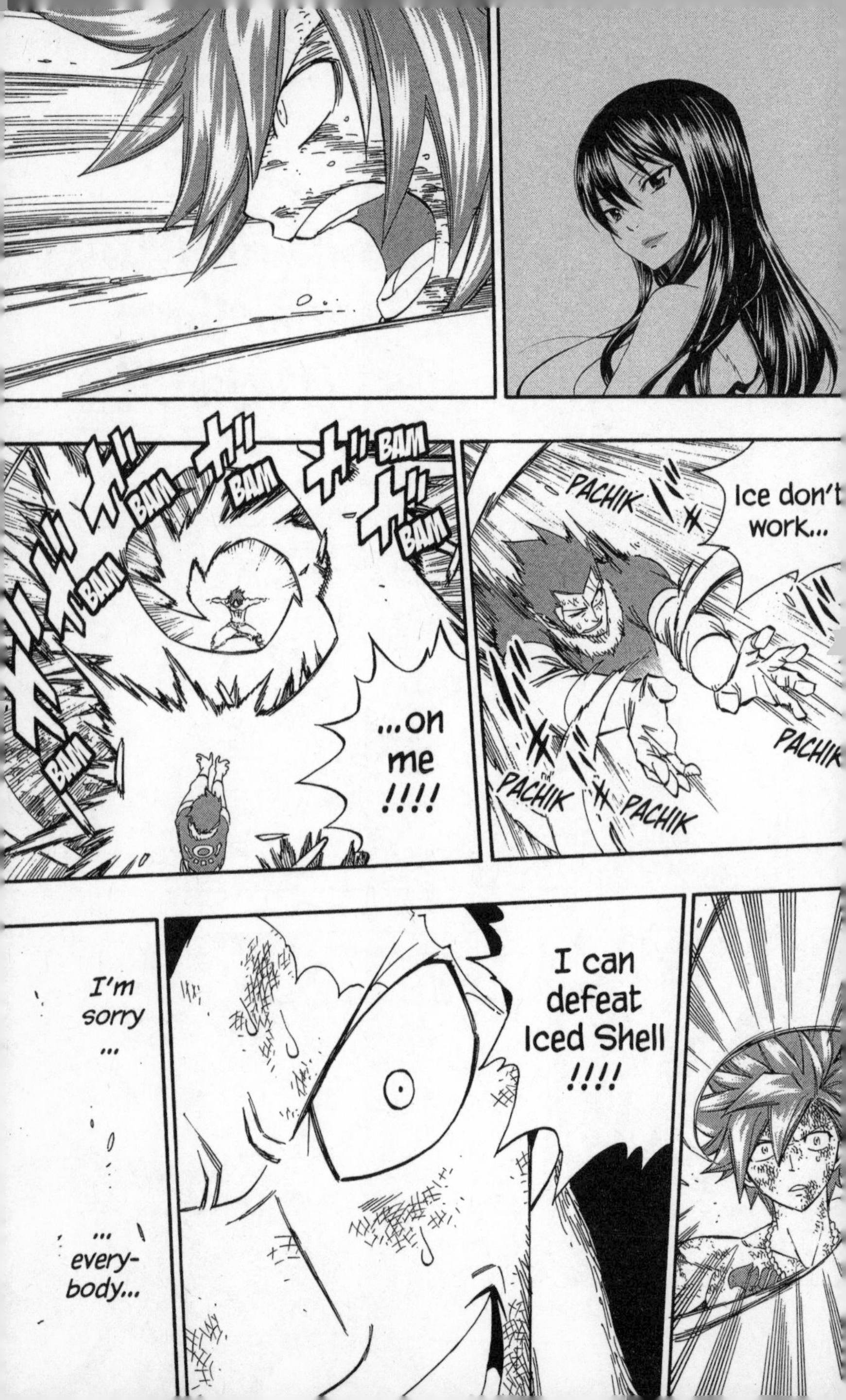
PACHIK
Ice don't work...
PACHIK
PACHIK
PACHIK
BAM
BAM
BAM
BAM
BAM
BAM
BAM
...on me !!!!
I can defeat Iced Shell !!!!
I'm sorry ...
... everybody...

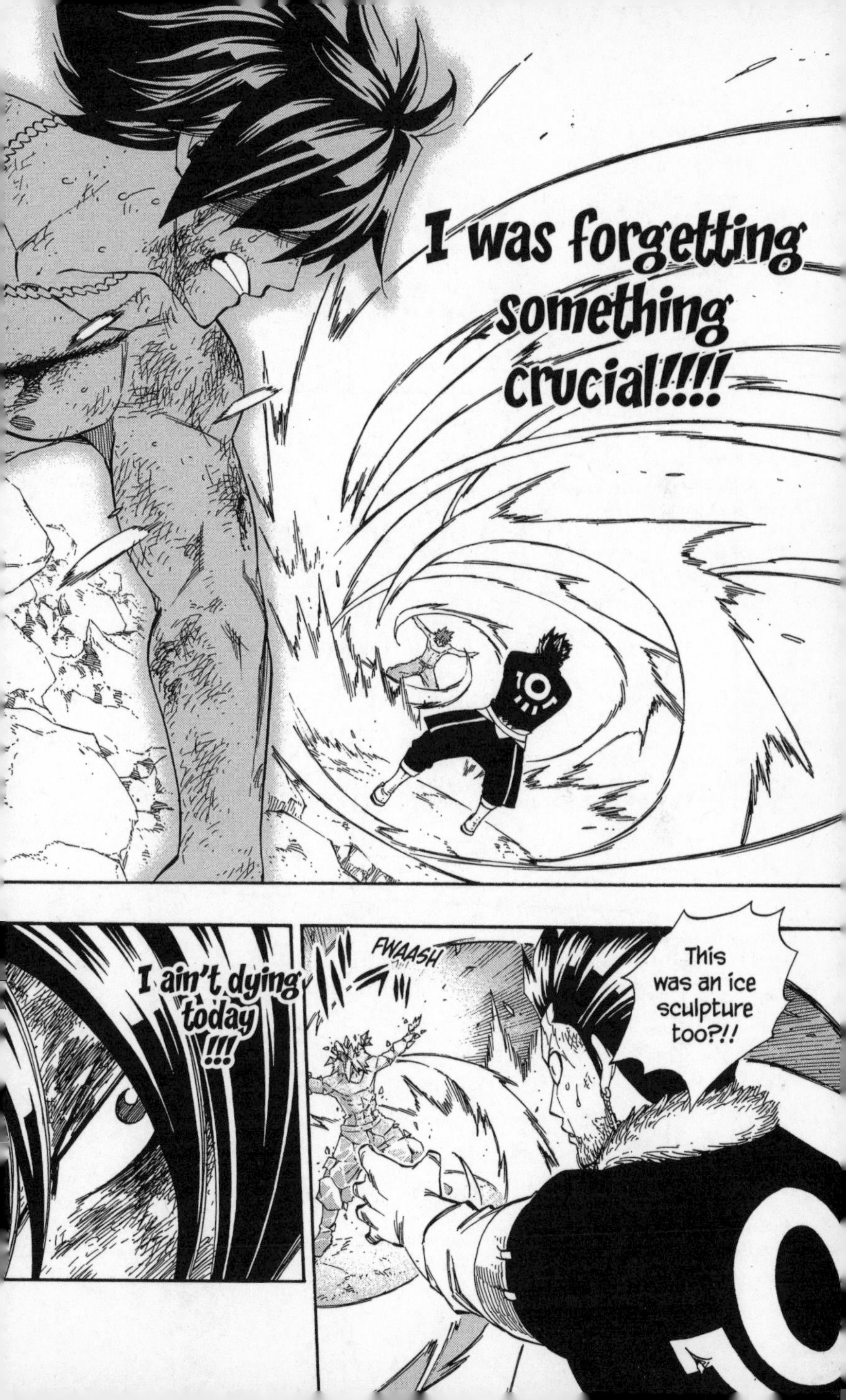
I was forgetting something crucial!!!!
This was an ice sculpture too?!!
FWAASH
I ain't dying today!!!

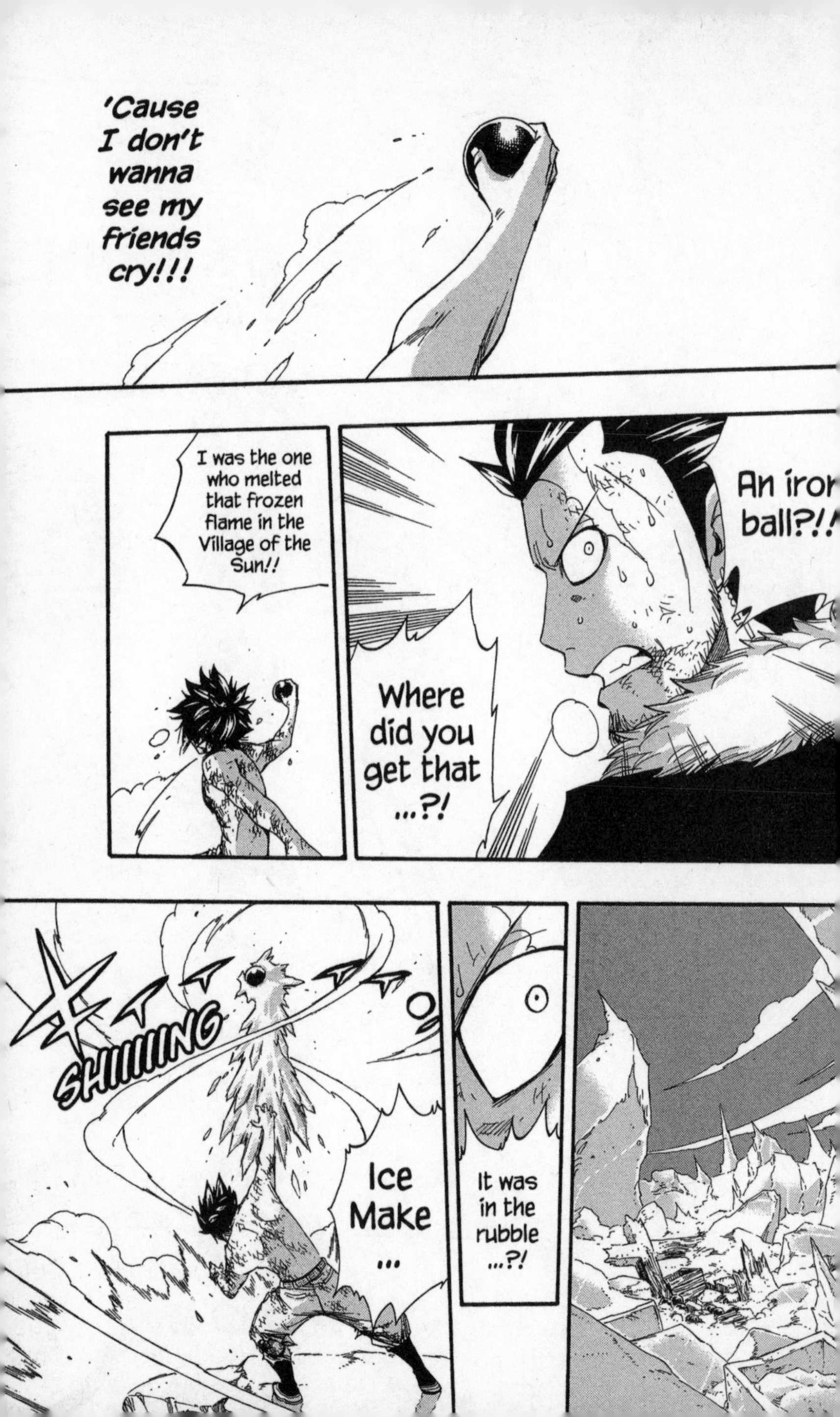
'Cause I don't wanna see my friends cry!!!
An iron ball?!!
Where did you get that ...?!
I was the one who melted that frozen flame in the Village of the Sun!!
It was in the rubble ...?!
Ice Make ...
SHIIIIING

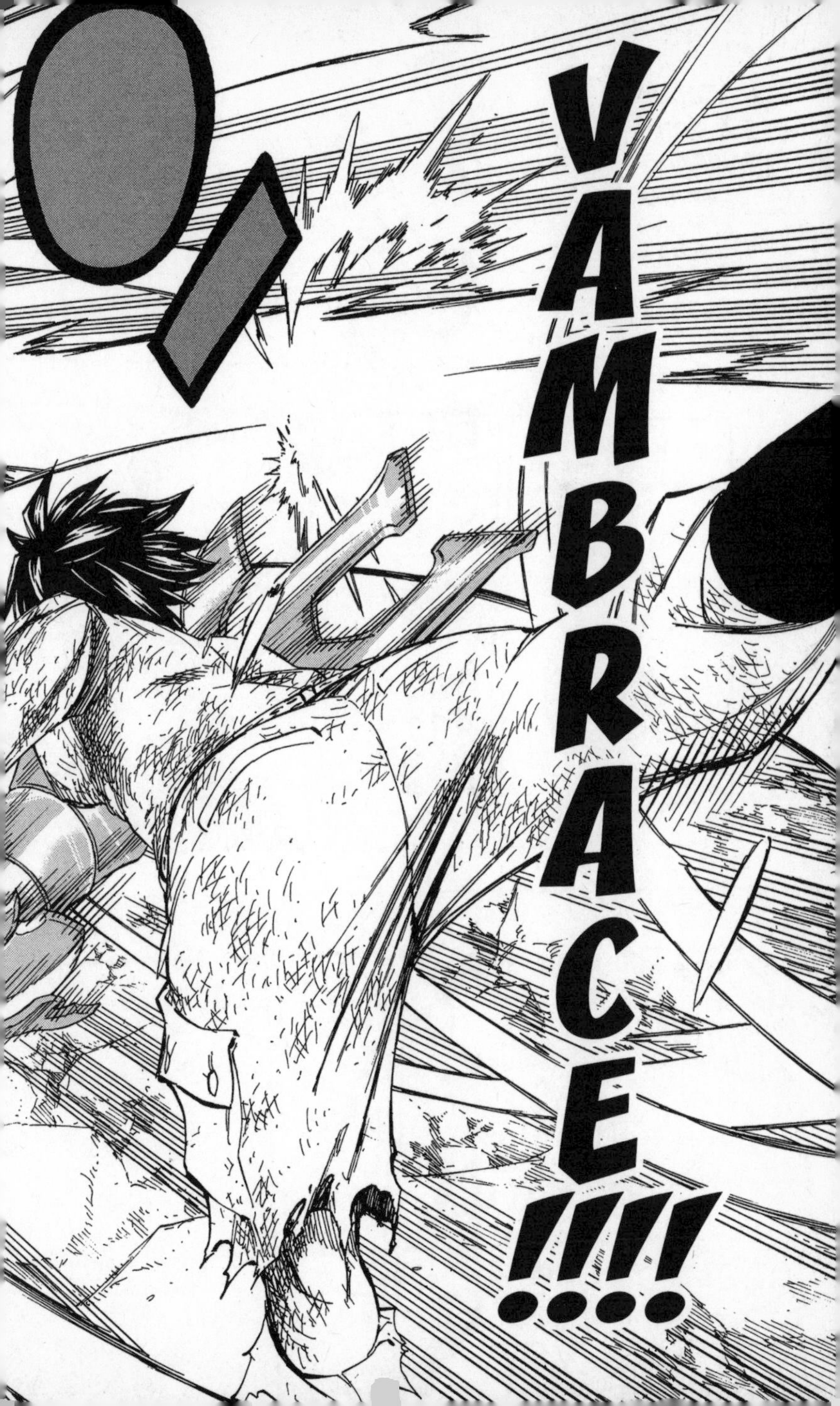
VAMBRACE!!!!

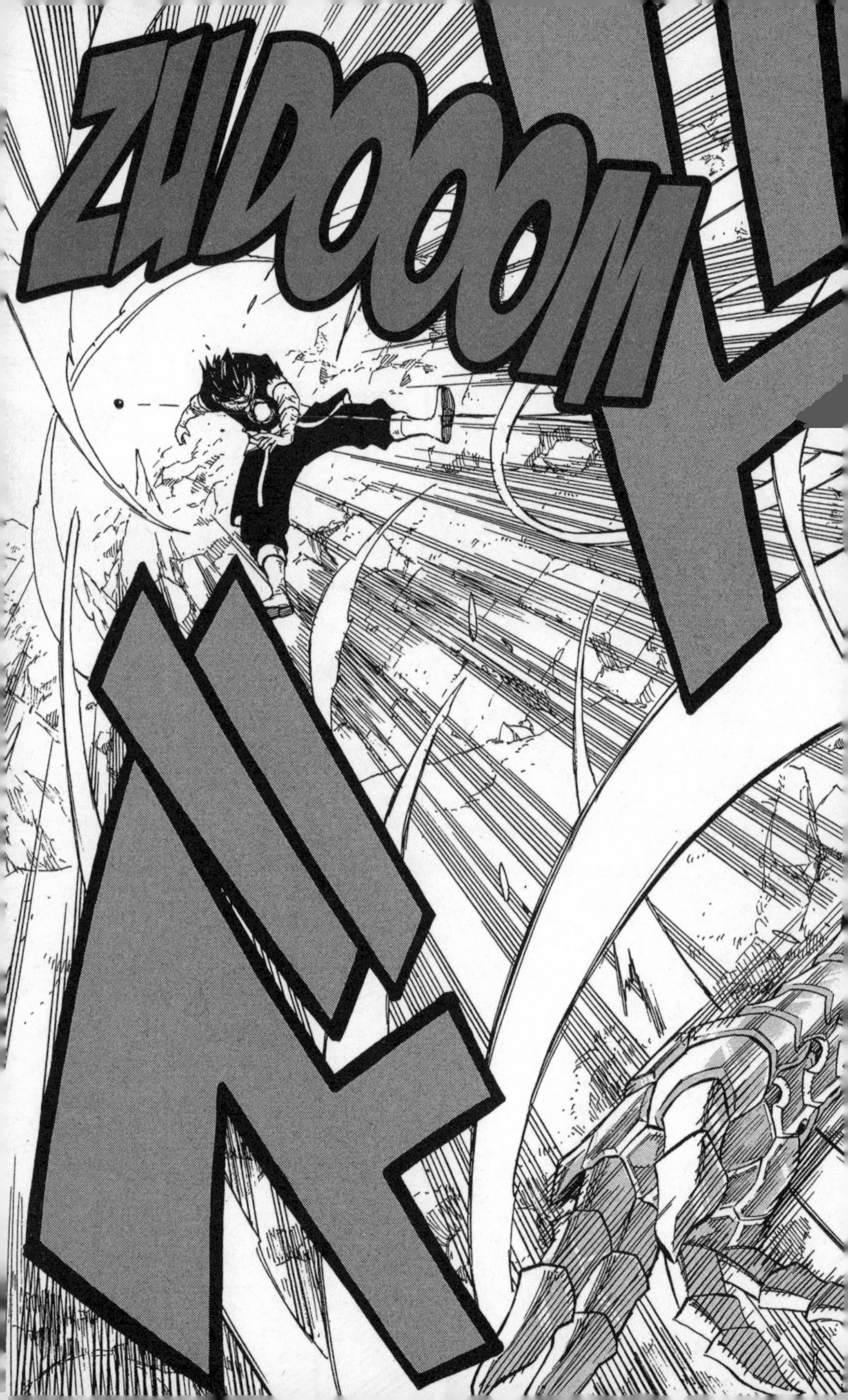
ZUDOOOM

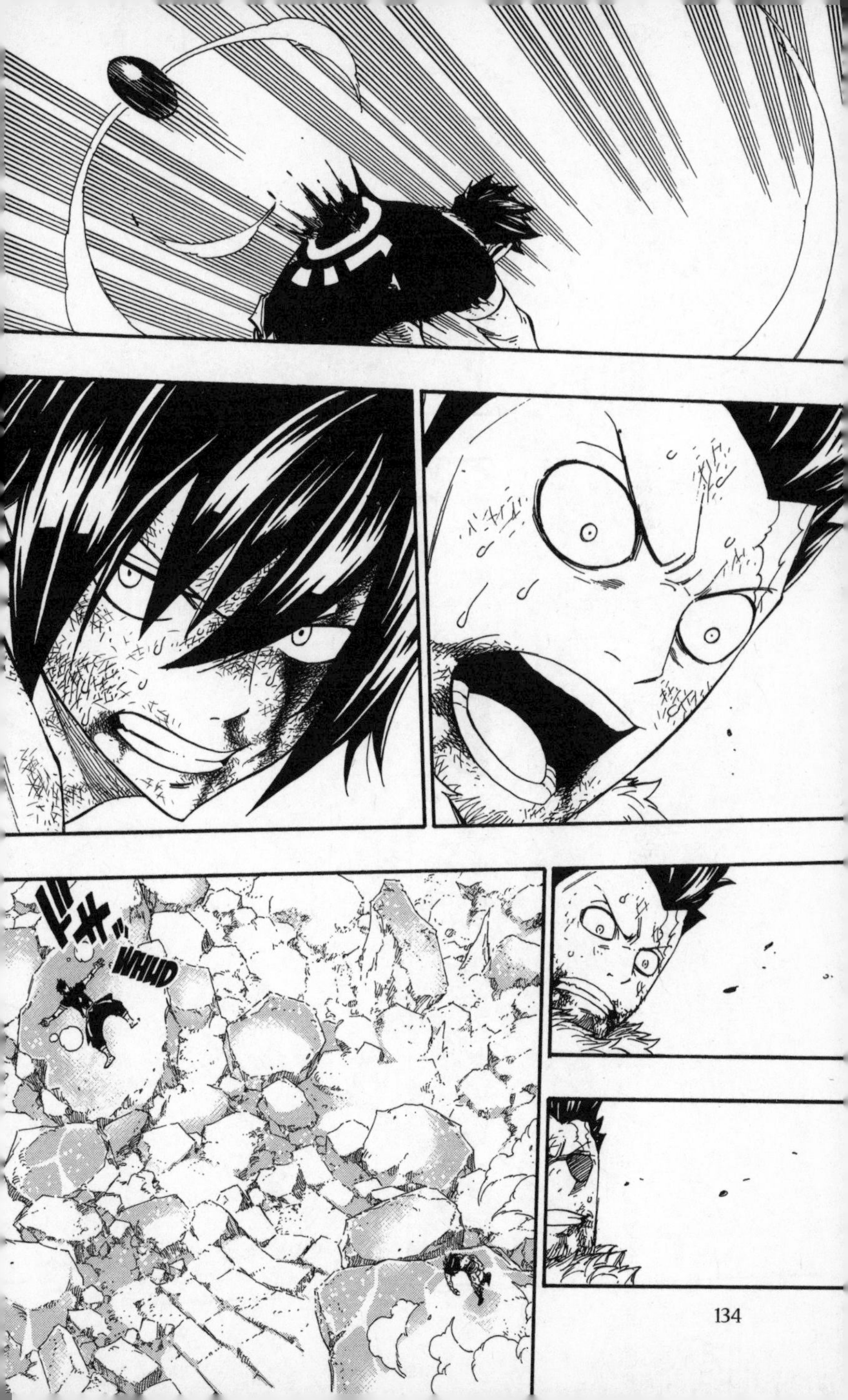
WHUD

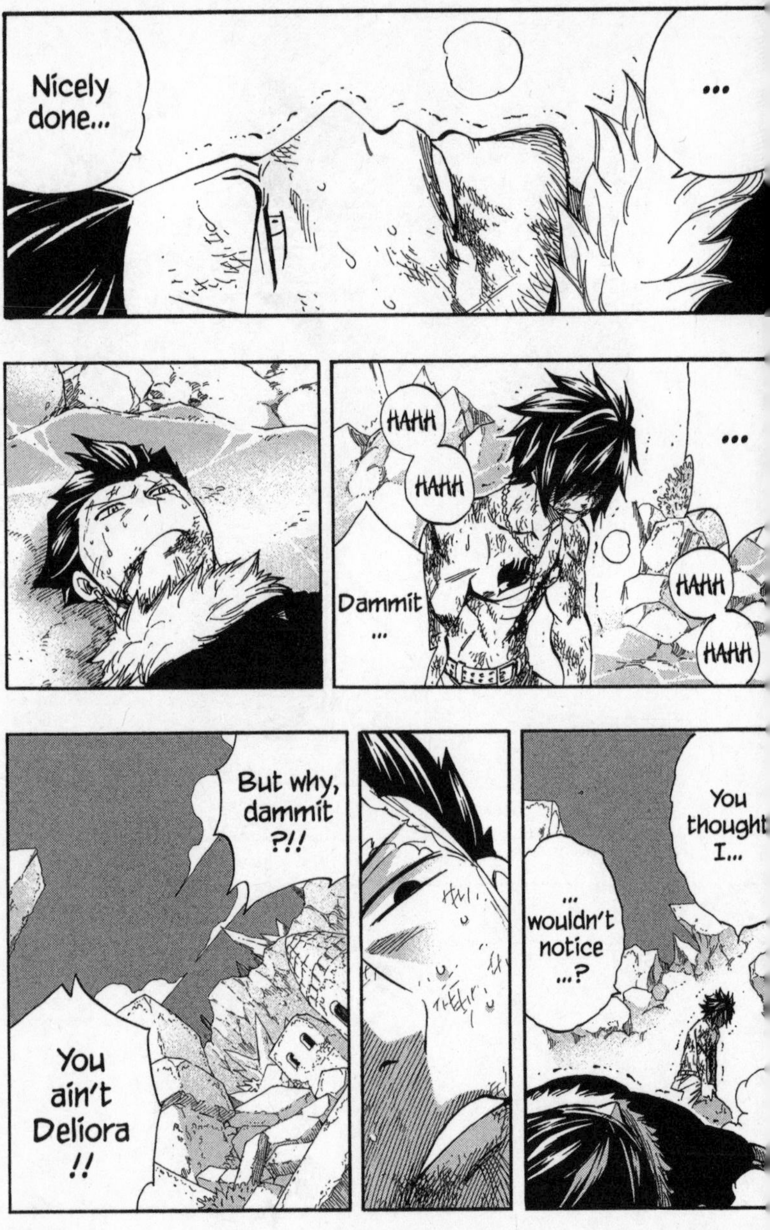
...
Nicely done...
...
HAHH HAHH
HAHH HAHH
Dammit ...
You thought I...
... wouldn't notice ...?
But why, dammit ?!!
You ain't Deliora !!

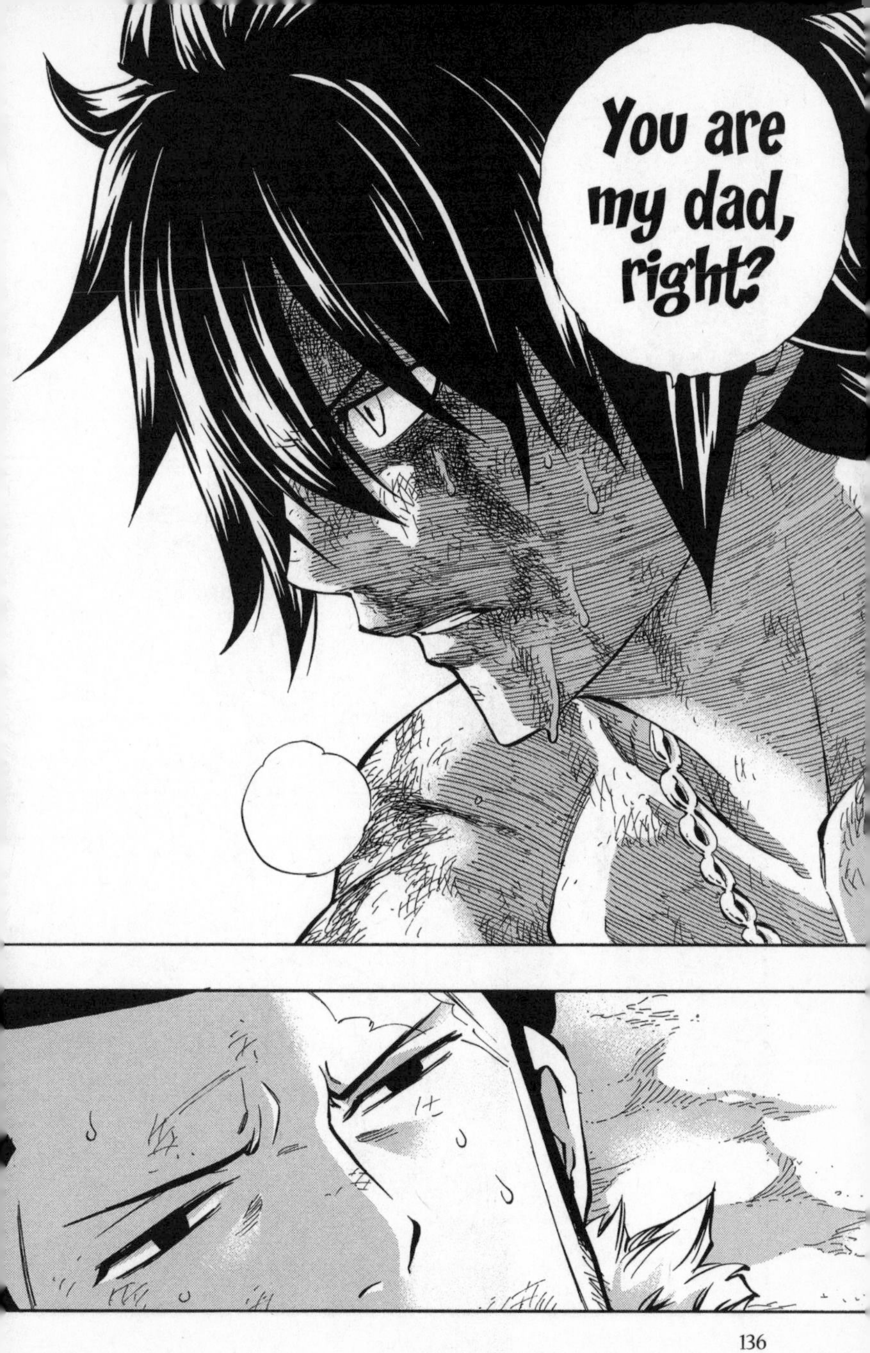
You are my dad, right?

FAIRY TAIL

フェアリーテイル

Chapter 393: Silver Memories

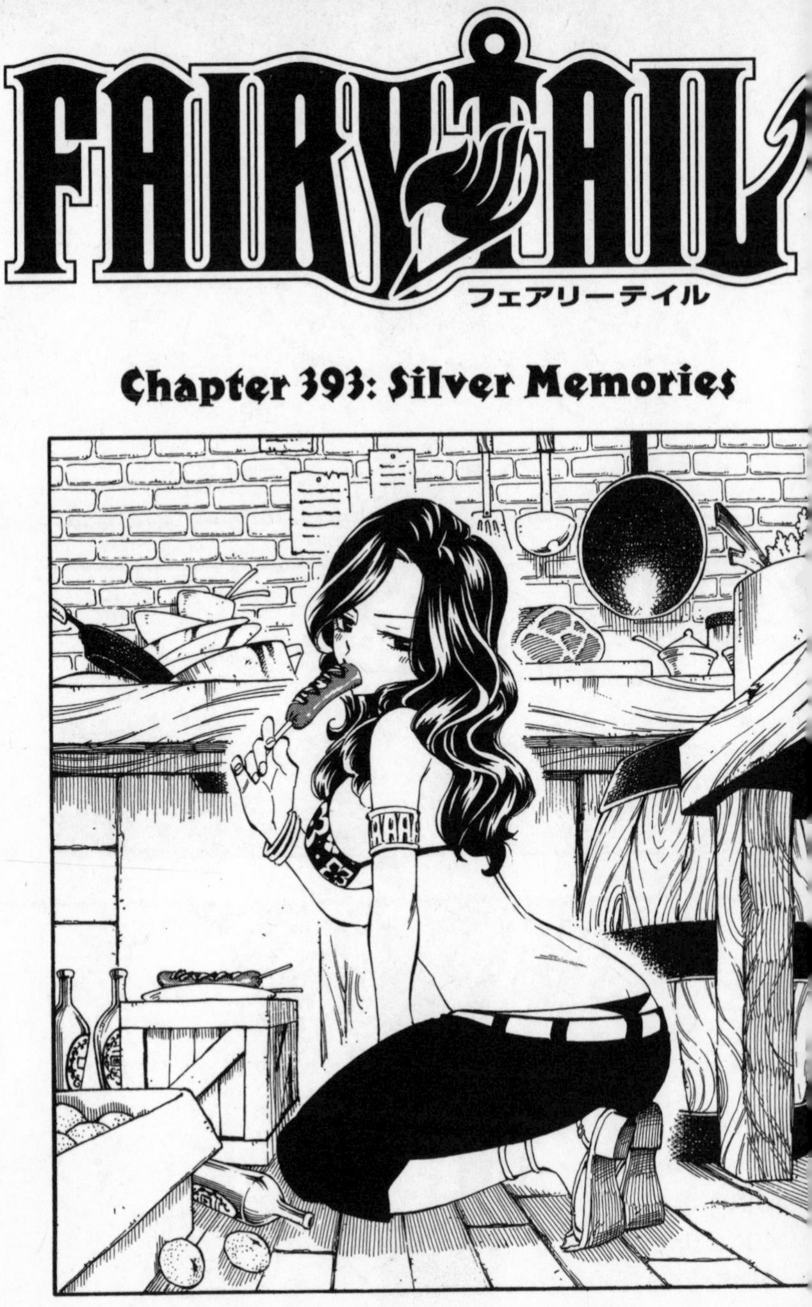

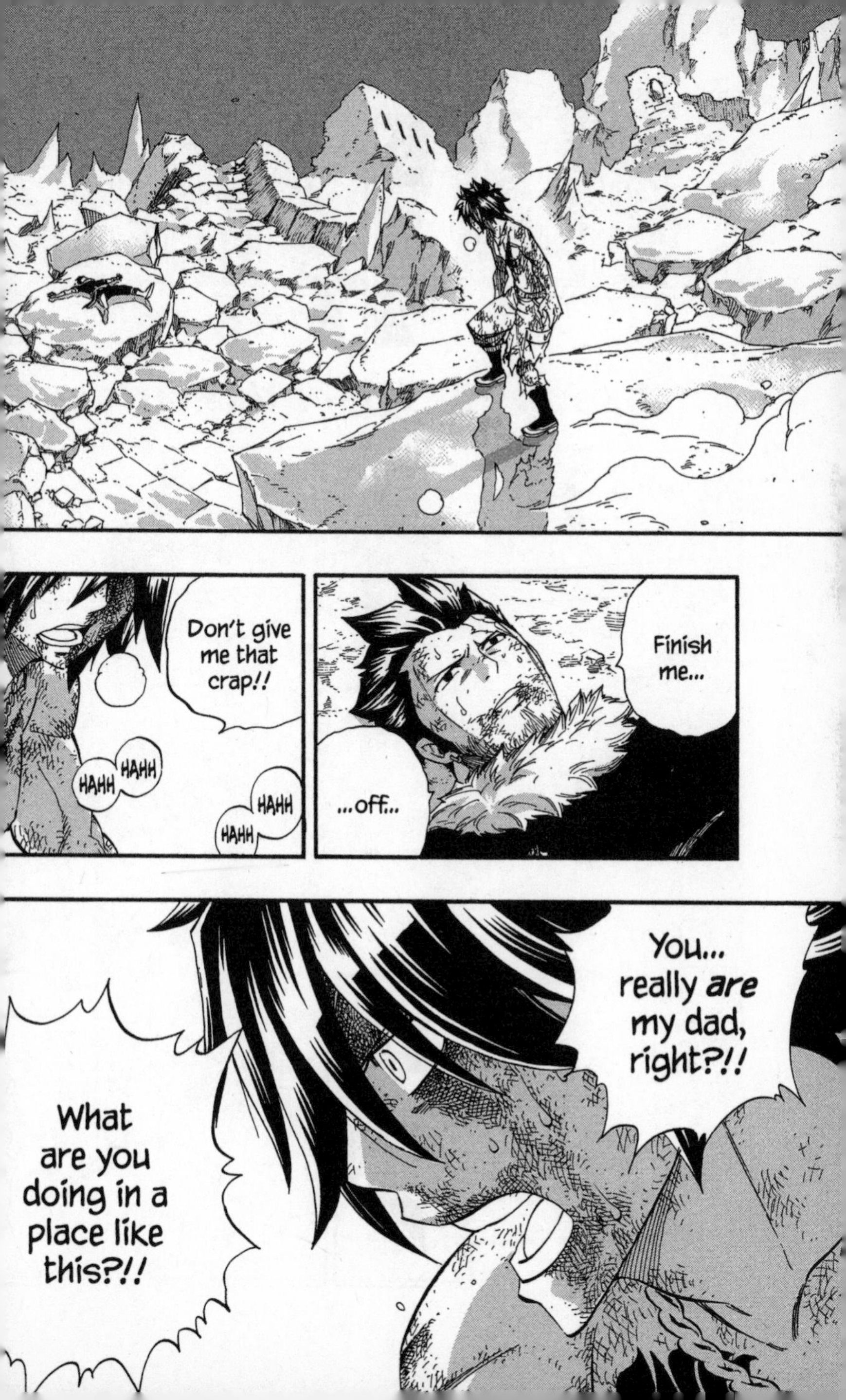

Finish me...
...off...
Don't give me that crap!!
HAHH HAHH
HAHH HAHH
You... really *are* my dad, right?!!
What are you doing in a place like this?!!

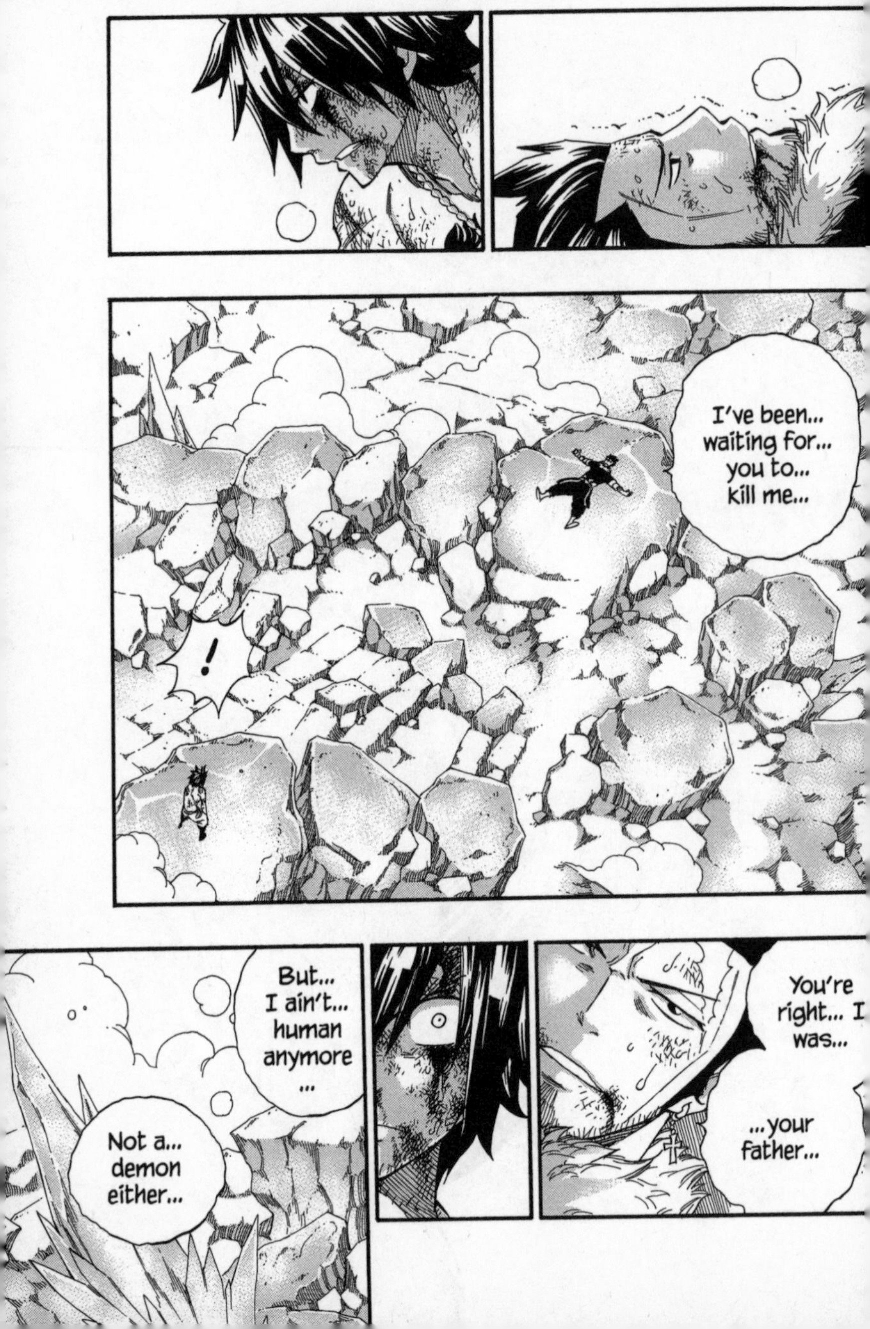
I've been... waiting for... you to... kill me...
!
You're right... I was...
...your father...
But... I ain't... human anymore ...
Not a... demon either...

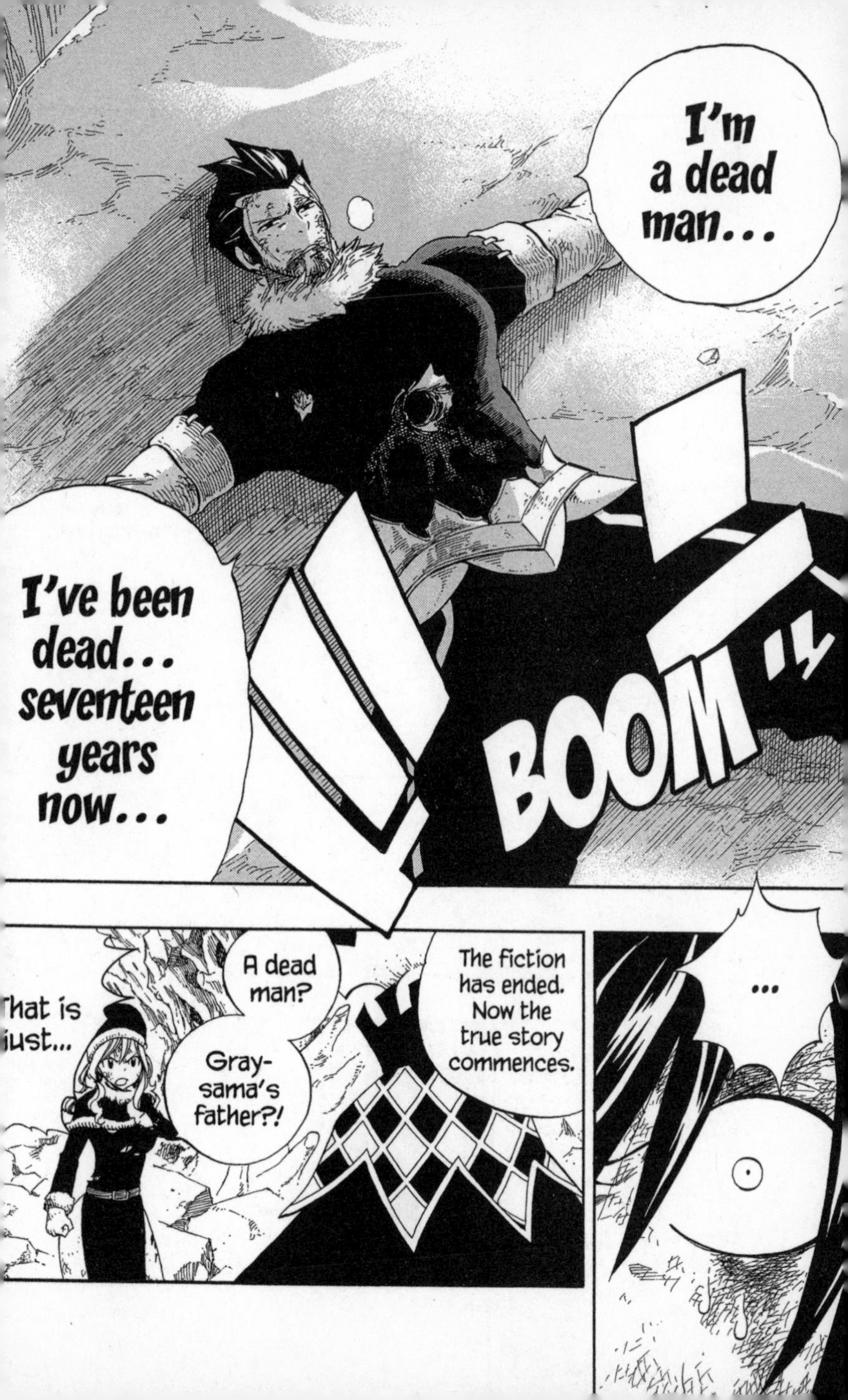
I'm a dead man...
I've been dead... seventeen years now...
BOOM
...
The fiction has ended. Now the true story commences.
A dead man?
Gray-sama's father?!
That is just...

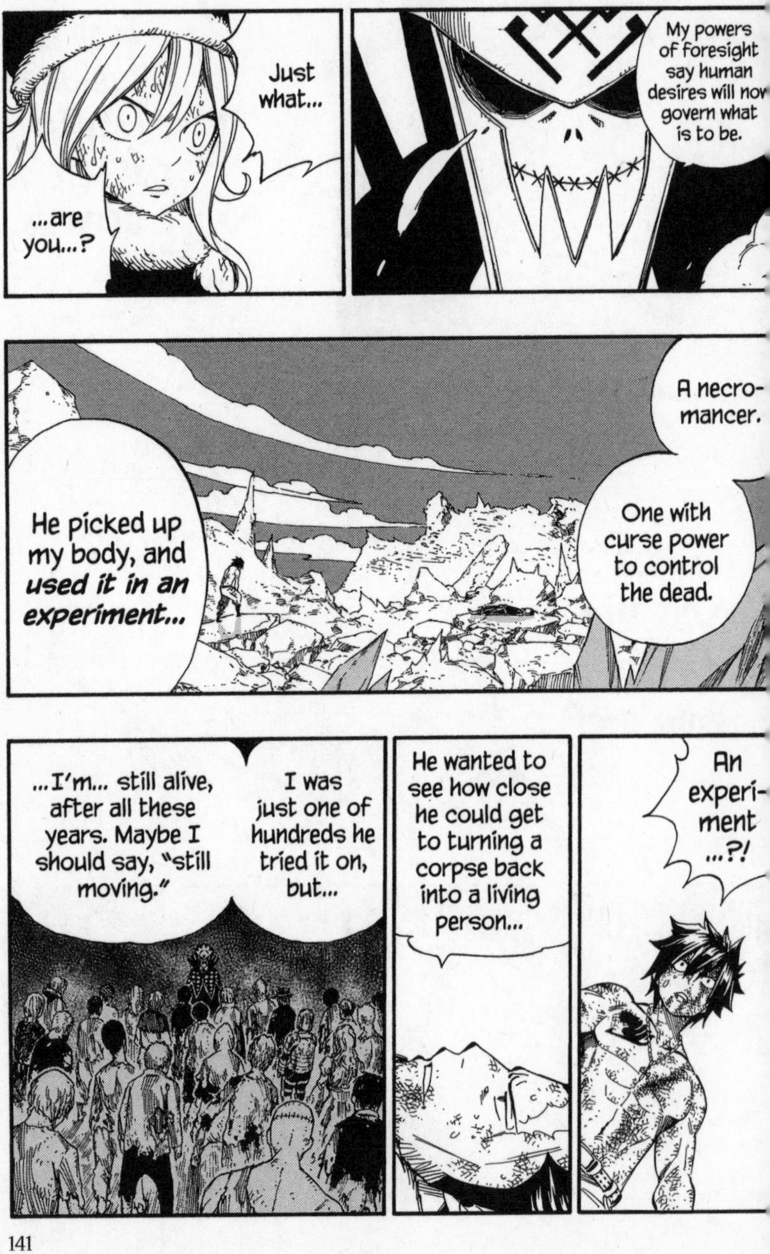
My powers of foresight say human desires will now govern what is to be.
Just what...
...are you...?
A necro-mancer.
One with curse power to control the dead.
He picked up my body, and ***used it in an experiment...***
An experi-ment ...?!
He wanted to see how close he could get to turning a corpse back into a living person...
I was just one of hundreds he tried it on, but...
...I'm... still alive, after all these years. Maybe I should say, "still moving."

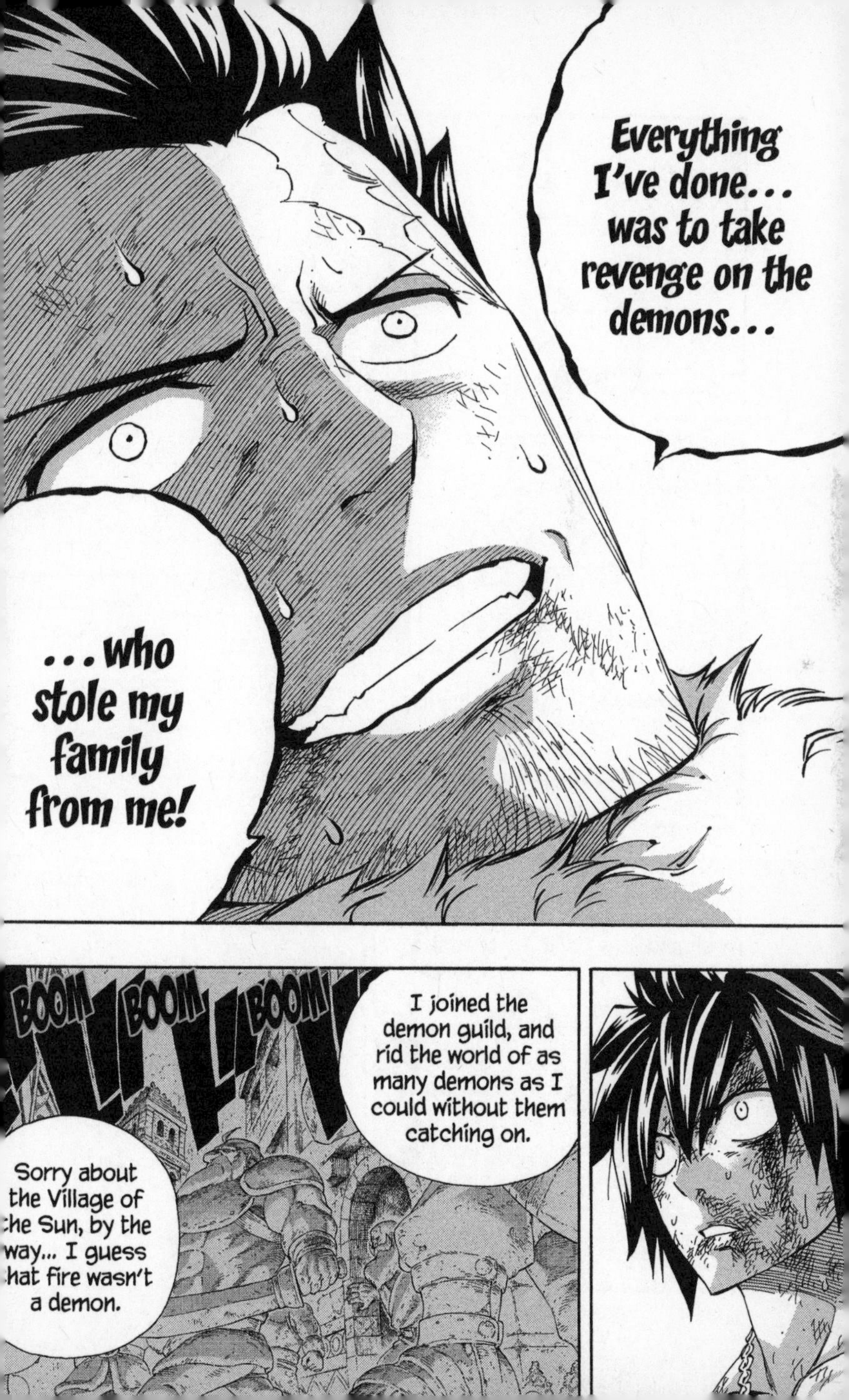
Everything I've done... was to take revenge on the demons...
...who stole my family from me!
I joined the demon guild, and rid the world of as many demons as I could without them catching on.
BOOM BOOM BOOM
Sorry about the Village of he Sun, by the way... I guess hat fire wasn't a demon.

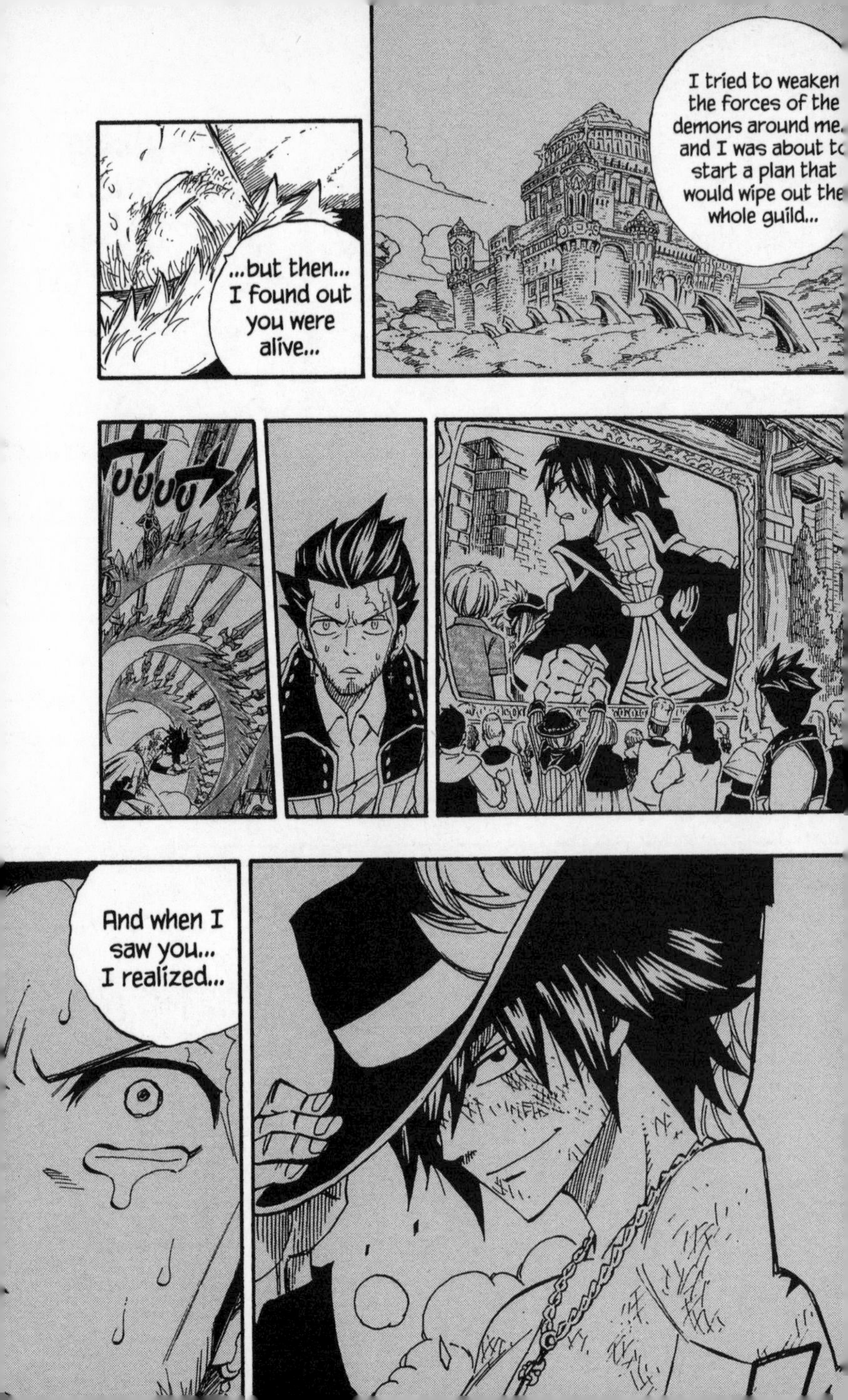
I tried to weaken the forces of the demons around me. and I was about to start a plan that would wipe out the whole guild...
...but then... I found out you were alive...
And when I saw you... I realized...

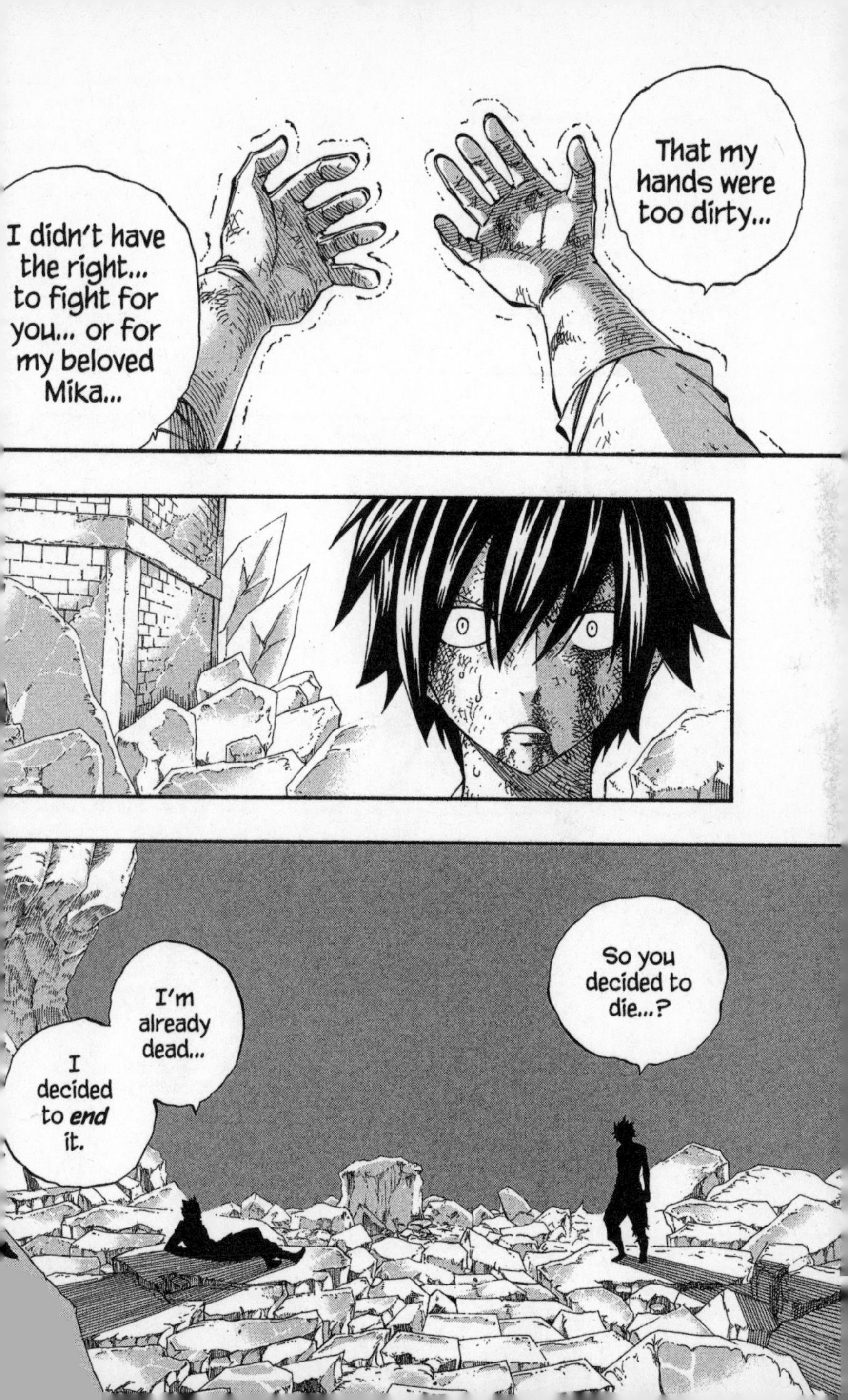
That my hands were too dirty...
I didn't have the right... to fight for you... or for my beloved Mika...
So you decided to die...?
I'm already dead...
I decided to *end* it.

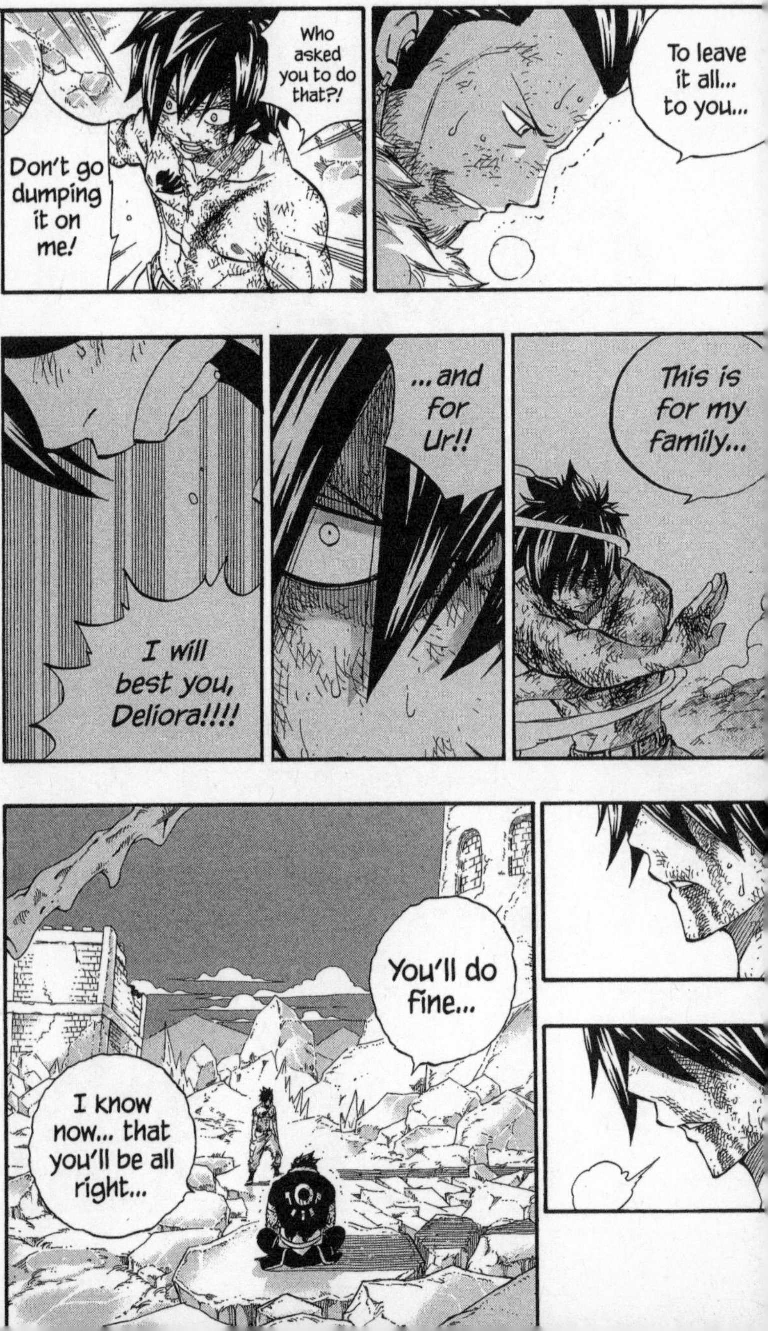
To leave it all... to you...
Who asked you to do that?!
Don't go dumping it on me!
This is for my family...
...and for Ur!!
I will best you, Deliora!!!!
You'll do fine...
I know now... that you'll be all right...

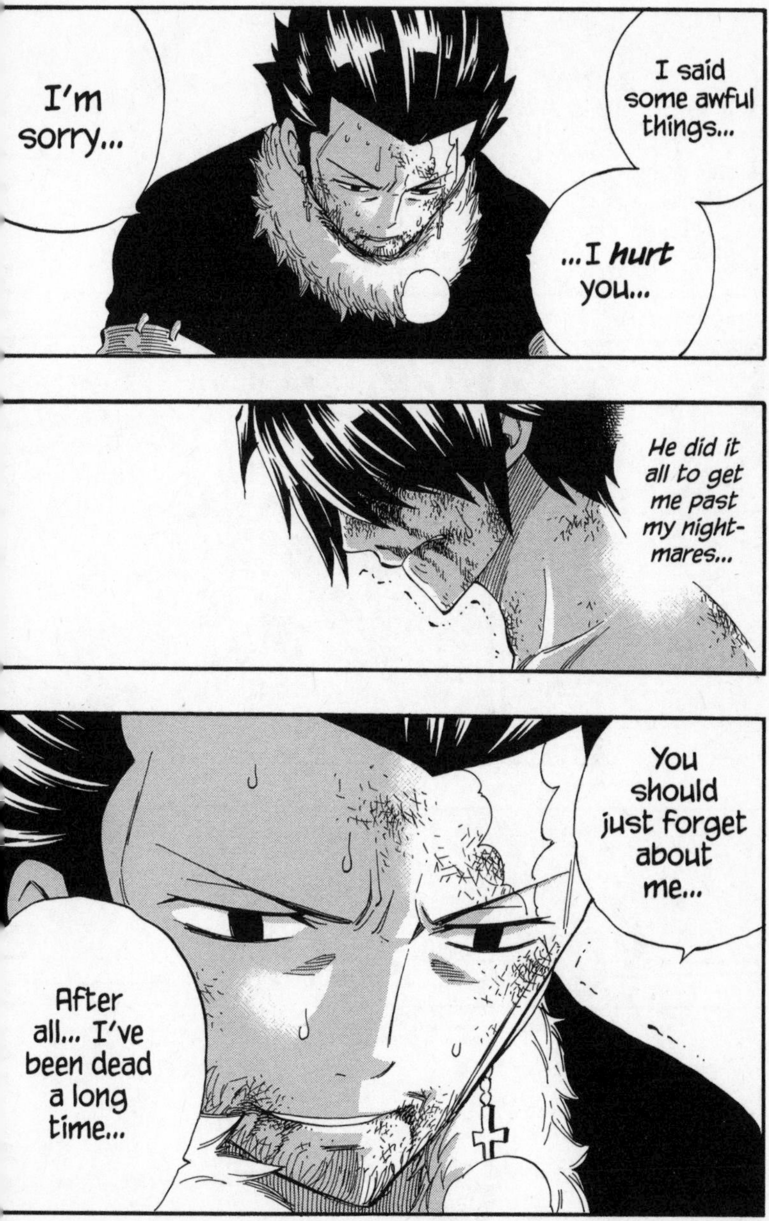
I said some awful things...
...I *hurt* you...
I'm sorry...
He did it all to get me past my night-mares...
You should just forget about me...
After all... I've been dead a long time...

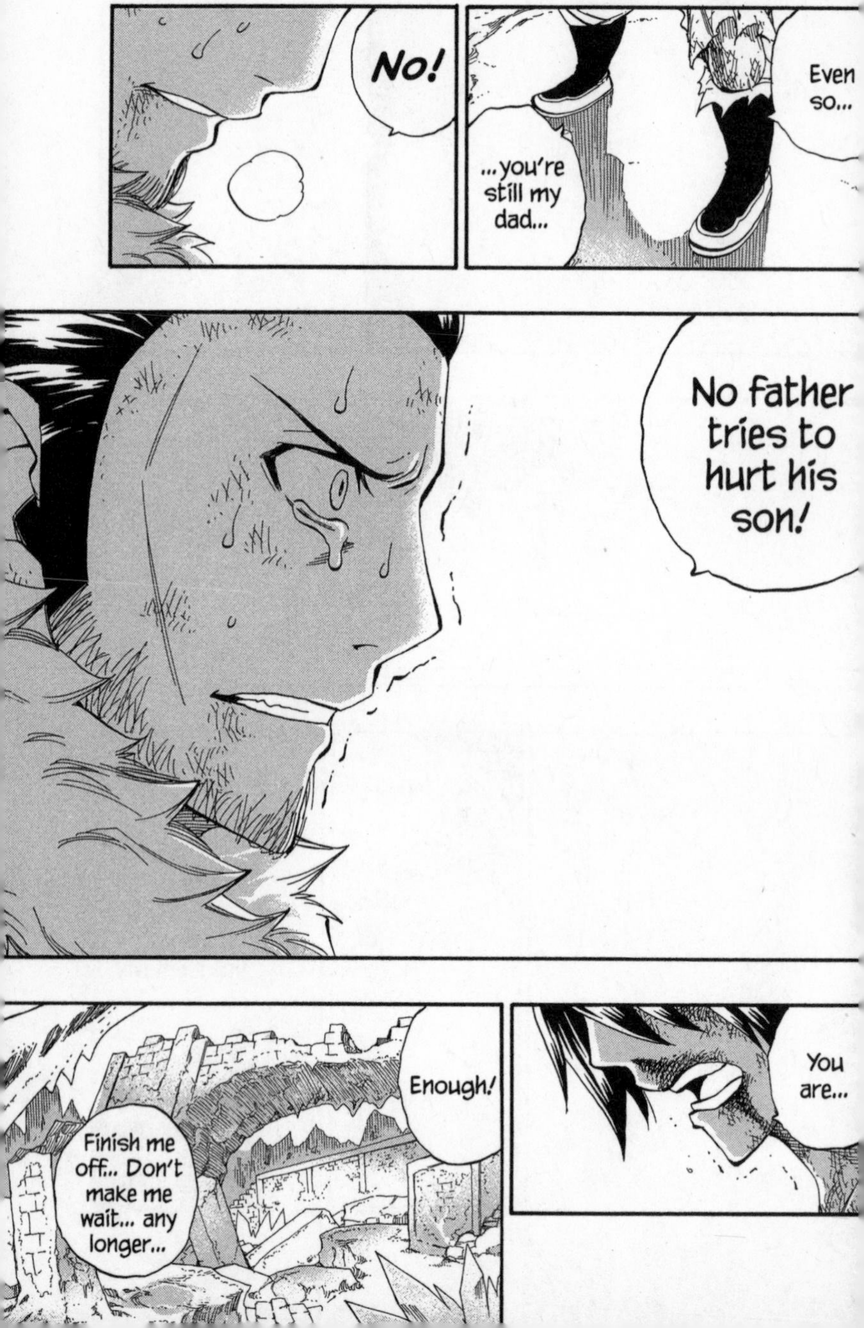
Even so...
...you're still my dad...
No!
No father tries to hurt his son!
You are...
Enough!
Finish me off... Don't make me wait... any longer...

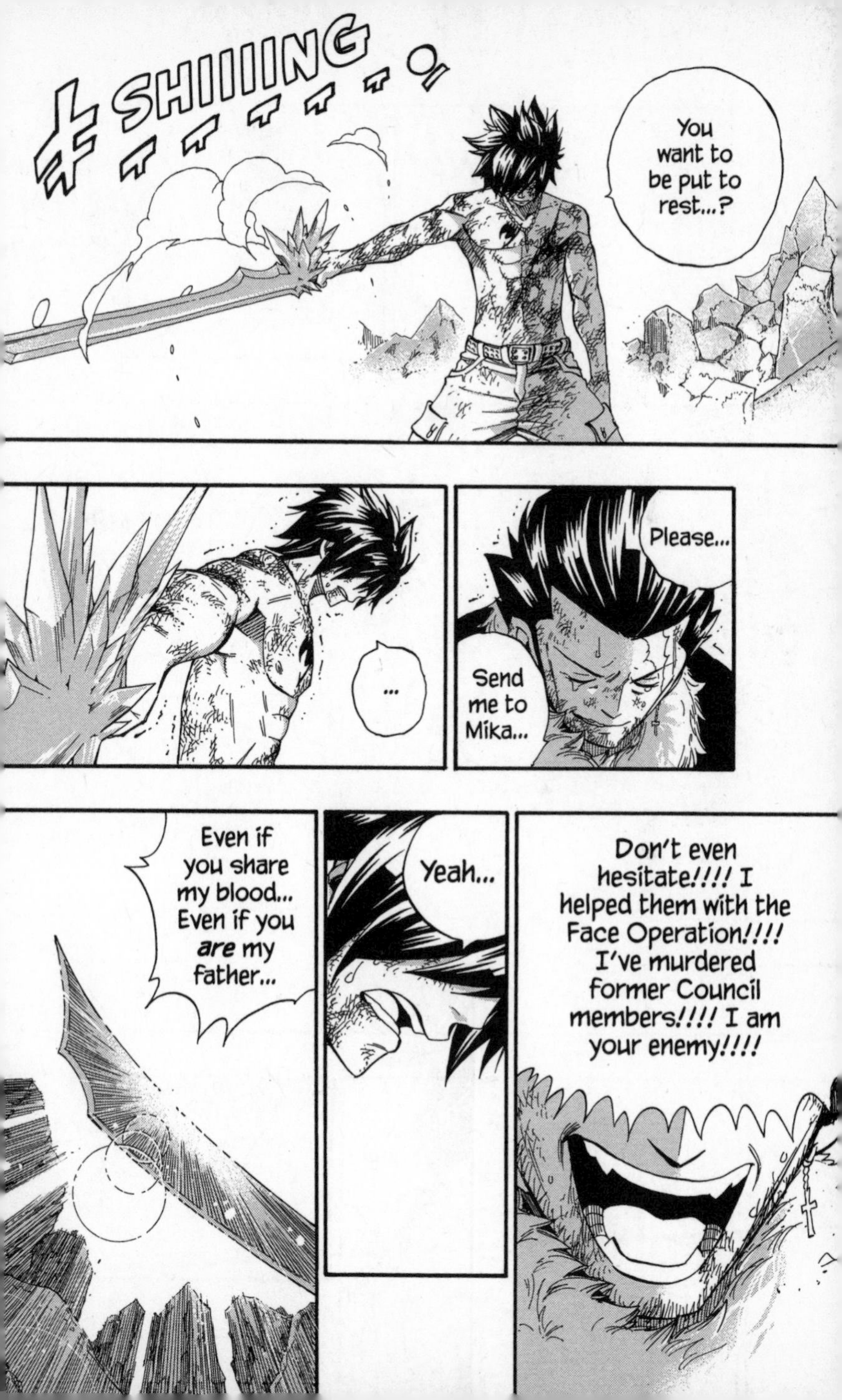
You want to be put to rest...?
SHIIIING
Please...
Send me to Mika...
...
Don't even hesitate!!!! I helped them with the Face Operation!!!! I've murdered former Council members!!!! I am your enemy!!!!
Yeah...
Even if you share my blood... Even if you *are* my father...

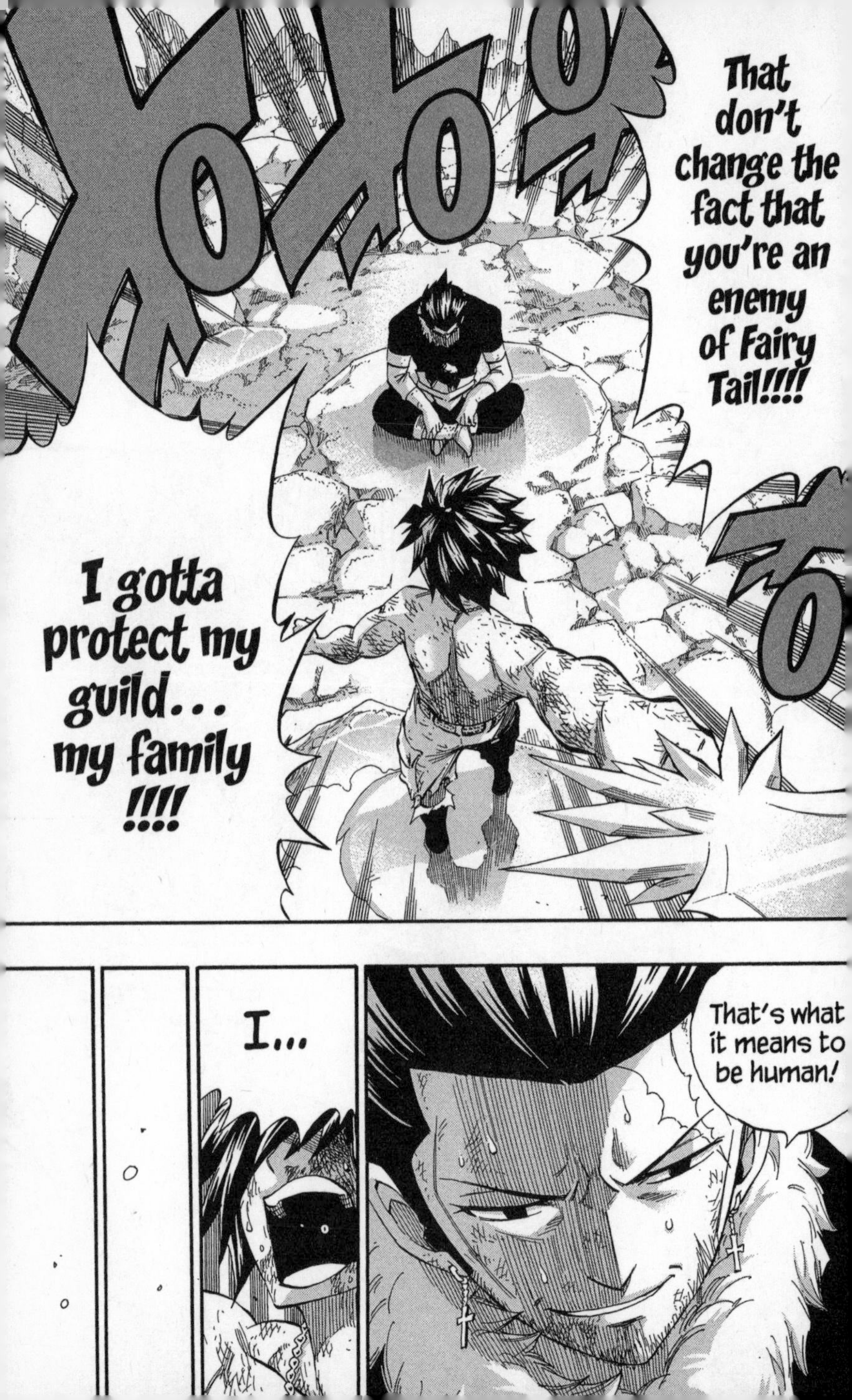
That don't change the fact that you're an enemy of Fairy Tail!!!!
I gotta protect my guild... my family !!!!
That's what it means to be human!
I...

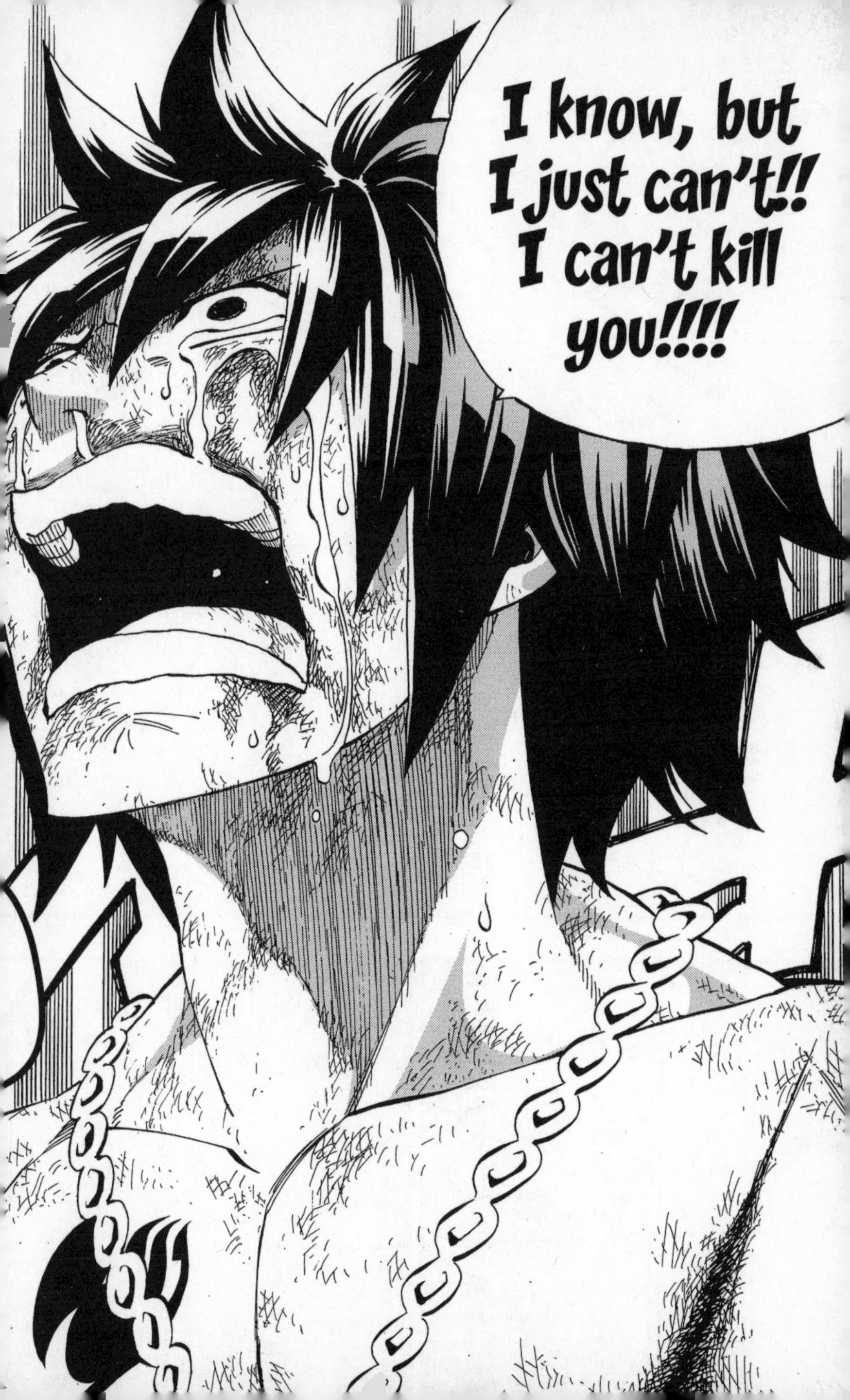
I know, but I just can't!! I can't kill you!!!!

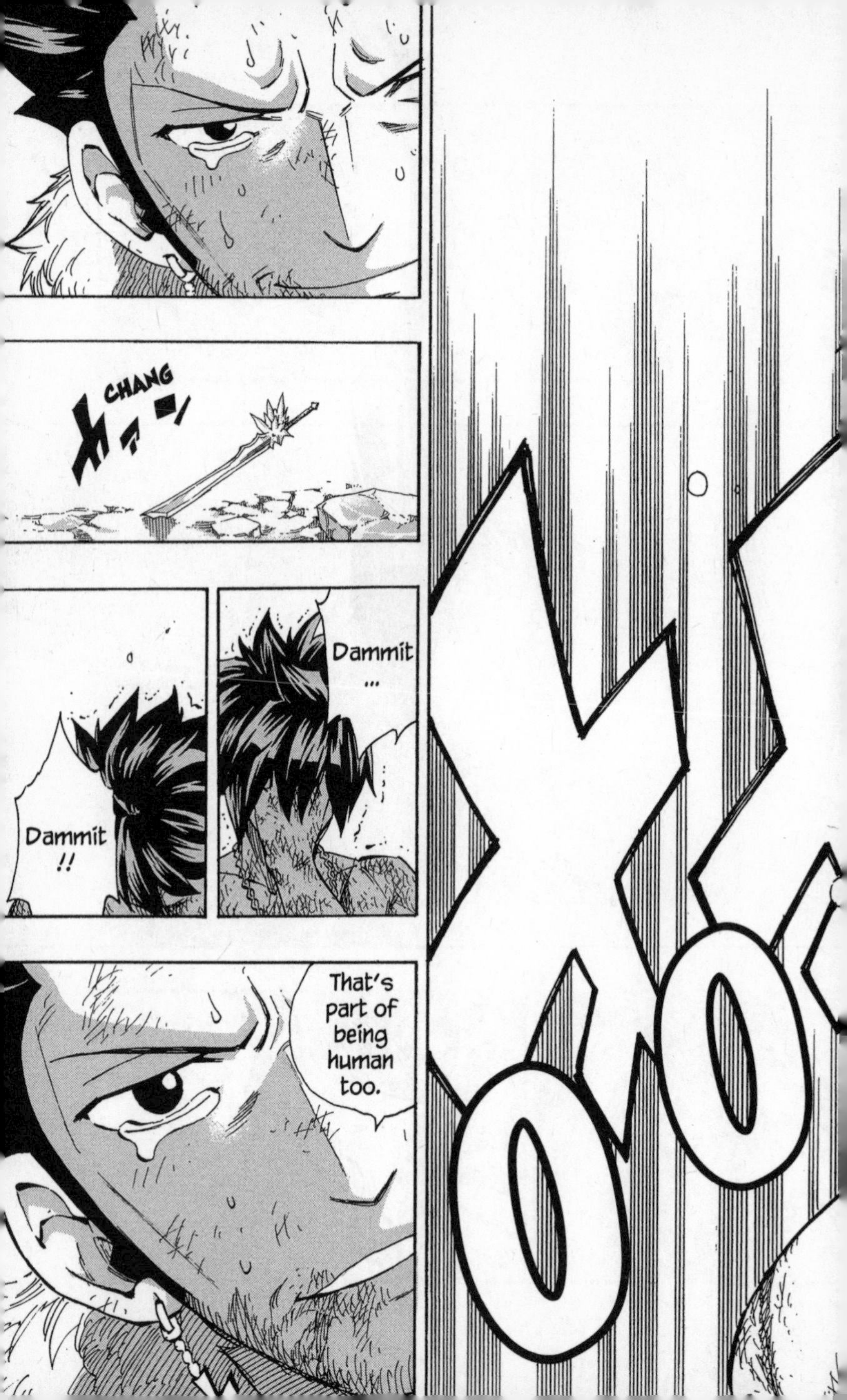
CHANG
Dammit ...
Dammit !!
That's part of being human too.

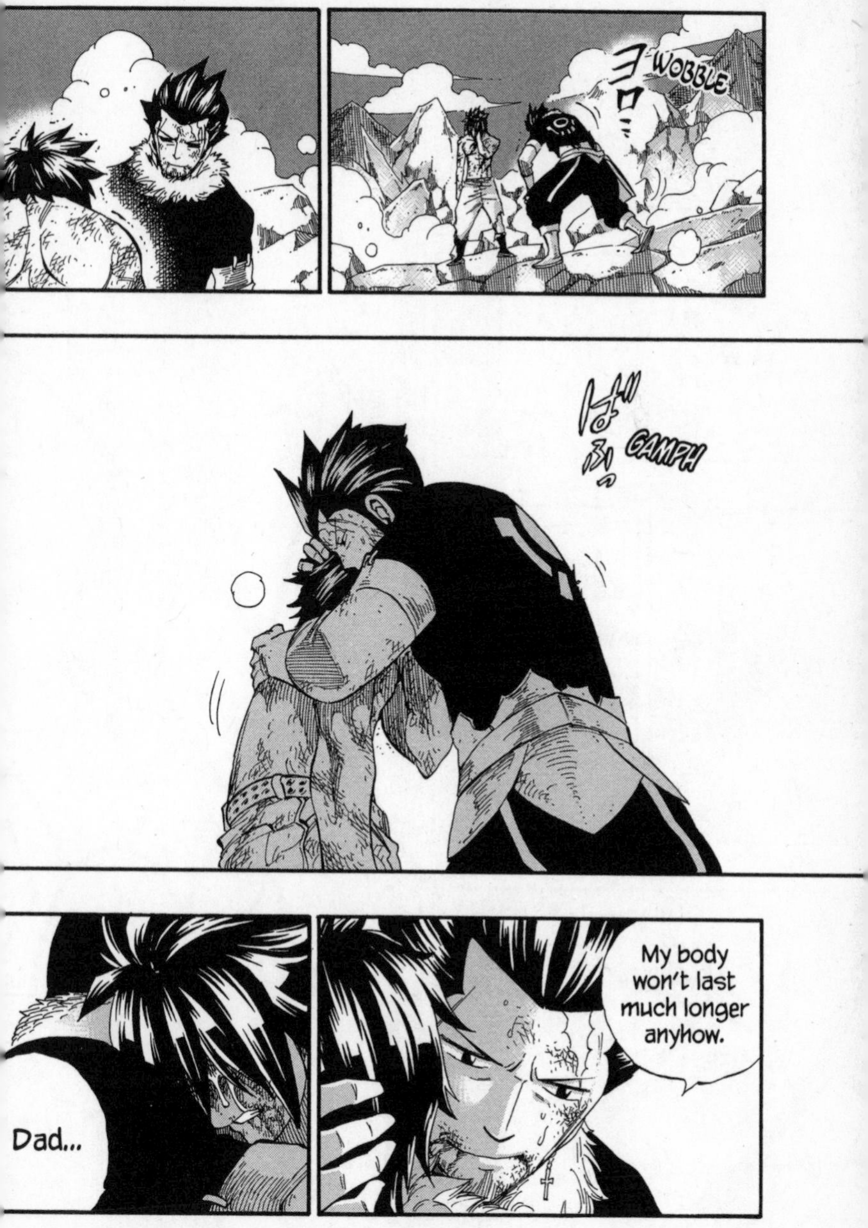
WOBBLE
GAMPH
My body won't last much longer anyhow.
Dad...

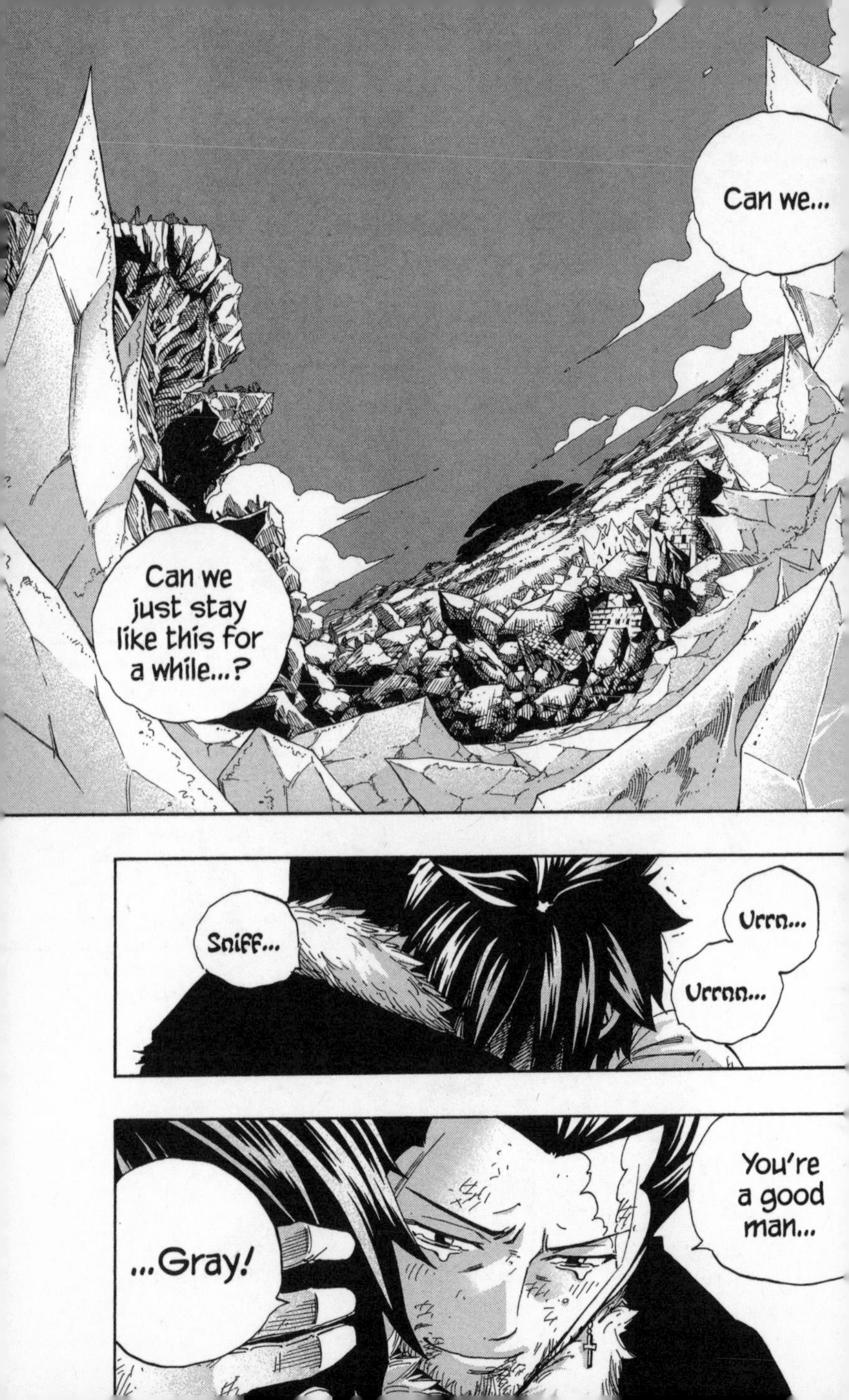
Can we...
Can we just stay like this for a while...?
Urrn...
Urrnn...
Sniff...
You're a good man...
...Gray!

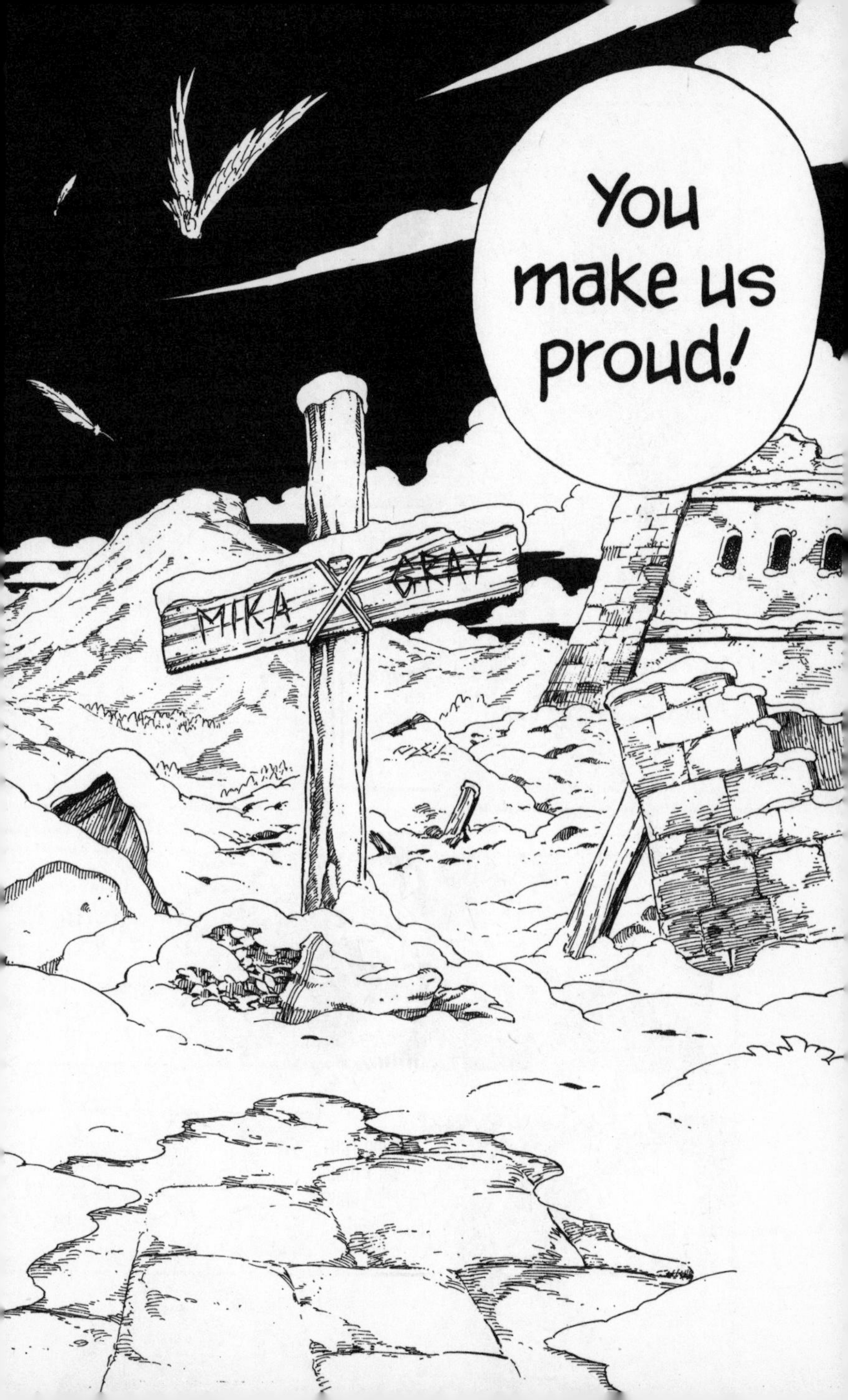
You make us proud!
MIKA
GRAY

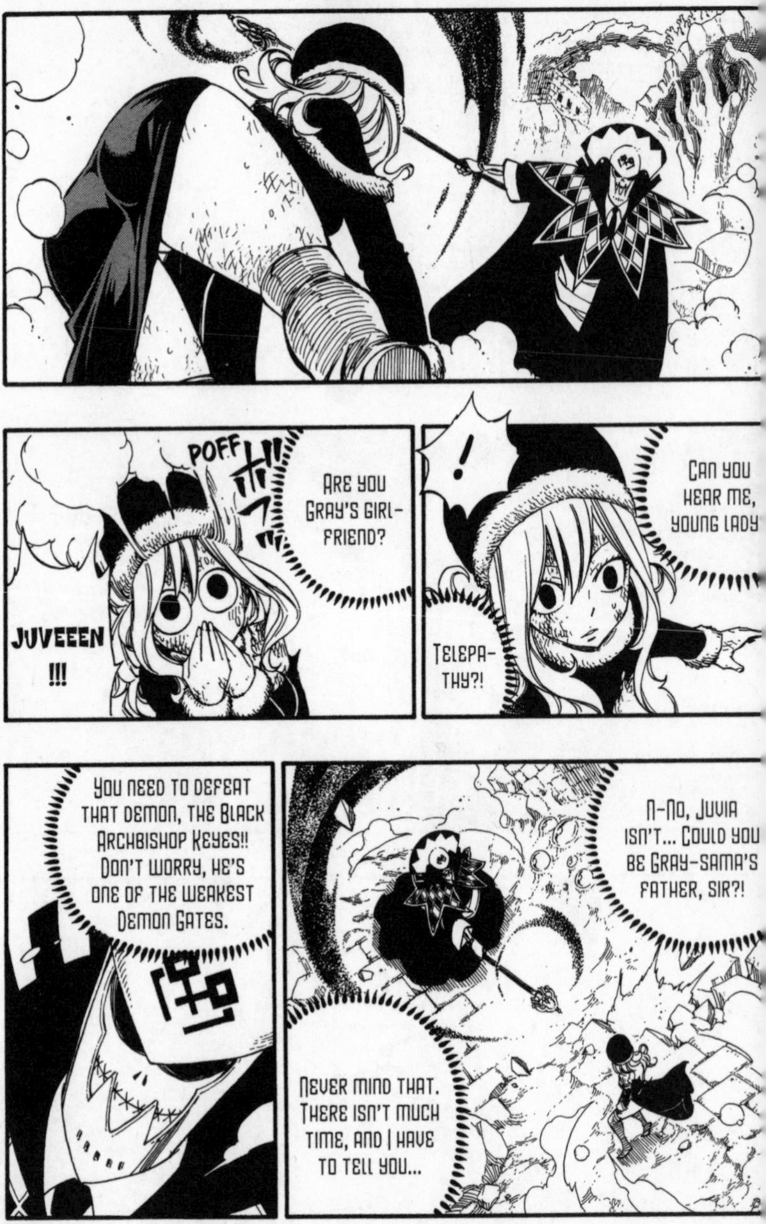
!
Can you hear me, young lady
Telepathy?!
Are you Gray's girlfriend?
POFF
JUVEEEN!!!
N-No, Juvia isn't... Could you be Gray-sama's father, sir?!
Never mind that. There isn't much time, and I have to tell you...
You need to defeat that demon, the Black Archbishop Keyes!! Don't worry, he's one of the weakest Demon Gates.

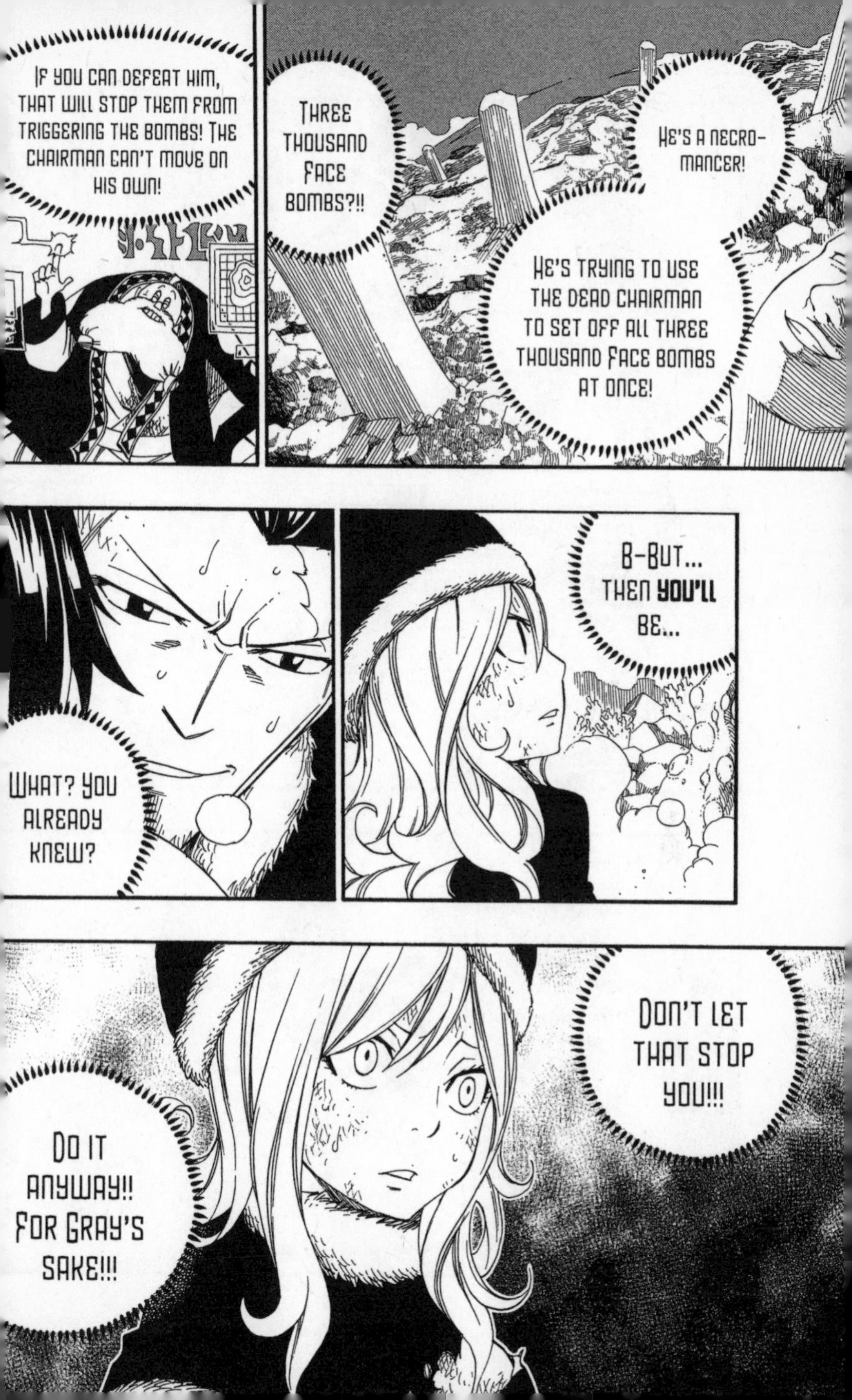
He's a necro-mancer!
He's trying to use the dead chairman to set off all three thousand Face bombs at once!
Three thousand Face bombs?!!
If you can defeat him, that will stop them from triggering the bombs! The chairman can't move on his own!
B-But... then **YOU'LL** be...
What? You already knew?
Don't let that stop you!!!
Do it anyway!! For Gray's sake!!!

FAIRY TAIL

フェアリーテイル

Chapter 394: Juvia vs. Keyes

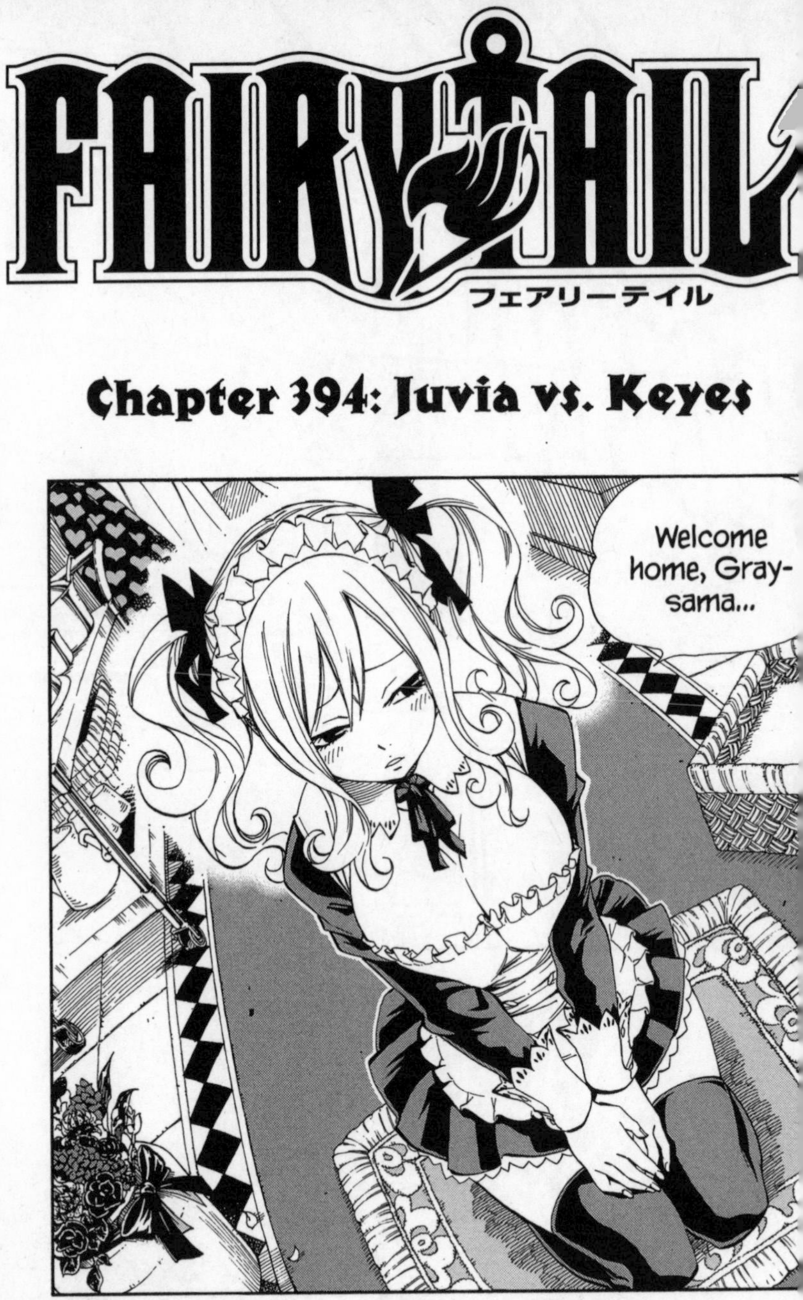
Welcome home, Gray-sama...

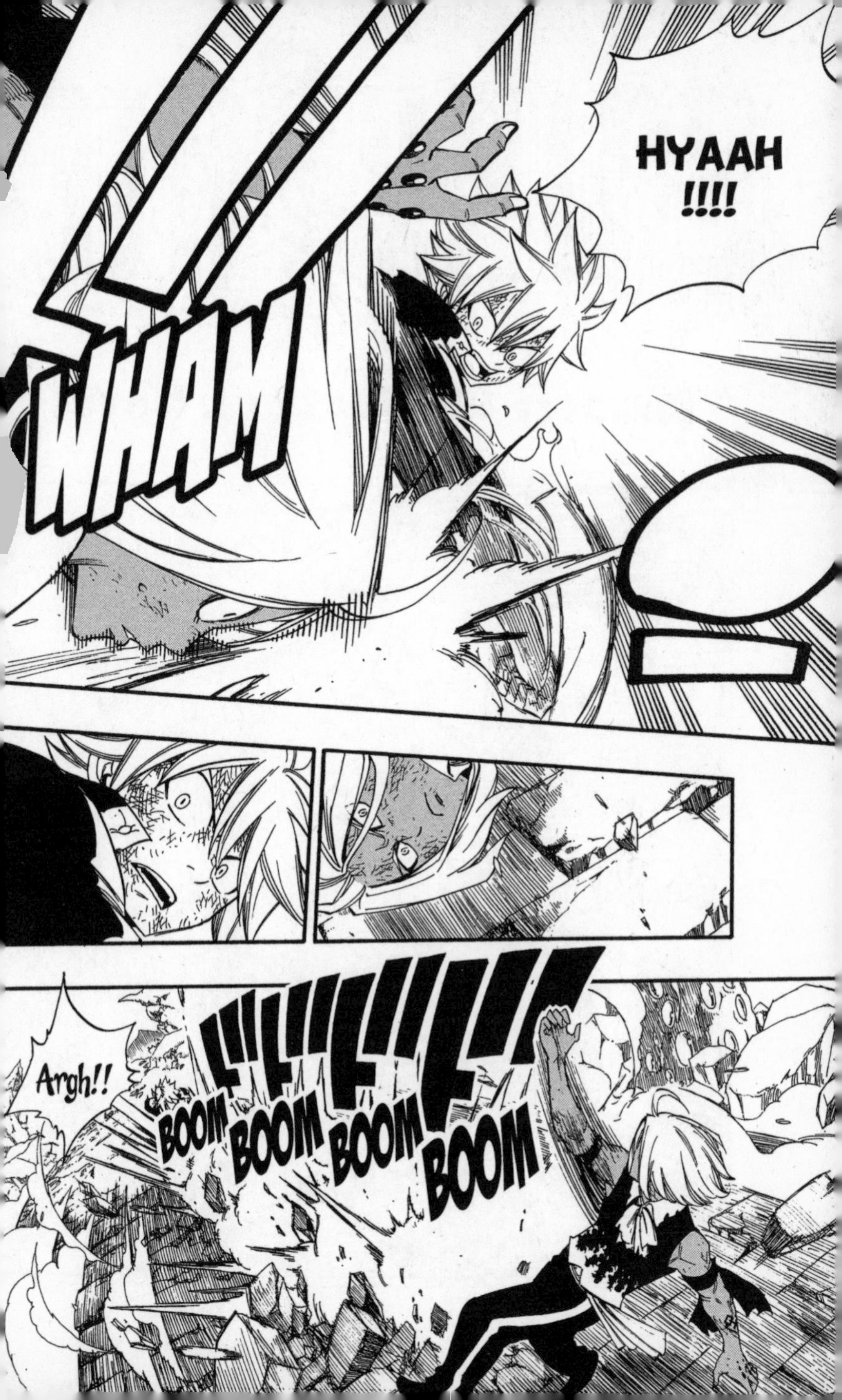
HYAAH !!!!
WHAM
Argh!!
BOOM BOOM BOOM BOOM

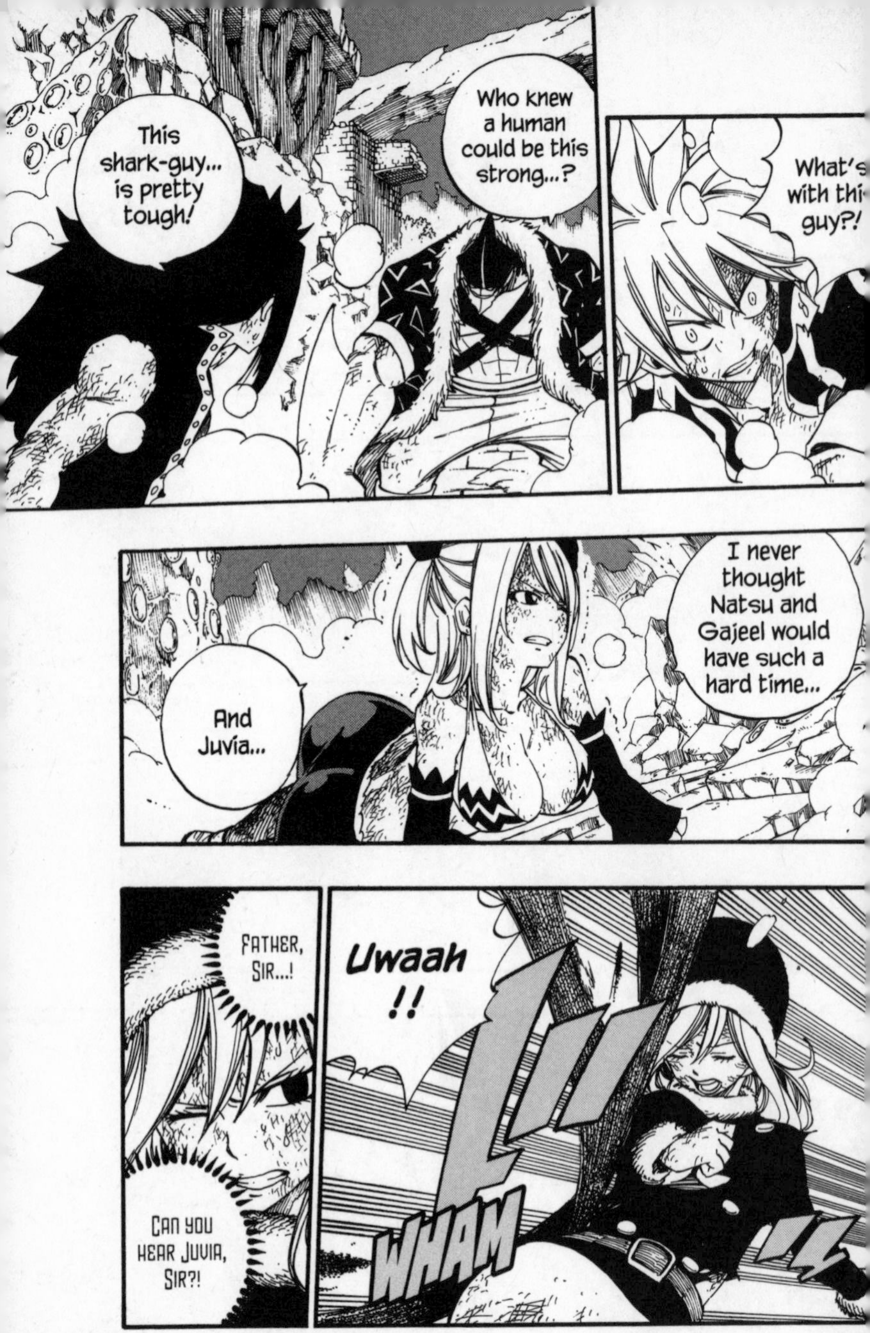
What's with thi guy?!
Who knew a human could be this strong...?
This shark-guy... is pretty tough!
I never thought Natsu and Gajeel would have such a hard time...
And Juvia...
Uwaah !!
WHAM
Father, Sir...!
Can you hear Juvia, Sir?!

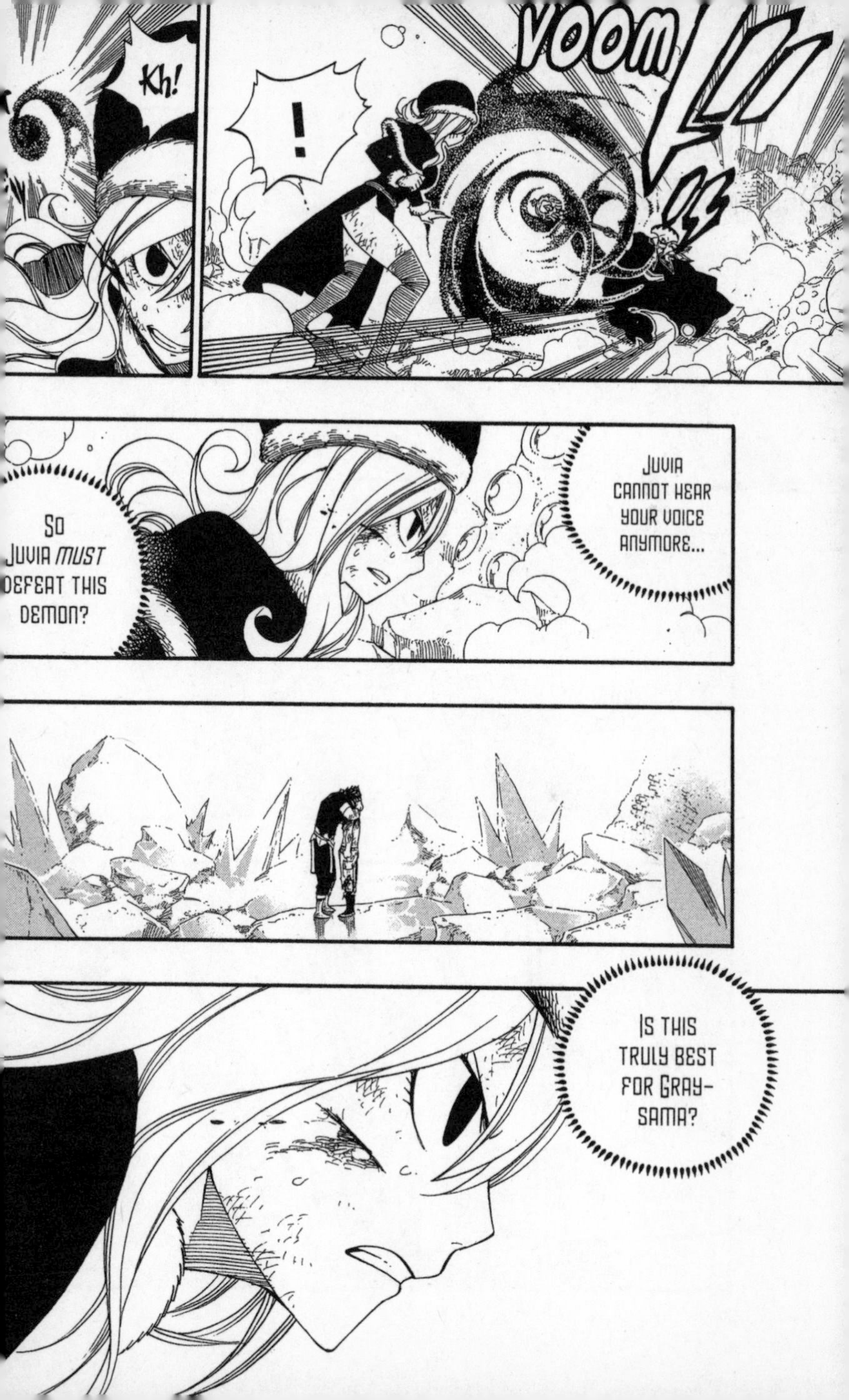
VOOM
!
Kh!
Juvia cannot hear your voice anymore...
So Juvia *must* defeat this demon?
Is this truly best for Gray-sama?

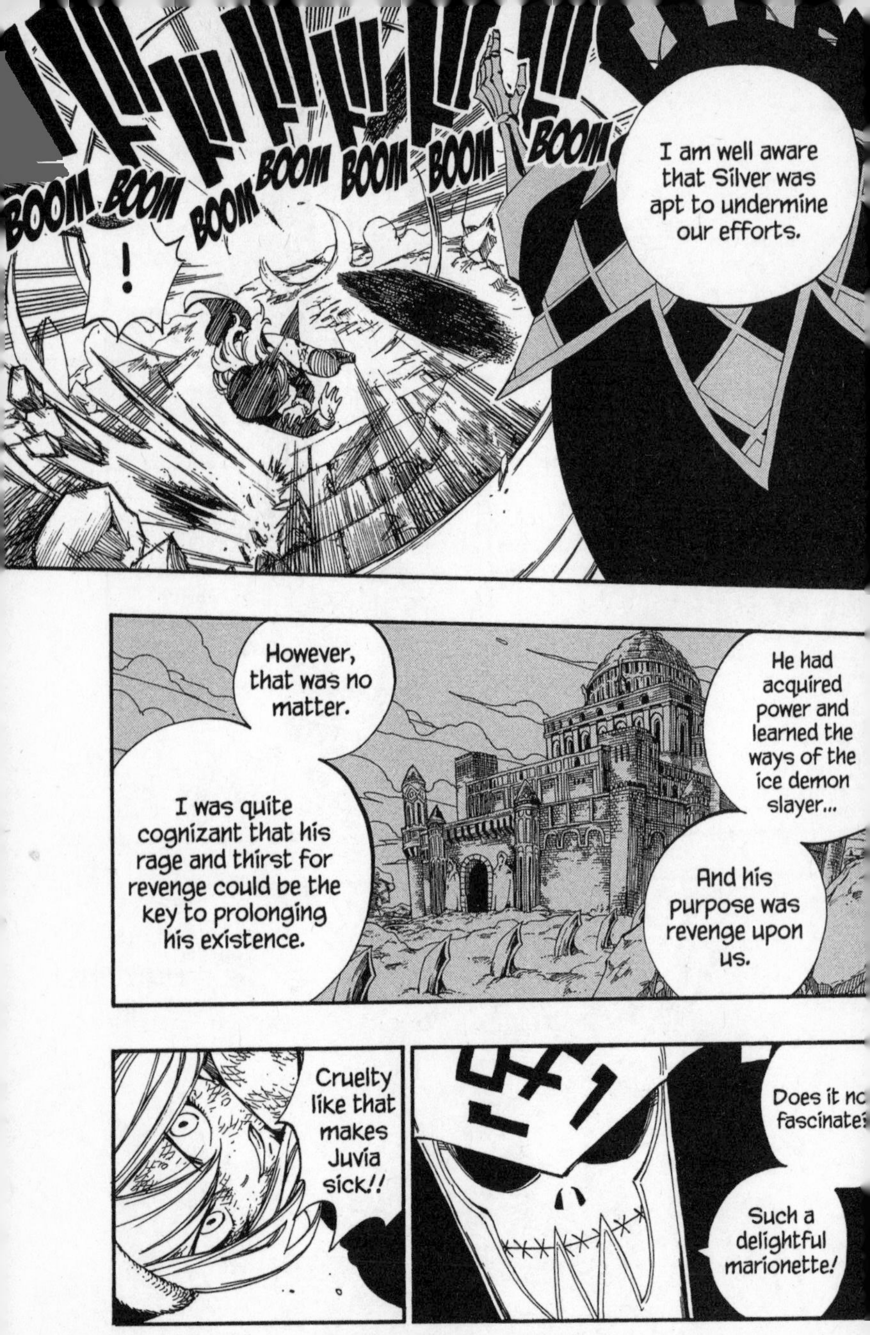
BOOM BOOM BOOM BOOM BOOM BOOM BOOM
I am well aware that Silver was apt to undermine our efforts.
!
He had acquired power and learned the ways of the ice demon slayer...
And his purpose was revenge upon us.
However, that was no matter.
I was quite cognizant that his rage and thirst for revenge could be the key to prolonging his existence.
Does it no fascinate?
Such a delightful marionette!
Cruelty like that makes Juvia sick!!

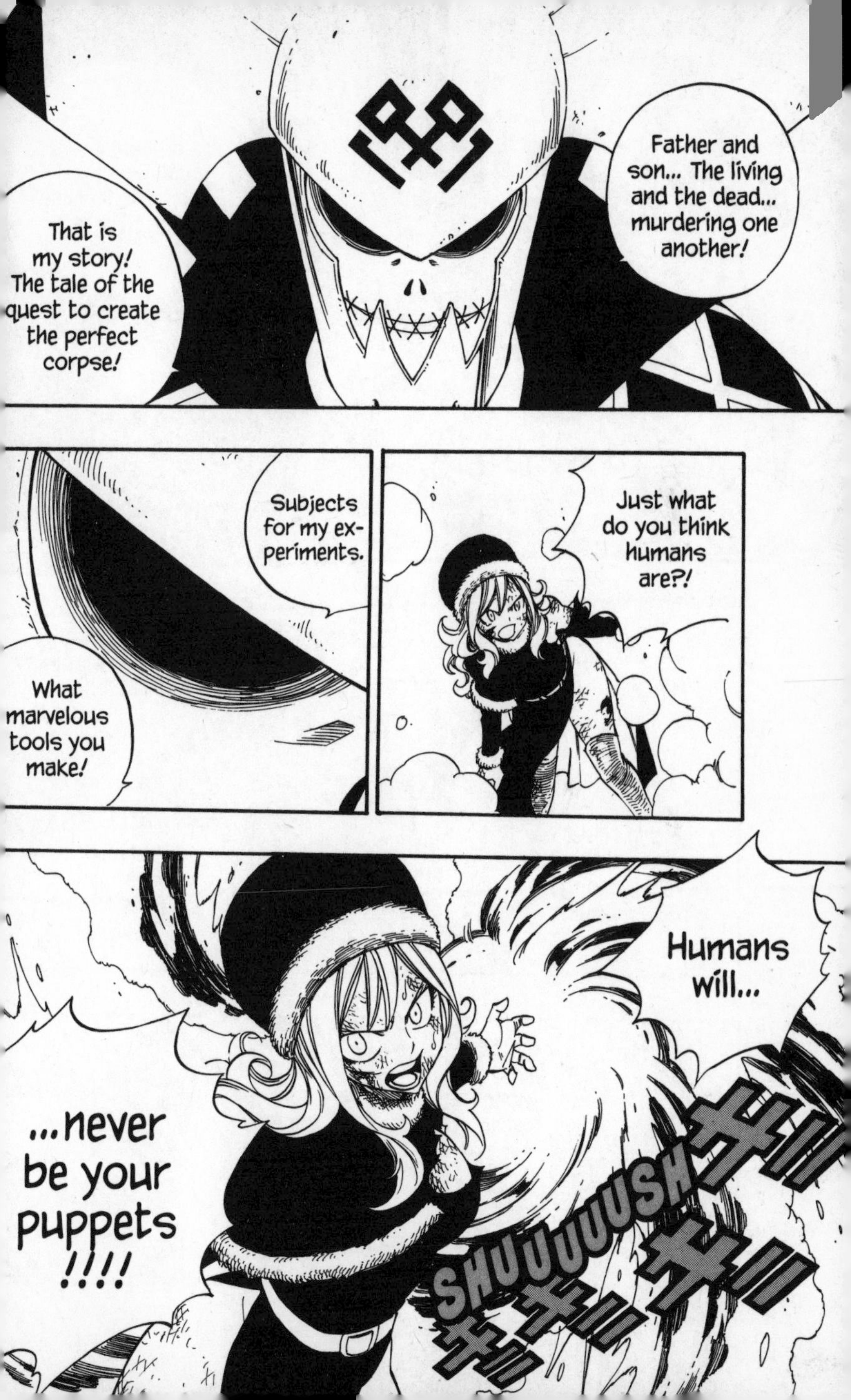
Father and son... The living and the dead... murdering one another!
That is my story! The tale of the quest to create the perfect corpse!
Just what do you think humans are?!
Subjects for my ex-periments.
What marvelous tools you make!
Humans will...
...never be your puppets!!!!
SHUUUUUSH

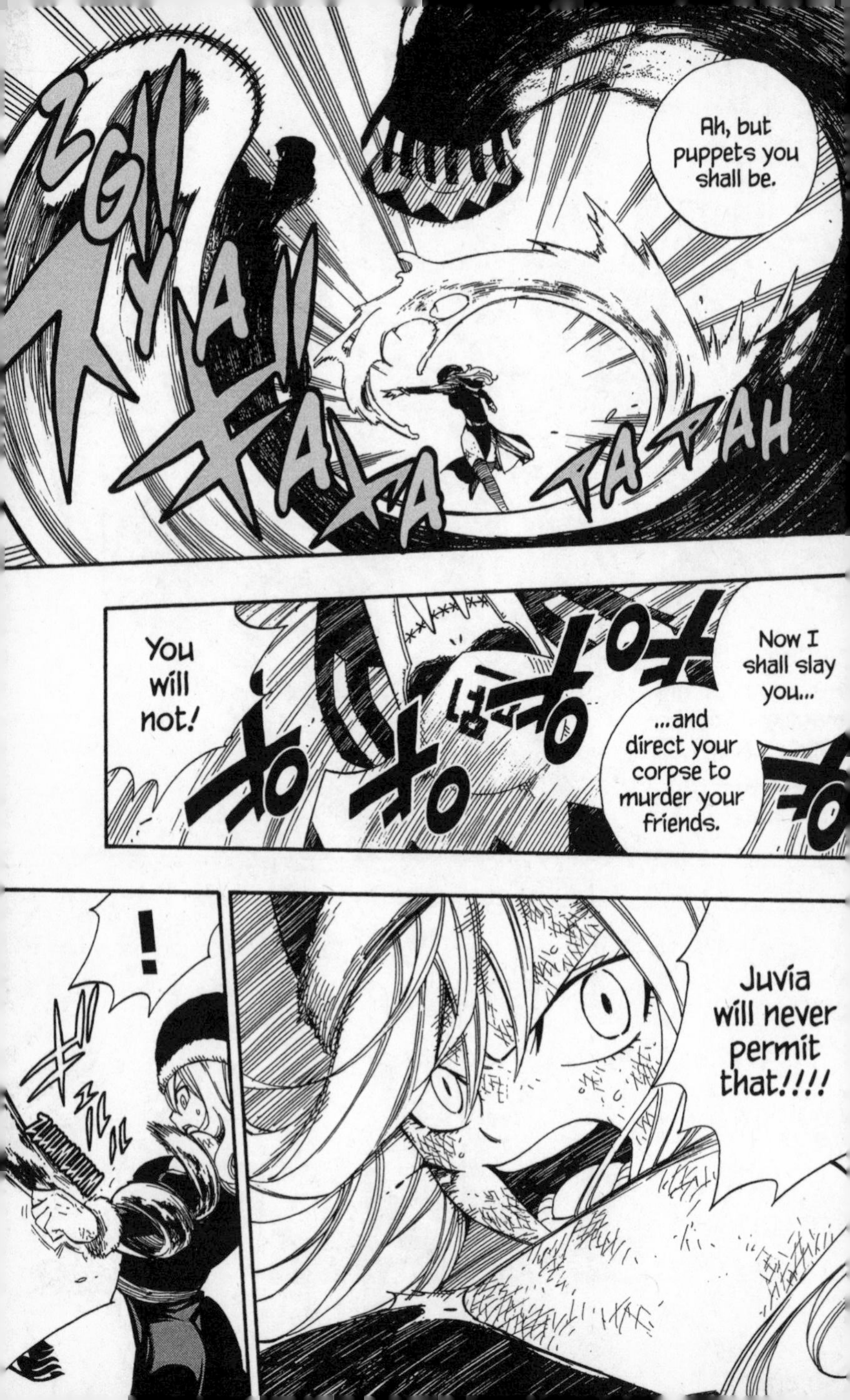
Ah, but puppets you shall be.
Now I shall slay you...
...and direct your corpse to murder your friends.
You will not!
Juvia will never permit that!!!!
!

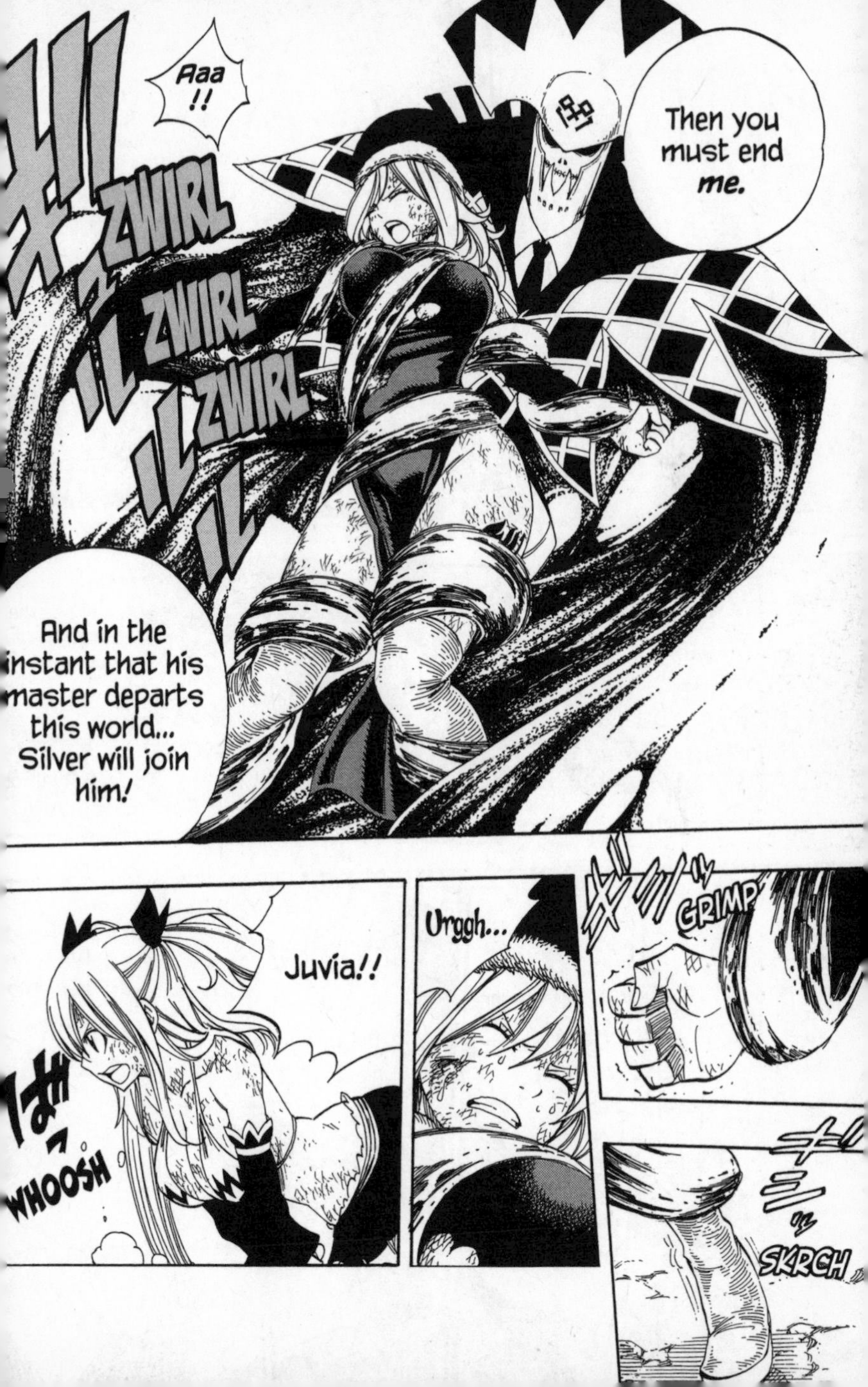
Then you must end me.
Aaa!!
ZWIRL
ZWIRL
ZWIRL
ZWIRL
And in the instant that his master departs this world... Silver will join him!
GRIMP
SKRCH
Urggh...
Juvia!!
WHOOSH

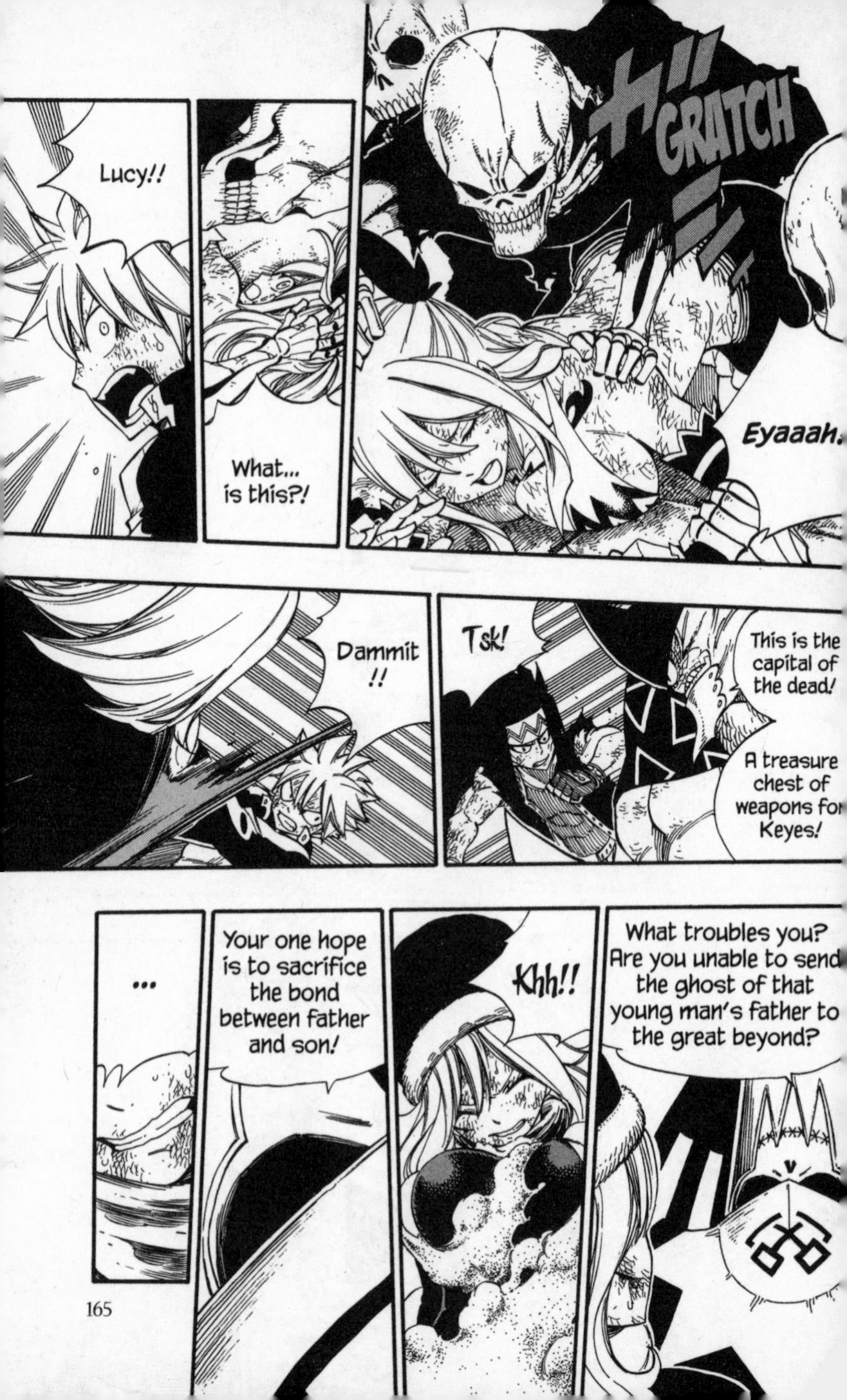
GRATCH
Eyaaah!
What... is this?!
Lucy!!
This is the capital of the dead!
A treasure chest of weapons for Keyes!
Tsk!
Dammit!!
What troubles you? Are you unable to send the ghost of that young man's father to the great beyond?
Khh!!
Your one hope is to sacrifice the bond between father and son!
...

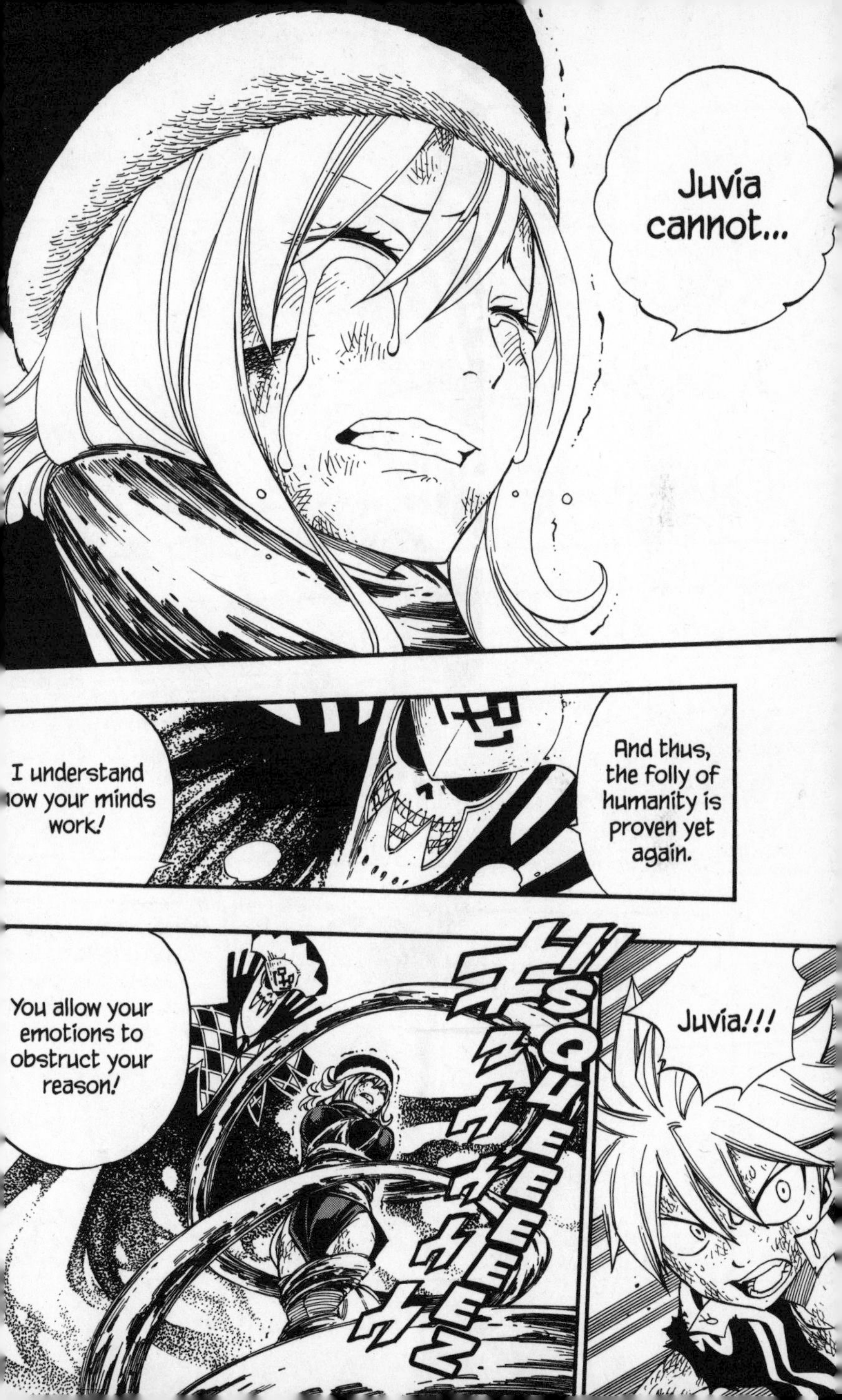
Juvia cannot...
And thus, the folly of humanity is proven yet again.
I understand ow your minds work!
Juvia!!!
SQUEEEEEZ
You allow your emotions to obstruct your reason!

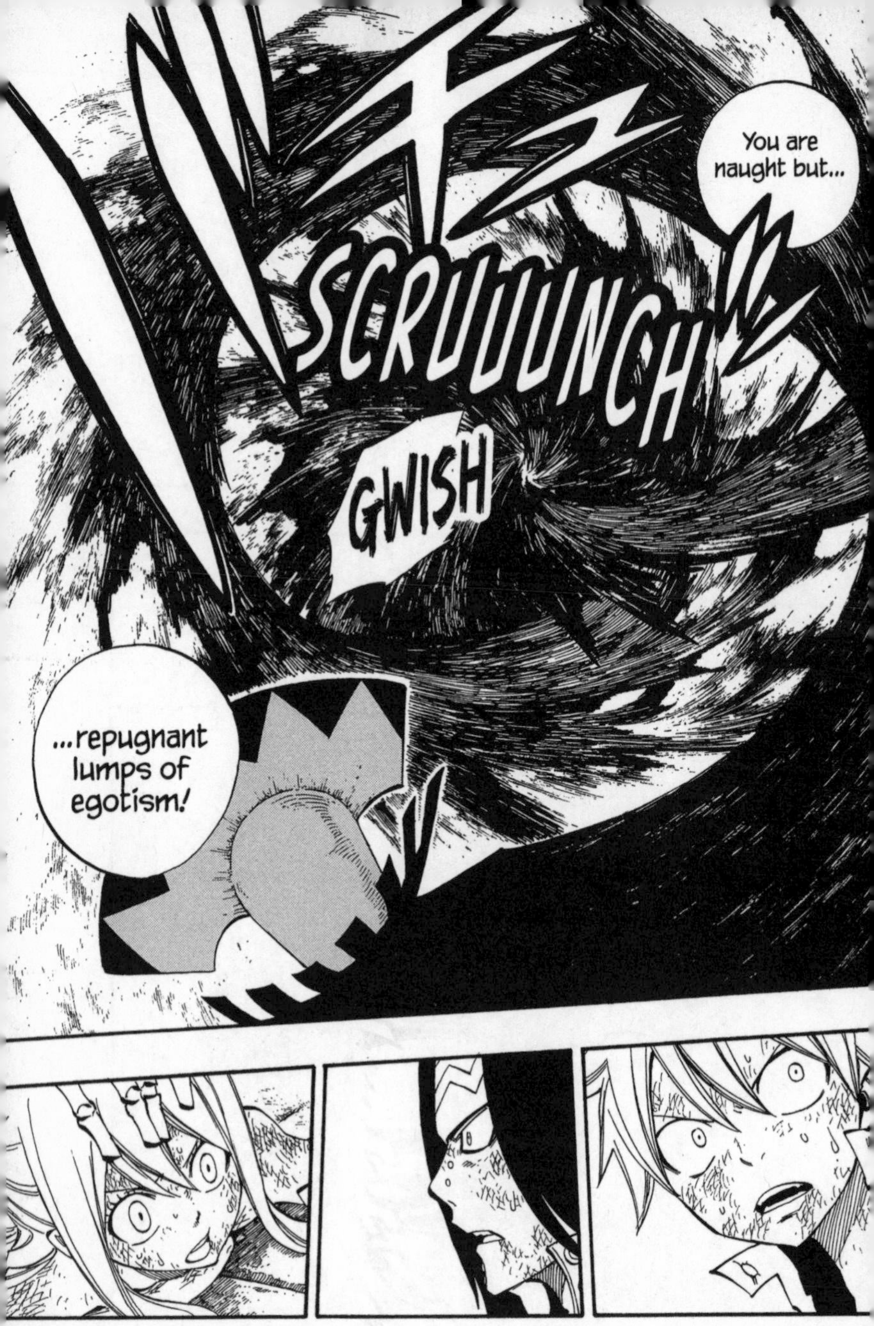
You are naught but...
SCRUUUNCH
GWISH
...repugnant lumps of egotism!

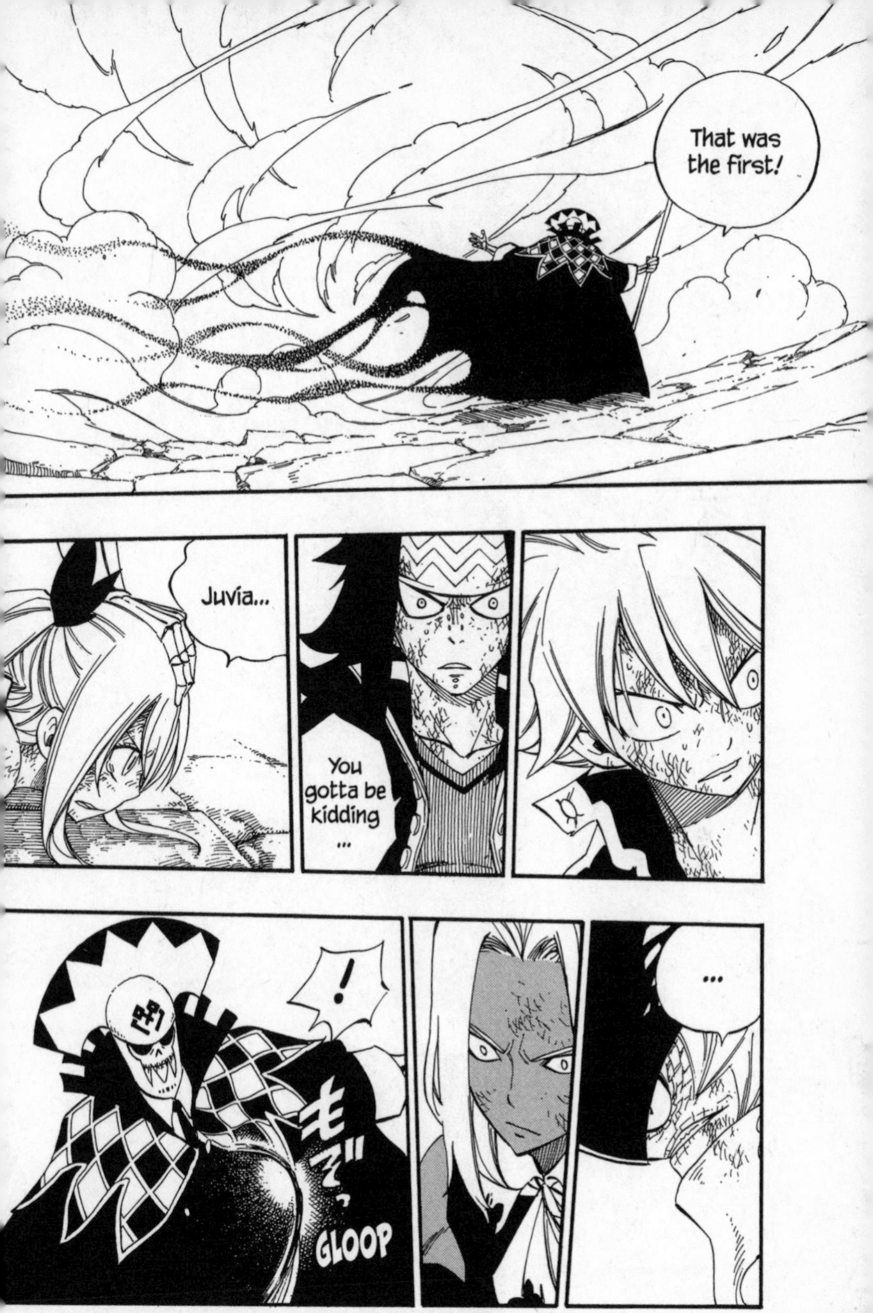
That was the first!
You gotta be kidding ...
Juvia...
...
!
GLOOP

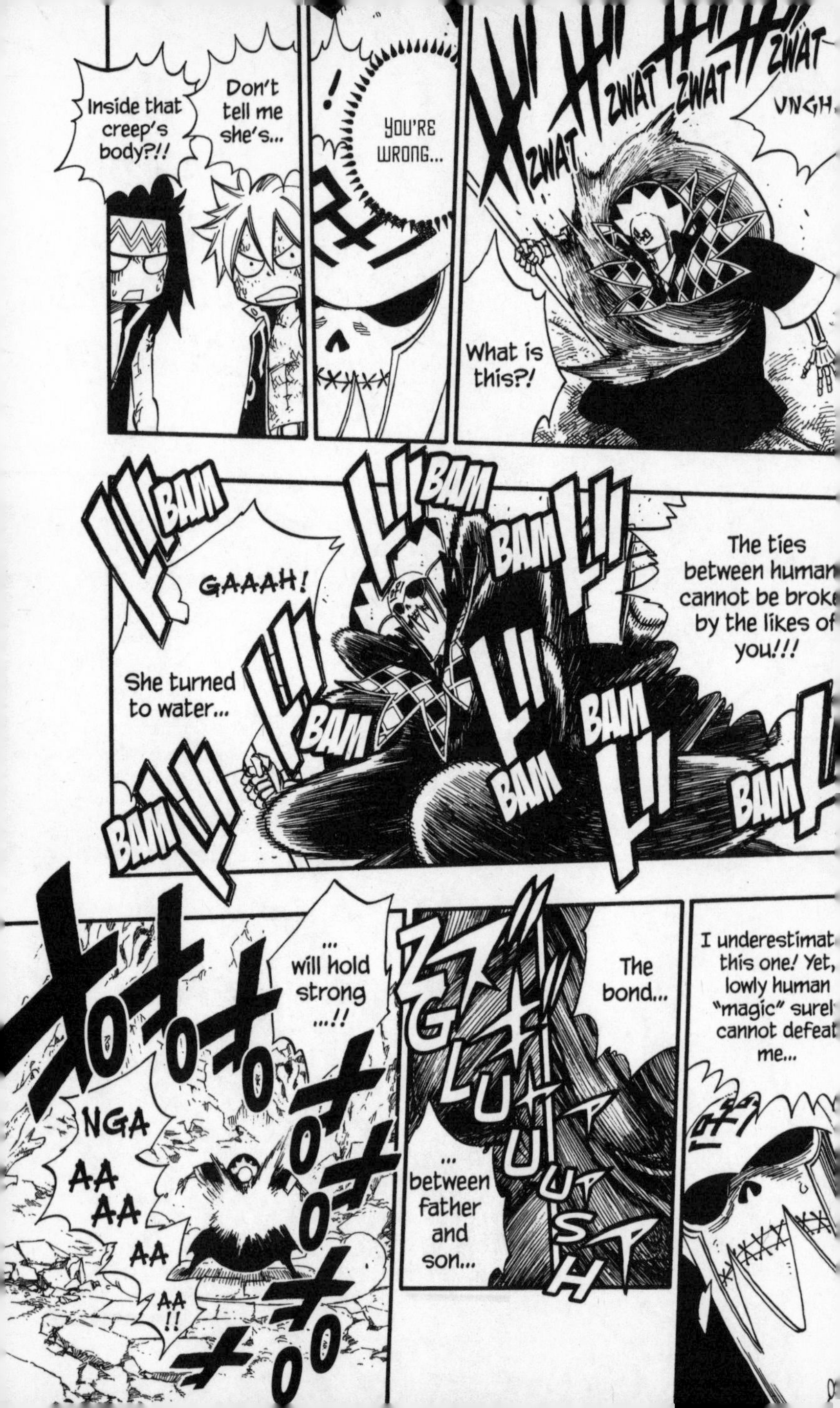
ZWAT ZWAT ZWAT ZWAT ZWAT
UNGH.
What is this?!
!
YOU'RE WRONG...
Don't tell me she's...
Inside that creep's body?!!
The ties between human cannot be broke by the likes of you!!!
BAM BAM BAM
GAAAH!
BAM BAM BAM BAM BAM
She turned to water...
BAM
I underestimat this one! Yet, lowly human "magic" surel cannot defeat me...
The bond...
... between father and son...
ZGLUUUUSH
... will hold strong ...!!
NGA AA AA AA AA!!

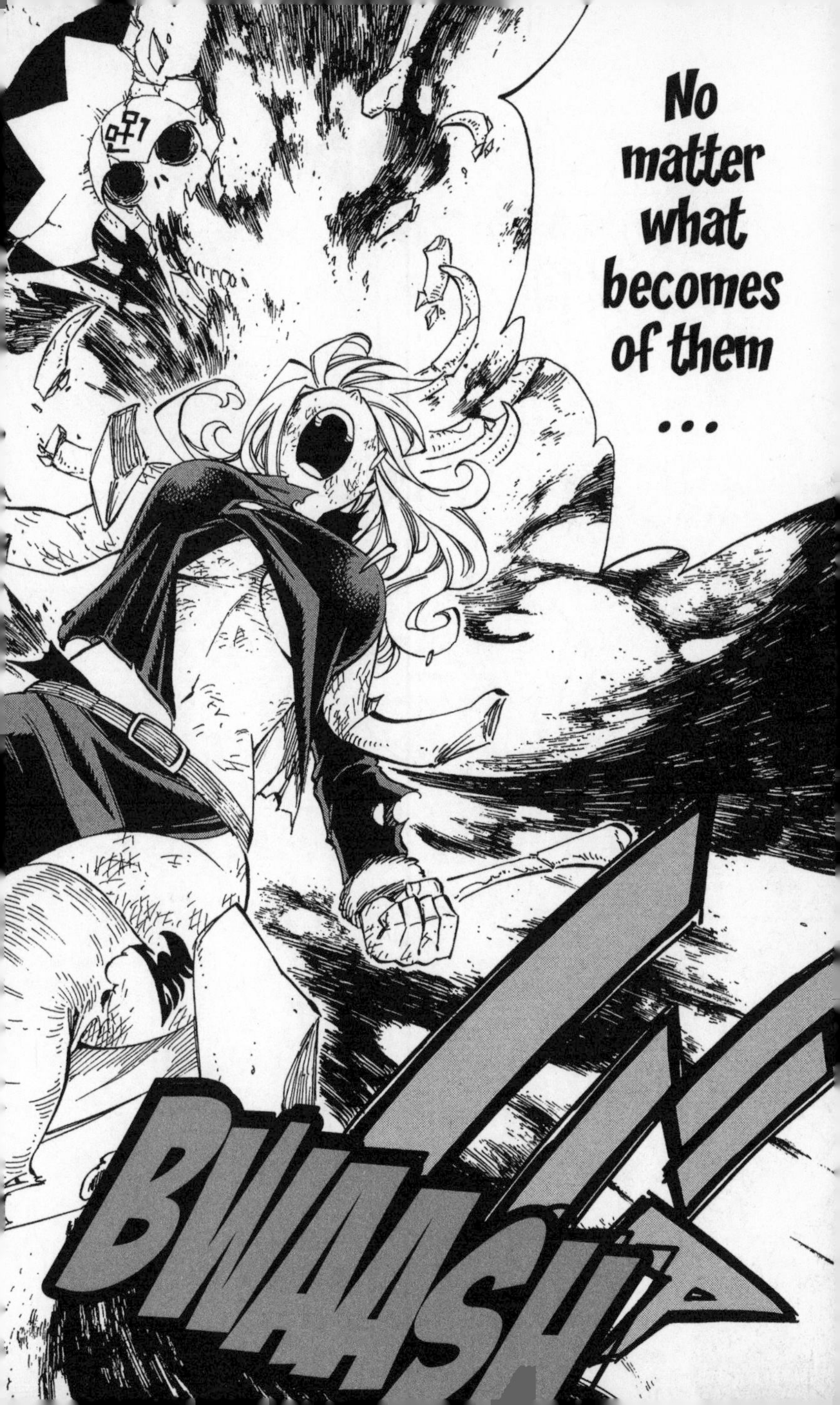
No matter what becomes of them ...
BWASH

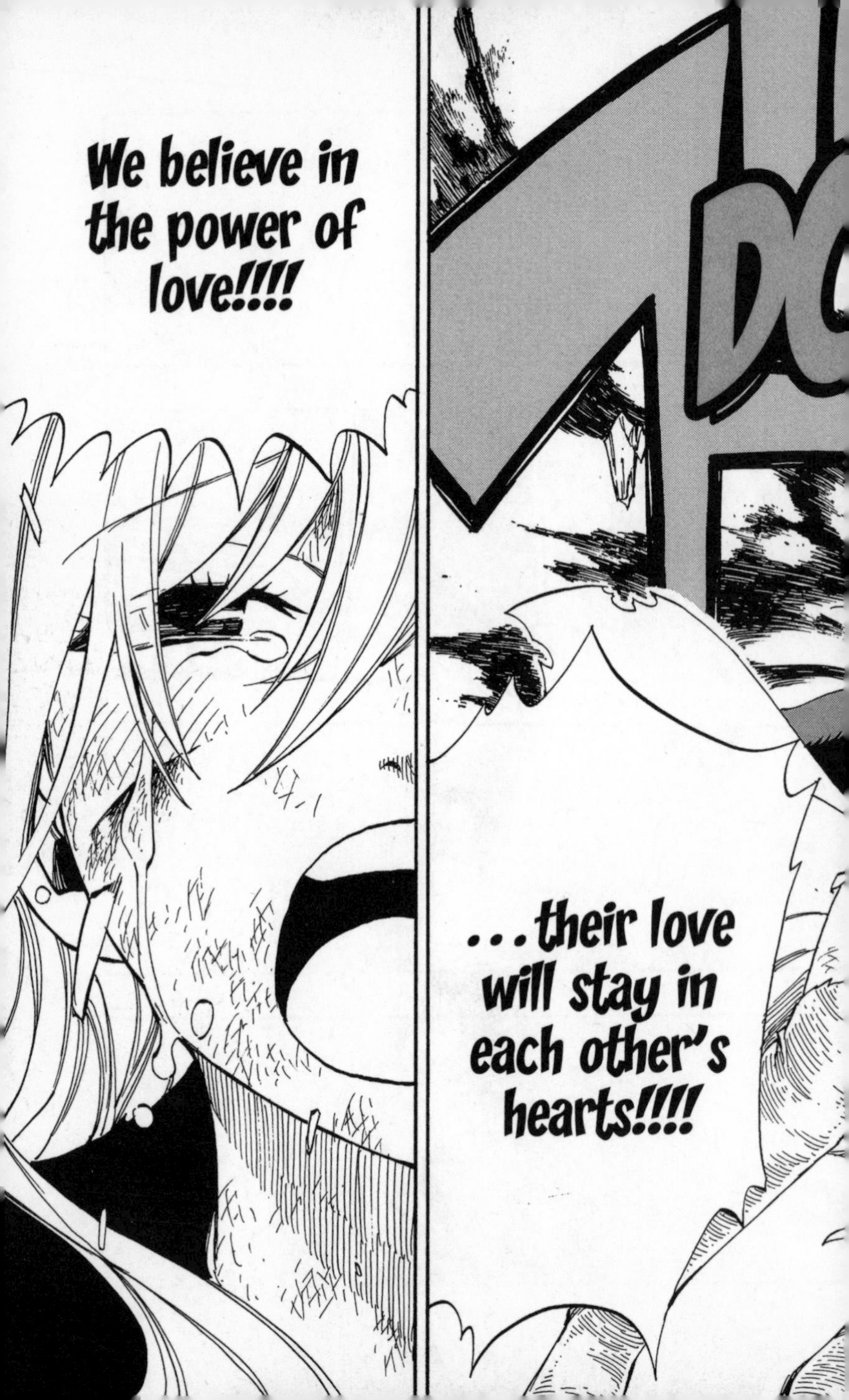
...their love will stay in each other's hearts!!!!
We believe in the power of love!!!!

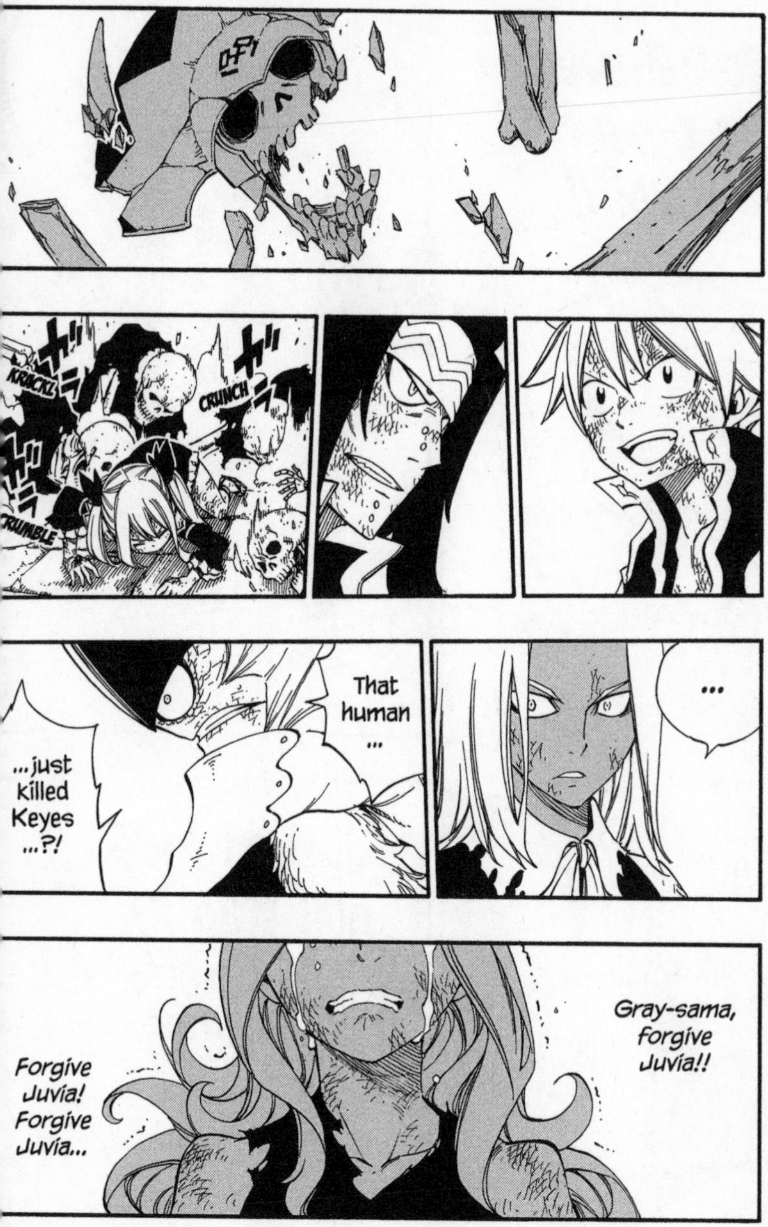
CRUNCH
KRACKL
CRUMBLE
...
That human ...
...just killed Keyes ...?!
Gray-sama, forgive Juvia!!
Forgive Juvia! Forgive Juvia...

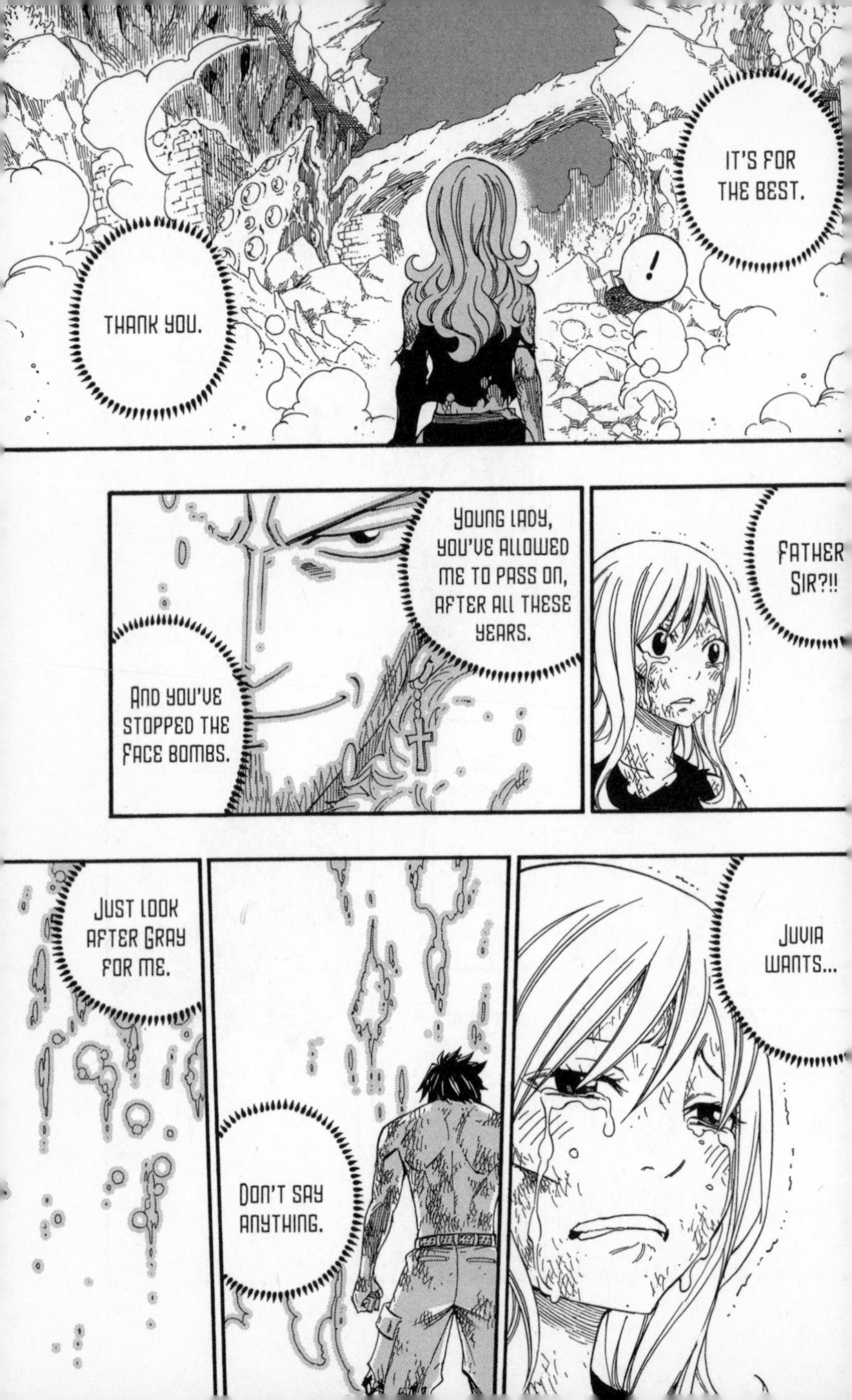
IT'S FOR THE BEST.
!
THANK YOU.
FATHER SIR?!!
YOUNG LADY, YOU'VE ALLOWED ME TO PASS ON, AFTER ALL THESE YEARS.
AND YOU'VE STOPPED THE FACE BOMBS.
JUVIA WANTS...
DON'T SAY ANYTHING.
JUST LOOK AFTER GRAY FOR ME.

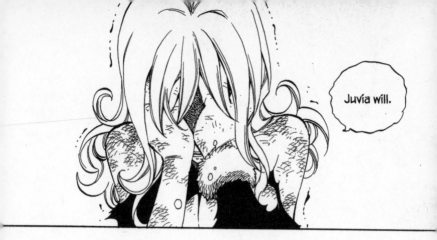

Juvia will.

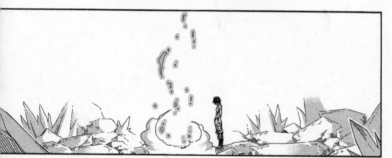

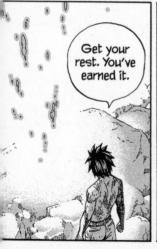

Get your rest. You've earned it.

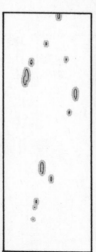

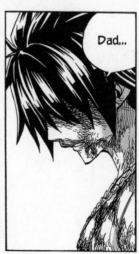

Dad...

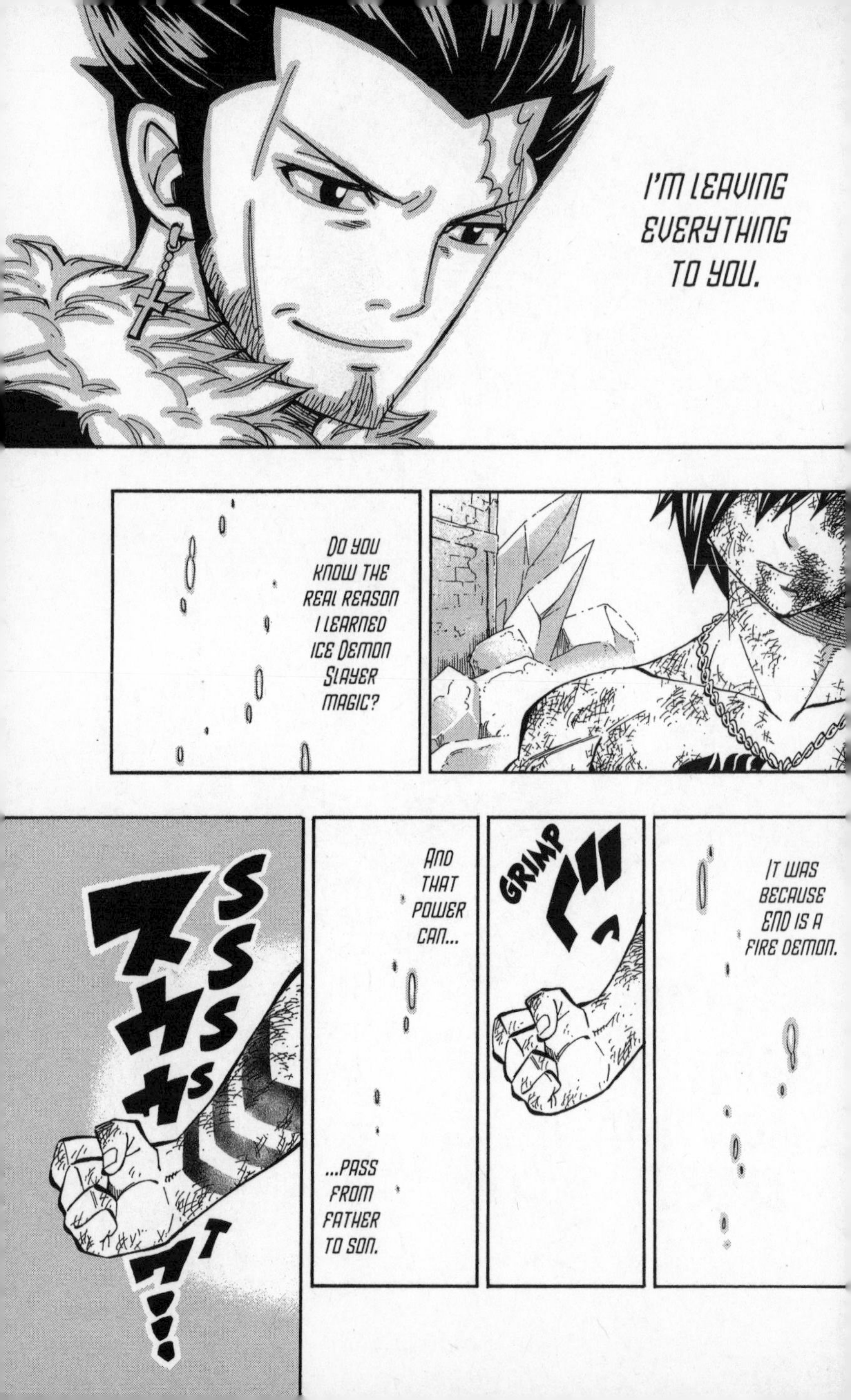
I'M LEAVING EVERYTHING TO YOU.
DO YOU KNOW THE REAL REASON I LEARNED ICE DEMON SLAYER MAGIC?
IT WAS BECAUSE END IS A FIRE DEMON.
GRIMP
AND THAT POWER CAN...
...PASS FROM FATHER TO SON.
SSSST

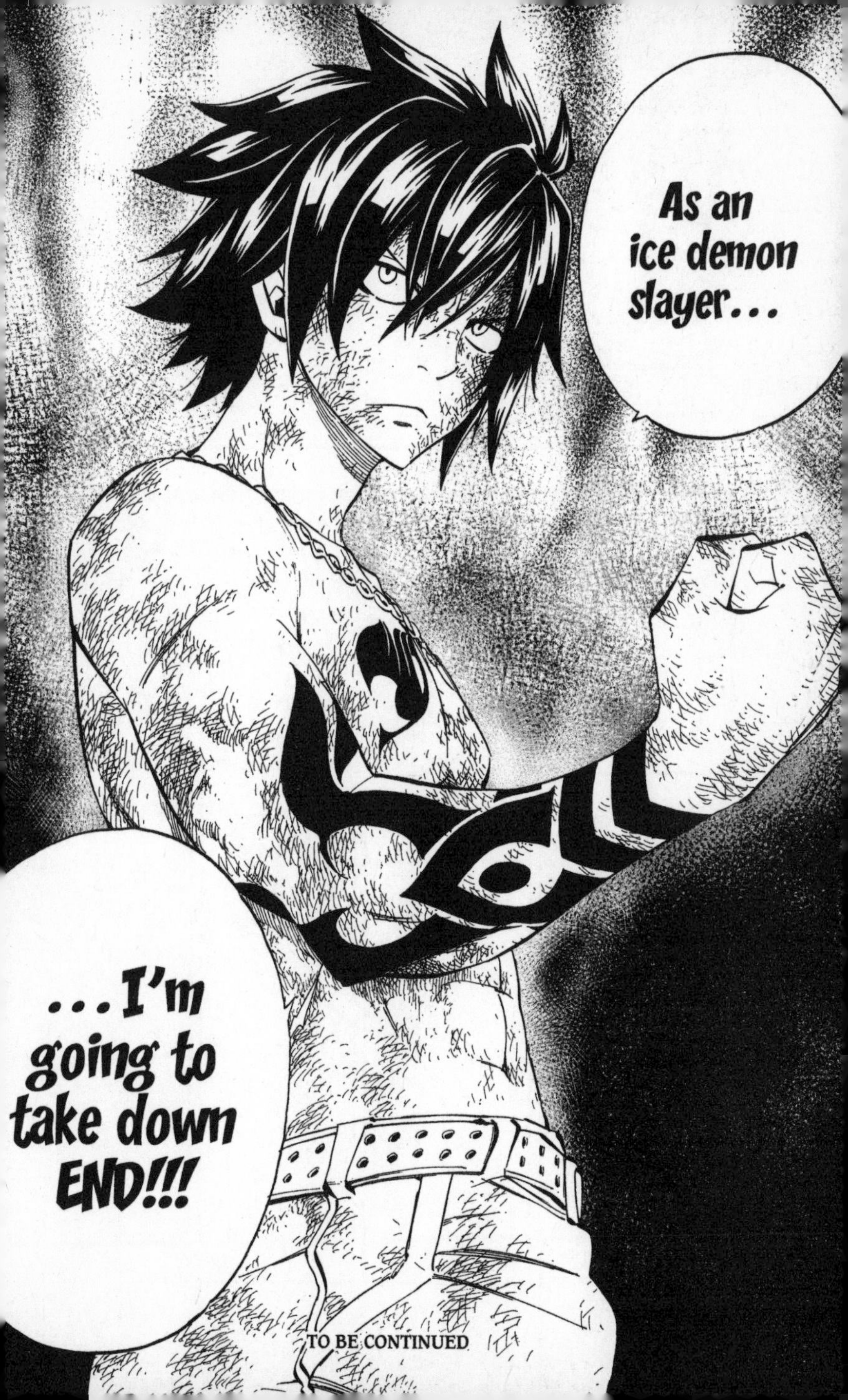
As an ice demon slayer...
...I'm going to take down END!!!
TO BE CONTINUED

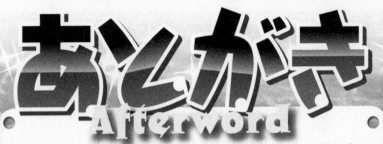

Afterword

I had thought up the story arc of Gray and Silver well before putting them in the Tartaros Arc, including pretty much how it ends, the ramifications, what becomes of Gray, and what becomes of Silver. They were all decided beforehand. And yet!!!! It was only right on the cusp before I started drawing their final battle that I realized **that something vital in the setup was wrong,** so to make sure that everything worked out logically, I had to change large portions of it in mid-stride. It was really rough! By the way, problems with the setup are a bad habit of mine.

In the past, too, I've had things wrong in the setup that caused a lot trouble and effort to patch. (Let this be a lesson that manga cannot be a slipshod affair.)

It really embarrasses me, so I won't go saying what it was in the setup that I got wrong or left out, but I think the final results didn't turn out too badly.

Now Gray is a demon slayer, but really, right from the very start, I figured that Gray would eventually become an ice dragon slayer, although that idea had to be rejected. I think it was rejected about the point when Gajeel showed up. But I recalled it about the time of his battle with Ultear because he had to stay an ice make wizard until at least that time. Then, just before the Grand Magic Games, I decided on making him a demon slayer. Now that Gray has obtained some really great power, keep your eyes on him!

The Gate to the Underworld, Tartaros

This is the dark guild that houses the Underworld King, Mard Geer and the Nine Demon Gates. Its master, END, is currently not acting in that capacity.

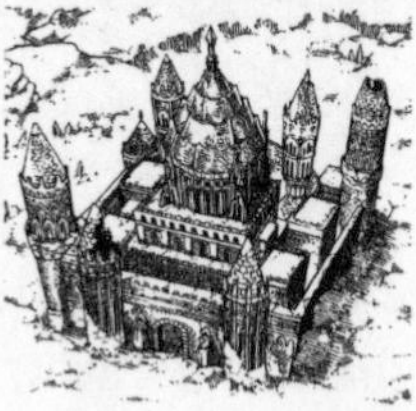

◀The guild exists on a huge chunk of floating earth called Cube.

Cube under the Alegria curse. It becomes a huge monster called Pluto's Grimm. ▶

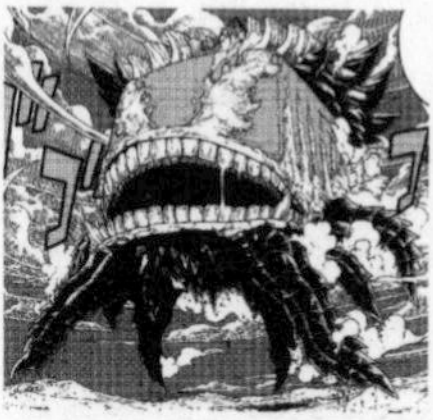

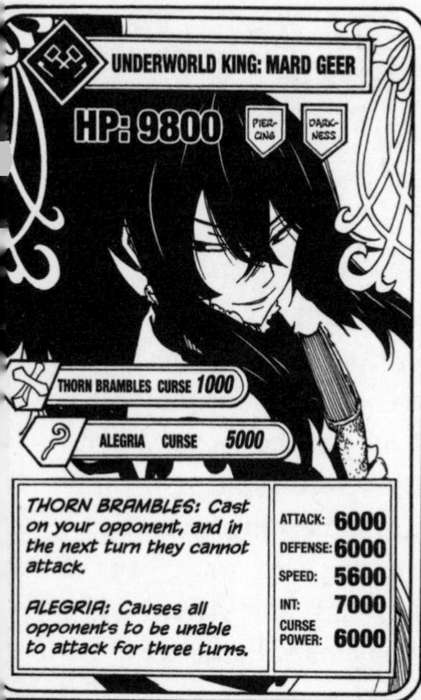
UNDERWORLD KING: MARD GEER
HP: 9800
PIERCING
DARKNESS
THORN BRAMBLES CURSE 1000
ALEGRIA CURSE 5000
THORN BRAMBLES: Cast on your opponent, and in the next turn they cannot attack.
ALEGRIA: Causes all opponents to be unable to attack for three turns.
ATTACK: 6000
DEFENSE: 6000
SPEED: 5600
INT: 7000
CURSE POWER: 6000

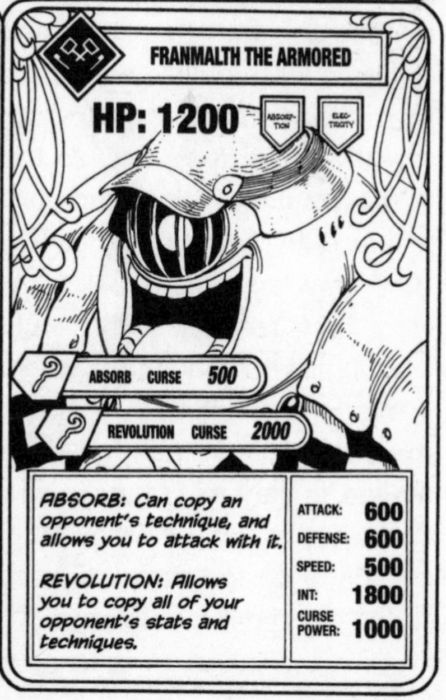
FRANMALTH THE ARMORED
HP: 1200
ABSORPTION
ELECTRICITY
ABSORB CURSE 500
REVOLUTION CURSE 2000
ABSORB: Can copy an opponent's technique, and allows you to attack with it.
REVOLUTION: Allows you to copy all of your opponent's stats and techniques.
ATTACK: 600
DEFENSE: 600
SPEED: 500
INT: 1800
CURSE POWER: 1000

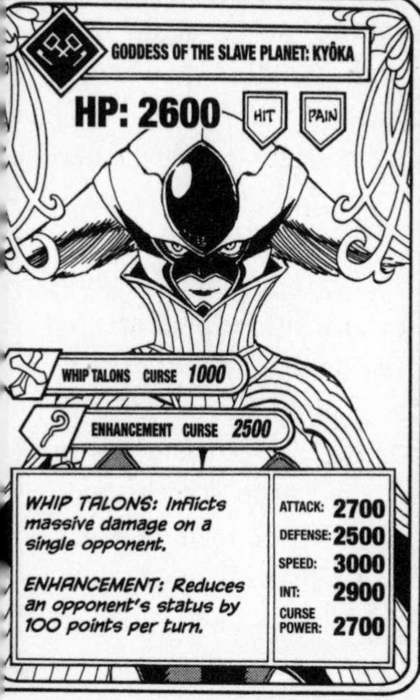
GODDESS OF THE SLAVE PLANET: KYÔKA
HP: 2600
HIT
PAIN
WHIP TALONS CURSE 1000
ENHANCEMENT CURSE 2500
WHIP TALONS: Inflicts massive damage on a single opponent.
ENHANCEMENT: Reduces an opponent's status by 100 points per turn.
ATTACK: 2700
DEFENSE: 2500
SPEED: 3000
INT: 2900
CURSE POWER: 2700

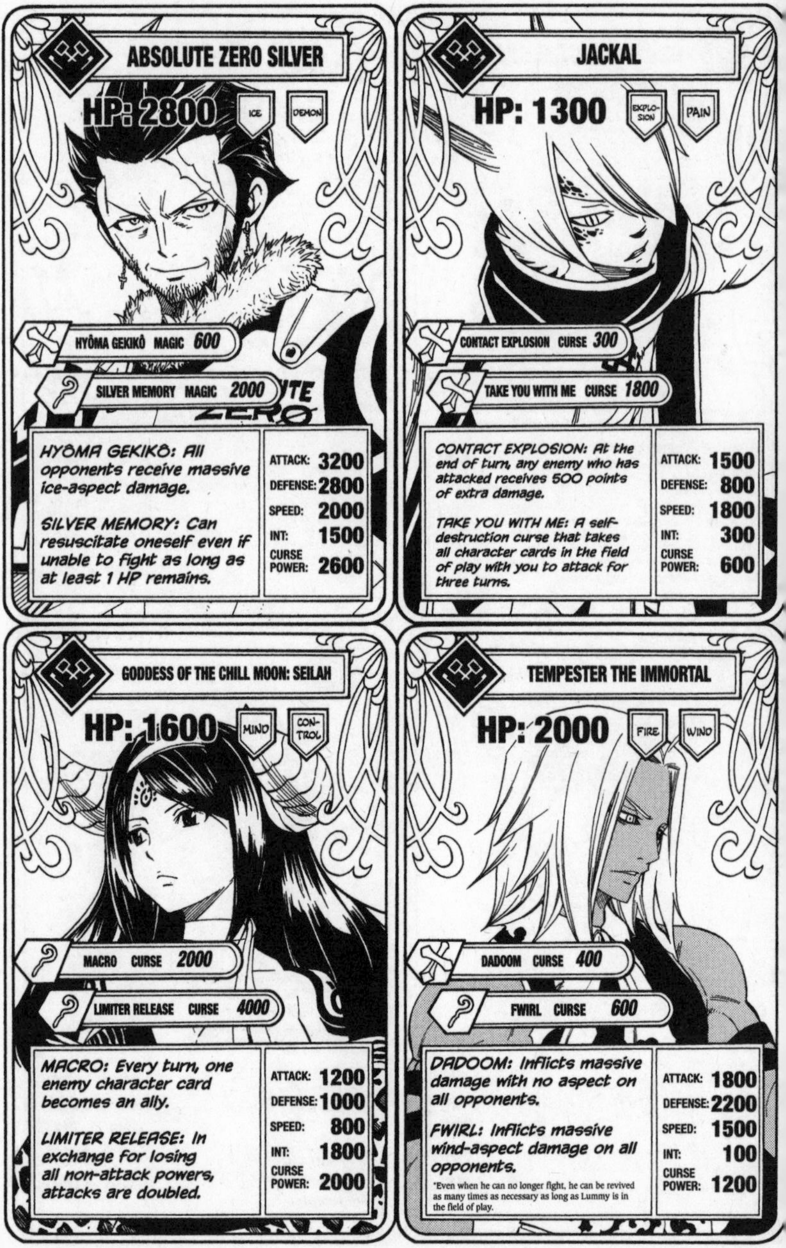
JACKAL
HP: 1300
EXPLOSION
PAIN
CONTACT EXPLOSION CURSE 300
TAKE YOU WITH ME CURSE 1800
CONTACT EXPLOSION: At the end of turn, any enemy who has attacked receives 500 points of extra damage.
TAKE YOU WITH ME: A self-destruction curse that takes all character cards in the field of play with you to attack for three turns.
ATTACK: 1500
DEFENSE: 800
SPEED: 1800
INT: 300
CURSE POWER: 600
ABSOLUTE ZERO SILVER
HP: 2800
ICE
DEMON
HYÔMA GEKIKÔ MAGIC 600
SILVER MEMORY MAGIC 2000
HYÔMA GEKIKÔ: All opponents receive massive ice-aspect damage.
SILVER MEMORY: Can resuscitate oneself even if unable to fight as long as at least 1 HP remains.
ATTACK: 3200
DEFENSE: 2800
SPEED: 2000
INT: 1500
CURSE POWER: 2600
TEMPESTER THE IMMORTAL
HP: 2000
FIRE
WIND
DADOOM CURSE 400
FWIRL CURSE 600
DADOOM: Inflicts massive damage with no aspect on all opponents.
FWIRL: Inflicts massive wind-aspect damage on all opponents.
*Even when he can no longer fight, he can be revived as many times as necessary as long as Lummy is in the field of play.
ATTACK: 1800
DEFENSE: 2200
SPEED: 1500
INT: 100
CURSE POWER: 1200
GODDESS OF THE CHILL MOON: SEILAH
HP: 1600
MIND
CONTROL
MACRO CURSE 2000
LIMITER RELEASE CURSE 4000
MACRO: Every turn, one enemy character card becomes an ally.
LIMITER RELEASE: In exchange for losing all non-attack powers, attacks are doubled.
ATTACK: 1200
DEFENSE: 1000
SPEED: 800
INT: 1800
CURSE POWER: 2000

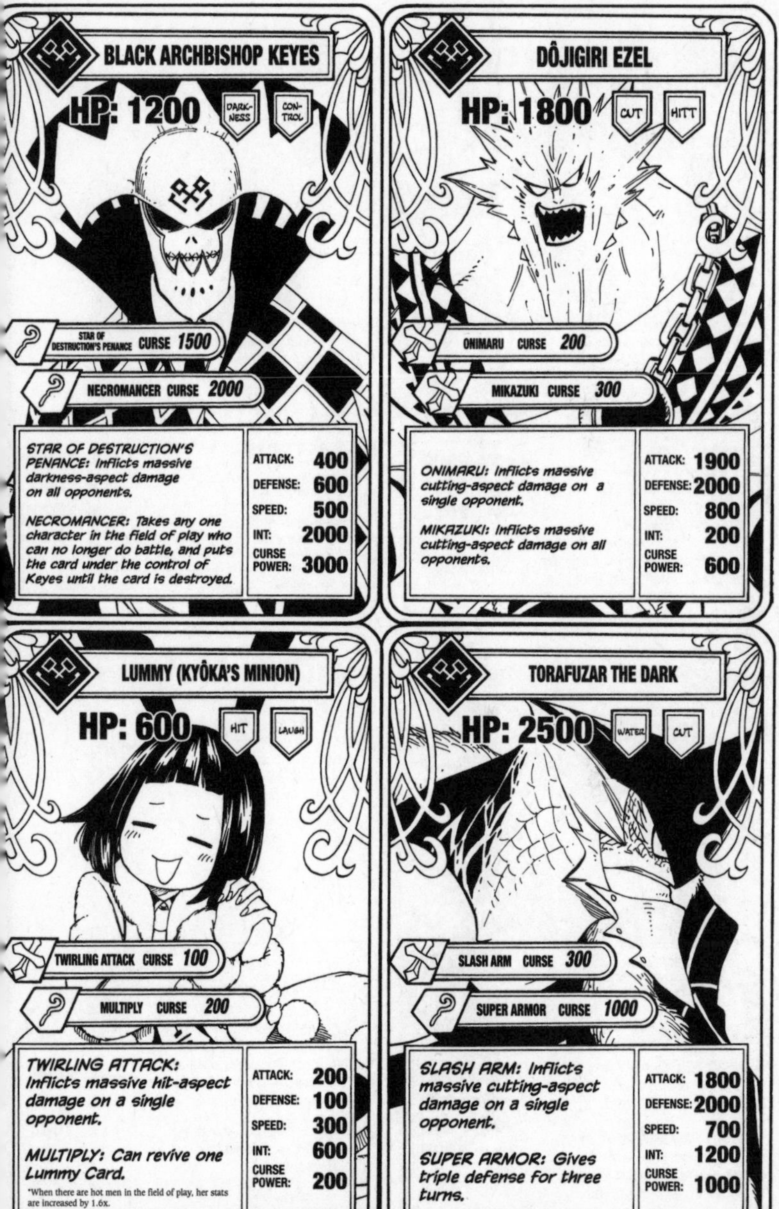
DÔJIGIRI EZEL
HP: 1800
CUT
HITT
ONIMARU CURSE 200
MIKAZUKI CURSE 300
ONIMARU: Inflicts massive cutting-aspect damage on a single opponent.
MIKAZUKI: Inflicts massive cutting-aspect damage on all opponents.
ATTACK: 1900
DEFENSE: 2000
SPEED: 800
INT: 200
CURSE POWER: 600
BLACK ARCHBISHOP KEYES
HP: 1200
DARK-NESS
CON-TROL
STAR OF DESTRUCTION'S PENANCE CURSE 1500
NECROMANCER CURSE 2000
STAR OF DESTRUCTION'S PENANCE: Inflicts massive darkness-aspect damage on all opponents.
NECROMANCER: Takes any one character in the field of play who can no longer do battle, and puts the card under the control of Keyes until the card is destroyed.
ATTACK: 400
DEFENSE: 600
SPEED: 500
INT: 2000
CURSE POWER: 3000
TORAFUZAR THE DARK
HP: 2500
WATER
CUT
SLASH ARM CURSE 300
SUPER ARMOR CURSE 1000
SLASH ARM: Inflicts massive cutting-aspect damage on a single opponent.
SUPER ARMOR: Gives triple defense for three turns.
ATTACK: 1800
DEFENSE: 2000
SPEED: 700
INT: 1200
CURSE POWER: 1000
LUMMY (KYÔKA'S MINION)
HP: 600
HIT
LAUGH
TWIRLING ATTACK CURSE 100
MULTIPLY CURSE 200
TWIRLING ATTACK: Inflicts massive hit-aspect damage on a single opponent.
MULTIPLY: Can revive one Lummy Card.
*When there are hot men in the field of play, her stats are increased by 1.6x.
ATTACK: 200
DEFENSE: 100
SPEED: 300
INT: 600
CURSE POWER: 200

*This is just a way to introduce the characters as if it were a trading card game. There aren't any actual rules in reality.

This is a special edition of Guild d'Art! There are three brand-new Fairy Tail spinoff manga, and the artists of each have graced us with character illustrations in their personal styles!!

GUILD d' ART DELUXE 3

デラックス

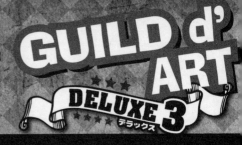

BOKU

"FAIRY GIRLS" started in the December 2014 issue of Magazine Special.

ジュビアはかわいくて描くのが
楽しいですね!!
グレイが羨ましいです(笑)
Boku
GRAY
LOVE

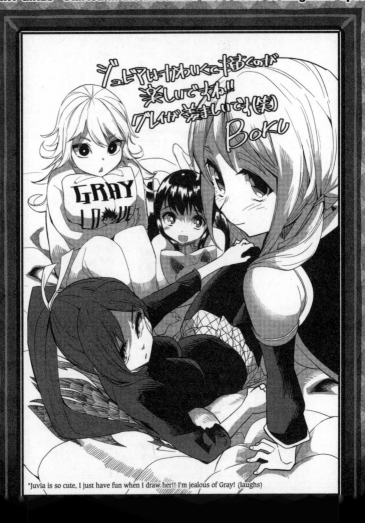

*Juvia is so cute, I just have fun when I draw her!! I'm jealous of Gray! (laughs)

GUILD d'ART

DELUXE 3

デラックス

YUUSUKE SHIRATO

Twitter Account: @yuusukeshirato

"TALE OF FAIRY TAIL: ICE TRAIL" runs in Monthly Fairy Tail Magazine.

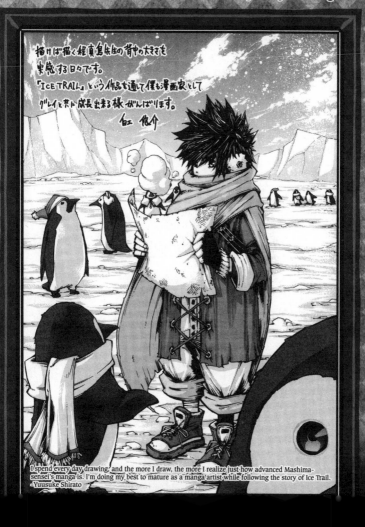

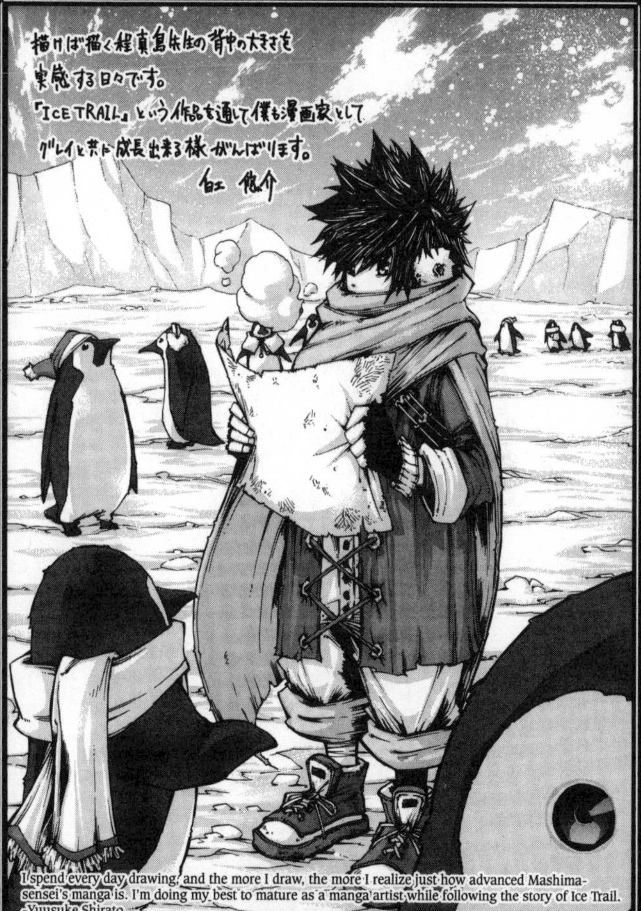
描けば描く程真島先生の背中の大きさを
実感する日々です。
「ICE TRAIL」という作品を通して僕も漫画家として
グレイと共に成長出来る様がんばります。
白土 悠介

I spend every day drawing, and the more I draw, the more I realize just how advanced Mashima-sensei's manga is. I'm doing my best to mature as a manga artist while following the story of Ice Trail.
-Yuusuke Shirato

GUILD d'ART DELUXE 3 デラックス

RUI WATANABE

Twitter Account: @naguwan

"FAIRY TAIL BLUE MISTRAL" is running in Nakayoshi.

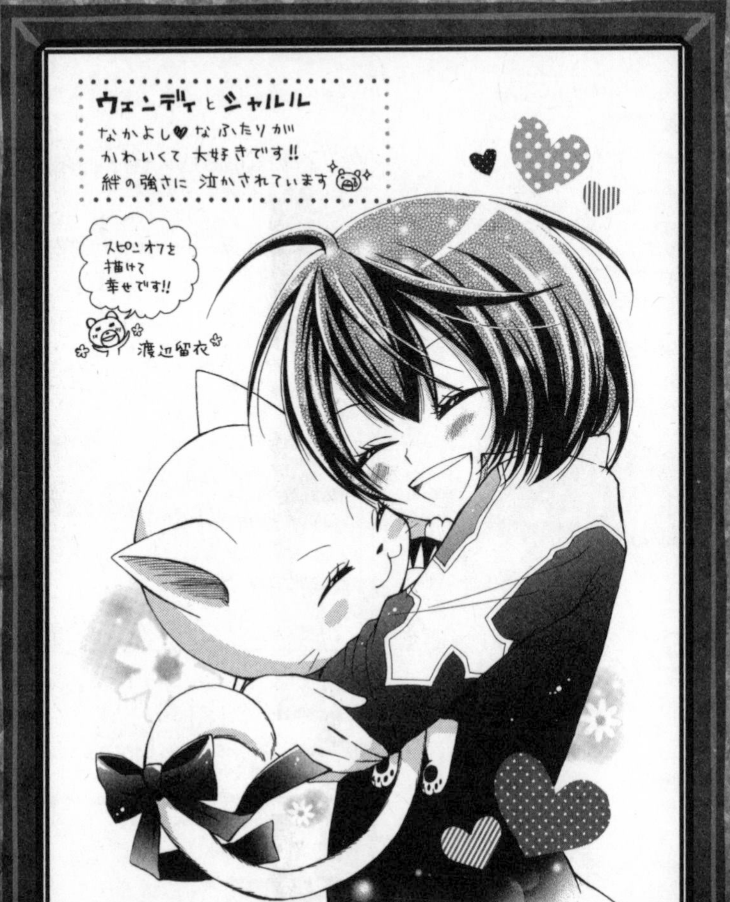

ウェンディとシャルル
なかよし♥なふたりが
かわいくて大好きです!!
絆の強さに泣かされています
スピンオフを描けて幸せです!!
渡辺留衣

Wendy & Carla
I love these two best [heart] friends!! They're just so cute!! Their bonds are so tight, it can even make me cry! I'm so happy to be doing this spinoff!! -Rui Watanabe

Continued from the left-hand page.

Lucy: No... I'm positive you'll play a really big role after this! I'm sure of it!

Mira: I think... I won't even show up again...

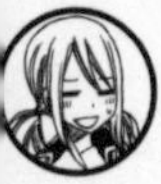
: No, no... See, I read a little bit ahead, so I know this for sure...

Mira: Really? Hold on. I'm checking Vol. 47...

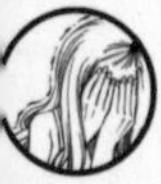
: WAAAH...

Lucy: Mira-san!! Pull yourself together!!

Mira: Yeah... I'm all right...

Lucy: The story arc's not over yet! I'm sure you'll do something great! You know?

Mira: Yeah... Okay. We'll have fun with the next question.

Will Wendy's hair ever go back to its original length?

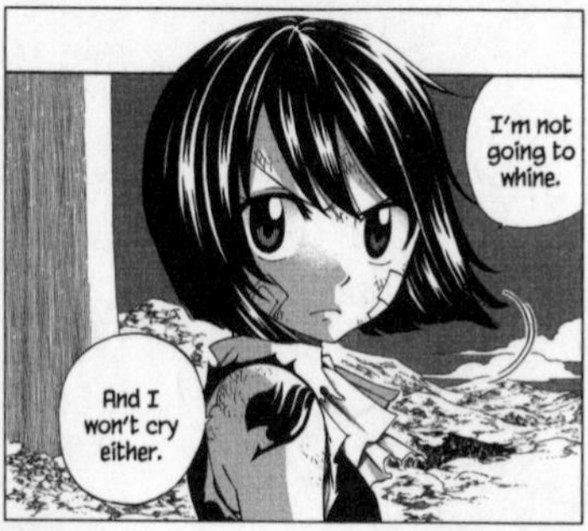
I'm not going to whine.
And I won't cry either.

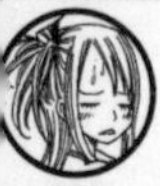
: Sniff...

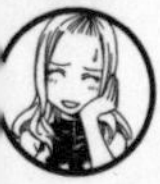
: Sniff, sniff...

Lucy: Wendy... really looked good in her long hair.

Mira: It'll grow back! Hey, there's even magic that will allow hair to grow back, right?

Lucy: Yeah, right! I could get Cancer on it!

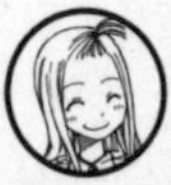
: Good! *This* is how we can have fun!

Lucy: He's a celestial spirit friend...

Mira: ?

Lucy: A celestial... Sniff...

Mira: Lucy?

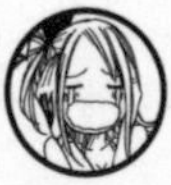
: Waaah! I want Aquarius back!! Waaah!

Mira: Oh, dear...

Lucy: I'm... sorry... I couldn't help it... Sniff...

Mira: This is our very last question, and we're going to have fun with it!

Lucy: Yes, ma'am!

Would you mind telling me Ichiya's measurements?

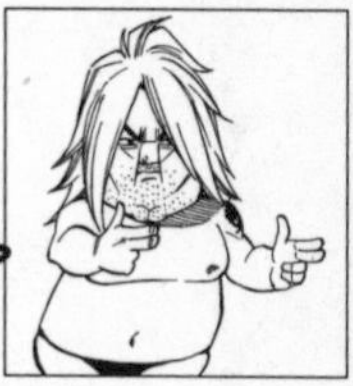

Mira: ...

Lucy: ...

Mira: Okay, I think that's enough for this time.

Lucy: But ***next*** time, we're going to have so much fun!

Mira: See you!

Lucy: Bye-bye!

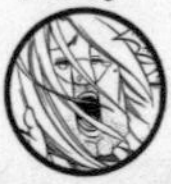
: Can't you guys answer a simple question?! Meeeeeeen!

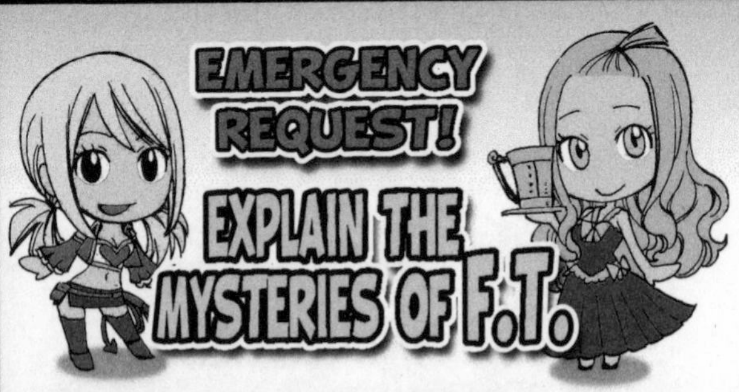
EMERGENCY REQUEST!
EXPLAIN THE MYSTERIES OF F.T.

In a certain café...

Mira: Hi there!

Lucy: Hi there!!

Mira: That's out of the way. So let's make this fun!

Lucy: Right!

Won't we ever see Aquarius again?

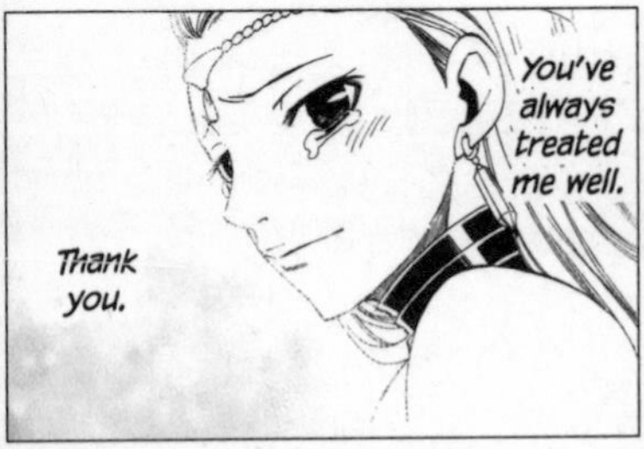
You've always treated me well.
Thank you.

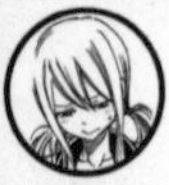 : Sniff...

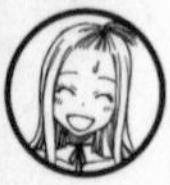 : Oh, dear...

Lucy: That's a question... I can't... have fun with...

Mira: We got a lot of this question.

Lucy: I... don't know what to say...

Mira: You don't need to say anything. I'm sure you'll meet again sometime. Let's trust in that.

Lucy: Yes... Yes, I guess so.

Mira: Now, let's get the fun back into this! Let's take the next question, and have fun! Fun!!

Mira-chan doesn't get to do very much during this story arc, does she?

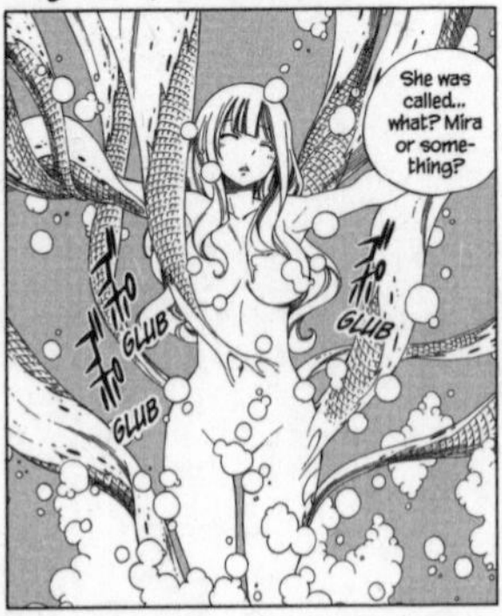
She was called... what? Mira or something?
GLUB
GLUB
GLUB

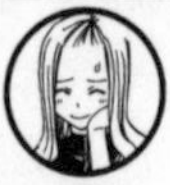 : Sniff...

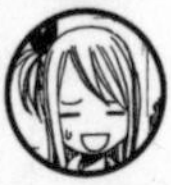 : Oh, dear...

Mira: Yes, I know that I was quickly captured right at the beginning, and that it was Elfman who came in at the end to finish the fight with Seilah...

Continued on the right-hand page.

TAIL d'ART International

We have a special expanded version of Guild d'Art this time!! We have thirty pieces of fan art from overseas fans to show you! But it's only because Fairy Tail has such passionate support that we can bring this art show to the printed page! So here is the hard work from dedicated fans of ten different nations! This proves that national borders are no hindrance for the love of Fairy Tail!!

France, Cécilia D

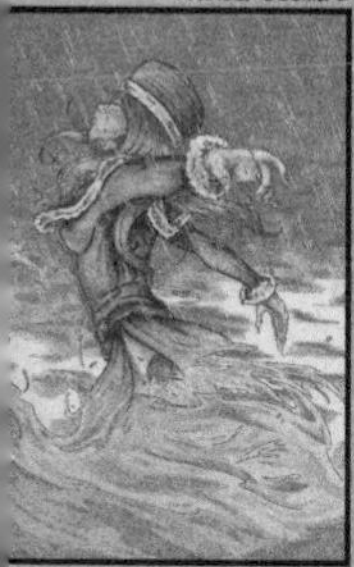

▲ This one is a beautiful ainting! It's too bad we an't print it in color!!

Brazil, Rafael Francoi

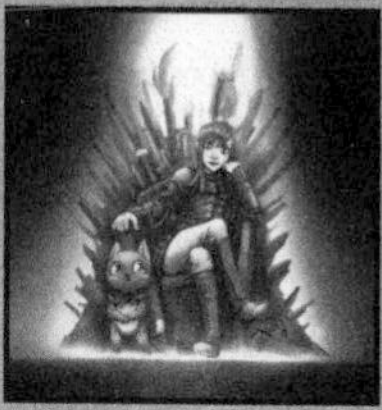

▲ Erza as a king! She wears it well! Happy looks cool too!

▼ There are the members of Fairy Tail in Brazil!! Yay!!

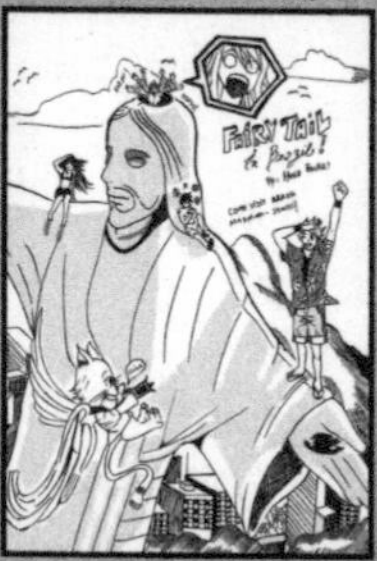

Brazil, Hugo Rocha

Brazil, Lucas Pedro Emiliano

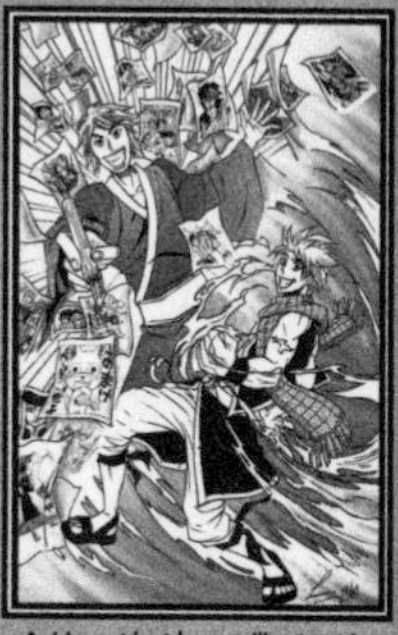

▲ Hey, that's an illustration of me (Mashima), isn't it? Thank you!!

That's really good!! A Natsu who looks like he's trying to talk a girl into dating him. That's a rare image! ▶

Italy, neeva

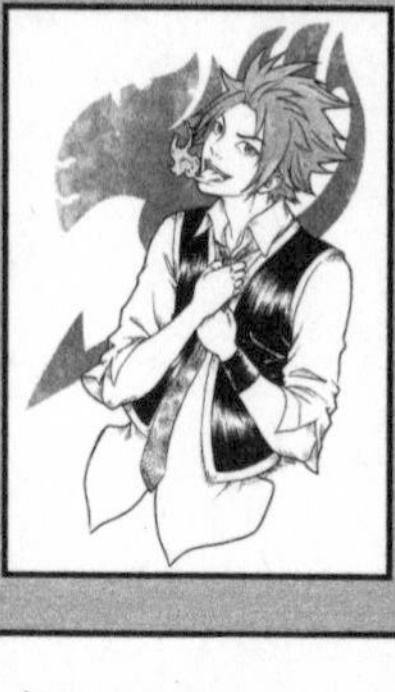

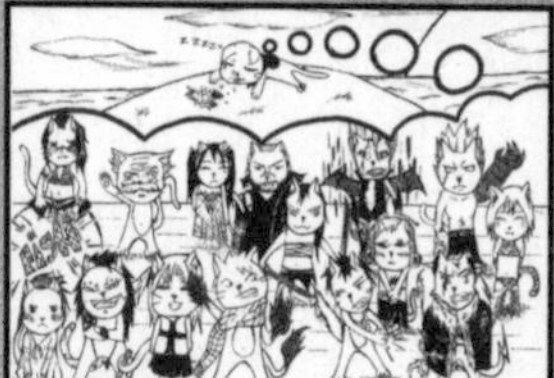

Italy, Damiano Mescia

What's this?!! ◀ Everybody's turned into cats!! Then suddenly I realize it's Happy's dream.

By sending in letters or postcards, you give us permission to give your name, address, postal code, and any other information you include to the artist as-is. Please keep that in mind.

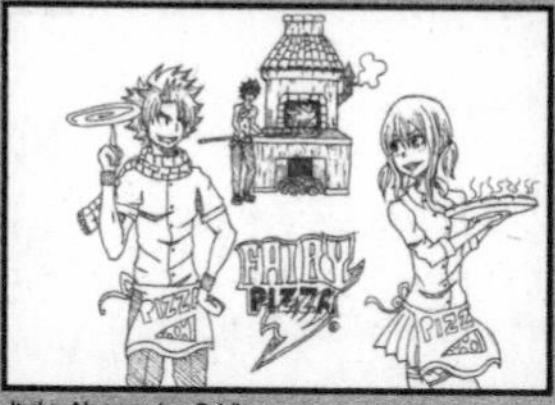
FAIRY
PIZZA

Italy, Alessandro Oddi

When ◀ you say, "Italy," the first thing you think of is pizza, right? It tastes soooo good!

Send to Hiro Mashima, Kodansha Comics

451 Park Ave. South, 7th Floor New York, NY 10016

FAIRY GUILD

Germany, Michelle Hauschild

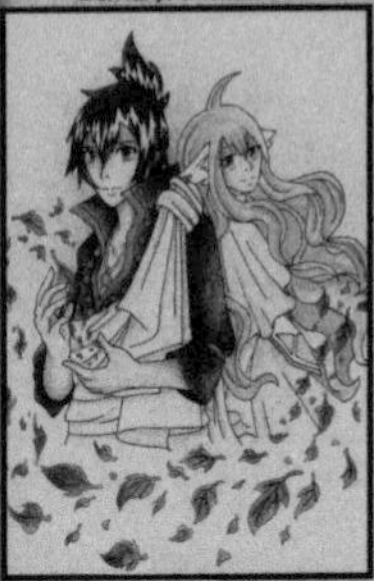

▲Zeref and Mavis. What is the relationship between these two?

▼The pretzel is Germany's best hot snack!! This piece of art makes me glad we're doing an international Guild d'Art!

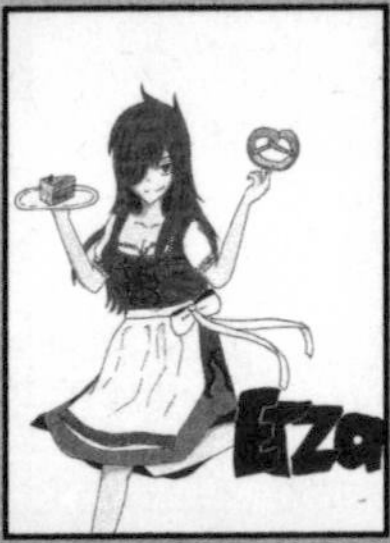
Erza

Germany, D. Placzek

France, Lucille M.t

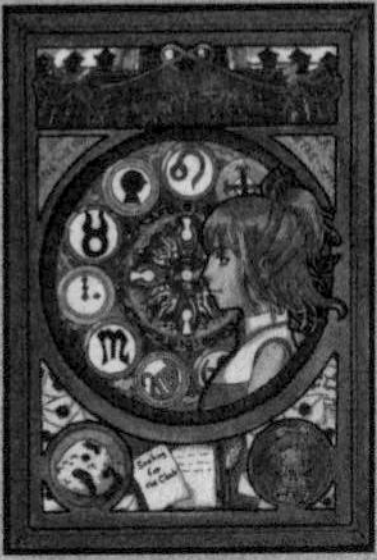

▲This piece is just gorgeous from layout and design all the way through!! Even the small elements are fully rendered!!

France, Laure

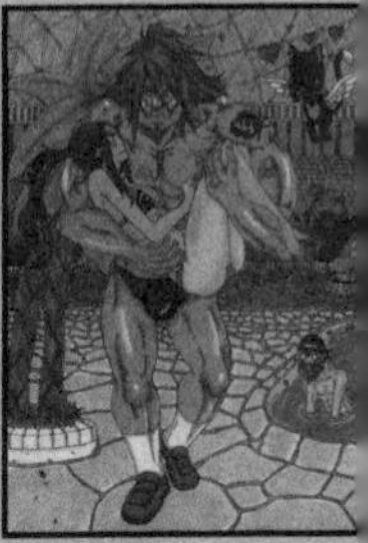

▲Ichiyaaaa!!! But why are you in socks and shoes? What wonderful perfume!!

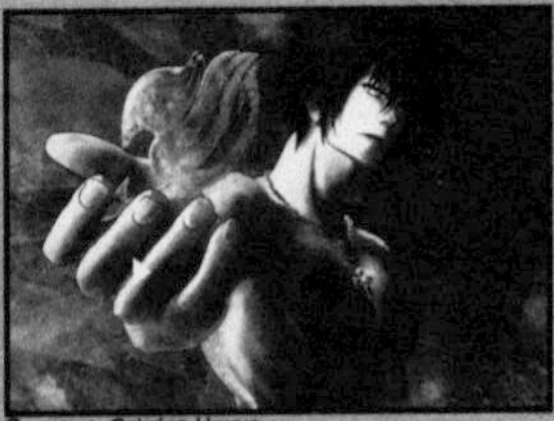

Germany, Sabrina Hoque

Whoa!! ◀ Cool!! Gray with an Ice Make of the Fairy Tail symbol! Great layout here!

Everybody ▶ on their way to school!! It seems kind of fun!!

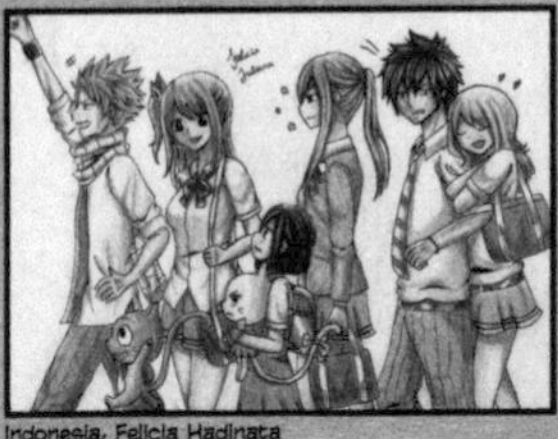

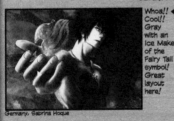

Indonesia, Felicia Hadinata

▼I love this for the warm feeling the colored pencils give the art!! Decisive Lucy!

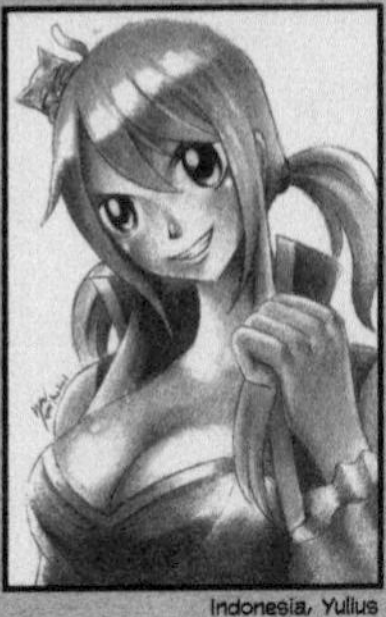

Indonesia, Yulius

Indonesia, Henry Trisula

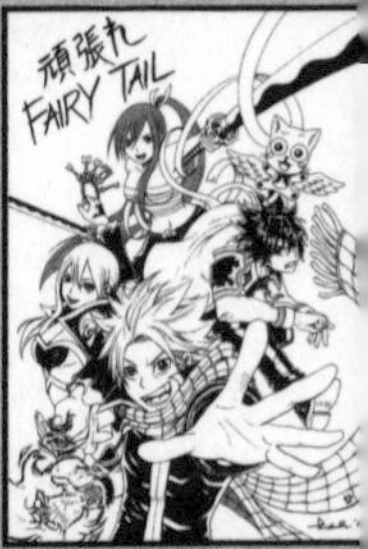
頑張れ
FAIRY TAIL

▲The stance a character takes when casting magic can be really cool! And go Japanese there!

TAIL d'ART International

The Fairy Tail Guild is looking for illustrations! Please send in your art on a postcard or at postcard size, and do it in black pen, okay? Those chosen to be published will get a signed mini poster! ♪ Make sure you write your real name and address on the back of your illustration!

▼ Wow, that's good!! Lisanna here is really cute!! And Natsu and Happy off to the side are really cute too!

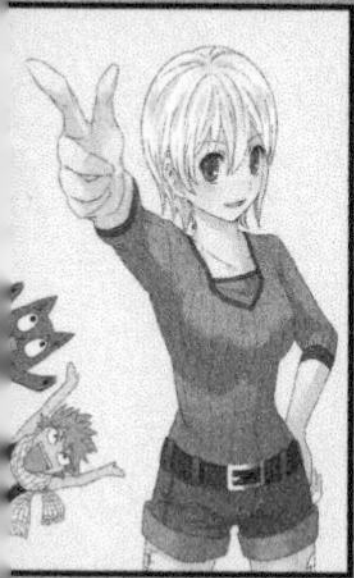

Taiwan, Ayakashi

Korea, Kim Teri

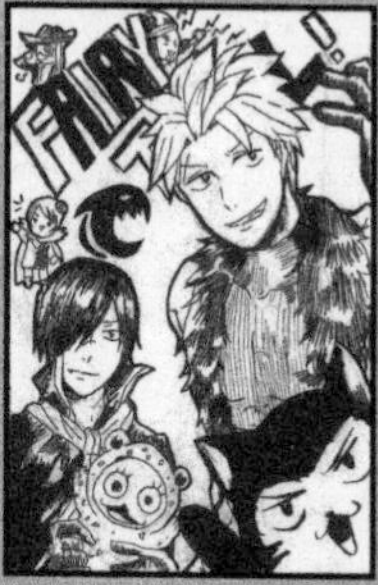

▲ All members of Saber Tooth, fall in!! I really like Rogue's face as he holds Frosch!

▼ Laxus when he was young! But even so, he's still plenty young now.

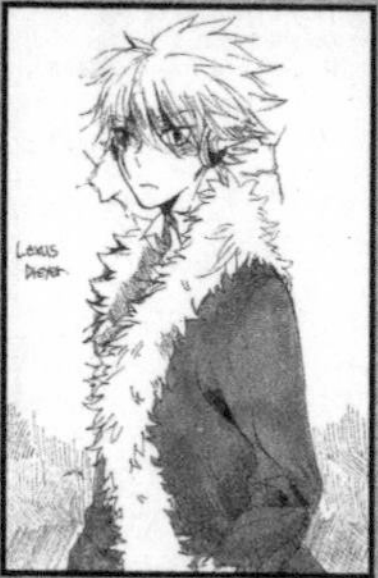

Korea, Puwa

Korea, NG

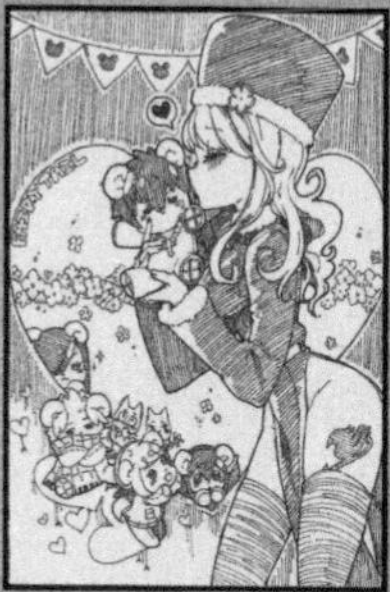

▲ A beautiful illustration of Juvia! That's a stuffed animal, huh? It all is so cute!

By sending in letters or postcards, you give us permission to give your name, address, postal code, and any other information you include to the artist as-is. Please keep that in mind.

Spain, Pol00

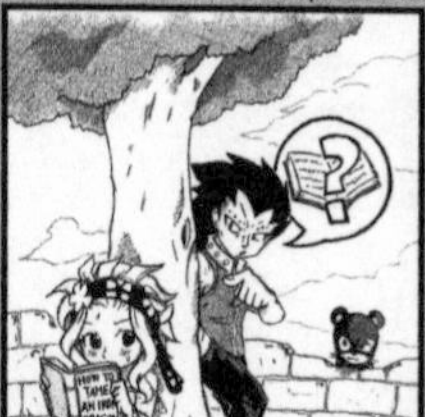

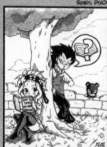

▲ Gajeel and Levy from Spain!! This pair is really popular overseas!!

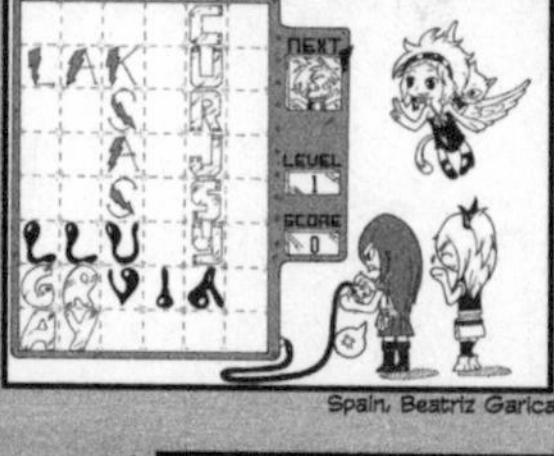
NEXT
LEVEL
1
SCORE
0

Spain, Beatriz Garica

I wonder ◀ what the rules to this game are. But it looks fun!

Lucy's ▶ really sexy here!! And behind her, Natsu and Happy are going strong!

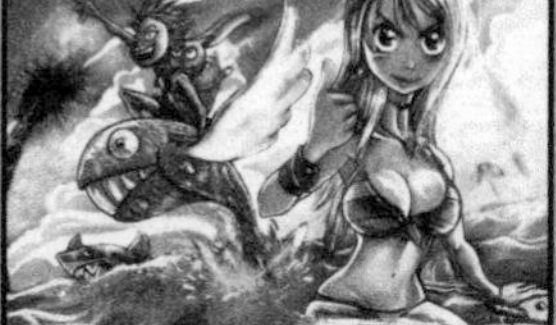

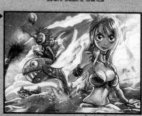

Spain, Charlie Casado

Send to Hiro Mashima, Kodansha Comics
451 Park Ave. South, 7th Floor New York, NY 10016

FAIRY
GUILD

▼An American Gajeel and Levy! Levy's clothes are really cute!!

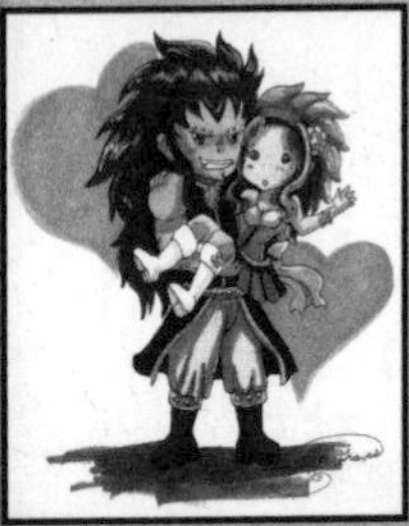

America, Amber Graves

All the dragon slayers have turned into cats! It looks good on Wendy! ▶

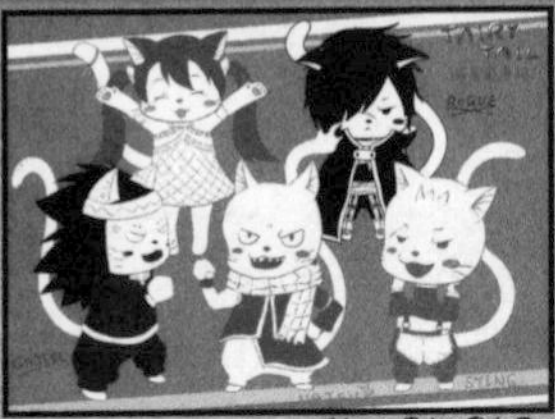

Taiwan, Flying Fish Roe

Taiwan, Miyako Ka

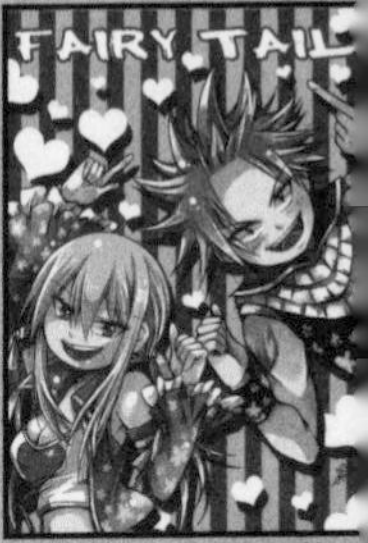
FAIRY TAIL

▲What a cool pattern!! Ar the texture of the clothes they're wearing is nice, too

Whoa, cute!! It makes me want to draw those clothes somewhere in the main story!! ▶

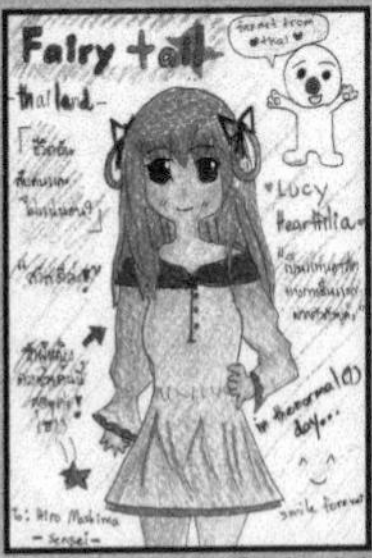
Fairy tail

Thailand, Nichnan Tangjitrapitak

Everybody when they were kids!! It brings back memories seeing Mirajane looking that way!! ▶

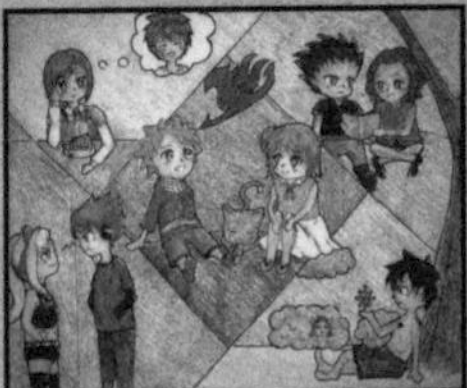

America, Angie Lin

Thailand, Isiya Reungboor

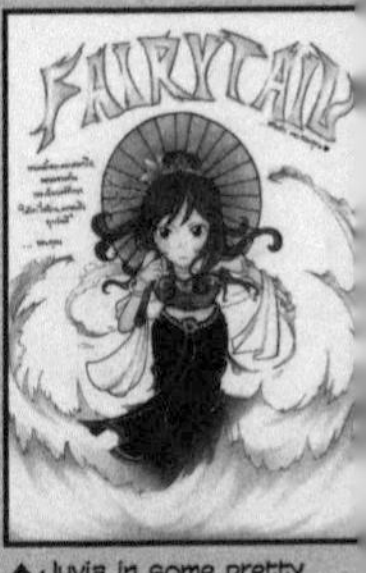
FAIRYTAIL

▲Juvia in some pretty exotic clothing! Thanks for the art all the way from Thailand!!

America, Devin Fuoco

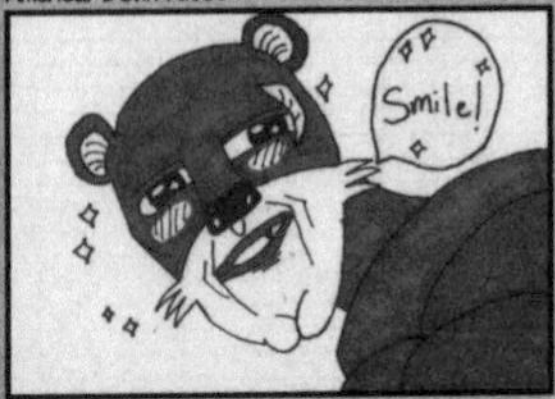
Smile!

▲ A Lily smile in America!! Meeeeeen!!

A fairy Natsu! The entire design actually shines!! ▶

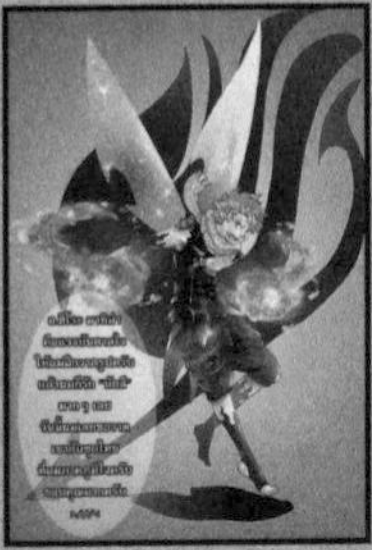

Thailand, Isiya Reungboont

Spot the Differences!

The page below looks just like page 48!!
But when you look closer, something's not right...

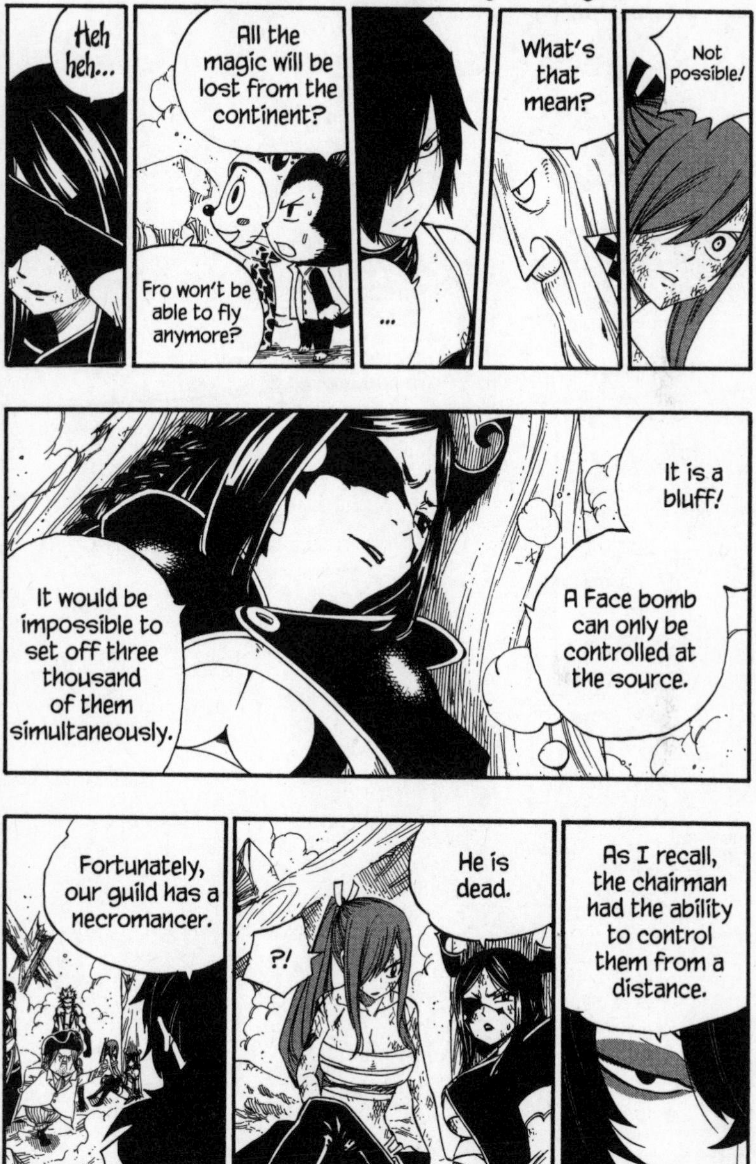
Not possible!
What's that mean?
...
All the magic will be lost from the continent?
Fro won't be able to fly anymore?
Heh heh...
It is a bluff!
A Face bomb can only be controlled at the source.
It would be impossible to set off three thousand of them simultaneously.
As I recall, the chairman had the ability to control them from a distance.
He is dead.
?!
Fortunately, our guild has a necromancer.

There are 10 differences in all!! Can you find them?

FROM HIRO MASHIMA

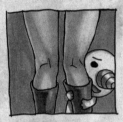

Recently, I've been chasing both weekly and monthly deadlines, so I've been incredibly busy. And at the end of each month, I have two deadlines at exactly the same time, and I have to have two different *name* (sketch manga for editorial review) ready for my editors. Hm… I think I need to get my act together better or my balloon's going to burst!

Original Jacket Design: Hisao Ogawa

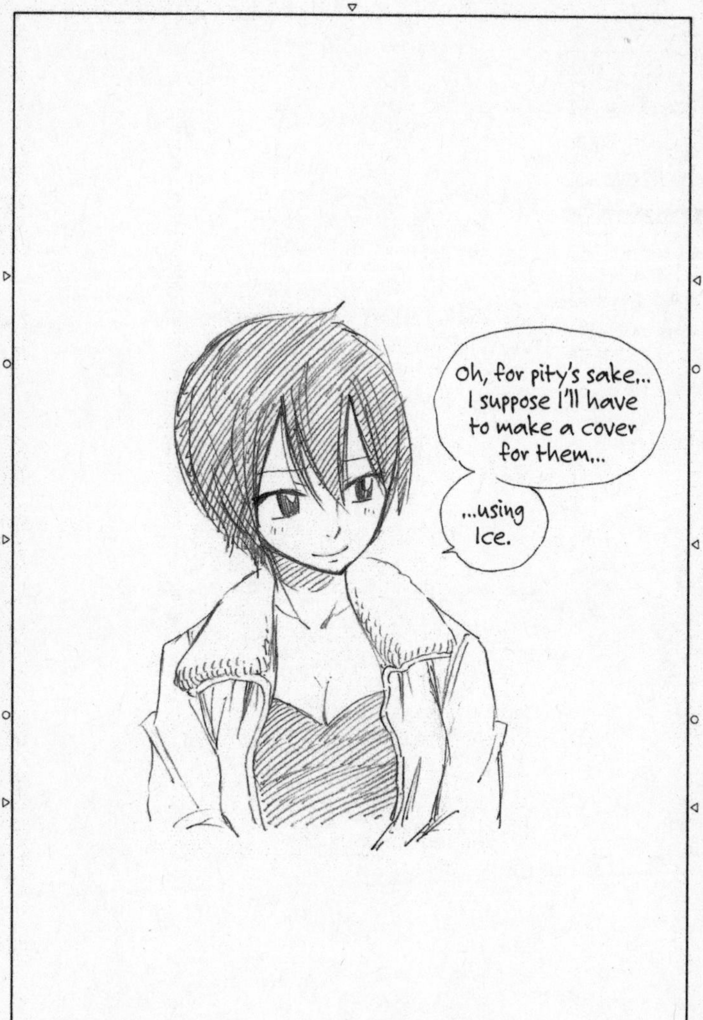
Oh, for pity's sake... I suppose I'll have to make a cover for them...
...using Ice.

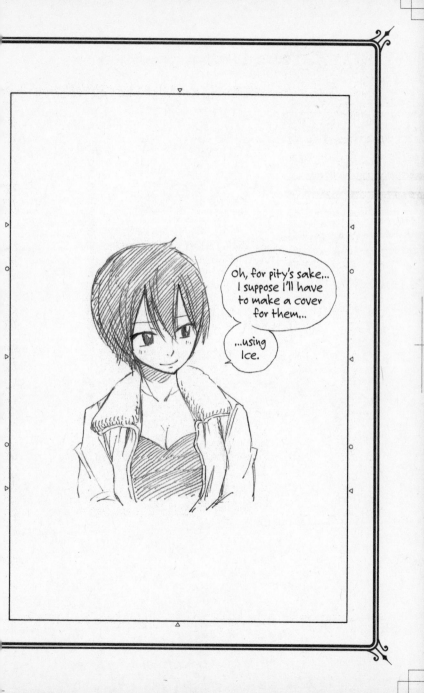

FAIRY TAIL

フェアリーテイル

46

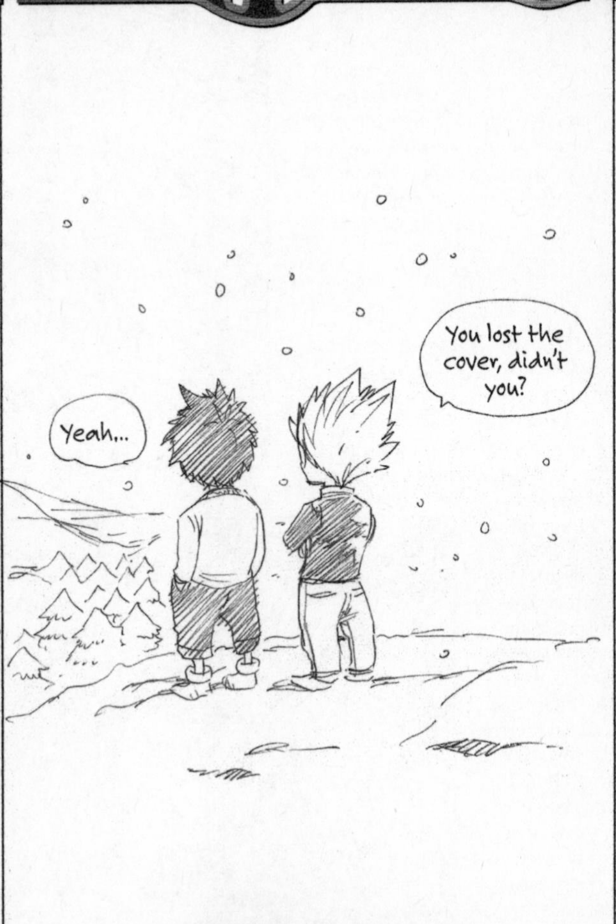

真島ヒロ

HIRO MASHIMA

Translation Notes:

Japanese is a tricky language for most Westerners, and translation is often more art than science. For your edification and reading pleasure, here are notes on some of the places where we could have gone in a different direction with our translation of the work, or where a Japanese cultural reference is used.

Page 132,
Vambrace

A vambrace is the piece of a suit of armor that covers and protects the wearer's forearm. In the manga's original *kanji*, it is written, "Demon King's Forearm Armor," however the entire attack name had a pronunciation guide which only had the English word "Vambrace"

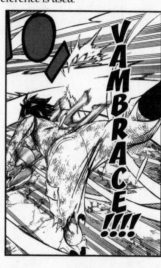

Page 157,
Welcome home, Gray-sama.

Over the past decade or so, maids have been a popular fetish in Japan. The concept of a pretty, young, obedient, servile girl in a revealing French maid's outfit is hardly new. But with the dawn of "maid cafés," where girls dressed up in maid costumes call the customer "Master" and make every effort to please, the concept went mainstream. The standard greeting when one enters a maid café can be translated to, "Welcome home, Master." That is the greeting that Juvia, in her maid costume, is alluding to on the title page of this chapter. (By the way, although some women visit maid cafés, the majority of their clientele is men. Butler cafés, which came later, cater more to a female clientele, and may be staffed by men or by women in drag.)

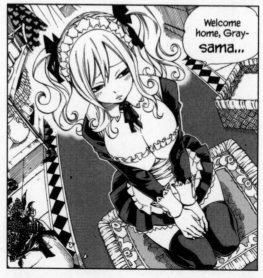

Welcome home, Gray-sama...

Preview of *Fairy Tail*, volume 47

We're pleased to present you with a preview from *Fairy Tail*, volume 47, coming in March. Check out our website (www.kodanshacomics.com) for details!

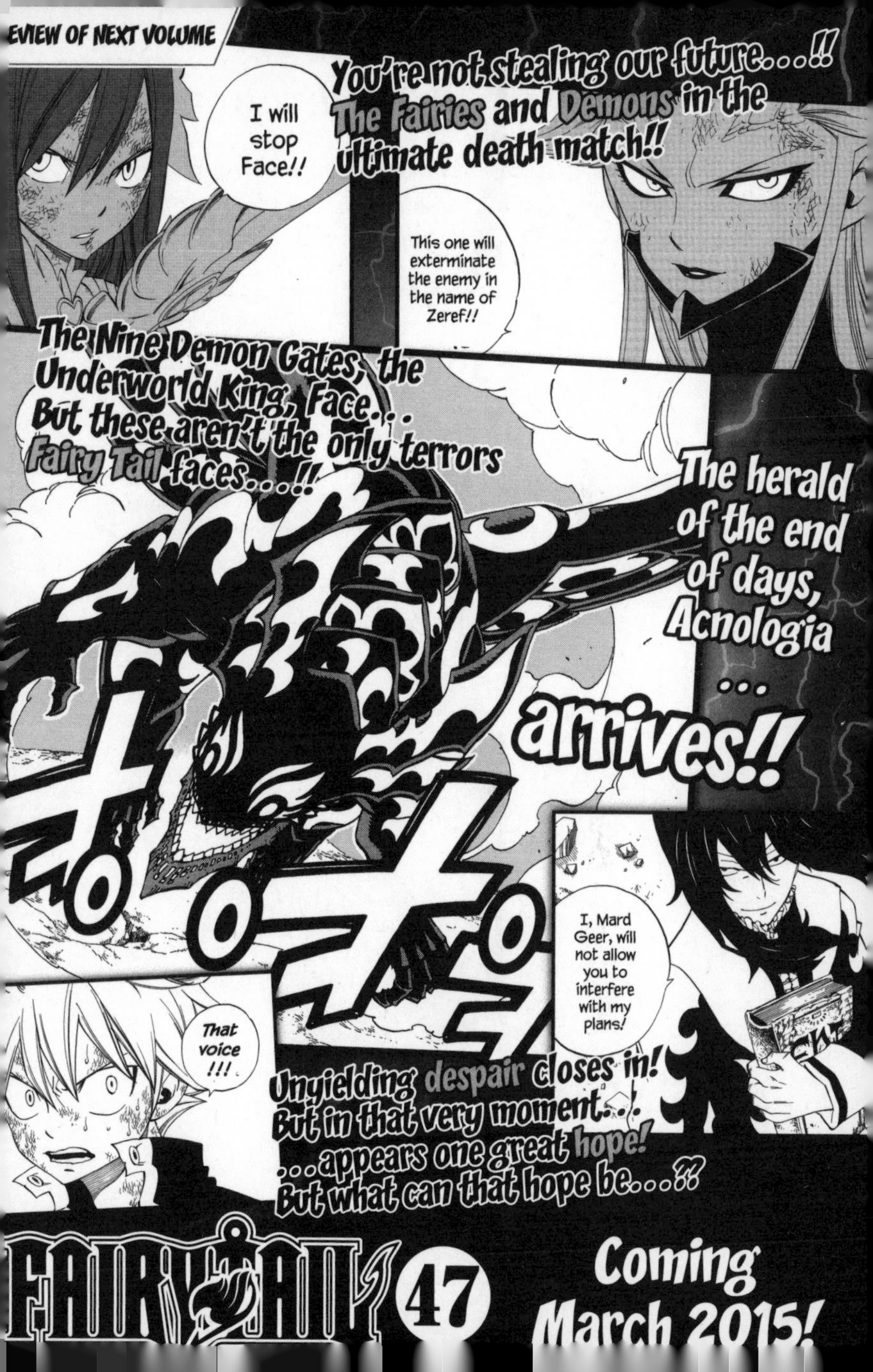
EVIEW OF NEXT VOLUME
You're not stealing our future...!! The Fairies and Demons in the ultimate death match!!
This one will exterminate the enemy in the name of Zeref!!
I will stop Face!!
The Nine Demon Gates, the Underworld King, Face... But these aren't the only terrors Fairy Tail faces...!!
The herald of the end of days, Acnologia ... arrives!!
I, Mard Geer, will not allow you to interfere with my plans!
That voice!!!
Unyielding despair closes in! But in that very moment... ...appears one great hope! But what can that hope be...??
FAIRY TAIL 47
Coming March 2015!

FAIRY TAIL
フェアリーテイル

Chapter 395: Tartaros Arc, Part Five: Ultimate Pain

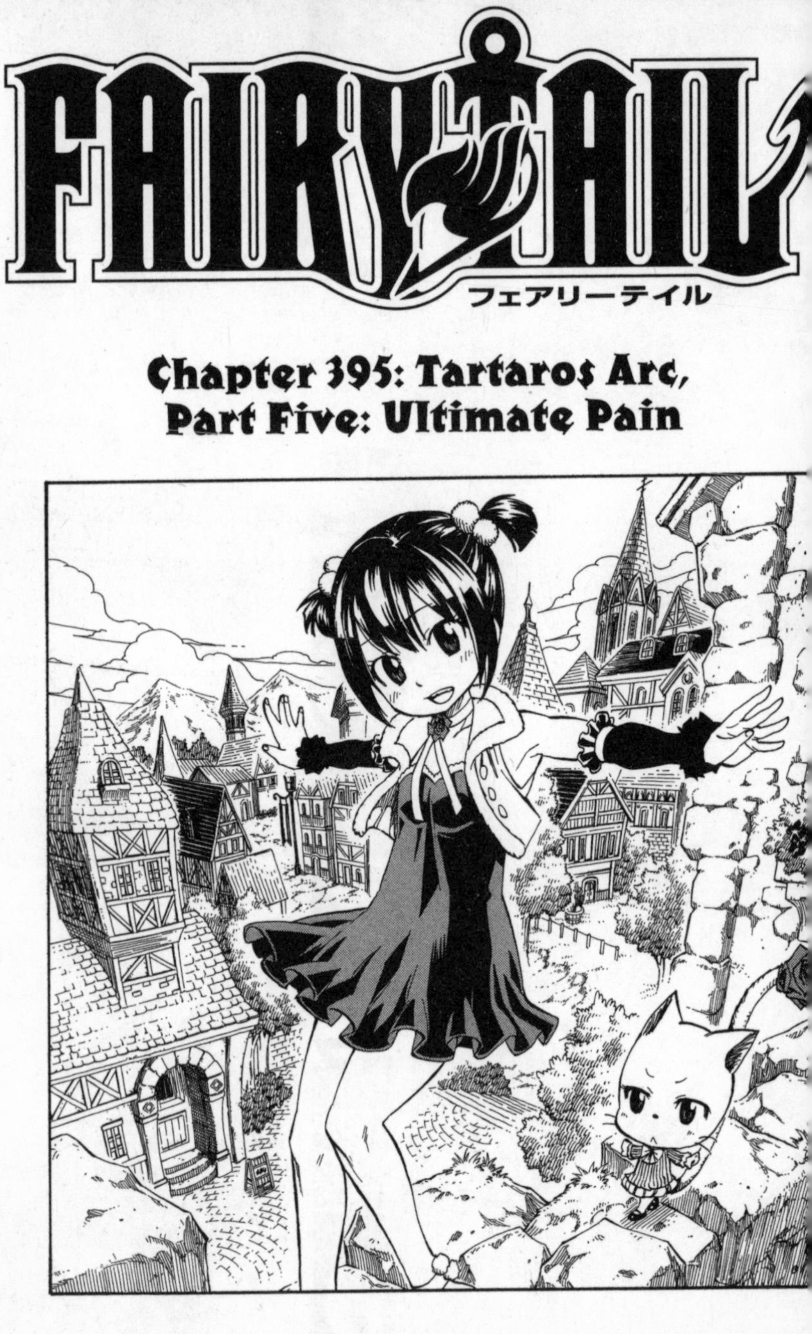

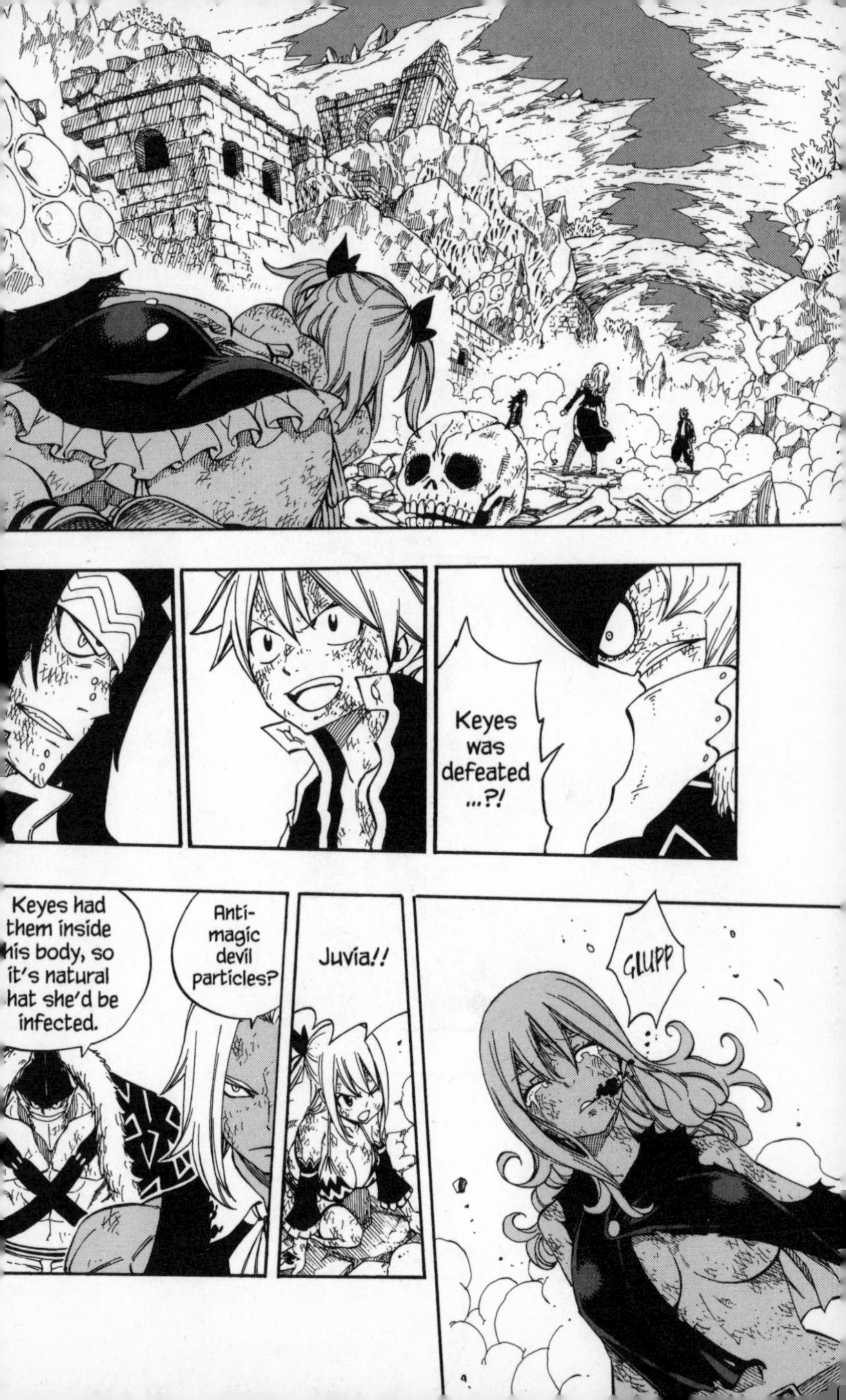
Keyes was defeated ...?!
GLUPP
Juvia!!
Anti-magic devil particles?
Keyes had them inside is body, so it's natural hat she'd be infected.

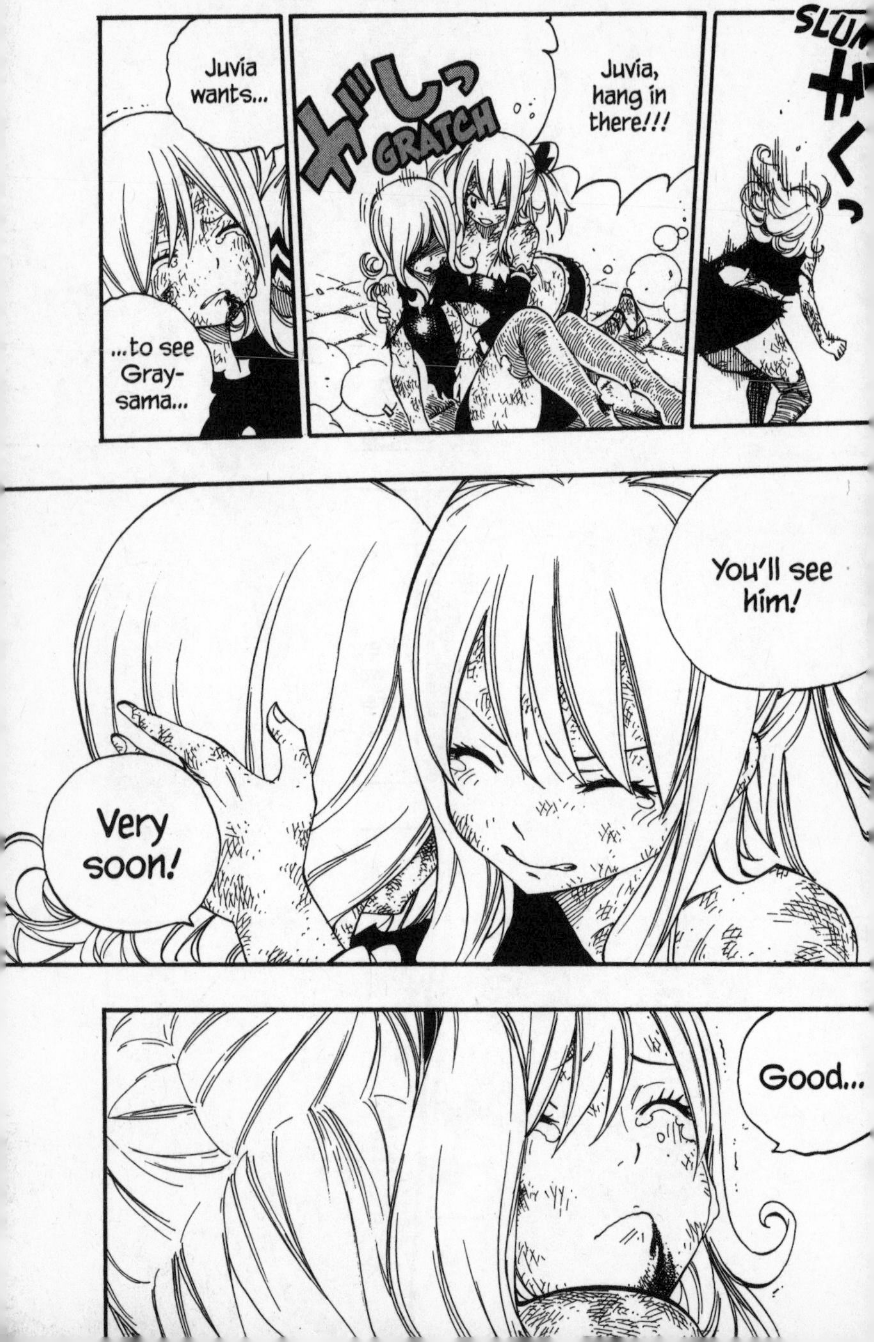
SLUM
GRATCH
Juvia, hang in there!!!
Juvia wants...
...to see Gray-sama...
You'll see him!
Very soon!
Good...

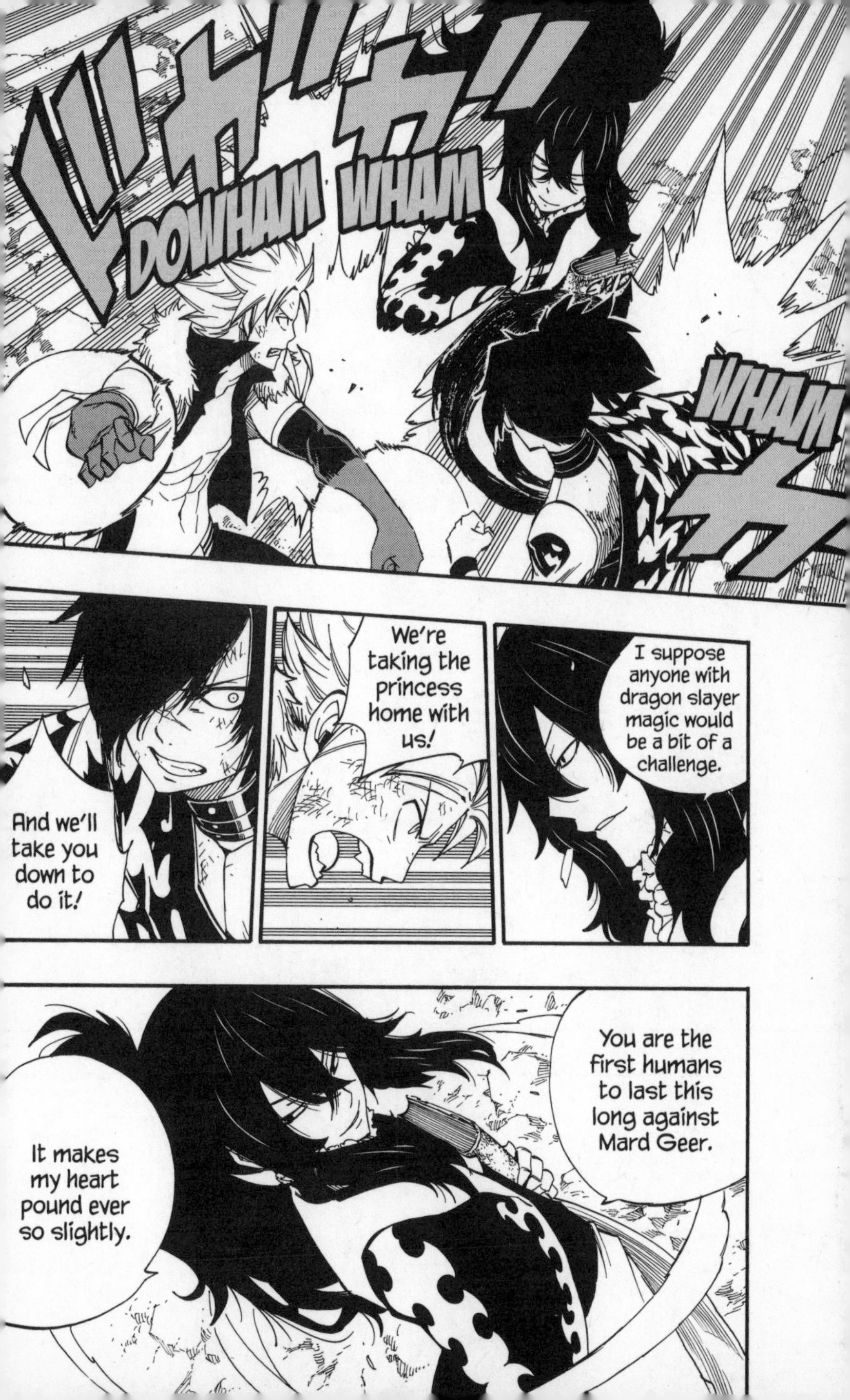
DOWHAM WHAM
WHAM
I suppose anyone with dragon slayer magic would be a bit of a challenge.
We're taking the princess home with us!
And we'll take you down to do it!
You are the first humans to last this long against Mard Geer.
It makes my heart pound ever so slightly.

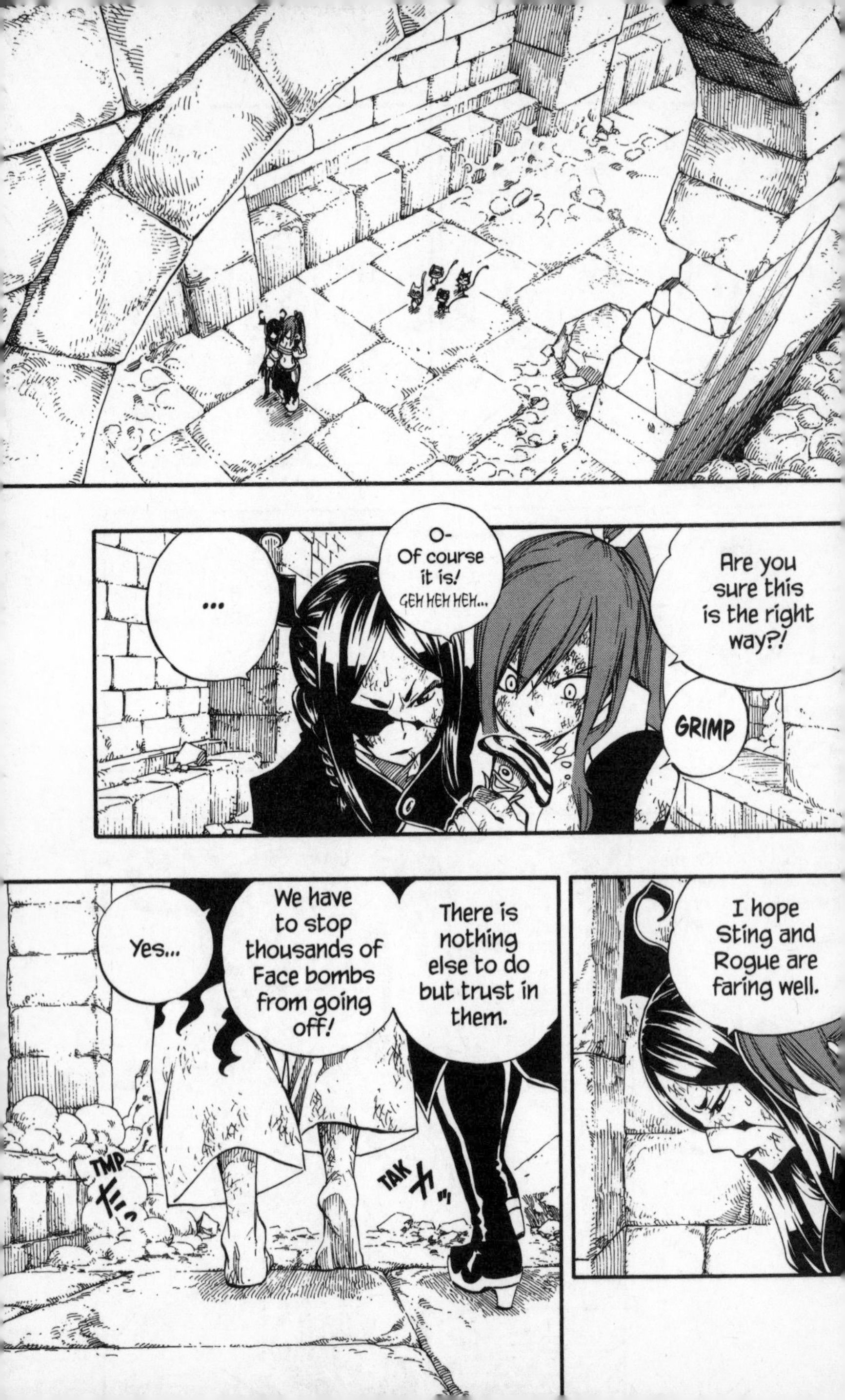
Are you sure this is the right way?!
GRIMP
O- Of course it is! GEH HEH HEH...
...
I hope Sting and Rogue are faring well.
There is nothing else to do but trust in them.
We have to stop thousands of Face bombs from going off!
Yes...
TAK
TMP

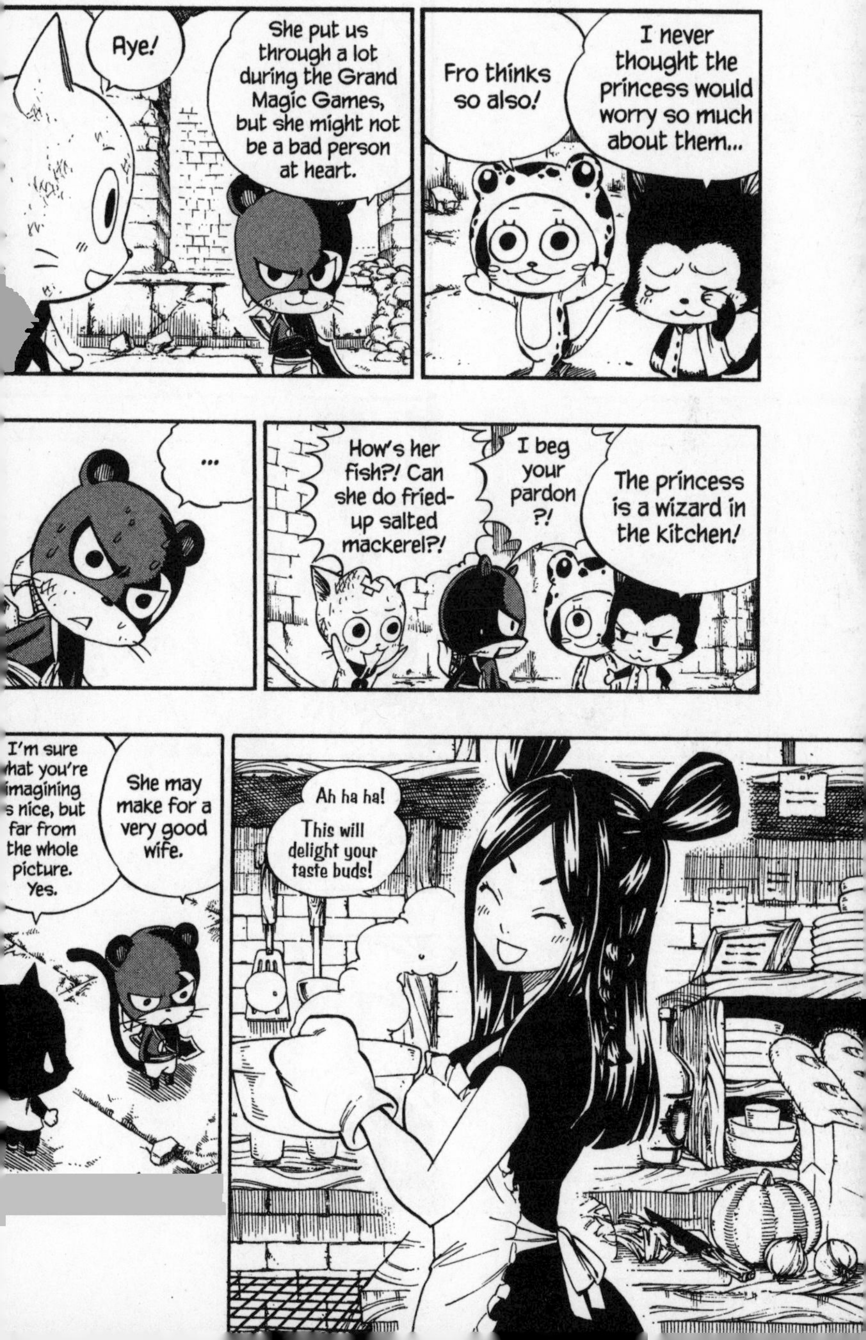
I never thought the princess would worry so much about them...
Fro thinks so also!
She put us through a lot during the Grand Magic Games, but she might not be a bad person at heart.
Aye!
The princess is a wizard in the kitchen!
I beg your pardon?!
How's her fish?! Can she do fried-up salted mackerel?!
...
Ah ha ha!
This will delight your taste buds!
She may make for a very good wife.
I'm sure hat you're imagining s nice, but far from the whole picture. Yes.

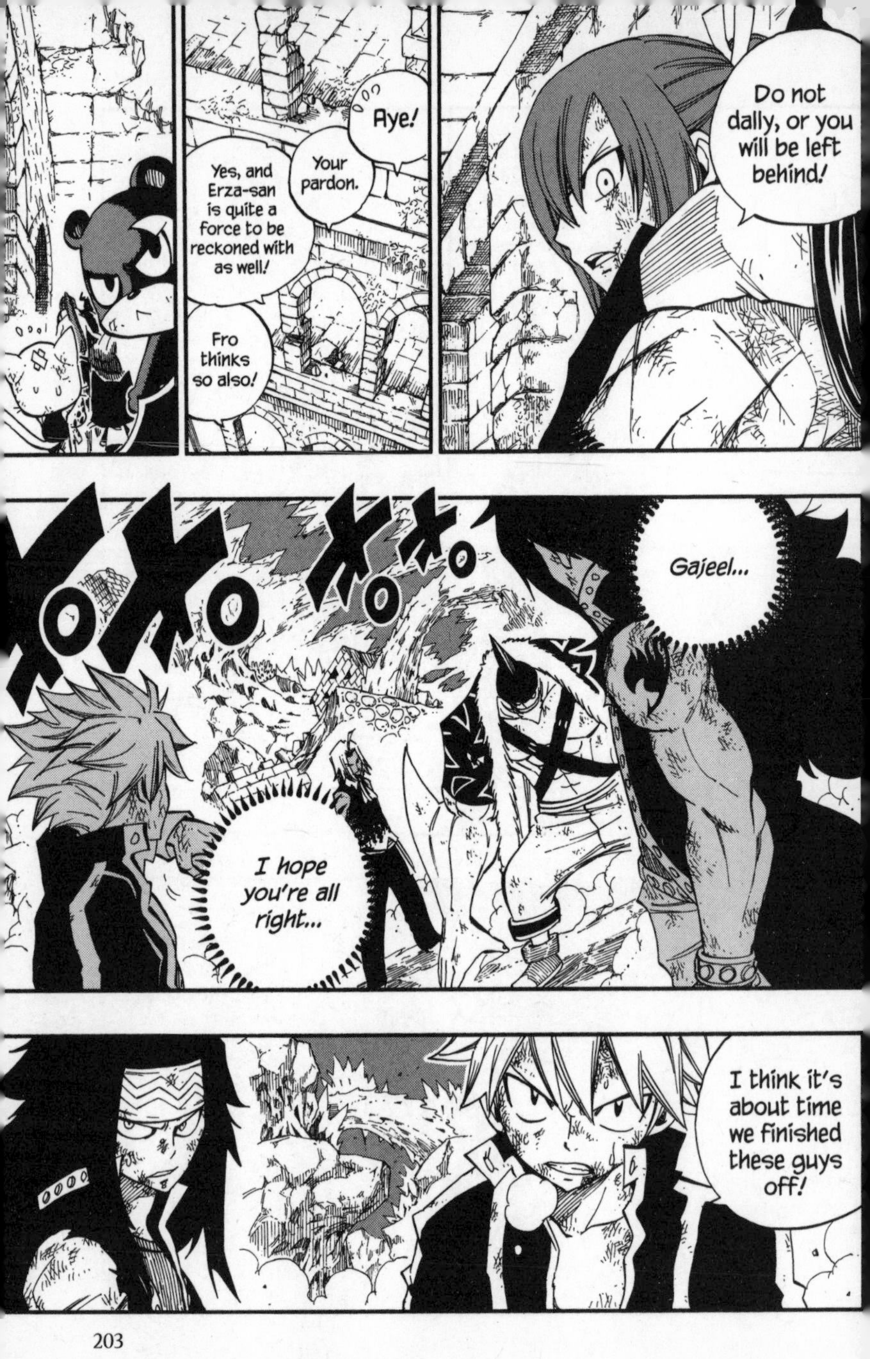
Do not dally, or you will be left behind!
Aye!
Your pardon.
Yes, and Erza-san is quite a force to be reckoned with as well!
Fro thinks so also!
Gajeel...
I hope you're all right...
I think it's about time we finished these guys off!

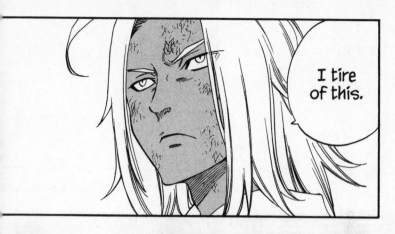

I tire of this.

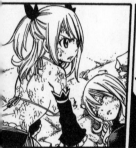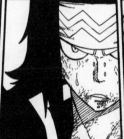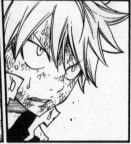

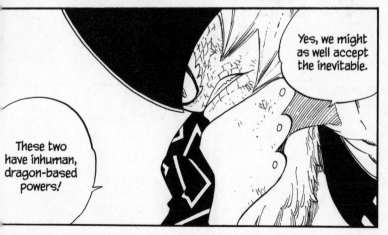

Yes, we might as well accept the inevitable.

These two have inhuman, dragon-based powers!

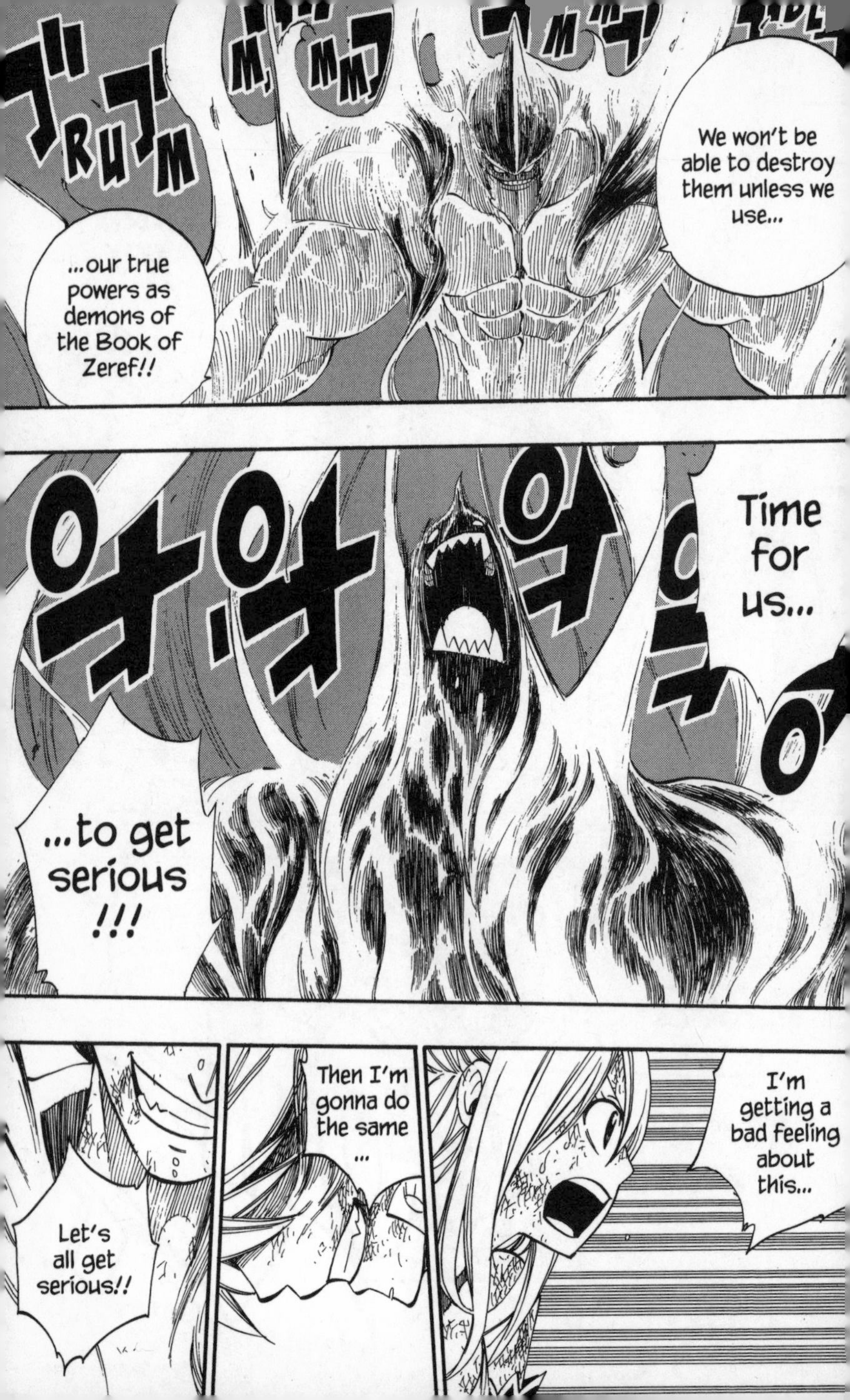
We won't be able to destroy them unless we use...
...our true powers as demons of the Book of Zeref!!
Time for us...
...to get serious!!!
I'm getting a bad feeling about this...
Then I'm gonna do the same...
Let's all get serious!!

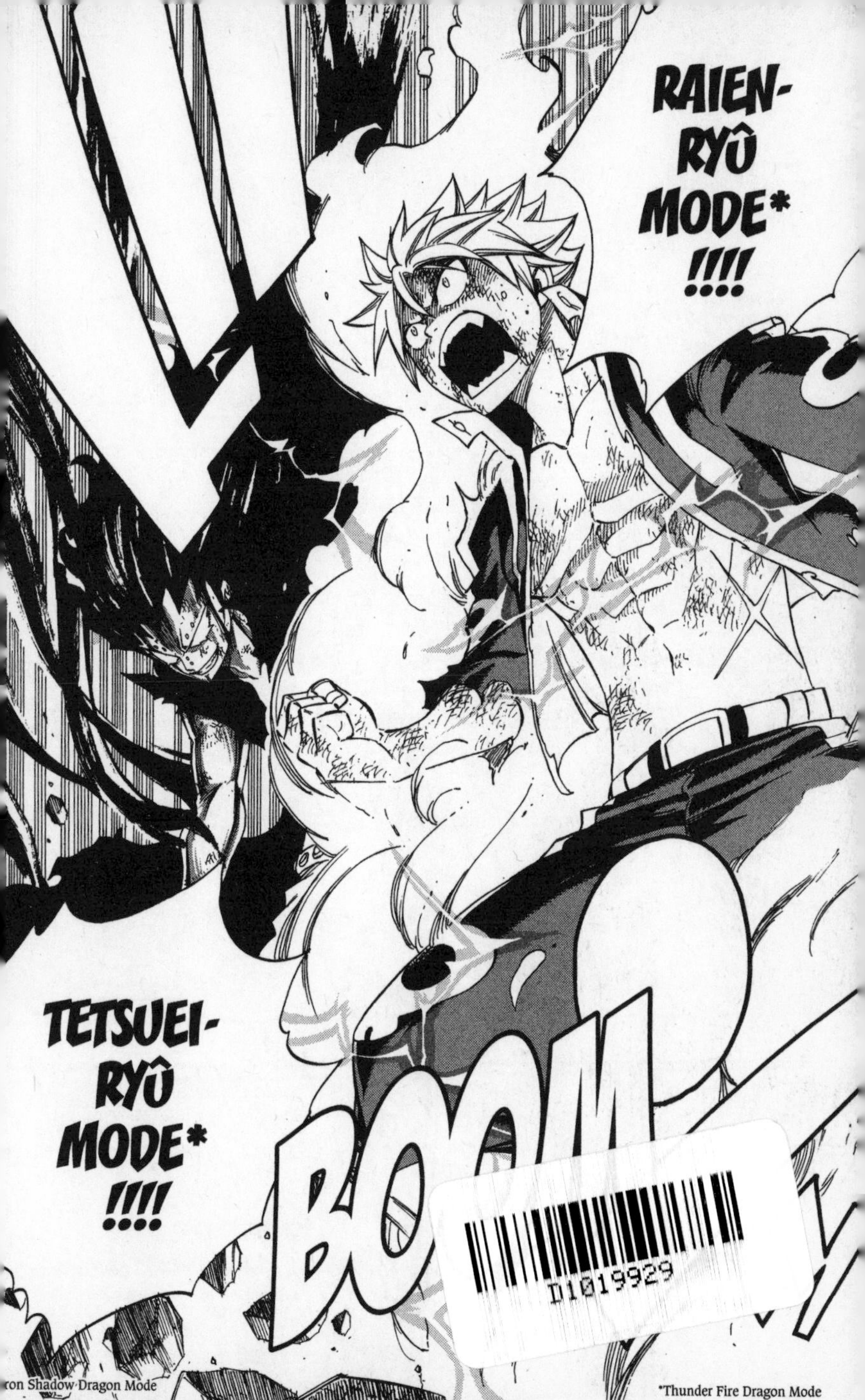
RAIEN-RYÛ MODE* !!!!
TETSUEI-RYÛ MODE* !!!!
BOOM

*Thunder Fire Dragon Mode

ron Shadow Dragon Mode